RADICAL

TRADITIONS

THEOLOGY IN A POSTCRITICAL KEY

SERIES EDITORS

Stanley M. Hauerwas, Duke University,
and Peter Ochs, University of Virginia

RADICAL TRADITIONS cuts new lines of inquiry across a confused array of debates concerning the place of theology in modernity and, more generally, the status and role of scriptural faith in contemporary life. Charged with a rejuvenated confidence, spawned in part by the rediscovery of reason as inescapably tradition constituted, a new generation of theologians and religious scholars is returning to scriptural traditions with the hope of retrieving resources long ignored, depreciated, and in many cases ideologically suppressed by modern habits of thought. RADICAL TRADITIONS assembles a promising matrix of strategies, disciplines, and lines of thought that invites Jewish, Christian, and Islamic theologians back to the word, recovering and articulating modes of scriptural reasoning as that which always underlies modernist reasoning and therefore has the capacity — and authority — to correct it.

Far from despairing over modernity's failings, postcritical theologies rediscover resources for renewal and self-correction within the disciplines of academic study themselves. Postcritical theologies open up the possibility of participating once again in the living relationship that binds together God, text, and community of interpretation. RADICAL TRADITIONS thus advocates a "return to the text," which means a commitment to displaying the richness and wisdom of traditions that are at once text based, hermeneutical, and oriented to communal practice.

Books in this series offer the opportunity to speak openly with practitioners of other faiths or even with those who profess no (or limited) faith, both academics and nonacademics, about the ways religious traditions address pivotal issues of the day. Unfettered by foundationalist preoccupations, these books represent a call for new paradigms of reason — a thinking and rationality that are more responsive than originative. By embracing a postcritical posture, they are able to speak unapologetically out of scriptural traditions manifest in the practices of believing communities (Jewish, Christian, and others); articulate those practices through disciplines of philosophic, textual, and cultural criticism; and engage intellectual, social, and political practices that for too long have been insulated from theological evaluation. RADICAL TRADITIONS is radical not only in its confidence in non-apologetic theological speech but also in how the practice of such speech challenges the current social and political arrangements of modernity.

Tradition in the Public Square

A David Novak Reader

Edited by

Randi Rashkover *&* Martin Kavka

WILLIAM B. EERDMANS PUBLISHING COMPANY
GRAND RAPIDS, MICHIGAN / CAMBRIDGE, U.K.

Published 2008 by
Wm. B. Eerdmans Publishing Co.
2140 Oak Industrial Drive N.E., Grand Rapids, Michigan 49505 /
P.O. Box 163, Cambridge CB3 9PU U.K.

and in the United Kingdom by
SCM Press
S9-17 St. Alban's Place, London N1 0NX

Printed in the United States of America

12 11 10 09 08   7 6 5 4 3 2 1

Library of Congress Cataloging-in-Publication Data

Tradition in the public square : a David Novak reader /
    edited by Randi Rashkover & Martin Kavka.
        p.   cm.   — (Radical traditions)
    ISBN 978-0-8028-3072-2 (pbk.: alk. paper)
    1. Novak, David, 1941-   2. Judaism — Doctrines.
    3. Jewish law — Philosophy.   4. Philosophy, Jewish.
    5. Rabbinical literature — History and criticism.
    I. Rashkover, Randi.   II. Kavka, Martin.

    BM602.T73   2008
    296.3 — dc22
                                            2007046555

www.eerdmans.com

Contents

Acknowledgments

We are deeply grateful to Stanley Hauerwas and Peter Ochs for their willingness to include this volume in the Radical Traditions series; to Linda Bieze at Eerdmans and Barbara Laing at SCM for helping to bring this book to fruition in as efficient a way as possible; and most of all, to David Novak for his instruction and friendship.

In addition, we gratefully acknowledge permission to print or reprint the following essays:

"Philosophy and the Possibility of Revelation: A Theological Response to the Challenge of Leo Strauss," in *Leo Strauss and Judaism*, edited by David Novak (Lanham, Md.: Rowman & Littlefield, 1996). Reprinted with permission.

"The Dialectic between Theory and Practice in Rabbinic Thought." Previously unpublished. Printed with the permission of David Novak.

"Heschel on Revelation." Previously unpublished. Printed with the permission of David Novak.

"Creation and Election," in David Novak, *The Election of Israel* (Cambridge: Cambridge University Press, 1995), pp. 115-37. Copyright © 1995 Cambridge University Press. Reprinted with permission.

"The Life of the Covenant," in David Novak, *The Election of Israel* (Cambridge: Cambridge University Press, 1995), pp. 143-44, 145-52. Copyright © 1995 Cambridge University Press. Reprinted with permission.

"The Role of Dogma in Judaism," *Theology Today* 45 (1988): 49-61. Reprinted with permission.

"Is There a Concept of Individual Rights in Jewish Law?" in *Jewish Law Association Studies VII: The Paris Conference Volume*, edited by S. M. Passamaneck and M. Finley (Atlanta: Scholars Press, 1994). Reprinted with permission.

"A Foundation for Jewish Philosophy: Preliminary Comments," *Journal of Reform Judaism* 26, no. 3 (1979): 83-113. Reprinted with permission.

"Persons in the Image of God," from David Novak, *Natural Law in Judaism* (Cambridge: Cambridge University Press, 1998), pp. 164-73. Copyright © 1998 David Novak. Reprinted with permission.

"Natural Law, Universalism, and Multiculturalism," in David Novak, *Natural Law in Judaism* (Cambridge: Cambridge University Press, 1998), pp. 151-54, 188-91. Copyright © 1998 David Novak. Reprinted with permission.

"Law: Religious or Secular?" *Virginia Law Review* 86 (2000): 569-96. Reprinted with permission.

"What Is Jewish about Jews and Judaism in America?" in *What Is American about the American Jewish Experience?* edited by Marc Lee Raphael (Williamsburg, Va.: College of William and Mary, 1993). Reprinted with permission.

"The Right and the Good," in *On Interpretation: Studies in Culture, Law, and the Sacred,* edited by Andrew D. Weiner and Leonard V. Kaplan (Madison: University of Wisconsin Press, 2002). Reprinted with permission.

"Is Natural Law a Border Concept between Judaism and Christianity?" *Journal of Religious Ethics* 32 (2004): 237-56. Reprinted with permission.

"The Treatment of Islam and Muslims in the Legal Writings of Maimonides," in *Studies in Islamic and Judaic Traditions,* edited by William M. Brinner and Stephen D. Ricks (Atlanta: Scholars Press, 1986). Reprinted with permission.

"A Jewish View of War" and "A Jewish View of Abortion," both from *Law and Theology in Judaism,* vol. 1 (New York: Ktav, 1974). Reprinted with permission.

"A Halakhic View of Responsibility," *Sh'ma* #270. Reprinted with permission.

"Religious Communities, Secular Societies, and Sexuality: One Jewish Opinion," in *Sexual Orientation and Human Rights in American Religious Discourse,* edited by Martha C. Nussbaum and Saul M. Olyan (Oxford: Oxford University Press, 1998). Reprinted with permission.

"Jewish Marriage and Civil Law: A Two-Way Street?" *George Washington Law Review* 68 (2000): 1059-78. Reprinted with permission.

"Can Capital Punishment Ever Be Justified in the Jewish Tradition?" in *Religion and the Death Penalty: A Call for Reckoning,* edited by Erik C. Owens, John D. Carlson, and Eric P. Elshtain (Grand Rapids: Wm. B. Eerdmans, 2004). Reprinted with permission.

"A Jewish Argument for Socialized Medicine," *Kennedy Institute of Ethics Journal* 13 (2003): 313-28. Reprinted with permission.

Editors' note: For the sake of uniformity in this volume, we have on occasion emended the citation format and transliterations in these previously published essays.

Introduction

One of the marks — perhaps the most important mark — of a great thinker is the ability to respond to the conditions and problems of one's time by changing the terms of the conversation. By this standard, David Novak ranks as one of the great American theologians of our time. His work, a response to the primary issue confronting modern Judaism (namely, what it means to be a part of Western culture yet separate from its secularized form of life), has helped to make Jewish theology and Jewish philosophy thriving fields in North American university life. It was not all that long ago that the project of a publicly engaged Jewish theology or philosophy seemed to be impossible within the strictures of North American culture. In his inaugural lecture as the J. Richard and Dorothy Shiff Chair of Jewish Studies at the University of Toronto, Novak recalled a philosophy class he took as a freshman at the University of Chicago in the late 1950s:

> We were assigned to write an essay on a section of a book which to this day I still think is the greatest philosophical work ever written, Aristotle's *Nicomachean Ethics*. At the same time, I was actively pursuing my Talmudic studies with a pious and learned rabbi who lived in the neighborhood of the university, although as far as the culture of the university was concerned, he could have been living on Mars. Anyway, in writing my essay for class, dealing with Aristotle's discussion of justice in the fifth book of the work we were studying, I was struck by certain similarities between what the great philosopher was saying and what some of the great rabbis were saying in the section of the Talmud, the tractate Baba Kama, I was studying with my rabbi. So, I decided to incorporate some of the Talmudic material into my essay in philosophy.

Well, the reaction of my professor, who himself happened to be, as he put it, "of Jewish origin," caught me quite unaware. He called me into his office and told me that normally he did not return a class essay to be re-written and resubmitted. However, he said he was doing so in my case because he thought I had intellectual potential, and he did not want me to "get into any bad academic habits." Then he said, "To put it to you straight, Mr. Novak, your Talmudic examples were inappropriate for this essay." Being a rather brash young man, I retorted, "But sir, weren't the rabbis and Aristotle employing very similar methods of analysis in dealing with the question of restitution?" He then smiled and said, "That may well be true, but you still don't get my point. To be blunt, the examples you brought are from a culture that has no place in the modern university except, perhaps, in the department of anthropology, where primitive practices are observed. This is not a yeshiva!" And by "yeshiva," which I suspected may have been a place he knew personally from his "Jewish origin," he meant a school where the Jewish ethical tradition has normative authority.

Somewhat shaken by this encounter as only the young and naïve can be, I went to my rabbi for reassurance. But, in effect, I went, as they say, "from the frying pan into the fire." My rabbi actually agreed with my professor, but for opposite reasons, of course. For him, too, my bringing the Talmud to the university class was inappropriate. In fact, he quoted a passage from the Talmud to me: *ye-lo tehe Torah shlemah shelanu ke-seehah betelah shelakhem,* namely, "Let not our perfect Torah be like your idle conversation" (B. Menahot 65b). In other words, for my rabbi, the Jewish ethical tradition, which Jews traditionally call "Torah," was too good to be exposed to the nonbelievers at the University of Chicago, or at any modern university, for that matter. Indeed, he went on gently to chastise me for studying something as "dangerous" as philosophy. He felt that if I were in the Business School, I wouldn't have this kind of problem. So, for the rest of my university education, I kept the Torah in one place and worldly wisdom in another, only relating the two in private thoughts and private conversations, neither with professors nor with rabbis, but with the very few traditional Jewish students at the university who were studying things like philosophy. It was a lonely life, let me tell you.[1]

The tension that Novak describes as existing between philosophy and Jewish religious life at the University of Chicago fifty years ago did not exist in a vacuum; it reflected a tension present in Western thought since at least the end of

---

1. David Novak, "The Jewish Ethical Tradition in the Modern University," *Journal of Education* 180:3 (1998): 21-39.

the Middle Ages. Dominant strains in Western philosophy since the work of David Hume have pressured believers and nonbelievers alike to choose within what William James, in a different context, referred to as a "forced option"[2]: choose "yes" or choose "no," but there is no third alternative. Use reason or live covenantally. Choose one or the other. Neither is it possible not to choose, nor is it possible to choose both, since the West has seen the two options as mutually exclusive. For what does Athens have to do with Jerusalem?

The Radical Traditions series, in which this reader appears, is devoted to undoing the centuries-old misdescription of the relationship between religion and reason as a forced option. Of greater significance still is, to use James's language again, the "momentous"[3] significance of tearing away at this false dichotomization. Books in this series presuppose "an unapologetic passion for theological work"[4] that in turn is premised on an awareness that theology literally works — that is, labors at the demands for problem-solving that characterize our time. There are few American theologians whose work better exemplifies the aims and efforts of this series than David Novak. His passion for theological work has been exemplified in his conversations with Christian theology and theologians over the last decades — conversations are represented by "Dabru Emet: A Jewish Statement on Christians and Christianity" (a Jewish rethinking of Christian theological categories) and the other essays included in *Talking with Christians*, which appeared in this series in 2005.[5] The unapologetic nature of his theology is also evident in his rigorous refusal to admit the impasse between religion and secularism that strangles North American culture in so many dichotomous forms (e.g., religion/philosophy, religion/state, religion/university).

Novak's reshaping of contemporary theological discourse is indebted to two intellectual traditions. Novak is a devoted student of Abraham Joshua Heschel, and his work reflects his rabbinic training at the Jewish Theological Seminary, where he completed the requirements for rabbinic ordination in the conservative movement. In addition, it is also deeply influenced by the canon of Western philosophy, represented by his undergraduate and graduate work in that discipline at the University of Chicago and Georgetown University.[6]

2. William James, "The Will to Believe," in *The Will to Believe and Other Essays in Popular Philosophy* (New York: Dover, 1956 [1897]), pp. 3ff.

3. James, "The Will to Believe," pp. 3ff.

4. Stanley Hauerwas, "Foreword: A Christian Perspective," in David Weiss Halivni, *Revelation Restored: Divine Writ and Critical Responses* (Boulder, Colo.: Westview, 1997), p. xxi.

5. Novak, *Talking with Christians: Musings of a Jewish Theologian* (Grand Rapids: Wm. B. Eerdmans, 2005).

6. One might also hypothesize that Novak's own idiosyncratic history in the academy also

Novak's dual training stands squarely within what can be called the ratio-nalist strain in Jewish philosophy, a strain that throughout the course of Western history has resisted the fast and easy dichotomy between Athens and Jerusalem by demanding the mutual interrogation of the one by the other. Seen from this vantage point, Novak's work offers Jewish readers and non-Jewish readers alike a critical reading and appropriation of the Jewish ratio-nalist tradition that includes the work of Saadia Gaon and Moses Maimo-nides in the medieval period, and that of Moses Mendelssohn and Hermann Cohen in modernity. Novak's reading showcases this rationalist tradition as a paradigm of resistance to the Athens-Jerusalem divide, all the while recasting many of the central categories dominant in this tradition in such a way as to catapult Judaism into a wider field of conversation whose members include Christians and Muslims, and whose range of topics goes beyond metaphysical questions and takes up vital matters of social ethics such as war, abortion, and worldwide desecularization.

To situate oneself within the tradition of Jewish rationalism waxes anach-ronistic today, when the categories and confidences of the Jewish rationalist tradition appear naïve at best. However, Novak appropriates this tradition in a postcritical key — that is to say, always retaining the tension between phi-losophy and traditional Jewish sources without either sacrificing the sources to the standards of a given school of thought or sacrificing reason to a naively positivist view of tradition. Central to this reshaping is Novak's ability to sift out, for example, Maimonides' structural recognition of the *ta'amei mitzvot* — that is, the notion that divine commandments are supported by good rea-sons — from his Aristotelian metaphysics. Similarly, Novak has recovered from Mendelssohn the value of a Jewish appropriation of social-contract the-ory, but has rejected his dwarfed account of Jewish covenantal life. From Hermann Cohen he has inherited the link between morality and Jewish life, but without falling prey to Cohen's rationally based teleology that leaves little room for a God who acts in history. Novak's insistence on the identification of reason both embedded within and on the boundary of a particular tradi-tion permits him to honor the philosophical limits exposed, and re-exposed, by various post-Cartesian turns in the history of Western philosophy.

Novak's recourse to the rationalist tradition counts as equally radical and potentially anachronistic in the context of Jewish thought as well. Yet here, ar-

---

has something to do with his refusal to engage in apologetics. Novak was primarily a pulpit rabbi in various locations — publishing numerous articles all the while, and teaching a class here and there at local universities — until 1989, when he became the Edgar Bronfman Profes-sor of Modern Judaic Studies at the University of Virginia, a position he held until 1996.

guably, the charge of anachronism poses a graver challenge. Jewish thought must now come to terms with Emil Fackenheim's post-Shoah re-evaluation of any Jewish philosophy that argues for more than fragmentary status, lest it be charged with neglect of the experience of the victims of the Shoah.[7] While Jewish philosophy has typically all too readily ignored the nature of evil attested to in memoirs of the Holocaust, Novak's thought in our view resists this reduction insofar as it derives from the very life-sustaining elements of the Jewish tradition.[8] While we will provide a more detailed account of Novak's use of the category of natural law in the following pages, here we can say that in Novak's account, "natural law" is the structure within Judaism that protects life. Natural law testifies to the finitude not only of the Jewish community but of all cultures. Without such an acknowledgment of finitude, there is no reason to hope that communities will not destroy one another. In addition, natural law enables Jewish communities (and, by extension, other religious communities) to critique the injustices that take place in those societies that fail to act within these normative limits. Natural law marks the difference between just and unjust worldviews; after the Holocaust, it is a matter of life and death. And so Novak's account of the relationship between philosophy and theology as lying at the cornerstone of human social existence is not simply a recapitulation of earlier strands in Jewish thought (especially, as we will later point out, the philosophy of Franz Rosenzweig); it is a recapitulation addressed to our world, which is essentially post-Holocaust.

We have divided *Tradition and the Public Square* into two parts: "Why Tradition?" and "Tradition and the Public Square." The selections of "Why Tradition?" showcase Novak's account of the inextricable relationship between matters philosophical and matters theological, although this intimacy does not as a result make them identical to each other. Religious particularity is illuminated in part by way of a philosophical approach to the structures of lived Judaism, while philosophy's quest for foundations requires the very contents of religious traditions. Novak's appreciation of the correlation between a philosophy of human nature and a theology of covenantal life grants

---

7. See Emil Fackenheim, *God's Presence in History* (New York: Harper & Row, 1974), and *To Mend the World* (New York: Schocken Books, 1982).

8. The Holocaust has not played an explicit role in Novak's own theological project; we describe his project as containing resources for post-Holocaust thought in order to cut off at the pass those critiques that require Auschwitz to play a role in Jewish thought as important as, if not more important than, that of Sinai. For Novak's most sustained article on this topic to date, see "Is There a Theological Connection between the Holocaust and the State of Israel?" in *The Impact of the Holocaust on Jewish Theology*, ed. Steven T. Katz (New York: New York University Press, 2005), pp. 248-62.

Judaism an unapologetic link to non-Jewish societies and persuades non-Jewish societies to recognize the presence of universal standards of human justice at work in the very fabric of Jewish practice.

The implications of Novak's philosophical theology are spelled out in his essays on social ethics and theopolitics. The essays selected for the second half of this volume diagram the impact of Novak's philosophical theology on the most pressing cultural questions of our day. What is the role of religion in the public square? What is the role of religion — both religion in general and any one specific religion — in a multicultural society? Novak's answers to these questions allow him to adjudicate the most pressing ethical issues of our day: abortion, war, capital punishment, sexual ethics, and health-care ethics.

We now turn to the arguments of the essays in these two sections in greater detail. Nevertheless, we admit that we focus more on Novak's larger philosophical-theological program than we do his positions on social-ethical issues. This is because many of his positions on these issues are quite well known, in part due to his publications in *First Things,* a culturally conservative magazine of theological ideas. Yet we also feel that the larger architectonic behind his social-ethical positions has been largely ignored by scholars in a way that has unjustly limited the audience of his work. For example, we surmise that many people who know of Novak's work primarily through his right-of-center positions on sexual ethics will be surprised by his quite left-of-center positions on socialized medicine and the ethics of war — especially his call, after the massacres in Sabra and Shatila in 1982, for Menachem Begin and Ariel Sharon to resign from their positions in Israel's government (reproduced here as Chapter 18). But these positions, which might appear at first glance to be ideologically diffuse, derive from one single stance about the relationship between philosophy and theology. By laying out that architectonic here and the way in which its logic can serve as a lifeline for religious traditions, we hope to persuade readers that Novak's logic can be detached from the positions on social-ethical issues that he holds.

Central to Novak's theology is an account of covenantal life as a communal process of testifying to the nearness of God while engaging in a world with others who are outside of this community. Yet as a human act of testimony to God in the world, covenantal life can be articulated in a variety of ways. What creates a meaningful reality for one individual or community will fail to create that reality for another individual or community. Consequently, we read Novak's social ethics as advancing a particular (and perhaps contingent) application of his broader portrait of covenantal life as perpetually negotiating between prior formulations of Jewish law (halakhah) and the evidence of the world in a way that permits a balance between halakhic responsiveness to change and sustained integrity to the legal tradition. Other approaches in modern Jewish thought, in addressing the apparent impasse of Judaism in the modern West and by extension the relationship between religious communities and the nation-state, have dishonestly sacrificed either the Jewish tradition to the world (in which case the descriptor "Jewish" has little or no purchase on the account), or the world to the Jewish tradition (in which case Judaism can no longer flourish in that world).

The path away from these conflicts leads through, and not around, Novak's philosophical theology. For example, those readers who believe that Jewish thought must begin with the Holocaust and culminate in the State of Israel will have to root such positions in Novak's account of covenantal life (or give another account of covenantal life) if they are to offer persuasive accounts of those positions as Judaic positions. Such is the method of philosophical theology that, in Novak's work, allows the claims of the Jewish tradition to remain distinct from claims abstracted from a sociological study of Jews' opinions.

Why Tradition?

In his essay "The Role of Dogma in Judaism," Novak describes Franz Rosenzweig as "the greatest Jewish theologian of this century." While most contemporary scholars of Rosenzweig pay attention to the impact of his phenomenology of Jewish life, Novak's work is more influenced by Rosenzweig's Copernican insight regarding the relation between philosophy and theology. Rosenzweig's 1919 magnum opus, *The Star of Redemption,* is as much a philosophical work as it is a work of Jewish theology. The first part of the *Star* is devoted to a philosophical account of the world as a clearing ground for establishing the possibility of theology. Similar to Kant's account of theoretical reason, philosophy for Rosenzweig establishes the possibility of transcendence and the religious life that testifies to it without itself being able to assert positive knowledge of transcendence. Theology needs philosophy to establish the plausibility of the divine-human relation in the world that we know. Philosophy needs theology, however, to account for the event of alterity in our experience, in terms of both our relation to God and our relation to others in our social fabric. Rosenzweig labeled this symbiotic relation between philosophy and theology "new thinking."[9] Novak's own "new

---

9. Rosenzweig, "The New Thinking," in *Philosophical and Theological Writings,* ed. Paul W. Franks and Michael L. Morgan (Indianapolis: Hackett, 2000), pp. 109-39, and *The Star of Redemption,* trans. Barbara E. Galli (Madison: University of Wisconsin Press, 2005), pp. 113-18.

thinking" owes a great deal to Rosenzweig's model, and yet it seems to us that Novak takes the link between the two areas even further. For Rosenzweig, philosophy acts as an epistemological gatekeeper to theology's more substantive determination of the coordinates of the divine-human and human-human relations; in the relationship between philosophy and theology, the former only anticipates the latter. Novak, on the other hand, does not leave philosophical thinking behind in theology, but asks after the mutual influence of philosophy and theology.

The first two essays in this reader, "Philosophy and the Possibility of Revelation: A Theological Response to the Challenge of Leo Strauss" and "The Dialectic between Theory and Practice in Rabbinic Thought," provide Novak's answer. The objective of the former essay is to underscore that philosophy and theology mutually affect one another's spheres of concern. This is not akin to the tradition of apologetic theology, which offers a defense of the rationality of religious belief. Instead, Novak begins the essay by asking whether or not theology matters to philosophy. Can theology make a claim to have any authority over philosophy? To speak of authority is to speak of politics, and so Novak argues that "we must ask just what philosophical understanding of political authority causes the philosopher not only to admit the possibility of revelation, but also to actually desire it." The key, according to Novak, is to appreciate political philosophy's paralysis around the question of the relation between communal duties and individual rights. While political philosophy has long sought to advance both the rights of institutions and normative standards for social well-being as well as the rights of individuals within a society to live according to their desires, political philosophy has infrequently been able to reconcile the rightful claims of both positions.

Revealed here is the more profound question of how can persons feel at home in a lawful world? "The human soul is restless" in a society that cannot of its own accord negotiate between individual needs and social demands. If as a social being I am necessarily limited by law, then to live in society is to be reminded of my finitude and my mortality. As mortal, I am alone; and yet as a social being, I am anything but alone, forced to meet the demands of others. The overcoming of this rift requires being in a relationship with others, recognized by them as the person I understand myself to be. Political life thus breeds the desire to be known. Nevertheless, political life cannot fulfill this desire, since people in society relate to each other through positive law, which claims an abstract understanding of personhood (as opposed to a specific understanding of *me*). The desire to be known is therefore best described as a theological desire, for as Novak points out, citing 1 Samuel 16:7, "humans only see appearances, but the Lord sees the heart." It is God who mediates between law and relationship in covenantal life. As the creator of the natural order, the transcendent God limits human pretensions and legitimizes law; but as revealer, God loves this same people, drawing them near in the world he has created. The lawful world is no different from the covenantal world, where persons dwell with the God who loves them. Novak's analysis suggests that even so-called secular law can be seen as theologically suggestive, since lawfulness implies theological desire.

If philosophy can and ought to acknowledge theological claims for the sake of politics, can philosophy claim some authority with respect to theology? Novak's work is driven by the conviction that philosophy matters to theology less as a theoretical justification for theology's epistemological plausibility and more as the practical reason which identifies the minimal normative conditions necessary for the survival of human life — what Novak calls "natural law." Human sociality is impossible without systems of law and without a prohibition against idolatry. Both constitute the "moral prerequisites of a society worthy of human loyalty," a society which limits the pretensions toward absolute freedom of any of its members at the expense of any other member. Societies that are willing to sacrifice the survival of any member for the sake of the freedom of another fail to satisfy the conditions of human flourishing, which minimally require that all persons be able to live.

Natural law is nothing other than the normative reminder of human finitude: "philosophy as practical reason, the practical reason that discerns natural law, is of most help to theology because it prevents theology from sinking from the level of the superrational to the level of the subrational — that is, to the level of superstition and fanaticism."[10] As the reminder of human finitude, philosophy generates and supports an impulse of natural (rational) justice in religious traditions that serves to guard against a tendency to identify the tradition itself with divine authority. Philosophy does not determine what can count as the legitimate content and/or *telos* of revelation. Natural law is not natural theology. It can, however, establish the normative limits that any particular law must at least meet in order to be considered just and justified. Novak's recognition of the role of philosophy deepens Rosenzweig's account, since philosophical awareness contributes to redemptive praxis and cannot be extricated from it.

For Novak, philosophy aids and accompanies theology not only as practical reason but as theoretical reason as well. In his essay "The Dialectic between Theory and Practice in Rabbinic Thought," published for the first time

---

10. See this volume, p. 17.

in this volume, Novak highlights what readers can identify as three aspects of theoretical reason's contribution to Jewish life and learning: the pragmatic, the theoretical, and the theologico-existential. The essay wrestles with the classic rabbinic question of whether or not learning is greater than practice. Citing the position of the kabbalist thinker Rabbi Isaiah Halevi Horowitz (referred to as Shela), Novak argues that the dominant rabbinic response, that learning is greater than practice because learning produces practice, "contradicts itself. . . . If the end is practice, isn't it obvious that the end is superior to what comes before it?!"

From here Novak follows Shela's own response, which takes up the language of philosophy to re-evaluate the character of the relationship between learning and practice, now from the position of the accounts of causality that have strong family resemblances with those found in Aristotle and Maimonides. Philosophy elucidates the sense of terms used in the tradition, and as such becomes an invaluable tool in rabbinic problem-solving. Agreeing with Maimonides that a philosophical account of causality points to "the absolute freedom of God," Novak then goes on to argue that learning about the acts of God in rabbinic aggadot, in order to walk in God's ways, cannot lead to a simple ethical formula. While not threatening the primacy of halakhah, Jewish norms also include "acts without measure" — that is, acts of neighbor-love, which require an evaluation of the situation at hand and not simply a predetermined act. Such acts are, for Novak, "devised on the spot, so to speak, depending on the existential needs of the personal object of this action."[11] The turn to Maimonides' account of causality opens up an account of learning that offers its own end. To study God's acts of freedom is an end in itself that prepares the believer for those situations in which already designated purposes are not yet known, and so learning is not simply an instrument for better practice. Philosophy here offers Judaism a resource into which Jewish life and practice may delve and deepen in its own self-understanding. Like Moses for Akiba, philosophy offers a teaching from which Jews may draw, as part of the perpetual unveiling of the Torah itself.

The fact that Novak's work showcases the invaluable place of philosophy in the religious life does not imply that Novak prizes philosophy over and against religious life. On the contrary, both practical and theoretical philosophy point toward the need for revelation; philosophy both intends revelation and is designed to fuel the creativity of the religious life that follows after the character of divine freedom. As a result, a phenomenological theology requires a developed phenomenological account of revelation and our response

---

11. See this volume, p. 30.

to it. In the subsection entitled "Revelation, Covenant, and Law," we have offered five selections from Novak's writings that outline this account.

The essay "Heschel on Revelation," published here for the first time, offers a transition into Novak's own constructive project by marking his appreciation of Heschel's account of the irreducibility of the revelatory God into rational terms. Unlike the reductionist accounts of revelation in the work of Mordecai Kaplan (who reduced revelation to patterns of human projection) and Joseph Soloveitchik (who reduced revelation to law), the foremost American Jewish theologies of the 1950s, Heschel's account was the first to appreciate revelation as an expression of God as the One who transcends human nature. For Heschel, the original content of revelation is indescribable through human language; in comparison, the Bible is a midrash. This, however, does not mean that revelation is unintuitable. What Novak appreciates in Heschel's account is Heschel's poetic description of the prophet as working through the limits of language to unveil the horizon beyond these limits. Heschel's phenomenology of revelation lends expression to Novak's conclusion that "our deepest feelings lie outside our constructing selves" and instead constitute our "cleaving to God." The God of absolute freedom is also the God we draw near to in feeling.

If Heschel can be credited with the retrieval of the concept of covenant in American Jewish thought, Novak alone can be credited for a more exacting philosophical recovery of the biblical doctrine of election. To showcase this recovery, we have drawn from the account Novak offers in *The Election of Israel.* Here Novak argues against a dominant strain in Jewish rationalism that interprets the biblical text singularly through the lens of the dominant ontology of the day. Lost in this approach that runs from Saadia Gaon through Maimonides up until and including the work of Hermann Cohen is the phenomenology of revelation revived by Heschel. Yet Novak recognizes — more deeply than Heschel, in our view — the value of a philosophical engagement with the biblical text:

> The one thing that this ontology has been able to do is to constitute the relation of the world to God as well as that of Israel to God. Calls for a simple return to biblical theology, without the philosophical detour of the rationalists, seem inevitably to lose sight of the factor of the world's relation to God. Yet this is a factor that is hardly ignored in Scripture itself, even though the primary concern is God's relationship with Israel.[12]

12. See Novak, *The Election of Israel* (Cambridge: Cambridge University Press, 1995), pp. 110-11.

It is the task of a postcritical biblical hermeneutics to highlight the unique character of historical revelation as this revelation relates to the world.

As we mentioned above in our discussion of the opening essay of this volume, persons need a God who reveals so that they feel at home in a world that is regulated and limited by law. In *The Election of Israel,* Novak locates the basis of this claim in a close reading of the biblical account of the Abrahamic covenant.[13] At the opening of Genesis 12, "The Lord said to Abram, 'Go forth from your native land and from your father's house to the land that I will show you. I will make of you a great nation, and I will bless you' . . . Abram went forth as the Lord had commanded him." Why does Abraham do what God says? According to Novak, his decision is not a mere leap of faith. Rather, Abraham had good reason to comply with God's command — namely, his desire to feel at home in the world which orders him. Abraham, Novak argues, already knows that the world is a given for which he cannot account, and that it is ordered according to laws both natural and social. What persons do not recognize prior to Abraham is the *person* that is the source of *tsedaqah* and *mishpat,* righteousness and justice.

Just as in the philosophical-political account above, so too in the biblical account, persons dwelling in a world of law seek out the source of this order as a personal presence. No mere philosophical quest, Abraham's quest is an existential one. What does it mean to live in a world that orders me? What does it mean to live in the world as a finite being? What is my purpose? Am I ultimately alone? Abraham longs to see his world as "an authentic dwelling place for humans. Abraham the bedouin is looking for home."[14] Theological desire exceeds philosophical desire; the latter searches for the conditions of the possibility of human survival, while the former searches for the conditions of the possibility of home, or existential comfort and purpose. This need, for Novak, can be met only through a covenantal relationship with the creator God. And so Abraham complies with God's command out of desire for the One who draws near, who "restores the lonely to their homes" (Ps. 68:7).

While Novak's philosophical recovery of the biblical doctrine of revelation appreciates revelation's role in relation to the minimal conditions of human survival, the meaning of historical revelation cannot be reduced to an account of worldhood. This recognition of the teleological and existential primacy of revelation informs Novak's understanding of Jewish law. In the essay entitled

---

13. This account of the Abrahamic covenant had already been present in Novak's work for two decades before *The Election of Israel* was published. See "A Theory of Revelation," in *Law and Theology in Judaism* (New York: Ktav, 1974-76), vol. 2, pp. 1-27, esp. pp. 19-22.

14. "A Theory of Revelation," p. 61.

"The Life of the Covenant," also excerpted from *The Election of Israel,* Novak applies his recovery of the doctrine of election to modern Jewish assessments of the meaning of Jewish observance. While the majority of modern American and German-Jewish philosophies located the meaning of Jewish observance in its ability to meet the demands of universal ethics, Novak by contrast argues that as the condition of the possibility of human survival, basic human morality is for the purpose of dwelling in the covenant. The life of the covenant is an end in itself; the justice practiced in covenantal life is for the sake of the people of Israel's "covenantal intimacy" with God. Law witnesses to this intimacy that constitutes the highest end of human life; the halakhic life performs it.

We end this section on "Revelation, Covenant, and Law" with two essays that illustrate the relationship between Novak's philosophical recovery of covenant theology and the halakhic tradition. To the extent that the halakhic life reflects the authentic dwelling in the world characteristic of covenantal intimacy, it counts as the primary datum of dogmatic belief. A philosophical retrieval of the doctrine of election poises Novak to retrieve the theological significance of halakhah insofar as Jewish law presupposes and thereby reflects the covenantal reality out of which it emerges: "Dogmas are not just propositions but laws, in the sense that they are propositions-to-be-affirmed," Novak writes in "The Role of Dogma in Judaism."[15]

Novak's position differs strongly from that of Soloveitchik, who, as stated above, reduced revelation to law. To identify Jewish thought with halakhah is to deny the engagement of halakhah practically and theoretically with history and the changing world. Not only does halakhah develop historically as a precedent-based system of law, but halakhah also reacts to historical change in its function as a generator of religious belief. The halakhic thinker is a problem-solver who addresses the questions of concern to the contemporary Jewish community. Pragmatic by nature, Jewish theology is motivated by the current set of problems and arrives at answers that are at the current moment unfalsifiable by the limits and/or datum of the halakhic system. The halakhic system therefore remains the touchstone of communal problem-solving. This is not equivalent, however, to saying that all decisions can be positively verified in and through the halakhic tradition as it is inherited. The halakhic system's ability to give rise to a range of responses over time reflects its function as a testimony to the primary covenantal reality that grounds it in and permits it to dwell in the changing world.

The essay "Is There a Concept of Individual Rights in Jewish Law?" exemplifies this facet of halakhic reasoning's elasticity with respect to the particu-

15. See this volume, p. 74.

lar question of individual rights. If one of the pressing questions of contemporary Jewish life has to do with the relevancy of Jewish law to democratic society, then it is incumbent upon halakhic thinkers to demonstrate how halakhah does or does not maintain the category of individual rights, which constitute the necessary basis of the democratic society. In keeping with the method of theological thinking described in "The Role of Dogma in Judaism," Novak demonstrates the link between individual rights and the non-legal texts (aggadah) of the Jewish tradition. While individual rights are not explicit in the halakhic material, neither does the halakhic tradition *prima facie* deny individual rights because of the presence of an implicit account of rights in the aggadic material of the Talmud. It so happens that the discovery of a belief in individual rights also points to what Novak takes to be the natural-law element within the halakhic system, because the right to private property comes from a midrashic treatment of the crime of the generation of the Flood, not from a dictum found in either Written or Oral Torah, or even a rabbinic pronouncement. Natural law is implicit in the act of rabbinic reasoning that opens up the principles underlying the insights of the tradition, and this applies not only to the reasoning of the Rabbis of antiquity portrayed in the Talmud but also to the reasoning of the responsa written by Rabbis in the centuries following the codification of the Talmud.

At one point in his *Natural Law in Judaism* (1998), Novak describes natural law as the "precondition of the covenant" in the sense of a Kantian *Bedingung*. What natural law does in this sense of a precondition is "make an opening in the world as we can experience it, for an entity to appear in it. But because such a precondition is in place does not mean there is any necessity for that entity to appear."[16] This view of natural law as a precondition deepens the account of the necessity of the relationship between philosophy and theology, the world and revelation, relationships in which the terms are irreducible to each other. On the one hand, to speak of natural law as a precondition of the covenant is to explain how the Israelites were able to see God's revelation as possessing normative value, so that they did not accept the covenant merely under threat of divine force. On the other hand, to speak of natural law as a precondition of the covenant is to acknowledge that natural law intends covenantal life as its highest end. In the first of the three essays we have included in the section entitled "The Precondition for the Phenomena: Noahide Law as Natural Law," Novak highlights the former sense of natural law as a precondition. In the latter two essays, both excerpts from *Natural Law in Judaism*, he attends to the latter sense.

16. Novak, *Natural Law in Judaism* (Cambridge: Cambridge University Press, 1998), p. 186.

Novak's account of natural law, when it first appeared in the 1970s, emerged out of his inquiry into rabbinic anthropology as it derives from the dynamic exchange between halakhah and extra-legal accounts of the human person. In an essay from this period, "Noahide Law: A Foundation for Jewish Philosophy," Novak points to the rabbinic category of the *ben Noah* or the Noahide, the non-Jew who according to the biblical story of the Flood is by definition a son of Noah, as the category by which the tradition develops an account of personhood in general. The rabbinic tradition views the Noahide as bound by seven Noahide commandments — six negative ones (prohibiting idolatry, blasphemy, murder, theft, sexual immorality, and eating the limb of a living animal) and one positive one, that of *dinim* — that establish a system of justice in one's society.

The category of the Noahide refers to non-Jews in two different senses. First, it refers to the people of Israel before they were chosen by God (what Novak calls in this essay "pre-Judaic man"); Jewish covenantal life requires that the content of revelation at Sinai comports with the minimal standards of human sociality as they existed prior to that time. Second, it refers to the non-Jews around whom Jews live (what Novak calls in this essay "co-Judaic man"). Halakhic life occurs against the larger backdrop of the human family. Novak begins his analysis by inquiring into the proper jurisdiction of the Noahide laws. Are gentiles responsible for their own enforcement of the Noahide laws, or is gentile conformity to the Noahide standards the responsibility of Jewish authorities? In a review of a debate between the medieval commentators Maimonides and Nahmanides, Novak sides with Nahmanides' claim that according to Jewish law, gentiles are responsible for enforcing their own adherence to courts of law. He deepens his defense of Nahmanides' position by noting how later commentators' interest in Nahmanides' position developed not so much as a technical identification over questions of enforcement but more so for the sake of constituting an account of universal morality that could then be used to evaluate Jewish law, especially such law as it pertains to the Noahides with whom Jewish communities interacted. It is thus the Jewish tradition's consideration of gentile normativity that aided medieval rabbinic efforts to reject any double standard with respect to Jewish treatment of non-Jews.

In addition, the category of the Noahide was also mobilized to formulate criteria under which non-Jewish rulers' authority over Jews would be rightful. It is the eleventh-century commentator Rashi who argues that, because non-Jewish nations are commanded as Noahides to construct systems of justice in their societies, the Talmudic ruling that "The law of the kingdom is the law" gains moral and not strictly political legitimacy. This, Novak says, "is not only a *de facto* recognition of Jews being subject to a non-Jewish regime; it is a *de jure* recognition that the state's right to rule is grounded in a law directed to the conscience of man. In other words, we now have a moral grounding for the positive law of the non-Jewish state."[17] Pressed to examine rabbinic anthropology in the context of contemporary diasporic life, Novak's account offers contemporary Jews a standard by which they may assess their relationship to the non-Jewish societies in which they live in a manner that comports with the rabbinic tradition. For Novak, natural law functions as the minimal standard to which both Jewish and non-Jewish law must adhere in order to be morally justified.

If by "precondition" Novak highlights natural law as the minimal normative limit of the contents of revelation, he also illuminates natural law as that which intends and/or points to the life of revelation as its highest end. To speak of natural law as needing revelation is to appreciate, first of all, that natural law never appears in the form of universal norms or laws that are shared by all persons. Rather, as in the case of rabbinic Judaism, natural law appears in the context of the positive laws of a particular culture. Natural law, Novak says, "is the constitution of a universal horizon by a thinker in a particular culture for his or her own culture."[18] Not only do particular cultures identify natural law only in the context of their reflection on their own tradition, but natural law is as well always expressed as the minimal standards necessary for the moral justifiability of that particular tradition, as above exemplified in the case of the Noahide laws. Second, as a universal horizon and/or limit on the pretensions of positive law, natural law is not the *telos* of positive law but strictly the limit or minimal conditions necessary for positive law to function justly. Natural law never determines the positive content of particular traditions.

In the essay we have entitled "Persons in the Image of God," Novak offers a phenomenological account of human sociality in order to establish the important link between natural law and teleology. If natural law does not provide the *telos* to which all positive law must conform, does this mean that natural law stands in no relation to teleological matters? Given that natural law concerns moral action and that moral action always assumes an end, there must be a relation between natural law and teleology. But what is it? Here Novak turns to a Kantian sense of "end," referring to a person as the object or end of an action. Compounding this Kantian turn with insights developed from the phenomenology of the presentation of the other person found in Emmanuel Levinas, in which the other person is herself the origin of my in-

---

17. See this volume, p. 138.
18. See this volume, pp. 157-58.

terest in behaving morally toward her, Novak concludes that the ground of my interest in behaving morally to others is the fact of human dignity grounded in another's being created in the image of God. The confrontation with another's desires confronts me with the limits of my freedom. And so at once the other is the reminder of my finitude and the object of my desire to feel at home in the world. The other person to whom I am obligated is a sign of my desire to be known by God; the obligation or limit placed on my freedom by the other becomes the occasion of my desire for God. I seek to do right by her because when so doing, I intend to draw near to the covenantal God I desire. Human existence intends transcendence when it desires to be known by and relate to another person. So my duty to another person before me is the condition of my desire for God and for the authentic dwelling place that this God alone affords for me and for all others. In this sense, natural law, the limit of my freedom, makes possible the pursuit of my ultimate end, God.

As a minimal account of natural law as the universal horizon that confronts a particular thinker within a particular tradition, Novak's position avoids charges of ontological and/or cultural imperialism. As something that is held in common, the natural-law strand of Judaism permits Novak to demonstrate Judaism's ability to function in a multicultural setting without itself falling prey to cultural relativism. In the second excerpt from *Natural Law in Judaism* that we have included in this section, Novak argues that natural law is a "cultural construct" that regulatively functions within Judaism (and, by extension, other traditions) to help it answer the question of the nature of the world that would make an account of revelation as God's self-presentation minimally persuasive. Natural law limits the pretensions of positive systems of law by virtue of its construction of a universal horizon, and delineates minimal conditions for justice in those cultures by virtue of its constituting act. Because cultures for Novak engage in such universal normative constructions, the work of comparative ethics between such constructions can situate different cultures into a conversation, the primary concern of which is to identify minimal standards of justice necessary for human sociality in an increasingly multicultural world.

Novak's account of natural law is part of a larger trend of the resurgence of natural-law thinking in scholarship on ethics and political theory, due in large part to the "new natural law" of John Finnis, Robert P. George, and his teacher Germain Grisez and others. To give a full account of the relationships between Novak and the new natural lawyers would dramatically expand this introduction. Nevertheless, we think it appropriate to make a preliminary point in this matter. One might want to describe Novak's account as further to the right than that of the new natural lawyers. Insofar as he argues that natural law does not exist outside of the constructs of particular cultures, lists of basic goods that are immediately grasped as good by the intellect apart from any cultural framework, such as those found in the work of John Finnis, do not come into play.[19] For Novak, only covenantal life structures the goods that members of a community pursue; while it may overlap with the accounts of human nature implicit in other communities' forms of life, this overlap is not in and of itself evidence that natural law can be divorced from accounts of divine grace and offered in the language of naked practical reason.[20] There is no view from nowhere.

Nevertheless, along with this increased rootedness in the theological tradition, the explicitly Kantian dimension of Novak's natural-law ethic mentioned above allows for a fruitful coupling of natural law (in contemporary North American society, an allegedly "conservative" approach to ethics) and a personalist existentialism (in academic Jewish philosophy, part of the allegedly "liberal" thought of Martin Buber and Emmanuel Levinas). Such a link is absent in the work of the new natural lawyers, in part because of the association of Kant with John Rawls's accounts of justice and public reason in political theory, opposed by Finnis and others.[21] While Novak certainly does not endorse Rawls's conceptions of public reason,[22] his personalism plays an important role in the construction of a natural-law ethic that can meet the needs of contemporary pluralist society, and raises the possibility of a resolution of the fraught relationship between liberal democracy and religious reasoning, which otherwise threatens to become a permanent rift based on incommensurable authority claims (e.g., the American Constitution versus the magisterium).

19. See Finnis, *Natural Law and Natural Rights* (Oxford: Clarendon, 1980), esp. pp. 59-133, and *Aquinas: Moral, Political, and Legal Theory* (Oxford: Oxford University Press, 1998), esp. pp. 56-102.

20. In this sense, we find Novak to be unexpectedly closer to Aquinas's account of natural law than are the new natural-law thinkers, because Novak (like Aquinas) refuses to divorce philosophy from theology. See Jean Porter, *Nature as Reason: A Thomistic Theory of the Natural Law* (Grand Rapids: Wm. B. Eerdmans, 2005), pp. 17ff.; and Mark D. Jordan, *Rewritten Theology: Aquinas after His Readers* (Malden, Mass.: Blackwell, 2006), pp. 136-53, esp. pp. 139-43.

21. For two examples, see John Finnis, "The Authority of Law in the Predicament of Contemporary Social Theory," *Journal of Law, Ethics, and Public Policy* 1 (1984): 115-37, esp. pp. 128-29; and Robert P. George and Christopher Wolfe, "Natural Law and Public Reason," in *Natural Law and Public Reason*, ed. Robert P. George and Christopher Wolfe (Washington: Georgetown University Press, 2000), pp. 51-74. Nevertheless, see also Finnis, *Aquinas*, p. 131.

22. See Novak, *The Jewish Social Contract* (Princeton: Princeton University Press, 2005), p. 1n.1 and p. 3n.6; and "The Right and the Good" in this volume.

Tradition in the Public Square

We begin the second half of this reader with a section entitled "Judaism and Multicultural Politics," consisting of five essays demonstrating the logic at work in Novak's theopolitics. Beginning with an essay offering a general claim regarding the affinity between natural law and the philosophical foundations of social contract theory, the section moves to more particular analyses of the relationship between contemporary democracy and Jews (and, by extension, other religionists), and ends with profiles of interreligious dialogue in a multicultural society.

"Law: Religious or Secular?" serves as a key example of how Novak applies his philosophical theology to the larger question of the relationship between religion and the public square. Questions concerning the proper place of religion within a constitutional democracy cannot, for Novak, be sufficiently addressed through a trail of court cases over instances of religious rituals in the public square; more productive for a democratic society is a philosophical analysis of the relation between religion and constitutional law within the social contract. At the heart of his philosophical analysis is the claim that constitutional law within a social contract presupposes a theological dimension. Why do we trust one another to follow law within the social contract? If Hobbes is right, we do so only because we fear punishment from the state. Nevertheless, a society premised on fear and/or coercion is anything but desirable; we want to live in a society where we can trust persons to behave lawfully (e.g., to keep their word) because they "are personally committed to a law or standard not of their own making," deriving from a lasting standard or "unchanging word."[23]

Reliable adherence to a lawful society demands that most persons feel obligated to some kind of deity. The question concerning the relation between secular and religious law is not whether a society admits theology or not but rather what kind of theology, "whose god" it acknowledges. That persons feel obligated to a standard that transcends their own making is, as several of the essays in the first half of the volume show, a central aspect of Novak's account of natural law. Any state that refuses to recognize its adherence to a standard beyond itself can freely assert its power at the expense of any of its citizens. By contrast, to base human rights on natural rights (natural law) is to have recourse to an order that transcends the autonomy of the state and challenges its unjust policies. Natural law is a necessary presupposition of a healthy democracy.

23. See this volume, p. 182.

In "What Is Jewish about Jews and Judaism in America?", published before he became a dual citizen of both the United States and Canada, Novak moves to the more specific arena of the relationship between Jews and American society. While few Jews question the value of American democracy for Jewish life, Jewish thinkers rarely if ever attempt to ground this affinity in anything more than the history of modern Jewry's effort to be accepted as citizens in the Western world. However, given Jews' need for America on the one hand, and the challenges facing America's own self-understanding as a democratic society on the other, contemporary Jews need to be able to articulate the Jewish grounds for their acceptance of American democratic society both as Jews within a covenantal community and as Americans engaged in the work of self-reflection. Are Jews happy in America because they are the lucky beneficiaries of a state that guarantees the freedom of private religion, or are Jews happy in America because their Judaism endorses the character of American democracy? The real issue here is one of authority. Are Jews obligated first and foremost to the nations in which they live and only derivatively free to practice their religion, or are Jews obligated first and foremost to their covenantal community and only derivatively committed to the nations in which they live? While justifying Judaism according to the criterion of the ethos of contemporary America contradicts basic Jewish self-respect in Novak's view, Jews nonetheless can (and ought to) ground their obligations toward America in natural law, since it is a rabbinic category that can test the moral legitimacy of the state on rational grounds. To the extent that American democracy meets the standards of natural law, American Jews can assert a moral (and not simply circumstantial) justification for their commitment to their country, without forfeiting their primary covenantal obligation.

These two essays showcase Novak's belief that there is a formidable link between rabbinic Judaism and participation in the modern democratic society. The remaining three essays in this section demonstrate how this link contributes to the current debate concerning the role of religion in public discourse. In "The Right and the Good" Novak applies his philosophical theology to tackle John Rawls's now-classic formula concerning the relation between the right and the good in democratic society. If Rawls's position advocates the promotion of only those goods that comport first with governing standards of justice, Novak by contrast argues that any primacy attributed to justice is not only qualified by the priority of the good but derives from it, when the good is understood to be a theological good, or the search for "transcendence."[24] If justice signifies theological desire, then it is also the case that

---

24. See this volume, p. 212.

Jews must challenge a Rawlsian notion of religious tolerance, premised as it is either on religion's adherence to conventional standards of justice or on the reduction of religion to merely private preference. Either of these standards of tolerance for Jews would be tantamount to idolatry, since they are both premised on the state's exclusive authority in determining what counts as a worthy human end. As a result, Novak calls on contemporary Jews to press for a less state-centered approach to tolerance, in which religious traditions can freely articulate their commitments to the good and identify the standards of justice that constitute the minimal normative conditions of the morality of their own traditions and the wider society at large.

In "Is Natural Law a Border Concept between Judaism and Christianity?" Novak provides an example of how the free articulation of religious commitments can foster the ethical health of conversation in a democratic society. Above we discussed Novak's interest in a comparative ethics based in tradition-specific exchanges regarding natural law. As mentioned earlier in this introduction, Novak argued in *Natural Law in Judaism* that tradition-based comparative ethics results from natural-law thinking. Such an inquiry should amount to more than sociological description, if comparative ethics is to be true to the prescriptive nature of ethics and to aid in contemporary societies' efforts to address ethical problems. Premised on the principle that any intercultural dialogue requires a common basis of conversation, this essay highlights how natural law (as expressed in tradition-specific terms) can function as the shared basis for a comparative ethics that retains prescriptive power.

While this account of comparative ethics is tradition-based, it is also philosophically driven. Points of overlap derive from commonalities in the minimal normative standards necessary to guarantee basic justice, rather than commonalities emergent out of overlapping themes and/or categories in revelatory accounts. Consequently, Novak's focus on Jewish-Christian relations in this essay is not an argument for a "Judeo-Christian ethic"; it does not preclude the inclusion of, say, Islamic conversation partners. Indeed, such inclusion has political benefits: "Conversations with Muslims on ethical issues would help Jewish and Christian ethical rhetoric to be more philosophically persuasive with the help of Muslims and the inclusion of Islam in public arguments," since those arguments could no longer be reduced to a particular — and putatively narrow — worldview. Nevertheless, the point remains that for Novak all comparative ethics is for the sake of asserting traditions' ethical claims "in and to the secular world."[25]

25. See this volume, p. 228.

We have closed the section on "Judaism and Multicultural Politics" with an article that Novak wrote in the 1980s entitled "The Treatment of Islam and Muslims in the Legal Writings of Maimonides" as a way to deepen Novak's own account of the possibilities of Jewish-Islamic relations. The centerpiece of Islamic-Jewish relations for Maimonides is monotheism. And while Maimonides indeed held Toraitic revelation to be superior to Qur'anic revelation on political and pragmatic grounds, these contrasting revelatory claims do not threaten the possibility of interreligious dialogue. It is philosophy — in this case, Maimonides' philosophical arguments for the correctness of monotheism — that grounds Maimonides' appreciation for Islam. Even if, as "Law: Religious or Secular?" shows, Novak's criterion for an ethically productive interreligious dialogue is not necessarily the Maimonidean one of monotheism, Novak's interpretation of Maimonides is instructive as a basis for the role of philosophy in his own work on interreligious dialogue and showcases the potential in the broader tradition of Jewish rationalism for encouraging the necessary development of scenes of interreligious dialogue that include Muslims.

The final section of this volume offers excerpts from Novak's work in social ethics, a testament to the problem-solving benefits of his postcritical philosophical and political theology. Unwilling to indulge divisions between theory and practice, the university and the community, religion and secularity, his approach to social ethics applies his postcritical form of rabbinic reasoning to the full range of contemporary social and ethical issues including war, abortion, capital punishment, marriage, and socialized medicine. We want to briefly identify three features of this methodology that come into play in these essays.

First, whether he is addressing questions of capital punishment or socialized medicine, Novak adjudicates these issues by recourse to the halakhic tradition. As we stated earlier in this introduction, while halakhah is not an exhaustive resource for ethical deliberation for Novak, as an account of testimony to the event of revelation it remains the most essential element in Jewish ethical deliberation. But halakhic deliberation also requires some world-based reflection, whether philosophical, scientific, or historical. Because it is designed to support a humane and just dwelling in the created order God has established, the halakhic tradition stands in conversation with the set of changing needs, beliefs, and knowledge characteristic of our contemporary scene. And so "A Jewish View of Abortion" indicates how rabbinic positions on this issue need be mindful of scientific evidence regarding the beginning of life as well as the challenges of a post-Holocaust Jewish life. The argument of "Religious Communities, Secular Societies, and Sexuality" depends upon a particular rendering of scientific impressions of homosexuality and evaluates it in halakhic terms. "A Jewish Argument for Socialized Medicine" challenges American attitudes on socialized medicine in view of Rashi's critique of the commodification of medical care. The combination of views on social ethics which Novak holds throws a wrench in North American culture's tired attempts to link religious reasoning, whether in fervent support or withering critique of it, with the ideology of a political party. In addition, the necessary conversation between halakhah and our world means that Jews and other religionists who want to critique Novak's conclusions on social ethics (including the two of us, on certain issues) need not oppose the *method* by which he comes to his conclusions. Neither need "secularists" dismiss religiosity when they express their opposition to the social policies that Novak supports. A Jewish view of abortion requires a judgment based on natural science, although that is not all that it requires. A Jewish view of homosexuality requires judgments based on both natural science and social science, although that is not all that it requires. A Jewish view of medicine requires a thick description of how medical care is delivered, although that is not all that it requires. Simply put, religious reasoning is not opposed to what John Rawls termed "public reason."[26]

Second, for this reason we understand Novak's recourse to natural law in these essays as offering significant guidance in determining what a normative Jewish response (yet one also accessible to non-Jews) is to these issues. As that which connects Judaism with the world, natural law offers Jews a standard of checks and balances regarding ethical issues that may be applied to Jewish and non-Jewish attitudes alike. Natural-law arguments against bloodshed and in favor of the preservation of human life stand at the cornerstone of Novak's ethical reflections on abortion, capital punishment, and war. The critique of idolatry implicit in his account of natural law funds his caution against abuses of power by medical professionals when they are paid directly by their patients or by insurance companies that are independent of the state, since these payments are structurally akin to bribes.

Finally, characteristic of all of Novak's work on social ethics is his commitment to the premise that traditional Judaism can thrive in a secularized society without either isolating itself or secularizing itself in turn. All the essays that we have included in this section demonstrate this commitment, but we would like to call especial attention to "Jewish Marriage and Civil Law," in

---

26. See John Rawls on the nature of Cardinal Bernadin's arguments for denying the right to abortion in *Political Liberalism,* rev. ed. (New York: Columbia University Press, 2005), p. liv, n. 32.

which Novak takes up the vexed problem of the *agunah* (the Jewish woman whose husband refuses to grant her a traditional divorce). On Novak's reading, traditional Judaism has in effect thrown up its hands in trying to resolve this issue as a religious problem, instead taking the path of treating Jewish marriage as a civil contract and sacrificing the covenantal nature of Judaism for halakhic expedience. Against such a blurring between religion and the state, Novak argues, following a minor strand of Jewish legal precedent, for the institution of marriage annulment in Judaism. This would hopefully have the effect of going "a long way toward restoring the confidence of both Jewish women and men in the moral power of their own religious authorities."[27] If it is to have this effect, it is only because Novak's commitment to active Jewish participation in public discourse on matters of social ethics reflects his recognition of the primacy of religious law for believers and the need and right to be able to articulate these positions rationally within the context of a multicultural society. For him, being beholden to Torah is prior to being beholden to a secular normative order, yet this does not make secularity irrelevant for traditional Jewish life: "I can accept only secondary secular authority because it has been justified as being in principle (if not always in specific practice) consistent with the primary religious authority for me."[28]

Modern Judaism's search for a middle way between a full embrace and a total ignorance of secularity is now in its third century. In the philosophical theology of David Novak, it has come closest to that golden mean.

September 2006   RANDI RASHKOVER
                                                  MARTIN KAVKA

27. See this volume, p. 326.
28. See this volume, p. 284.

I WHY TRADITION?

The Role of Philosophy

1 Philosophy and the Possibility of Revelation: A Theological Response to the Challenge of Leo Strauss (1996)

There are three basic ways that one can hear or read the words of a particular thinker: one, as a disciple; two, as a student; and three, as an opponent. The disciple believes that everything (or almost everything) this thinker says and writes is the truth. What the disciple does not understand is what is not yet true for him or her; the present lack of understanding is his or her own problem, and it is hoped that it will be only temporary.[1] The student, on the other hand, believes that some of what the thinker says and writes is true and some of it is not true. Even what the student does not believe is true in the words of the thinker is still respected as a challenging alternative that calls for a respectfully reasoned response. Finally, there is the opponent, who believes that nothing or almost nothing that thinker says or writes is true. The response of the opponent is usually one of dismissal, often involving personal ridicule or contempt.

Leo Strauss, *zikhrono li-vrakhah* (may his memory be blessed), has cer-

---

1. Based on Strauss's own criteria, it seems paradoxical for anyone to claim to be his disciple, that is, to be a "Straussian." Let it be remembered that the only two valid forms of ultimate knowledge, for Strauss, are philosophy and theology. If Strauss was a philosopher, then philosophers only know what is true by their own "unassisted efforts" (*Natural Right and History* [Chicago: University of Chicago Press, 1953], p. 85). They cannot be the disciples of anyone else in the strict sense of the term, nor can their students *qua* philosophers be their disciples. So, in order to be his disciples, Straussians must see Strauss as a theologian, that is, someone who transmitted a tradition based on revelation, which is the necessary aid to anyone who desires to know that revealed truth. Whether Strauss saw himself as a philosopher or not is subject to speculation; however, I do not see how anyone can see him as a theologian, whatever his respect for theology, especially Jewish theology, happened to be. Hence, could one not see "Straussianism" as a misplaced desire for revelation and, accordingly, inconsistent with everything we do know about Strauss's own position?

tainly inspired disciples, students, and opponents. And, at least among the disciples and the students, there are internal disputes.

Among Strauss's disciples, both those who learned from Strauss himself and those who have learned from them or, by now, from their disciples — those who either call themselves or are called by others "Straussians" — there are disputes over what the master really *meant*. Among those who have learned from Strauss, there are disputes over what exactly is true in Strauss's teaching and can be accepted, and what is not true in it. As for Strauss's opponents, who are most often the opponents of *both* Strauss's disciples and students, the usually categorical character of their dismissal of him does not seem to admit enough doubt for there to be internal disputes among them.

I would classify myself as a sympathetic student of Leo Strauss, one who learned much from his lectures that I was privileged to hear as an undergraduate at the University of Chicago, much from the few personal conversations I was honored to have had with him, and much from his writings that seem to be always at hand in my own research and thought. Therefore, unlike Strauss's opponents, I am not here to either refute him or — God forbid — dismiss him. Unlike his disciples, I am not here to explicate what Strauss himself *really* meant, what his own point of view *truly* was. Frankly, I am unclear about that; in fact, greater clarity on that is something I have long hoped to learn from Strauss's disciples in their ongoing intramural disputes.[2] For what Strauss *himself* really meant, what his *own* point of view really was, is far from clear and evident. If it were, there would be much more unanimity among his disciples than there currently is. So, in the interim anyway, what I want to do is to respectfully respond to the challenge to theology that Strauss seems to present, specifically to the challenge to the traditionalist Jewish theology I espouse — although Christians and Muslims might well respond to this challenge to their theologies similarly. In fact, I believe that responding to the challenge Strauss seems to present might well be one of the most powerful stimulants available to Jewish theology today.[3]

---

2. The main point of these intramural disputes among Straussians seems to be how important Judaism was in Strauss's thinking. For the view that Judaism is peripheral in Strauss's thought, see Thomas L. Pangle's introduction to Strauss's *Studies in Platonic Political Philosophy* (Chicago: University of Chicago Press, 1983), pp. 19-24. For the view that Judaism is more central in Strauss's thought, see Harry V. Jaffa, "Crisis of the Strauss Divided: The Legacy Reconsidered," *Social Research* 54 (1987): 583; and K. H. Green, *Jew and Philosopher: The Return to Maimonides in the Jewish Thought of Leo Strauss* (Albany, N.Y.: SUNY Press, 1993), esp. the preface. Here again, I do not know enough about Strauss to decide who is right as regards his thought. However, it is only the latter reading of his thought that could possibly make it a matter of serious interest to contemporary Jewish thinkers.

3. See David Novak, "Jewish Theology," *Modern Judaism* 10 (1990): 322-23.

Strauss's Challenge to Theology

Where might we find the *locus classicus* of Strauss's challenge to Jewish theology? In first preparing myself for these reflections, I needed the counsel of
someone who knew Strauss far better than I. So, I consulted my friend Joseph Cohen of St. John's College in Annapolis, who had been a graduate
student of Strauss for a number of years at the University of Chicago, and
who had enlightened me before about other aspects of Strauss's work. He
wisely suggested that this locus is found in Strauss's little-known essay from
the early 1950s, "The Mutual Influence of Theology and Philosophy."[4] (Let
it be remembered that this essay began as a lecture Strauss gave in Jerusalem, a city — and not just an idea — he loved.[5]) After studying it, I agree
with Professor Cohen's judgment, although as in all of Strauss's statements,
it is difficult to locate Strauss's own opinion. But, since that is not my concern, I will only take some of the statements made there and respond to
them. If what I am quoting is not what Strauss himself really meant, it is
still an insightful presentation of what someone else meant, someone else
worth responding to.

At the beginning of this great essay, Strauss writes about "the philosopher [being] open to the challenge of theology or the theologian [being]
open to the challenge of philosophy."[6] At the end of the essay, Strauss writes
that "philosophy must admit the possibility of revelation."[7] My questions are
these: What is the challenge of philosophy to theology? And what can it
mean for theology that philosophy admits the possibility of its prime datum,
which is revelation? Let me begin my response with the second question, the
one about the possibility of revelation, and conclude with the first question,
the one about philosophy's challenge to theology. I can only hope that my
responses will be worthy of the greatness of the thinker who has elicited
them.

---

4. Published posthumously in the *Independent Journal of Philosophy* 3 (1979): 111-18.

5. A Hebrew translation of the original English lecture appeared long after it was given in
Iyyun: Hebrew Philosophical Quarterly 5 (1954): 110-26. For all of Strauss's love of Jerusalem,
note: "In this city and in this land, the theme of political philosophy — 'the city of righteousness, the faithful city' — has been taken more seriously than anywhere else on earth. Nowhere
else has the longing for justice and the just city filled the purest hearts and the loftiest souls with
such zeal as on this sacred soil" (*What Is Political Philosophy?* [Westport, Conn.: Greenwood
Press, 1959], p. 9).

6. Strauss, "The Mutual Influence of Theology and Philosophy," p. 111.

7. Strauss, "The Mutual Influence of Theology and Philosophy," p. 118.

The Possibility of Revelation

The insistence that philosophy must admit the possibility of revelation implies that there are philosophers who would deny any such possibility. Who are they? Strauss, who sees philosophy as a way of life, states that "the right way of life cannot be fully established except by an understanding of the nature of man, and the nature of man cannot be fully clarified except by an understanding of the nature of the whole."[8] Then, speaking of Socrates as the paradigm of one who lived the philosophical life, Strauss says that Socrates was one "who knew that he knew nothing, who therewith admitted that the whole is not intelligible, who merely wondered whether by saying the whole is not intelligible we do not admit to have some understanding of the whole."[9] So, in other words, philosophers who deny the possibility of revelation are those who are convinced, unlike Socrates, that they do have understanding of the whole and that revelation could not possibly be part of it, let alone the apex of the whole as the theologians usually assert. However, after Hegel, I am unaware of any philosopher who seems to have thought that he or she could explain the whole.[10] Moreover, even Hegel, who seems to have made such a claim in his later thought, did not dismiss the possibility of revelation; he, like Spinoza before him, only denied its ultimacy, reserving that distinct honor for philosophy alone.[11]

It seems, therefore, that it is not the case that some philosophers deny the possibility of revelation, since the only impossibility one can cogently deny is logical impossibility. Yet there is nothing inherently illogical about the doctrine of revelation. What most philosophers do deny, however, is revelation's importance. Even if the possibility of revelation is admitted — which means it *could* occur — such an occurrence would make little or no difference to the quest for truth that animates authentic philosophers. Revelation could easily be relegated to the realm of the accidental, where it would be as far as possible from the realm of the essential. If the matter, then, is left at this impasse, philosophy and theology could not have any mutual influence at all. To cite two prominent modern examples, what influence could a philosopher like Bertrand Russell have on a theologian like Karl Barth, and vice versa? Accord-

8. Strauss, "The Mutual Influence of Theology and Philosophy," p. 113.

9. Strauss, "The Mutual Influence of Theology and Philosophy," p. 114.

10. See *Hegel's Logic*, trans. W. Wallace (Oxford: Clarendon, 1975), sec. 14: 19-20; sec. 24: 41-42.

11. See Hegel, *Phenomenology of Spirit*, trans. A. V. Miller (Oxford: Oxford University Press, 1977), pp. 453ff.; and Spinoza, *Tractatus Theologico-Politicus*, trans. S. Shirley (Leiden: E. J. Brill, 1991), chaps. 13-15.

ingly, the question is not just one about the possibility of the event of revelation; rather, it is one about the possibility of the authority of revelation. Is that something a philosopher could authentically admit? It is the authority of revelation that challenges everybody, philosophers included.

Now when one speaks of authority, one is in the realm of political philosophy, the realm where Leo Strauss did his work as a scholar and a thinker; and the Hebrew Bible, the record of revelation accepted as authoritative by traditional Jews (and Christians *mutatis mutandis*), is a consummately political book. (So is the Qur'an.) The Bible is the constitution of a covenant between God and the world, and particularly between God and the people of Israel. The question, then, is this: What philosophical understanding of authority admits the possibility that its ultimate truth could only come from revelation? Only a question like this could indicate why theologians should be open to the influence of philosophy. Without a question like this, there is simply no commonality in which influence, either way or both ways, could possibly take place.

Revelation and Political Authority

If the common nexus between philosophy and theology lies in the question of political authority, then we must ask just what philosophical understanding of political authority causes the philosopher not only to admit the possibility of revelation, but also to actually desire it. Revelation's importance as a ground of human action presupposes that it is desired as good — indeed, the *summum bonum*.[12] So the Psalmist says, "As for me, the nearness of God is good for me" (Ps. 73:28). That nearness of God is the nearness of God's authoritative word. So the Deuteronomist says, "For the Word is very close to you, in your mouth and in your heart to be done" (Deut. 30:14).

Modern discussions of political authority usually see the main issue as being that of autonomy versus heteronomy. However, only when we get ourselves out of this modern dichotomy can we see a real nexus between philosophy and theology. Nevertheless, we must first work our way through and out of this dichotomy because it is ours.[13]

Autonomy recognizes the self as the ultimate authority. It holds that the only commands having moral validity are those that the self issues to itself.

12. See David Novak, *Jewish Social Ethics* (New York: Oxford University Press, 1992), pp. 27ff.

13. Novak, *Jewish Social Ethics*, pp. 45ff.

Minimally, autonomy means independence. The mode of society that autonomy posits is that created by *contract* — that is, morally valid political standards are those that are or can be agreed upon by equally independent selves
as authoritative for all. Heteronomy, on the other hand, recognizes the self as
being part of a larger structure and thus having to conform to commands not
of its own making but of an external authority. Minimally, heteronomy
means dependence. The mode of society that heteronomy posits is one having pre-existent hierarchy — that is, morally valid political standards are ones
that assign to a person his or her rightful *status* in a society, a status existing
prior to one's individual entrance into it. This distinction between autonomy
and heteronomy underlies a number of important modern theories about society and its institutions, such as Sir Henry Maine's distinctions between ancient and modern law, and Ferdinand Tönnies's distinctions between *Gemeinschaft* and *Gesellschaft*.[14] Nevertheless, despite the modern preference for
this distinction, its roots are surely ancient.

The most cogent philosophical defense of heteronomy was made by Plato
and his student Aristotle. Plato regarded the very notion of "self-mastery" —
later understood as "autonomy" — to be absurd because it violates the distinction between subject and object that is presupposed by any coherent notion of transitive action. Therefore, he emphasizes that rule must be by the
better part over the worse part, be those parts of the soul or of the city.[15] In
order for rule to be beneficial, reason must rule over what is not rational. In
the soul, reason must rule both the passions and the appetites. In the city,
more rational persons must rule less rational persons. In both realms, that relation is inherently unequal.[16] Aristotle argues on both empirical and normative grounds that "to rule [*archein*] and to be ruled [*archesthai*] is both necessary and beneficial." As such, hierarchy is inevitable (pure anarchy being in
the human world as much a phantom as a pure vacuum in the physical
world). The only question is what form of hierarchy is best.[17] However, in
contrast to what we shall be examining next, this hierarchy does not terminate in the human subject; rather, the human soul orients itself toward an end
above itself, and by that criterion it rules what is below it.[18]

---

14. See Maine, *Ancient Law* (Oxford: Oxford University Press, 1931); and Tönnies, *Community and Society*, trans. C. P. Loomis (East Lansing: Michigan State University Press, 1957).

15. Plato, *Republic*, 431a. See Aristotle, *Magna Moralia*, 1213a7.

16. See Plato, *Republic*, 433ab, 441a, 494a.

17. Aristotle, *Politics*, 1254a20.

18. Hence *autarkeia*, "self-rule," for Aristotle, means the reasoned self-control of the rational person. Even when he speaks of such a person being "like a law unto himself" (*hoion nomos
ōn heauton* — *Nicomachean Ethics*, 1128a10 — my translation), he does not mean that this per-

The most cogent philosophical defense of autonomy comes from Kant, although, as we shall soon see, its roots long predate him. He emphasizes that it is the "law-making" power of the rational will "which determines all value."[19] That power is the ability to make rules that could apply to oneself as well as to any other rational person in the same situation. Since, for Kant, great philosophical ability is not required to make rational moral judgments, one can assume an inherent equality among all persons having at least ordinary mental ability.[20] This is because Kant makes moral action more important in the human world than speculation about the basic structures of nature. By doing this he inverts 180 degrees the priorities of Plato and Aristotle.

This emphasis of Kant can be better understood by looking at the very etymology of the word *autonomy*. It comes from two Greek words: *autos*, meaning "self," and *nomos*, meaning "law." The problematic term is *autos*. Does it means "self" in the sense of "self-identity," as in A = A, or does it mean "self" in the sense of "self-awareness"? In other words, is "self" a point of reference, or is it a person who refers? If it means the former, that is, "the rule of law *itself*," then are we not back to the classical natural-law position that asserts that reason is itself inherently normative?[21] It seems that Kant means something more radically innovative than that. He seems to mean that the self is capable of constructing a rational order in which it is both sovereign and subject. Accordingly, it seems that when Kant speaks of the rational human person as *Zweck an sich selbst*, the word *selbst* refers both to the irreducible selfhood of the human subject of the act as well as to the irreducible selfhood of the human object of the act, which begins by being located within the same person. Hence, suicide is the first moral situation Kant deals with in both the *Groundwork of the Metaphysics of Morals* and *Metaphysics of Morals*.[22] That oscillating role of sovereign/subject is the condition that makes for human equality in Kant's ideal democracy.[23] It is the ideal condition of every normal person. Authority, which is of course required by the division of labor in any

---

son's will is the ultimate criterion of his or her action. Rather, he means that this person's *nomos* is modeled after the greater *physis* in which it participates by its aspirations. (See *Nicomachean Ethics*, 1141a20, 1177a25-30, 1177b25-30.) *Nomos* originates in humans, but *physis* is prior to it and is its ultimate standard. (See below, n. 47.)

19. Kant, *Groundwork of the Metaphysics of Morals*, trans. H. J. Paton (New York: Harper & Row, 1964), p. 103.

20. See Kant, *Critique of Practical Reason*, trans. L. W. Beck (Indianapolis: Indiana University Press, 1956), pt. 2: 157.

21. See Thomas Aquinas, *Summa Theologiae*, 2/1, q. 90, a. 1.

22. See David Novak, *Suicide and Morality* (New York: Scholars Studies Press, 1975), pp. 83ff.

23. See Kant, *Groundwork of the Metaphysics of Morals*, pp. 102ff.

society, even an ideal one, is relative and not absolute, as it is for Plato and Aristotle. Every person, being primarily an end-in-himself/herself, is always to transcend any use of his or her labor as a means.

Nevertheless, attempts to constitute society on exclusively heteronomous grounds or exclusively autonomous grounds are subject to serious philosophical critique. The philosophical notion that individual human persons are to find their total fulfillment in an all-encompassing, heteronomous, social order, the root of which comes from Plato (the Plato of the *Republic,* that is), has most recently been the target of Karl Popper.[24] Popper sees this notion as the most original philosophical justification of the totalitarianism of ideologues, which has brought such mind-boggling suffering to humankind in our own century especially. But, if Popper's critique is too colored by modernist prejudices for some, let me remind them that Aristotle had similar suspicions. For Aristotle, unlike Plato, the person's relationship with family is something the state must honor with restraint.[25] Furthermore, for Aristotle, also unlike Plato, the true metaphysician is able to transcend even the best society by becoming godlike, never to be morally obligated to serve any society again.[26]

The philosophical notion that an adequate human society can be constituted on the basis of autonomy alone has also been the target of philosophers since Hegel.[27] Most recently, philosophers such as Mary Ann Glendon and Michael Sandel have argued against John Rawls's view of autonomous justice, pointing out that the coherent survival of society requires that society be able to make claims on its citizens that are not themselves reducible to the individual right to contract — even to contract a social contract.[28]

So it seems that the best order philosophers can constitute for society is a mixture of heteronomy and autonomy — for autonomy alone seems to lead to anarchy, and heteronomy alone seems to lead to tyranny. Autonomy alone does not bring with it enough society; heteronomy alone brings with it too much society. Thus in democratic societies, which are the only places in the world where such debates can be conducted in public, philosophical debates

24. See Popper, *The Open Society and Its Enemies,* 5th rev. ed. (Princeton: Princeton University Press, 1966), vol. 1, pp. 86ff.

25. See Aristotle, *Politics,* 1262a5ff.

26. See Aristotle, *Nicomachean Ethics,* 1177a25-30, 1177b30-1178a1.

27. See Hegel, *Philosophy of Right,* trans. T. M. Knox (Oxford: Oxford University Press, 1952), sec. 324.

28. See Glendon, *Rights Talk: The Impoverishment of Political Discourse* (New York: Free Press, 1991); Sandel, *Liberalism and the Limits of Justice* (Cambridge: Cambridge University Press, 1982). For Rawls's debt to Kant on the question of autonomy, see his *A Theory of Justice* (Cambridge, Mass.: Harvard University Press, 1971), pp. 251ff., 563ff.

(in the broadest sense of the term) are generally about how the rights of the majority are balanced by the rights of minorities and vice versa, the most basic minority being the individual person. The rubric of these debates is essentially the same not only for positivists but also for adherents of natural law.[29] As Charles Taylor has recently demonstrated so powerfully, moral discourse in our society becomes almost unintelligible if not conducted with a vocabulary in which human selfhood is central.[30]

So far, the level of political philosophy that we have been examining does not seem to have any opening for theology at all. For the subject of theology, who is God, specifically the God of biblical revelation, is certainly neither a majority nor a minority, neither a society nor an individual. This God is not a majority because God is One *(ehad)*, whereas a majority is many. This God is not a minority because God is Unique *(ehad)* and thus could not become part of any society as an individual can and must become.[31] Where, then, does political philosophy provide an opening for the God of biblical revelation, whether it is aware of it or not? I think that for this opening we must return to the ancients (who were so preferred by Leo Strauss), especially to Plato, the Plato of the *Republic*.

It will be recalled that at the beginning of this work, Socrates shows the inherent inconsistencies of three views of justice, those of Cephalus, Polemarchus, and Thrasymachus. However, when he is confronted by the view of Glaucon, he has no such logical refutation. For Glaucon basically presents the social contract theory that Socrates himself had accepted as the argument of the laws of Athens in the *Crito*.[32] The argument is that society can make claims on individuals who have already given their tacit consent to that society's authority. In Socrates' particular case, this meant that he would restrain himself from escaping from the death sentence of the Athenian court because by remaining in Athens of his own free choice, he thereby accepted the authority of Athenian legal institutions. These institutions, nevertheless, could not make unconditional, total claims on him or any citizen. They could not stop him from being a philosopher.[33] Thus, his life and those of his fellow

29. See, e.g., Ronald Dworkin, *Taking Rights Seriously* (Cambridge, Mass.: Harvard University Press, 1978), pp. 171-72, 205; John Finnis, *Natural Law and Natural Rights* (Oxford: Oxford University Press, 1980), pp. 223ff.

30. See his *Sources of the Self: The Making of the Modern Identity* (Cambridge, Mass.: Harvard University Press, 1989), pp. 511ff.

31. See Hermann Cohen, "Einheit oder Einzigkeit Gottes," *Jüdische Schriften*, ed. B. Strauss (Berlin: C. A. Schwetschke, 1924), vol. 1, pp. 87ff.

32. Plato, *Republic*, 358aff.; *Crito*, 51d. See Strauss, *Natural Right and History*, p. 119.

33. See Plato, *Apology*, 29d.

Athenians were involved in a delicate balance between personal rights and communal duties. In a somewhat different context, Freud called the balance of psychic demands made by what he called the pleasure principle and the reality principle the "economics of the libido," and sadly concluded that this is the best that civilization and its discontents could come up with.[34]

Unlike the first three views of justice, the view of Glaucon is not one that is necessarily false; it is only one that is humanly insufficient. It is insufficient because it sees the human person as essentially schizoid, unable to devote himself or herself to anything or to anyone with a full soul. At this level, though, the human soul is restless, a restlessness that only a fool would deny.[35] Plato's constitution of his philosophical polity is his answer to this restlessness of the human soul. Theology cannot accept his constitution as the solution, as we shall presently argue, but the very recognition of the question is the only opening that theology needs. At this level, philosophy and theology can at long last truly take each other seriously. Both philosophy and theology now believe that the solution to the human predicament lies in humans being properly related to that which surpasses them but which cannot itself be surpassed, or as Anselm unforgettably put it: "that which nothing greater can be conceived" *(id quo maius non cogitari nequit)*.[36] And *that* certainly surpasses humans, whether they are taken individually or collectively. The difference between theology and philosophy lies in whether the relationship with that greatest reality originates from below (as in philosophy) or from above (as in theology).

Creation and Revelation

Let us now see why theology can share Plato's question while simultaneously rejecting his answer. In the Mishnah, which is the second most authoritative book in Judaism after the Bible, we find a principle that appears in numerous rabbinic discussions thereafter. It is this: "One may benefit another person without their consent [*zakhin l'adam she-lo bi-fanav*], but one may not obligate [*ein havin*] another person without their consent."[37] An example of this would be: I may accept money on your behalf without your consent, but I may not pledge money on your behalf without your consent. My right to ben-

34. See Freud, *Civilization and Its Discontents*, trans. J. Riviere (Garden City, N.Y.: W. W. Norton, 1958), p. 25.

35. See Augustine, *Confessions*, 1.1.

36. See Anselm, *Proslogion*, chap. 2.

37. M. Eruvin 7.11.

efit you without your consent assumes that I know what is beneficial to you, a benefit you yourself acknowledge in principle. However, if it turns out that what I thought was beneficial to you is not acknowledged by you in principle, then my assumed benefit for you is in fact a detriment, which may be refused. (In rabbinic Hebrew, *hov* is the same word for "detriment" and "obligation."[38]) The reason behind this formulation is that I have more authority over my own life than you do because I have more knowledge and concern for my own interests than you do. The converse is equally true — that is, you have more authority over your own life than I do because you have more knowledge and concern for your own interests than I do.

If left at this level alone, we seem to have the epistemological foundation of moral autonomy — namely, I am transparent to myself just as you are transparent to yourself. However, there are times when you are required to act for my benefit even without my consent, even contrary to it. Such action is required when I am in danger of harming myself. When this is the case, then "you shall not stand idly by the blood of your neighbor" (Lev. 19:16). When this is the case, I do not know what my benefit truly is; I am not transparent to myself.[39] Furthermore, the other in the person of society itself is authorized to enact rules for the common good of which I am a part, even if that part is an unwilling minority. In other words, society is at times authorized to act heteronomously. The balance of heteronomy and autonomy is based on the assumption that no one is totally transparent, even to themselves. On the other hand, though, the inevitable anarchy of autonomy is based on the erroneous assumption that individuals are totally transparent to themselves; and the inevitable tyranny of heteronomy is based on the equally erroneous assumption that individual persons are totally transparent to society — at least to the ideal society run by savants. It can be argued that the schizoid social contract qua social compromise described by Socrates in the *Crito* and advocated by Glaucon in the *Republic,* and then followed more or less by modern social contract theorists, is preferable to both of these extreme political options.

However, the reason that this balance in a society constituted by revelation does not lead to the schizoid state of human life that we have just seen is that both the individual person and the society itself are totally transparent to God. "For humans only see appearances, but the Lord sees the heart" (1 Sam. 16:7). "Above all, the heart is deceitful; it is wounded [*v'anush hu*]. Who knows it? I

38. See, for example, B. Baba Metsia 19a; B. Berakhot 27b; Maimonides, *Mishneh Torah:* Rebels, 2.9.

39. See Maimonides, MT: Gerushin, 2.20.

the Lord get to the bottom of the heart" (Jer. 17:9-10).[40] It is revelation that makes this fundamental truth known to the people — both collectively and individually — to whom God has chosen to reveal God's self and God's law. Revelation is from the creator God who alone has perfect vision of the whole and everything in it — we humans included — because "He made us and not we ourselves" (Ps. 100:3). God's commandments are addressed to all created entities: human and nonhuman, individual and collective. The only way of life, then, that is truly sufficient to our nature must come from the Unique One (ehad), who transcends the limits of created nature itself. As the Mishnah puts it, "Beloved are Israel having been given a desirable vessel [the Torah], and it is an additional act of love that it is made known to them [by God] that this desirable vessel is that through which the world is created."[41] Israel's revelation thus privileges her to be aware of what is the true fulfillment of human nature, a nature that reflects the nature of the whole created universe.

God's authority is the total authority unique to the creator of the universe. Obviously, it is not "autonomous" in the modern anthropocentric (and ultimately atheistic, in my opinion) sense of that word that we have seen above. It is not "heteronomous" either because it does not come from an "other" (heteros). It does not come from a stranger, whose authority, as we have also seen above, is only valid when limited and distributed, but invalid when unlimited and ubiquitous. God is closer to our nature than any of us are to ourselves (autos). With all "other gods," however, we are essentially alienated from our nature.[42] As the Talmud puts it, "God does not deal with his creatures as a tyrant."[43] That is why the Mishnah teaches, "God wanted to benefit [le-zakkot] his people, so he multiplied commandments for them."[44] God can benefit the people much more than they can ever benefit themselves.

For theologians who have been open to the influence of philosophy, the natural law that humans can discern from the dim mirror of nature is part of the larger divine law that is revealed more directly by God. We see this in theologians as otherwise disparate as Maimonides, Aquinas, and Calvin.[45]

40. See Hannah Arendt, The Human Condition (Garden City, N.Y.: Doubleday, 1959), 302n. 2 regarding Augustine, Confessions, bk. 10.

41. M. Avot 3.14. See Bereshit Rabbah 1.1.

42. See Mekhilta: Yitro re Exod. 20:3 and Isa. 46:7, ed. Horovitz-Rabin (Jerusalem: Bamberger & Wahrman, 1960), p. 223.

43. B. Avodah Zarah 3a. See also B. Shabbat 88a.

44. M. Makkot 3.16 re Isa. 42:21.

45. See Maimonides, MT: Kings, 8.11-9.1; Thomas Aquinas, Summa Theologiae, 2/1, q. 94, a. 4, ad. 1; John Calvin, Institutes of the Christian Religion, trans. F. L. Battles (Philadelphia: Westminster Press, 1960), 2.7.10, 4.20.16.

However, unlike later rationalists, they do not think natural law and divine law are identical.[46] Unlike later fideists, they did not think that natural law and divine law are antithetical.[47]

For philosophers who have been open to the influence of theology, natural law is seen as coming to nature from the divine lawgiver, even though these philosophers can be agnostic about any particular historical revelation. Indeed, as Strauss's oldest disciple Harry V. Jaffa has shown, the very term *natural law* is itself an oxymoron in ancient pagan philosophy, for *natura* or *physis* is the opposite of *lex* or *nomos*.[48] Hence that term could only enter philosophical discourse that is open to the influence of theology. When the word *law* is used nonfiguratively, it presupposes that there is a lawgiver.[49] Therefore, natural law presupposes, in the words of the Declaration of Independence, "Nature's God," who, being the *creator,* is not the same as "the God *of* Nature." Nevertheless, natural law is the province of philosophy and not theology precisely because it is not directly derived from the words of revelation but, rather, from reflection on the limits or ends of the human condition itself. To confuse theology and philosophy at this key juncture is to commit a most disastrous category error.

46. Thus Kant replaces *Gebote Gottes* with *göttliche Gebote* (*Critique of Pure Reason,* B847), which means that whatever is divine is ipso facto rational and, conversely, whatever is not rational is ipso facto not divine. Along these lines, he is followed by his greatest Jewish disciple, Hermann Cohen. See his *Religion of Reason Out of the Sources of Judaism,* trans. S. Kaplan (New York: F. Ungar, 1972), chap. 16, pp. 338ff.

47. One of the most influential expressions of this kind of fideistic antinatural law position in Judaism today is that of Marvin Fox in his widely discussed 1972 essay, "Maimonides and Aquinas on Natural Law," *Dinē Israel* 3 (Eng. sec.), now reprinted and slightly revised in his *Interpreting Maimonides: Studies in Methodology, Metaphysics, and Moral Philosophy* (Chicago: University of Chicago Press, 1990). The following quote epitomizes his views: "In ancient Hebrew thought there is only one source of the knowledge of good and evil — the commandments of God as they are revealed to man" (p. 126). For a critique of both Fox, who errs on this point for theological reasons, and Strauss, who errs on this point for philosophical reasons, see Novak, *Jewish Social Ethics,* pp. 25-33.

48. See his article "Natural Law" in *The International Encyclopedia of the Social Sciences,* 17 vols., ed. David Sills (New York: Macmillan, 1968), vol. 11, p. 80; also Helmut Koester, "The Concept of Natural Law in Greek Thought," in *Religions in Antiquity: Essays in Memory of Erwin Ramsdell Goodenough,* ed. J. Neusner (Leiden: E. J. Brill, 1968), pp. 521ff.

49. Thus, Spinoza, who wanted to sever philosophy from any connection to theology, distinguished between *lex,* when used for nature, and *ius,* when used for human society. *Ius* presupposes a temporal will; *lex* expresses the eternal natural order. See *Tractatus Theologico-Politicus,* chap. 4.

Philosophy's Challenge to Theology

Strauss was quite astute to see that the philosopher's problem with revelation derives from the question he raised in his article "The Mutual Influence of Theology and Philosophy," namely, "Is the tradition reliable?" — that is, the tradition through which revelation is transmitted to all of us who are not prophets.[50] (The assumption of the Bible and the Rabbis is that all the people of Israel, at least when the first two commandments of the Decalogue were uttered, were themselves prophets for that moment.[51]) Moreover, he raises the question of "one particular divine code [being] accepted as truly divine" and "all other allegedly divine codes [being] simply denied."[52] In other words, there are competing revelations, and even if there were only one, how do we know that it is accurate?

Philosophy, of course, cannot answer either of these questions. A philosophical answer would have to judge which revelation, if any, presented the best law inasmuch as revelation for the three religions of revelation — Judaism, Christianity, and Islam — is explicitly normative. But, as Strauss rightly points out in this essay (speaking as a Jew about Judaism), "If this is the case, is then the allegedly revealed law not in fact the product of reason, of human reason, the work of Moses and not of God?"[53] It is one thing for philosophy to admit the possibility of revelation; it is quite another thing for philosophy to claim that it can validate revelation. No true theologian could ever accept such external validation. As the Bible puts it, "There is no wisdom, there is no understanding, there is no counsel, over above [le-neged] the Lord" (Prov. 21:30).[54] Revelation is only validated by the experience of responsively hearing the voice of God, or by the trust one has for those who have transmitted the story of revelation and its normative content.

However, what philosophy can do for theology is to elucidate its *conditio sine qua non*, its minimal condition, without judging its *conditio per quam*, its ultimate ground.[55] Philosophy and theology can agree on what the moral

---

50. "The Mutual Influence of Theology and Philosophy," p. 115.

51. See B. Makkot 23b-24a; also, Maimonides, *Guide of the Perplexed*, 2.33.

52. "The Mutual Influence of Theology and Philosophy," p. 112.

53. "The Mutual Influence of Theology and Philosophy," p. 115.

54. See B. Berakhot 19b.

55. One can see this distinction in the way Aristotle relates justice and friendship, As he writes, "Friends do not need justice, but the just need friends" (*Nicomachean Ethics*, 1155a26 — my translation). What he seems to mean here is that justice is presupposed by friendship; hence it is already in place before persons can be friends to each other. It is tacitly assumed. However, justice per se is insufficient for a fulfilling human life. It is form, not content. *Philia* is the

prerequisites of a society worthy of human loyalty are to be. Strauss speaks of "a broad agreement between the Bible and Greek philosophy regarding both morality and the insufficiency of morality; the disagreement concerns that 'x' which completes morality."[56] The Rabbis speak of the area of interhuman relations *(bein adam le-havero)* with which part of the Torah is concerned as being most akin to the workings of human reason, as being that "which even if it were not written, it should have been written."[57] Aristotle saw custom *(ethos)* as being capable of rational explanation *(ēthikē).*[58] And both the Rabbis and Aristotle, *mutatis mutandis,* saw the realm of the interhuman as ultimately subordinate to the realm of the divine-human. Here philosophy as practical reason, the practical reason that discerns natural law, is of most help to theology because it prevents theology from sinking from the level of the superrational to the level of the subrational — that is, to the level of superstition and fanaticism. So also does practical reason prevent metaphysics — theoretical philosophy — from sinking to the level of irresponsible flight into fantasy. In our day, practical reason prevents both *Torah* and *theōria* from sinking to the level of ideology, which argues neither from revelation nor from nature, both of which are public (as Maimonides emphasized), but only from the private vision of the ideologue. In other words, the enemy of both *Torah* and *theōria,* in both ancient and modern times, is gnosticism, of which ideology is only its modern manifestation.[59]

Let me give one example of how this philosophical influence on theology works from the writings of Strauss's favorite Jewish theologian, Maimonides. The Torah commands the people of Israel to exterminate the Amalekites. "Blot out the memory of the Amalekites from under the heavens" (Deut. 25:19). Two grounds for this command seem to be found. One is that of revenge for the unprovoked attack of the Israelites by the Amalekites when they left Egypt (25:17-18a), an attack on noncombatants as well as on combatants. The second is that the Amalekites "did not fear God" (25:18b), fear of God being a biblical term for elementary human decency and restraint.[60]

---

ground and content (for Aristotle, the *telos*) of *dikaiosynē;* and *dikaiosynē* is its necessary condition. For my own more Kantian treatment of the logical relation of ground and condition in the ontological relation of revelation and reason, see David Novak, *Jewish-Christian Dialogue: A Jewish Justification* (New York: Oxford University Press, 1989), pp. 129ff.

56. Strauss, "The Mutual Influence of Theology and Philosophy," p. 111.

57. See M. Yoma 8.9; B. Yoma 67b; M. Baba Batra 10.8; and R. Israel Lipschütz, *Tif'eret Yisra' el,* n. 84 thereon.

58. Aristotle, *Nicomachean Ethics,* 1103a17.

59. See Hans Jonas, *The Gnostic Religion,* 2d ed. (Boston: Beacon Press, 1963), pp. 320ff.

60. See Gen. 20:11; Exod. 1:17.

If the ground of revenge is emphasized, then the present moral condition of the Amalekites is irrelevant: an old score is to be settled. Israel is to do to Amalek as Amalek did to Israel. To use a rabbinic term, it is "measure for measure" *(middah ke-neged middah)*.[61] However, if the ground of fear of God is emphasized, then what if the present moral condition of the Amalekites has changed? What if they have repented of their evil, either all of them or even only some of them?[62] To interpret the commandment as being categorical rather than hypothetical would be blatantly unjust. Therefore, Maimonides, basing himself on earlier rabbinic speculation — not legislation per se — writes in his code of Jewish law, the *Mishneh Torah:* "Even though Scripture says about Amalek 'Blot out the memory of Amalek' (Deuteronomy 25:19) that only pertains to those who did not accept peace terms [*she-lo hishlimu*]."[63] Thus he changed what appeared to have been a categorical imperative into a hypothetical imperative, As the commentator on Maimonides, Joseph Karo, pointed out, basing himself on Maimonides' whole ethical approach, "this means they accepted the seven Noahide laws . . . thus removing themselves from the moral category of 'Amalek' and becoming proper [*ha-kesherim*] Noahides."[64] "Noahides" is the rabbinic name for humankind; and "the seven Noahide laws" is the rabbinic term for natural law, as I have argued elsewhere.[65]

In other words, criteria of rational morality are invoked to interpret revelation. But, unlike modern Jewish thinkers such as Hermann Cohen, against whose approach to Judaism Strauss argued more than once, the criteria of rational morality do not constitute revelation.[66] There is much more to revelation than morality, but not anything less. As Maimonides emphasized elsewhere, all philosophers are not prophets, but all prophets are first philosophers.[67] In the end, the theologians can account for philosophy, but the philosophers cannot account for revelation.

Thus Deutero-Isaiah in his messianic vision states:

All the nations are gathered together, the peoples are assembled. Who among them can tell this and let us understand the first things? Can they

61. B. Sanhedrin 90a.

62. See Gen. 18:23-25; Jon. 3:8-10.

63. Maimonides, MT: Kings, 6.4. Rabbinic sources for this ruling are *Sifre* no. 204 and Y. Shevi'it 6.1/36c.

64. *Kesef Mishneh* on Maimonides, MT: Kings, 6.4.

65. See David Novak, *The Image of the Non-Jew in Judaism: An Historical and Constructive Study of the Noahide Laws* (New York and Toronto: E. Mellen Press, 1983), esp. pp. 275ff.

66. See *Spinoza's Critique of Religion*, trans. E. M. Sinclair (New York: Schocken Books, 1965), introduction and pp. 15ff.

67. See Maimonides, MT: Foundations, 7.5, *Guide of the Perplexed*, 3.29.

put forth their witnesses and be justified so that they will be heard and say "it is truth" [*emet*]? You are My witnesses, says the Lord, My servants whom I have chosen, so that you may know and be certain of Me and understand that I am He, before Me no god has been and after Me none will be. (Isa. 43:9-10)

In the earliest translation of the Bible, that of the Septuagint into Greek, we see that "first things" — *ri'shonot* — of the Hebrew text is translated *ex archēs*. Since it is not unreasonable to assume that the Greek translators were aware of the earlier philosophical use of *archē*, for example by Aristotle, we can see a text like this laying the groundwork for philosophical theology from Philo on. That is, this theology insists that it can recognize the authentic insights of the philosophers about the "first things" and then witness the revelation that shows what the philosophers alone could not see.[68] To do this, these theologians themselves have to already be philosophers. Being in this tradition myself, I must therefore respectfully disagree with Strauss, who insists that philosophers cannot be theologians and vice versa. In this tradition, theology presupposes philosophy, and philosophy intends theology. Furthermore, theology itself admits of philosophical analysis every bit as rigorous as that which is applied to the study of any other area of significant human experience. Revelation itself is a prime datum.[69] Being itself a creation of God, like nature, revelation cannot be inconsistent with what we know about nature, and thus there must be significant commonality between the methods used to study both data.[70]

68. See H. A. Wolfson, *Philo* (Cambridge, Mass.: Harvard University Press, 1947), vol. 2, pp. 439ff.

69. As such, my difference with Strauss can be specifically connected to the debate among scholars about whether Maimonides' reference to his major legal work *Mishneh Torah* as "our great compilation" (*Guide*, III:29 — Arabic: *ta'alifana al-khbir;* Hebrew: *hiburenu hagadol*) is a statement about its quantity or its importance in relation to the *Guide*. The latter is Strauss's view; see *Persecution and the Art of Writing* (Glencoe, Ill.: Free Press, 1952), pp. 39-40. For the former view, see Isadore Twersky, *Introduction to the Code of Maimonides* (New Haven: Yale University Press, 1980), pp. 18-19. Over and above what Maimonides' true opinion was, *Mishneh Torah* is in many ways — including theological ways that include philosophy — the more perennially interesting work. For its reflections are more beholden to the most perennially interesting Jewish data: the Commandments. The *Guide*'s reflections, on the other hand, are far more beholden to an ontology that presupposes a by now irretrievable natural science and an ethics that presupposes a by now irretrievable political order. See David Novak, *The Election of Israel: The Idea of the Chosen People* (Cambridge: Cambridge University Press, 1995), pp. 237ff., esp. pp. 239-40n. 151; also, *Law and Theology in Judaism* (New York: Ktav Publishing House, 1974), vol. 1, pp. 142-43. This specific question was the subject of my very first conversation with Leo Strauss, sometime in the spring of 1960 in Hillel House at the University of Chicago.

70. See Maimonides, *Guide of the Perplexed*, 1.65, 1.55.

Conclusion

Since I have learned much from Leo Strauss, learning that directly pertains to Torah itself, I am duty-bound to pay him honor — a duty that is also a pleasure.[71] Let me close with a rabbinic word about what our relationship to a deceased teacher might be. "Levi bar Nazira said that whoever quotes a teaching in the name of the one from whom he heard it, the lips of that teacher move along with his, even in the grave."[72] In order to explain this cryptic dictum, the interpretation of a later scholar is brought by the editor of the same text. He says, "It is like drinking good old wine: even after the wine has been drunk, its taste remains in one's mouth." With such a taste in one's mouth, one not only continues to enjoy the wine; one will also be much better prepared to distinguish good wine from bad, the true from the false. After drinking this good old wine, he or she will never again be the same. So it was, so it is, and so it will be when we are privileged to learn from Leo Strauss.

71. See M. Avot 4.1 re Ps. 119:99 and M. Avot 6.3 re Ps. 55:14.
72. Y. Berakhot 2.1/4b re Song 7:10.

2 The Dialectic between Theory and Practice in Rabbinic Thought (2004)

Theōria and *Praxis*

It would seem that the question of the dialectic between the theoretical and the practical is a perennial philosophical question. It is a question that has been asked time and time again in the history of philosophy. It is still being asked today. It is a question of the relation of what the Greeks (the first philosophers per se) called *theōria* (in Latin *contemplatio*) and *praxis* (in Latin *actus*): How does one distinguish between them? How does one connect them? Is it correct to say that each discipline is on its own, as Hume would say?[1] Is it correct to say that *theōria* takes precedence over *praxis*, as Aristotle would say?[2] Is it correct to say that practical reason takes precedence over pure (speculative) reason, as Kant would say?[3]

However, there is a question that Jewish thinkers must ask themselves before ever embarking on this type of questioning of classical Jewish sources, namely: Is it possible to ask adequate questions about issues in classical Jewish texts when the very questioners are formulating their questions using Greek philosophical terminology (or any other terminology), which was unknown to the authors of these classical Jewish texts, especially to the Rabbis of the Talmudic period? Indeed, these Rabbis are the prime example of tradi-

1. See Hume, *A Treatise of Human Nature*, 3.1.1, ed. L. A. Selby-Bigge (Oxford: Clarendon Press, 1888), pp. 455-70.
2. See Aristotle, *Nicomachean Ethics*, 1128b16-1139b14.
3. See Kant, *Critique of Pure Reason*, B596-599.

This essay was originally presented as a lecture, delivered in Hebrew, at Ben-Gurion University of the Negev, Beer Sheva, Israel, in June 2004.

tional Jewish thinkers who lived in a historical period before the introduction of academic philosophy and its language into normative Jewish discourse.[4]

All this notwithstanding, I think it is possible to ask philosophical questions, like the one about the dialectic between the theoretical and the practical, when pondering rabbinic literature, and that it is even possible to find some appropriate answers to these questions. In fact, there are definite precedents to this approach in our traditional Jewish literature, even literature not usually classified as "Jewish philosophy." I would now like to demonstrate this point by reading a well-known rabbinic anecdote and the teaching it contains. This reading is done by utilizing the interpretation of this anecdote and its teaching by a great pre-modern Jewish thinker of the seventeenth century, who explained it using Aristotelian philosophical terminology (which he no doubt learned from the Hebrew writings of medieval Jewish Aristotelians). But what is important to keep in mind is that this later thinker is not writing Aristotelian philosophy; he is only using Aristotelian terminology in the service of Jewish conceptuality. The Jewish conceptuality is essential; the Greek terminology only functions for it secondarily. Nonetheless, because of her Greek service to her Jewish mistress, the maidservant is still needed and cannot be sent away as having only performed a onetime service.[5] Her service is continually required once introduced. She becomes a permanent guest among us, as it were. That is, without this philosophical terminology being regularly kept in mind, the deeper meaning of this rabbinic teaching diminishes in intellectual value. Therefore, one can ask the question of the mutual relation of *theōria* and *praxis* in a philosophical way within the domain of normative Judaism and do so with profit. One can, moreover, formulate or begin to formulate an answer to the question there, an answer that could not be formulated elsewhere.

This rabbinic anecdote (with certain minor textual variations) is found in several places in rabbinic literature. Here I quote the version of *Sifre* on Deuteronomy:

---

4. Although it is quite likely that Palestinian Rabbis were familiar with various intellectual aspects of the Graeco-Roman culture of their time and place (generally called *hokhmah yevanit*), there does not seem to be any evidence of their use of Greek philosophical texts or even of formal philosophical terms, as was the case with Philo and some other Hellenistic Jewish authors. See my late revered teacher, Prof. Saul Lieberman, *Greek in Jewish Palestine*, 2d ed. (New York: Feldheim, 1965), pp. 15-28; *Hellenism in Jewish Palestine*, 2d ed. (New York: Jewish Theological Seminary of America, 1962), pp. 100-114. The use of formal philosophy per se did not come into rabbinic Judaism until the encounter with Greek philosophy via the Arab *falasifa* beginning in the ninth century.

5. See H. A. Wolfson, *Philo* (Cambridge, Mass.: Harvard University Press, 1947), vol. 1, pp. 143-63.

Rabbi Tarfon, Rabbi Akibah, and Rabbi Yose the Galilean were already din-
ing in the home of Aris in Lydda when the following question was put before them: What is greater, learning [*talmud*] or practice [*ma'aseh*]? Rabbi
Tarfon said practice is greater. Rabbi Akibah said learning is greater. But
those assembled all answered by saying learning is greater because it brings
one to practice. Rabbi Yose the Galilean says learning is greater since Israel
was learning the law of the dough-offering [*hallah*] forty years [in the Wilderness before having to practice it in the land of Israel].[6]

One must understand "learning" *(talmud)* not as "study" in the modern
sense, which can often be a private activity, but as an essentially public act of
communal education.[7]

As a question of political history, there are two approaches one could take
in regard to this text. First, during the Roman persecution of the Jews at the time
of the Bar Kokhba revolt (around 135 C.E.), the Roman government looked upon
public Judaism, especially public Torah instruction and the political meanings
inherent in its very publicity, as being itself revolutionary activity. (The fact that
Rabbi Akibah, the most prominent sage of his time, was an open supporter
of the Bar Kokhba revolt no doubt lent credence to these imperial fears.) So it
seems that for reasons of political security, Rabbi Tarfon was convinced that it
was necessary to temporarily cease from public Torah instruction *(talmud
torah),* and that despite this, Judaism could survive in the long run. After all,
most of the commandments could be kept clandestinely, away from the prying
eyes of the government and its informers. Rabbi Akibah, though, disagreed.
He was convinced that without uninterrupted public Torah learning, Judaism
as a living reality was doomed. Without this regular public activity, even in
dangerous times, the Jews would become like fish out of water, who after fleeing
their natural aquatic pursuers realize to their sorrow that what seemed like a
place of refuge is in fact "a place of our death."[8] As is well known, Rabbi Akibah
paid for his conviction, which he not only preached but practiced, with his own
life, having been gruesomely killed as a martyr by the Romans because of his
insistence on "assembling groups in public" for Torah instruction.[9]

---

6. *Sifre al Devarim,* no. 41, ed. Louis Finkelstein (New York: Jewish Theological Seminary
of America, 1969), p. 85. For parallels and variants, see n. 13 thereon.

7. For the priority of public over private learning so that the latter is taken to be a means to
the former, see B. Baba Kama 17a and Rashi, s.v. "le-migmar," and Tos., s.v. "ve-ha'amar"
(Rabbenu Tam's interpretation); B. Avodah Zarah 19a and Rashi, s.v. "u-ktiv" (2d opinion).

8. B. Berakhot 61b.

9. B. Berakhot 61b. See also my late revered teacher, Prof. Louis Finkelstein, *Akibah* (Philadelphia: Jewish Publication Society of America, 1936), esp. pp. 195ff.

The answer of the other Rabbis (all who answered to resolve the impasse between Rabbi Tarfon and Rabbi Akibah) demonstrates the victory of Rabbi Akibah's point of view. That is, practice is contingent on learning in a way learning is not contingent on practice: learning brings one to practice, but practice does not bring one to learning. Along these lines, Rabbi Yose the Galilean cited as proof that in the past there had been a hiatus between the giving of some commandments and their actual practice, but there had been no such hiatus between the giving of these commandments and their being learned. That was done immediately and perpetually. Thus there are times when the Jews can survive without the actual practice of a commandment, but they cannot survive with the continual learning of the commandment: what it is and how it is to be practiced when the opportunity to do so arises sooner or later.

The medieval commentators (at least as many as I have been able to check) did not delve into the debate between Rabbi Tarfon and Rabbi Akibah as a pragmatic political problem in a certain period of past Jewish history. They did not seem be concerned with this as a question of public policy. They did not seem to be concerned with the obvious question: Does saving Jewish lives take precedence over Judaic public instruction or not? Quite the contrary. These commentators delved into the debate as an intellectual matter, which for them could only be theological. Especially in the conclusion of the rest of the Rabbis present at the debate, these commentators saw a glaring contradiction in the attempt of these Rabbis to synthesize the view of Rabbi Akibah with the view of Rabbi Tarfon. But what is the contradiction? It is as follows: If learning is "greater" (*gadol*), why does one have to justify its greatness with the reason "it brings one [*mev'i*] to practice"? By giving such a reason for the greatness of learning Torah, is it not the case that they are making it a means functioning for an end outside itself and greater than itself? Is not the end always greater than the means to it? So, in a parallel text in the Babylonian Talmud, the primary medieval glossators (*tosafot*) say in the name of the most famous medieval commentator, Rashi: "One has to say practice is greater [*adif*]."[10] But then the question remains: If practice is greater, then it is as Rabban Simeon ben Gamliel put it a generation later: "Not enquiry [*he-midrash*] but practice is of the essence."[11] If so, then by what logic did the other Rabbis come to the conclusion that "learning is greater"? How could Rashi say, "Who depends on whom? Is it not that the lesser [*ha-qatan*] de-

10. B. Baba Kama 17a, Tos., s.v. "ve-ha'amar." Cf. B. Yoma 72b and Rashi, s.v. "ve-ta'r'a"; also, M. Avot 3.9.

11. M. Avot 1.7.

pends on the greater [*ha-gadol*]?!"[12] Isn't the means dependent on its end in a way that the end is not dependent on its means? Nevertheless, the medieval commentators seem to evade this inner contradiction. In effect, they dissolve it by interpreting it in a way that assigns Rabbi Tarfon's view to one kind of situation and Rabbi Akibah's view to another.[13] In other words, they took a direct dispute of an identical point ("either/or" logic) and turned it into two noncontradictory views about two different kinds of situations ("both/and" logic). Thus these glossators advocated that in some situations learning ought to precede practice, whereas in other situations practice ought to precede learning. Hence each situation calls for a different mode of action, so that Rabbi Tarfon's opinion pertains here and not there, and Rabbi Akibah's opinion pertains there and not here. To use the language of Aristotelian logic: the excluded middle has been re-included.

Causality: Teleological or Creative?

The first (and perhaps the only) exegete to grab the bull by the horns, so to speak, by attempting to solve the inner contradiction in the compromise made out of the views of Rabbi Tarfon and Rabbi Akibah by their colleagues is Rabbi Isaiah Halevi Horowitz, the author of the widely read quasi-kabbalistic work, *Shnei Luhot ha-Berit* ("The Two Tablets of the Covenant"). Horowitz is most widely named according to the acronym of his magnum

---

12. Quoted by the gloss on B. Kiddushin 40b, Tos., s.v. "talmud."

13. However, they do this following Bavli's resolution of a contradiction between two different texts. The first text (B. Kiddushin 40b) emphasizes the priority of *talmud*, being a variant of the *locus classicus* we have been examining. The second text (B. Baba Kama 17a) is based on an anecdote about Rabbi Yohanan bar Nappaha performing several practical commandments before answering a halakhic question from his pupil, Rabbah bar bar Hanah, which Bavli seems to infer as a normative precedent for the priority of *ma'aseh*. Rashi and Rabbenu Tam (see n. 7 above) assume that the anecdote about Rabbi Yohanan refers to his private study that is trumped by his individual practice, which wouldn't be the case were he being called to engage in truly public instruction. Were that the case, *talmud* would take precedence since public need trumps private need (see, e.g., B. Berakhot 47b). But, the gloss on B. Baba Kama 17a (Tos., s.v. "ve-ha'amar") quotes what seems to be a lone opinion, that of *Sheiltot*, which gives priority to private study. Hence Rabbi Yohanan performed these practical commandments before instructing his pupil, which does seem to be a matter of public instruction. Were he confronted, though, with the choice of first engaging in his own private study, he would have made that his priority, since this is what would bring him to *ma'aseh*. See *Sheiltot de-Rav Ahai Gaon*, ed. Kenig (Jerusalem: n.p., 5700/1939-40), pp. 8b-9a. Maimonides (MT: Torah Study, 1.3), in effect, ignores the anecdote about Rabbi Yohanan and concludes that in all cases *talmud* takes precedence over *ma'aseh*.

opus: *Shela*. (He shall be so called throughout this discussion.) As an exegete and a theologian, he is not usually seen to be a Jewish "philosopher," which might be a title reserved for those Jewish theologians who make explicit and continual use of philosophical literature in their work. Nevertheless, in his brief treatment of the rabbinic text we have been discussing, *Shela* shows a remarkable use of philosophical logic. So he writes:

> The well-known difficulty that earlier and later thinkers struggled so with is that the reason "because it [learning] brings one to practice" contradicts its own premise. If the end is practice, isn't it obvious that the end is superior [*me'uleh*] to what comes before it [as its means]?! . . . We are able to answer that by saying "learning brings to practice" does not mean this matter is in the category of an end with a means thereto. Rather, it is in the category of a cause [*sibbah*] and its effect [*mesovav*]: learning is the cause and practice is the effect. The superiority of cause over effect is already assumed.[14]

What is the difference between learning as a means for the sake of practice as its end and learning as a cause of which practice is its effect? For the solution to this problem, which will lead to the solution of the inner contradiction of the rabbinic compromise of the views of Rabbi Tarfon and Rabbi Akibah, we need to understand how *Shela* is using two different models of causality and how he is raising one of them to a higher theological level than the other. As such, we have a model of philosophical theology conducted with logical sophistication and rigor. The first model of causality used is Aristotelian; the second seems to be more dependent on the creation theory of Maimonides (and perhaps of Crescas too).

According to Aristotle, there are four essential points in any causal order (what he calls under the general name *aitia*, meaning "irreducible first principles").[15] All four points function together in one unified process. They are: (1) the material cause (*homer* in Hebrew); (2) the efficient cause (*ha-po'el* in Hebrew); (3) the formal cause (*ha-tsurah* in Hebrew); and (4) the final cause (*ha-takhlit* in Hebrew). For Aristotelians, the causal process is best illustrated by the building of a house. (1) There are building materials at hand. (2) The builder takes these materials and begins to build something from them, based on (3) the image of the house before his eyes. (4) The end result is the house as the physical reality intended in the first place by the builder. The emergence of the house is the completion of the whole causal process. Therefore, in more philosophical terms: the efficient cause brings what is potential

---

14. *Shnei Luhot ha-Berit* 3: R'eh (ed. Amsterdam, 1648), 82b-83a.
15. See Aristotle, *Physics*, 194b16-36.

(dynamis) into actuality *(energeia)* or teleological fulfillment *(entelecheia)*.[16] This actuality is envisioned from the start by the efficient cause through vision of the formal cause as archetype. First is thought, then comes the act.

In this example, Aristotle describes a tangible effect: a thing. But in reflection that is more pertinent to our reflection on the mutual relation between learning and practice, we have to infer how this causal process operates in the area of intelligent human action, especially as discussed in Aristotle's *Nicomachean Ethics*. There we can see four interrelated loci: (1) the innate moral nature of human beings, which is their initial capacity for moral development in a morally constituted human society; (2) the moral agent himself, who is the human being capable of moral development by engaging in teleologically intended action; (3) the form, which is the idea of the good, which the moral agent wants to attain by actualizing it in himself; and (4) the end, which is the act itself that is done for its own sake and not as a means or an instrument for the sake of something external and superior to it, which is something better than it.[17] As a genuine process, this is the final goal, the ultimate purpose beyond which there can be nothing of greater worth. To borrow a rabbinic phrase to make this point: "What is last is most precious."[18]

When this precise philosophical terminology is brought into the domain of Talmudic Judaism (which is the Judaism operative from the close of the biblical canon until the present day), as *Shela* has done, we see the following scheme: (1) The material cause is the Torah, whose commandments are waiting to be actualized by (2) the Jews who have accepted them. They are the efficient cause. (3) The formal cause is the practical meaning of the Torah — that is, *how* the commandment is to be practiced *(halakhah le-ma'aseh)*. (4) The final cause is the actual practice of the commandment itself as a fully intelligent act, one whose actor is aware of its intentionality and makes that intentionality evident in any public context when and where he or she is so acting.

One might say that the end becomes fully actual when as action per se it makes an intelligent statement in the world. With this type of scheme in mind, Maimonides writes: "Thus one finds throughout the Torah the commandment 'you shall learn them' (Deuteronomy 5:1), and thereafter 'to do them.' Learning [*ha-talmud*] is prior [*qodem*] to practice because through learning one will come to practice."[19] Therefore, practice is better *(adif)*, as

16. Aristotle, *Physics*, 201a5-15.

17. Aristotle, *Nicomachean Ethics*, 1103a25-30; 1139a20-32.

18. *Bereshit Rabbah* 78.8 re Gen. 33:2.

19. *Commentary on the Mishnah:* Introduction, trans. Y. Kafih (Jerusalem: Mosad ha-Rav Kook, 1976), 1.23.

Rashi too explained in the Babylonian Talmud's version of the story of the dinner party in Lydda.

A fundamental feature of the Aristotelian causal scheme is that all four causes are included in one finite process that is known from start to finish, and that everything is for the sake of the final cause or end *(telos)*. Yet, when *Shela* distinguishes between teleology and causality per se, he seems to be basing himself on the ontological-cosmological theory of Maimonides and somewhat on that of the anti-Aristotelian cosmology of Hasdai Crescas, even though he does not mention Maimonides or Crescas in his brief statement.[20] Thus Maimonides, in the *Guide of the Perplexed,* claims that the doctrine of *creatio ex nihilo* — which he calls there "the necessary foundation of the whole Torah" — does not correspond to Aristotle's theory of causation.[21] If God is the cause of all causes, who is not included in the finite causal process, there is no limit to the number of effects of his causality inasmuch as God is the creator who absolutely transcends his entire creation, being the creator who is not limited within any cosmic entelechy. As creator of a world or even of worlds out of nothing, God causes effects that are impossible for any creature to create or even anticipate. No creature could envision such effects *ab initio,* since they do not yet exist, even potentially. And no human being could know the final end for which these effects are intended, since its form could not be known by any created being *ab initio.* Creative intelligence seems to be spontaneous. We are here in the realm of infinite possibility, not finite potentiality.[22] Along these lines, Maimonides explains the rabbinic term "the matter has feet" *(raglayim le-davar)* to be denoting limitless possibilities. "The matter has possibilities [*ha'efshariyot*] which, if pursued, would lead us to no definite conclusion [*le-l'o takhlit*]."[23]

Although in ordinary language potentiality and possibility are often used interchangeably, in philosophically more precise language they are very different. Potentiality is defined by the end for whose sake it is prepared to be informed by the image of that end. Potentiality is correlated with the actuality that is its end — that is, the end the efficient cause intends for it. Potentiality

20. See *Or Adonai,* 1.2.3; H. A. Wolfson, *Crescas' Critique of Aristotle* (Cambridge, Mass.: Harvard University Press, 1929), pp. 129-38.

21. Maimonides, *Guide of the Perplexed,* 2.27ff.

22. For the distinction between potentiality (whose correlate is actuality) and possibility (whose correlate is realization), see David Novak, *Jewish-Christian Dialogue* (New York: Oxford University Press, 1989), pp. 129-38.

23. *Commentary on the Mishnah: Nazir* 9.3, trans. Kafih, 2:136. Cf. Maimonides, *Guide of the Perplexed,* 1.28 (and the discussion of Abravanel thereon concerning Maimonides' concept of causality).

is implicit in actuality; indeed, potentiality is inferred from actuality *post factum,* not vice versa. To use rabbinic language: "What is earlier is explicated retroactively [*yesh breirah*] by what comes afterwards."[24] Taken by itself, though, potentiality has no discernable existence, since it is totally uninformed, which means it could not be an object of our experience inasmuch as it is infinite and we can only experience what is finite. (Even revelation is experienced through the finite word of God that God reveals.)

Conversely, there is no limit to the active power of the creator, since this power has an infinite number and range of possibilities. Here the conceptuality, perhaps even the causal terminology, is unmistakably Hebraic. There is no Creator God in the cosmology of Aristotle, and not even in the cosmology of Plato (which Maimonides at times seems to prefer to that of Aristotle).[25] Accordingly, when these effects will be caused, how they will be caused, and why they will be caused — all this is what "no eye but God's can see."[26] The uniqueness of the biblical idea of divine creativity, which found philosophical expression in the idea of *creatio ex nihilo,* is that of the absolute freedom of God to do whatever he will, all things being possible for him. This is what the great Israeli Bible scholar and philosopher of history Yehezkel Kaufmann so emphasized as being the most original idea in the Hebrew Bible.[27]

How are we to understand a causality that is not delimited in the context of the dialectic between learning and practice in rabbinic thought? Following *Shela's* causal distinction, there are two kinds of causality of which one can speak there.

One, there is the usual personal causality when the Torah commands us to do a certain commandment. Halakhic reasoning explains how it is to be properly done. Aggadic speculation — sometimes — explains why it is to be done. Here learning *(talmud)* is the preparation for the act to be predictably done afterward, hopefully with sufficient ultimate intentionality. Learning here is practical instruction *(hora'ah).*[28] And, even though the situation in which the act is to be done could arise suddenly, there is no real spontaneity in what our knowledge of what is to be done, that is, according to the law and its method already codified.

---

24. B. Betsah 37b and parallels.

25. See Maimonides, *Guide of the Perplexed,* 2.13.

26. B. Berakhot 34b re Isa. 64:3.

27. See Kaufmann, *The Religion of Israel,* trans. M. Greenberg (Chicago: University of Chicago Press, 1960), pp. 60ff., 127ff.

28. Thus there are certain laws that can only be discussed theoretically, but which are not to be publicly advocated for actual normative practice. See, e.g., B. Betsah 30b; B. Berakhot 33b and Rashi, s.v. "halakhah"; B. Baba Batra 130b; also, Y. Kilayim 4.2/29b.

Two, there is causality that is unusual, whose method of doing is not learned from the commandments written in the Torah as God's explicit decrees. Rather, this method of doing is learned from the acts of God. For the Rabbis, these acts of God are learned from history — that is, from the scriptural narratives about the relationship between God and humanity, especially between God and his people Israel. These stories and their elaborations constitute the core of aggadah. As for human acts modeled after these acts of God — that is, human acts of *imitatio Dei* — it is impossible for a person to adequately prepare for them in advance. From these narratives *(aggadot)* normative action is learned, but not action that can be permanently codified as law to be officially practiced *(halakhah le-ma'aseh).*[29] The method of action is ad hoc, devised on the spot, so to speak, depending on the existential needs of the personal object of this action, whose manifestation itself is often unpredictable. Thus it states in *Sifre* on Deuteronomy:

> "To walk in all His ways" (Deuteronomy 11:22): these are the ways of God — "the Lord, compassionate and gracious" (Exodus 34:6) . . . But how is it possible for any human to be called by the name of God? Well, as God is called compassionate and gracious, so you are to be compassionate. . . . Those who expound the narratives *(dorshei aggadot)* say that if you want to apprehend He-who-spoke-and-the-world-came-to-be, study *aggadah* since out of that you will recognize Him-who-spoke-and-the-world-came-to-be, and you will cleave to His ways.[30]

When a person learns Torah for its own sake *(li-shmah),* one's intention is not to prepare oneself for a definite act as the purpose of that learning. Torah learning is an end in itself, even though one might not understand that when first engaging in such learning.[31] But when one learns the commandments of the Torah in a practical halakhic way *(halakhah le-ma'aseh)* as preparation for a specific act, one then comes to know just how he or she will be able to properly perform that act whenever the occasion for so doing will arise in the foreseeable future.[32] One can even imagine what is to be properly done in the far

29. See Y. Peah 2.4/17a; also, B. M. Lewin, *Otsar ha-Geonim: Hagigah,* nos. 67-69 (Jerusalem: Hebrew University, 1931), vol. 4, pp. 59-60. Nonetheless, there are numerous case where *haggadot* inspired individual action, some of which eventually did become codified (see, e.g., B. Shabbat 127a; B. Sotah 14a).

30. Sifre al Devarim, no. 49, p. 114. See also *Mekhilta:* Shirata 3 and B. Shabbat 133b re Exod. 15:2.

31. See B. Nazir 23b and parallels.

32. See, e.g., B. Megillah 4a. Cf. B. Sanhedrin 71a and parallels.

off messianic future *(hilkhata le-meshiha).*[33] Therefore, in the concluding part of the rabbinic text we had been examining earlier, Rabbi Yose the Galilean does not solve the inner contradiction in the answer of the Rabbis that "learning is greater because it brings one to practice." Rabbi Yose the Galilean only shows the chronological precedence of learning over practice. (Israel had to wait forty years to be able to practice the law of the dough-offering, but Israel did not have to wait at all to learn that law, or ever cease at all from learning that law, even when that law could not be practiced at times in Jewish history.) Nevertheless, this denotation of priority is not the ontological priority that the word *greater (gadol)* might well imply.[34]

When a person learns the acts of God, those revealed (and perhaps those concealed), as Torah for its own sake, he or she is unable to imitate God in definite acts whose modus operandi can be anticipated and prepared in advance. A person does not know how or when the divine exemplar will influence or inspire one, to lead him or her in relationships of loving-kindness *(gemilut hasadim),* acts which "have no measure."[35] All that depends on the spontaneous situation of a neighbor he or she is commanded to love as they are there and then.[36] As such, this is not like Israel in the Wilderness who already know from their learning just how they would be able to practice the commandment of the dough-offering when they would come into the land of Israel after forty years. But a person does not really know in advance just how to love his or her neighbor like oneself prior to the time when that neighbor stands before one face to face. Here God is the cause and the human being imitating God is the vessel through whom this new effect itself becomes a world as a new creation out of nothing. In this regard, we are engaging in ontology and not just in ordinary morality (as would seem to be Maimonides' view at the very end of the *Guide of the Perplexed).*[37] In my humble opinion, this is the intended meaning of *Shela* in his explication of the theological dialogue at the dinner party in Lydda. It would seem that this is the result of his delving into Greek philosophy (albeit filtered through Hebrew translations

---

33. See B. Zevahim 45a and Tos., s.v. "hilkhata."

34. See Y. Nedarim 9.4/41c re Gen. 5:1.

35. M. Peah 1.1.

36. See Maimonides, MT: Mourning, 14.1 re Lev. 19:18. So, e.g., in comforting mourners, which is a major act of *gemilut hasadim,* one is to wait for the spontaneous speech of the mourner himself or herself before expressing one's own words of comfort in response thereto. Indeed, one does not know how to comfort a mourner, which is to truly address his or her sorrow, until that mourner reveals his or her own particular sorrow on the spot to those coming to comfort him or her. See B. Moed Qatan 28b re Job 2:13–3:1.

37. Maimonides, *Guide of the Perplexed,* 3.54 re Jer. 9:23.

and transpositions) as a supplement and aid to the higher wisdom of the To-rah. Nevertheless, can one say that this is the intended meaning of the opin-ions of Rabbi Akibah and the other Rabbis who attempted to reconcile his opinion with that of Rabbi Tarfon?

To answer this question, we need to learn something from the well-known legend in the Babylonian Talmud about Moses in the academy of Rabbi Akibah. As we know, Moses became depressed when he did not un-derstand the discourse of Rabbi Akibah. But he regained his composure when he heard from the mouth of Rabbi Akibah himself that the basis of his teaching is "a law given to Moses at Sinai" (halakhah le-mosheh mi-sinai).[38] Now there are two ways to explain why Moses (that is, the "Moses" of the imagination of whoever thought up this legend) felt better about the teach-ing of Rabbi Akibah. One, there is the minimal explanation. Moses saw that Rabbi Akibah's teaching did not contradict his own teaching. Likewise, one could say that the philosophical interpretation of Shela does not contradict the teaching of the Rabbis' reconciliation of the views of Rabbi Akibah and Rabbi Tarfon. Two, there is the maximal explanation. Moses saw in the teaching of Rabbi Akibah the further development of his own teaching, something that could only be seen post factum. To use more precise philo-sophical language, one could say that in the first instance Moses' teaching is the necessary cause or condition for the teaching of Rabbi Akibah; it is the conditio sine qua non. And in the second instance one could say that the teaching of Moses is the sufficient cause or ground of the teaching of Rabbi Akibah; it is the conditio per quam.[39] In the first instance, the earlier teaching is essentially a negative limit on the later teaching; hence that later teaching need only not contradict the evident meaning of the earlier teaching. In the second instance, though, the earlier teaching is essentially a positive source of the later teaching; hence the later teaching needs to regularly return to that source in order to be sustained by it and to search it again for heretofore hidden meanings.

In the second instance, though, do we have the right to develop the teach-ing of our ancestors and to carry it to lengths they themselves did not imag-ine? Isn't this, in fact, using their teaching as a mere pretext (asmakhta) for our own ideas?[40] Quite the contrary! If we do not develop the teaching of our ancestors, which means letting their teaching cause new effects long after they themselves have had nothing more to teach, that teaching will remain, as the

---

38. B. Menahot 29b.

39. See Immanuel Kant, Critique of Pure Reason, Bxxiv-xxv.

40. See Judah Halevi, Kuzari, 3.73; also, B. Menahot 92b and Tos., s.v. "girsa."

Talmud strikingly puts it, "folded up and lying in some corner."[41] It is only possible for us to draw from the past by putting its content into new vessels in the present. It is always the case that the past is brought to us, but we are not able to return to it as it was in its own time. Only naive historicists think we can know the past "as it really was" *(wie es eigentlich gewesen)*. So, in this or any philosophical retrieval, be it *Shela's* retrieval of rabbinic teaching or our retrieval of his retrieval of rabbinic teaching, what is retrieved does change like anything that moves; but, nonetheless, it does not change into something else so as to lose its own coherent identity entirely. (Moses can still recognize his teaching as being essentially within the teaching of Rabbi Akibah.) It would thus seem that there is a causality in this development that not only operates on potential but, even more so, realizes truly future possibilities, operating as it were in an open rather than a closed universe (of discourse, that is). To use a rabbinic metaphor: Do not these developments occur more like water gushing from a fountain than water drawn from a sealed cistern?[42]

Looking at the mutual relation between teaching and practice in rabbinic thought through the philosophical prism of the dialectic between *theōria* and *praxis* has enabled us, I think, to see the ontological dimension of this question over and above its more immediate moral or political meaning. This prism has helped us formulate the question more precisely. Yet, by looking for an answer within the theological domain of Judaism, we do find an answer (or perhaps only an approach to an answer) that could not be found anywhere else. Philosophy has served the Torah well.

41. B. Kiddushin 66a.
42. M. Avot 2.8.

Revelation, Covenant, and Law: The Phenomena of Tradition

3   Heschel on Revelation (1999)

Students of great minds are often given to making what seem to be exaggerated claims about their teachers, especially to those who did not know these teachers in person. That is because the oral Torah of any great mind is always superior to his or her written Torah. Indeed, it is the oral Torah that makes the written Torah possible. As someone privileged to have sat at the feet of Professor Abraham Joshua Heschel, may the memory of the righteous and holy be blessed *(zekher tsaddiq ve-qadosh li-vrakhah)*, and who was privileged to have heard some of his oral Torah even before it became written Torah, I wish to now make what might seem to be an exaggerated claim: Without the Torah of Abraham Joshua Heschel, specifically the Torah he taught in America during the last half of his life, no English-speaking Jewish thinker today could utter the name "God" and expect anyone to listen to him or her seriously. When Heschel came to America in 1940, what little Jewish thought there was then seemed to have forgotten how to truthfully utter the name "God" altogether. Heschel's legacy, which has enabled English-speaking Jewish thinkers to remember what they had previously forgotten, is something I am convinced will continue to inspire Jewish thought irrespective of how many subsequent Jewish thinkers will or can accept the specific points of Heschel's *Gotteslehre,* his *theo-logy.* So, it is important for that reason alone to revisit Heschel's written teaching on the divine *(torat ha-elohut)* to see how he enabled such a profound return to God *(teshuvah)* to take place in English-speaking Jewish thought.

But where do we look most intensely for this? After all, Heschel was himself, to use the name of his first book, *Der Shem ha-Mefoirash Mentsh,* someone so *Gottgetrunken* that Novalis could have well called *him* that rather than Spinoza — that is, had Novalis known Heschel. Like the Kabbalah in which he was so long and so early nurtured, there is nothing but God in all of Heschel's thought. Nevertheless, if we wish to see Heschel *in situ* — that is, where and when he had his most profound influence on us who live in this place and speak this language (which was Heschel's fourth language) — then I think it is best for us to turn to what is his major theological statement in English, *God in Search of Man,* first published in 1955. About that book the Toronto journalist Rick Salutin recently wrote in his newspaper column that no other "religious" book has ever given him the sense of exhilaration he received as a teenager when first reading *God in Search of Man.* I know how he feels. I first read it at age fifteen and determined then and there to some day become Heschel's student. I even wrote him a rather impassioned "fan" letter, to which he politely replied. About six years later he did accept me as his student.

What sort of Jewish world did this book fall into in 1955? Well, I am old enough to remember it and tell you about it. Most Jewish thought at the time — whose "Jewishness" and whose "thoughtfulness" are both arguable — expressed itself as if Jews had never spoken the name "God" at all. It was concerned with such things as locating the origins of anti-Semitism in religious fanaticism, showing how Judaism anticipated democratic ideals, and making American Jews feel better about their cultural identity. *(Plus ça change, plus c'est la même chose.)* As for more traditional segments of the Jewish community, those who still uttered the name of God among themselves in their Hebrew prayers at least, most of their more public discourse consisted of harangues about how too many Jews were carelessly abandoning ancient Jewish traditions. For both of these extremes, though, serious talk about "God" sounded too much like what Christian preachers do too much of in public. Both extremes seemed to be little concerned with the intention *(kavvanah)* of any Jewish act; both of their advocates were what Heschel derisively called "behaviorists" — "religious" or otherwise.

Of course, there was some Jewish theology at the time, but it avoided as much as possible the whole question of revelation. It still tried to talk about "God," but without an adequate treatment of revelation, what could a Jew really say about God that would be authentically Jewish? Jewish theology, more than any other type of Jewish discourse, has to be a fundamental retrieval of biblical teaching. And in the Bible we certainly learn that virtually anything we say about God is because of God's self-revelation to us. But without an adequate constitution of the experience of revelation, we were left, at least at that time, with two alternatives.

One was the approach of Mordecai Kaplan, Heschel's colleague at the Jewish Theological Seminary, who assumed that anything the Bible (or anyone else, for that matter) said about God is a human construction. This assumed that human beings speak about God the way they think God *ought to be*. Because of this, the experience of revelation was demythologized through a process of philosophical theology (having some affinity with the way Charles Hartshorne has demythologized the Bible for Christians by using Whitehead's ontology). It was thus assumed that God did not make himself known to man, but that man projected his own image of God onto reality. Revelation, then, is only a metaphor. The problem, of course, is that this approach is defenseless against the critique of Feuerbach, Marx, and Freud — namely, is not all of this the unconscious projection of the image of man onto reality instead of man taking responsibility for his own life and destiny? Can one still believe a myth when it has now been uncovered as a mythical construction of reality? So, doesn't assigning to revelation a source other than the one it proclaims for itself, doesn't that make the retrieval of the Bible impossible, since it destroys the phenomenological integrity of the revelatory events presented in the Bible? As such, is the God we are left with still the God of Abraham, Isaac, Jacob — and of Sinai? Is this God, or any God like it, still the Lord God of Israel? Were the biblical writers either liars or fools?

The second alternative was the approach of Joseph Soloveitchik, Heschel's rival at Yeshiva University, who certainly believed that the Torah, and especially the law of the Torah structured into the halakhah, comes from God, not from man. (To be sure, in the mid-1950s Soloveitchik had not yet begun to write in English. Yet his great theological essay, *Ish ha-Halakhah* [*Halakhic Man*], was known to a number of Jewish thinkers; in fact, I remember having a long conversation with Professor Heschel about it that indicated how very carefully and very critically he had studied it.) Nevertheless, Soloveitchik's *Gotteslehre*, at least at that time, did not deal with the experience of revelation. It was simply assumed that the content of revelation is divine law. But without a phenomenology of revelation itself, what prevents us from taking the divine factor of the law *(torah min ha-shamayim)* as being itself a halakhic requirement? In other words, do we affirm God's revelation *because* the halakhah so enjoins us, or do we affirm the sanctity of the halakhah *because* of God's revelation? Do we believe the Torah is from God, or do we believe God is from the Torah? In terms of our chronological experience, everybody after Moses first learns of God from the Torah; but, ontologically speaking, God is certainly prior to *his* Torah. Soloveitchik's *Ish Ha-halakhah* is an ideal construction of the mind-set of the exemplary *ba'al ha-halakhah*, but it is not a phenomenology of the revelation that originally made such a mind-set possible.

It seems to me that Heschel entered his phenomenology of revelation as a better philosophical alternative to these two prevailing theological options at the time. As opposed to Kaplan, revelation for Heschel is from God to man, not from man to God. In distinction from Soloveitchik, Heschel assumed that the question of the *how* of revelation precedes the *what* of revelation, even though as a traditional Jew he affirmed the *what* of *that* revelation, and in great opposition to his teacher, Martin Buber. With this background (highly conjectural, to be sure), we now need to look at some key passages from the chapter in *God in Search of Man* entitled "The Mystery of Revelation." I think the preceding points help locate this chapter in Heschel's oral Torah, whose written remains are still with us and for us to decipher, perhaps even elaborate.

The most central passage of this chapter, to my mind anyway, is this sentence: "As a report about revelation the Bible itself is a *midrash*."[1] Against the background of Kaplan on his left and Soloveitchik on his right, and in the immediate context of the rest of this chapter, he seems to be saying the following: In considering revelation, there are four elements: one, the God who reveals himself; two, the human being who is the recipient of that revelation; three, the original content of that revelation; and four, the subsequent result of that revelation.

To better appreciate what Heschel means by this sentence, by way of contrast let us try to reconstruct it in the way Kaplan could have said it: "Biblical revelation is itself a human *midrash* about God." That is, revelation is the human projection of what God is. Kaplan would make man the subject and God the object of revelation, and he would make the revelation and the *midrash* one and the same. By phenomenological criteria, Heschel would fault Kaplan on two counts: one, Kaplan has inverted the proper subject/object relation within the phenomenon; and two, he has conflated two distinct elements of the phenomenon itself — namely, revelation the *explicand* and *midrash* the *explicans*.

Let us now try to recast Heschel's sentence the way Soloveitchik could have said it: "*Midrash* is the human understanding of God's revelation which is the Bible (most fully, the Written and Oral Torah)." By phenomenological criteria, Heschel would have no dispute with Soloveitchik about *who* is the subject and *who* is the object of revelation. The constitution of the divine-human relation is intact, and consistent with the whole rabbinic tradition. Moreover, *midrash* is certainly human understanding of the divinely given *explicand*. But Heschel would have to fault Soloveitchik for his conflation of the event of revelation with the content of revelation written down in the Bible. For Heschel, the Bible itself is the *explicans*, and the event of revelation is the *explicand*.

1. Abraham Joshua Heschel, *God in Search of Man* (New York: Farrar, Straus & Giroux, 1955), p. 185.

Soloveitchik could very well have retorted that Heschel conflates the biblical *explicand* with the midrashic *explicans*. Following a line closer to Soloveitchik than to Heschel, one could say that the divine element in revelation is discovered by speculating on what God *meant* there. To use Husserl's language, what was God's *Bedeutung* in saying what he did in revelation? That is, *why* did God say what no creature could have possibly meant? In other words, how does the midrashic *Bedeutung* get us back to the creative divine *Sinn* assumed to be there *ab initio*? But, as far as I know, Soloveitchik himself was not given to such *ta'amei ha-mitsvot*-type thinking.

Since the specific difference is between Heschel and Soloveitchik, and since it is more theologically fecund than the generic difference of Heschel *and* Soloveitchik contra Kaplan, it is the more interesting difference for us to explore. Furthermore, Heschel and Soloveitchik both claim Maimonides as their most important theological influence. In his treatment of the event of revelation in *God in Search of Man*, Heschel's primary quote (along with the majority of his references) is from Maimonides' *Guide of the Perplexed*. As such, like a tannaitic debate over a biblical passage, if Heschel reads Maimonides one way for his theology of revelation, then Soloveitchik would have had to read the same passage differently for his different theology of revelation. Our question now should be this: How does Heschel's distinction between the event of revelation stem from (as a *derashah*) or extend to (as an *asmakhta*) Maimonides' theology of revelation? (Not knowing Soloveitchik's oral Torah, I cannot answer for Soloveitchik.)

I think Heschel's key reference to Maimonides is the following from the *Guide of the Perplexed*:

> The general consensus of our community on the *Torah* being created [*beru'ah*] . . . is meant to signify that His speech that is ascribed to Him is created. It was ascribed to Him only because the words heard by *Moses* were created and brought into being by God, just as He has created [*bera'o*] and brought into being [*ve-hidsho*] everything. . . . There is a divine science [*mada elohi*] apprehended by the prophets in consequence of God's speaking to them so that we should know that the notions transmitted by them from God to us are not . . . mere products of their thought and insight. . . . He, may He be exalted, never spoke using the sounds of letters and a voice. . . . His sayings [at the creation of the world] were volitions [*retsoniyim*] and not speeches [*ma'amariyim*] . . . [since] speech may only be addressed to an existent that receives the command [*ha-tsivui*] in question.[2]

2. Maimonides, *Guide of the Perplexed*, 1.65.

I would now like to suggest that Heschel's reading of this text from Maimonides is significantly kabbalistic, and that recognizing this goes a long way in explaining Heschel's own view of revelation.

Heschel is convinced that the original content of revelation is wordless. "The nature of revelation, being an event of the ineffable, is something which words cannot spell, which human language will never be able to portray."[3] Now it will be remembered that whereas the Rabbis only said "the Torah speaks by human language" (dibbrah torah ke-lashon bnei adam) when looking at atypical biblical expressions, Maimonides said that this is true of the words of the Torah itself typically, indeed ubiquitously. That is because the written text of the Torah is addressed to human hearers already there. They can only appropriate a created entity because their intelligence is limited to the work of creation (ma'aseh bereshit, what others have called ens creatum).

So, if the prophets perceive something divine that is ineffable, what could that be? Is it what we would call "thought"? But if so, how does that thought differ from audible speech? Doesn't the "linguistic turn" of modern philosophy, which we see beginning in Frege, Rosenzweig, Heidegger, and Wittgenstein (maybe going as far back as Socrates) and then extending into the present — doesn't that turn show that thought is internalized speech, that "in the beginning was the word" (en archē ēn ho logos), what others have called verbum uncreatum? Isn't thought but second-order speech? Why would thought be so privileged as to make it an act of God ontologically prior to the creation of words and things (dvarim) and not just the transitive intentionality creation seems to logically presuppose? How is the truth of God's thought apprehended prior to the comprehension of its meaning for us? That is a question both for Maimonides and for Heschel.

If revelation, then, is the revelation of that which is truly prior to the act of creation, we can see why Heschel says, "It is just as improper to conceive revelation as a psycho-physical act as it is to conceive God as a corporeal being."[4] Furthermore, he says, "Our goal, then, must not be to find a definition, but to learn how to sense, how to intuit the will of God in the words. The essence of intuition is not in grasping what is describable but in sensing what is ineffable." He speaks of this as being "that which lies beyond reason."[5] Does thought lie beyond reason? Well, of course, Plato too insists that those who finally perceive the eternal forms, for which (like Maimonides and Heschel) an event of revelation is required, do so by a process beyond reason, what Plato

3. Heschel, God in Search of Man, pp. 184-85.
4. Heschel, God in Search of Man, p. 187.
5. Heschel, God in Search of Man, p. 189.

calls seeing with "the eye of the intellect" *(tēs dianoias opsis).*[6] (Like Maimonides and Heschel after him, Plato refuses to describe this event or let it be described by others.) Nevertheless, how does a prophet know that he or she is experiencing that which lies beyond all reason and, all the more so, beyond all utterable words? That question is especially pressing since revelation does, as it were, *create* utterable words subsequently (at least for Maimonides and for Heschel).

The answer to this question, at least for Heschel, lies in the character of the words the Bible uses to "describe" revelation. Heschel writes, "This is why all the Bible does is to state *that* revelation happened; *how* it happened is something they only convey in words that are evocative and suggestive."[7] In other words, the Bible doesn't *describe* revelation at all in that it does not put forth theological propositions *about* revelation, propositions that *enclose* revelation *within* words or concepts. Evocative language is the language of poets, not that of philosophers or theologians. Do not poets experience more than they can understand, and even more than they can convey to others? Heschel knew a lot about the language of poets, being a poet himself in his beginning and in his end. Yet isn't poetry the Achilles' heel of Heschel's thought? How well I remember those who wished to dismiss him and his work by saying, "Heschel is only a poet" or a "rhetorician."[8] In fact, just recently a certain veteran Jewish writer told me, with undisguised disdain, that he had long ago dismissed Heschel as being "sentimental."

One has to remember that circa 1955 English-speaking philosophy was still being inundated by the death gasps of a school of thought called "Logical Positivism." For these philosophers, still uncritically enchanted by everything they thought natural science signified, only "verifiable propositions" were truly intelligible. Everything incapable of experimental validation was beyond the pale. Everything else — even ethics, let alone religious language — was merely "emotive" — that is, one could say anything he or she wanted inasmuch as it had no public meaning anyway. The only ethical imperative was not to take any of this nonverifiable language seriously — that is, thou shalt not act on it, not ever. (It was Heschel's misfortune that this type of thinking dominated the philosophy department of his closest academic neighbor, Columbia University.)

However, in this postmodern day and age, when all canons of meaning

---

6. Plato, *Republic,* 519b.

7. Heschel, *God in Search of Man,* p. 185.

8. See, for example, Arthur A. Cohen, *The Natural and Supernatural Jew* (New York: Pantheon, 1962).

are open to critical reappraisal, we might finally be able to give Heschel the poet the posthumous intellectual honor that mostly eluded him in his all too brief life. We are now in a better position to appreciate that a poet is not someone who senses less than we do; he or she senses more than we do. Poets stand at the very frontier of language, not at its back door. A poet uniquely participates in the very creation of the word-thing *(davar)*. Without the continual infusion of poetry into any language, our language itself becomes but our tool for the manipulation of the world, that which carries our world to its immanent dissolution rather than what celebrates its transcendent source. And a poet who has apprehended such creation as truly divine, that poet is God's spokesperson, God's *navi*. And just as the challenge of poetry makes more bad poets than good ones, so there are more bad prophets than good ones. The Bible calls them *nib'ei ha-shaqer*, "the prophets of falsehood."

Both Maimonides and the kabbalists would say that it is not the word of God *(dvar hashem)* that finally reaches the ears of all the people which the prophets sense. Instead, it is God's experience of himself that they, as it were, *overhear*, and then translate it down as best they can *(keveyakhol)* into human language that is ethically evocative and, finally at the lowest level, into human language that is descriptively propositional.[9] Again, as Heschel puts it, "Never is our mind so inadequate as trying to describe God. The same applies to the idea of revelation."[10] (His use of the adjective *inadequate* is purposeful, I think. Remember the scholastic designation of truth is *veritas est adaequatio intellectus ad rem* — namely, the full *correlation* of subject and object.) Since that inner divine experience is beyond words, it is beyond anything we could mean by thought. Could it not be pure feeling, the divine *pathos*, whose evocation in his dissertation, *Die Prophetie*, launched Heschel on his remarkable theological journey? Could we not say, therefore, along with Heschel that the prophetic apprehension of the pure divine pathos *(Gefühl)* is "sympathy" *(Mitgefühl)* — that is, feeling with God himself? And couldn't we say that the translation of this sympathy into humanly appropriated language is "empathy" — that is, the projection of this original feeling-with into the experience of someone else *(Einfühlung)* — that is, feeling-into *(Einwurf)?* Are not our deepest feelings ineffable, and do we not sense that the source of our deepest feelings lies outside our constructing selves? Isn't our inner experience a reliving *(Erlebnis)* of what has been lived prior to us? Wouldn't claiming full responsibility for these deepest feelings ultimately throw us into Nietzschean

---

9. See Rashi re Num. 7:89.
10. Heschel, *God in Search of Man*, p. 187.

madness? (Remember that in the Bible, "to make oneself a prophet," *le-hitnav'ei*, is to become mad like King Saul [1 Sam. 19:24].)

This "reading" of Maimonides is kabbalistic because it assumes that there is a multifaceted inner life of God. It is also kabbalistic in that the procession from self-feeling (what we might call *Gefühl an sich selbst*) to feeling-with *(Mitgefühl)* to feeling-into *(Gefühl für sich)* is more a matter of emanation *(atsilut)* than *creatio ex nihilo (beri'ah)*. It is a progression *(hitpashtut)* of the divine being, not an interruption of it *(tsimtsum)*. It is not a holy nothing-ness, which one might finally infer from what Maimonides could be implying in his *Gotteslehre;* instead, it is holy plenitude, so intense that one can only allude to it, only evoke it lest one be consumed by it. That is why Heschel the poet, by refusing to suppress his poetic insight, is the one who has carried us farther in our quest for God (what the kabbalists called *itar'uta de-le-tatta*) than most others. By his language, which either enchanted or repelled, he forces us to settle for nothing less than cleaving to God *(devequt)*, which has no synonyms in anything we have otherwise experienced in this world.

I apologize if this presentation has been overly personal when it should have been more strictly academic. But I had a teacher who gave me gold, so forgive me for not pretending I only got silver.

4 Creation and Election (1995)

In the narrative of Scripture the election of Abraham, the progenitor of the covenanted people of Israel, comes suddenly and without warning. It seems to catch us unprepared:

> The Lord said to Abram: "You go away from your land, from your birthplace, from your father's house to the land that I will show you. I will make you a great nation and bless you; I will make your name great and you will be a blessing. I will bless those who bless you and those who curse you I will curse. Through you [*vekha*] all the families of the earth will be blessed." And Abram went as the Lord had spoken to him. (Gen. 12:1-4)

In this elementary text there seems to be no clue as to why God elects Abraham and his progeny or why Abraham obeys the call to respond to being elected by God. Unlike in the case of Noah, who is elected to save humankind and the animal world from the Flood "because [*ki*] I have seen that you are righteous [*tsadiq*] before Me in this generation" (Gen. 7:1), and who obviously responds to God's call because of the biological drive for self-preservation, there is no reason given here for either God's choice or Abraham's positive response to it. Any righteousness attributed to Abraham is seen as subsequent, not prior, to God's election of him.[1] It is thus a result of election, not a reason for it. And unlike Noah, Abraham does seem to have the alternative of staying where he already dwells. He seems to have a reasonable alternative to obedience to God's call. From the text of Scripture itself it

---

1. See Gen. 26:5; Neh. 9:7-8.

seems as though Abraham could have stayed home. In his case, there is no destruction like a universal flood on the imminent horizon.

Simply leaving the matter at this mysterious level — does it not preclude speculation about the deeper meaning of the covenant established by this election and its acceptance? In the case of God's reason for electing Abraham and the people of Israel as his progeny, the answer seems to be yes. At that side of the covenant, Scripture itself seems to imply "My thoughts [*mahshevotai*] are not your thoughts" (Isa. 55:8) when it states,

> For you are a people consecrated to the Lord your God; the Lord your God chose you [*bekha bahar*] to be unto him a treasured people from out of all the peoples on the face of the earth. It was not because you were more numerous than all the other peoples that the Lord desired you [*hashaq bakhem*] and chose you, for you are the least [*hame'at*] of all the peoples. It was because of the Lord's love for you [*me'ahavat adonai etkhem*] and his keeping the promise [*ha-shevu'ah*] he made to your ancestors. (Deut. 7:6-8)

Of course, taken by itself this statement is a tautology: God loves you/chooses you/desires you because God loves you/chooses you/desires you. For there is no reason given as to why he made his promises to Abraham and to Isaac and Jacob in the first place.[2] And the people of Israel themselves cannot claim any inherent qualities that could be seen as reasons for their election by God.[3]

2. See R. Judah Loewe (Maharal), *Netsah Yisra'el* (Prague, 1599), chap. 11; *Gevurot Ha-Shem* (Cracow, 1582), chaps. 24, 39, 54.

3. See H. Wildberger, *YHWH's Eigentumsvolk* (Zurich: Zwingli, 1960), p. 111; N. W. Porteous, "Volk and Gottesvolk in Alten Testament," in *Theologische Aufsatze: Karl Barth zum 50, Geburtstag* (Munich: C. Kaiser, 1936), p. 163. Cf. H. H. Rowley, *The Biblical Doctrine of Election* (London: Lutterworth, 1950), pp. 38-39n.2. Rowley sees Israel's election being based on teleology (pp. 35ff.) — that is, God chose Israel because she had qualities useful for universal divine purposes. However, Rowley's supersessionist assumptions lie just beneath the surface of his scholarship. For when Israel fails God, then her election is annulled (pp. 49ff.). The implication, of course, is that the church will have better qualities, so that it will replace Israel in and for God's universal plan. Porteous and Wildberger, conversely, being under the influence of Karl Barth (and, it seems, Calvin too), see God's electing promise and covenant to Israel as unconditional and never annulled or to be annulled. (See Barth, *Church Dogmatics*, 2/2, sec. 34, trans. G. W. Bromiley et al. [Edinburgh: T&T Clark, 1957], pp. 195ff.; Calvin, *Institutes of the Christian Religion*, 2.10.1ff., 2 vols., trans. F. L. Battles [Philadelphia: Westminster Press, 1960], vol. 1, pp. 428ff.) Whatever differences Calvinist and Barthian Christians have with Judaism over the ultimate meaning of election — and they are crucial — these Protestants are not offended by the Jewish doctrine of the unconditional election of Israel, which is not the case with most of their more liberal co-religionists. Along these lines, see K. Sonderegger, *That Jesus Christ Was Born a Jew* (University Park: Pennsylvania State University Press, 1992), pp. 161ff.

This is consistent with the logic of creation. In Scripture, unlike other ancient sagas, we are not told about any life of God prior to creation. Indeed, only the God to whom "all the earth is mine" (Exod. 19:5), to whom "the heavens and the highest heavens" (Deut. 10:14) belong — only this God has such absolute freedom from any natural necessity to create a singular relationship like the covenant with Israel. There is nothing that could be considered a divine *a priori* from which one could infer the possibility of a nondivine world, much less the reality of any such world. All of God's relations with the world are, therefore, *a posteriori*. From revelation we learn some of the things God wants to do with the world, most especially what God wants his human creatures to do with the world along with him, but we do not learn why he made the world the way he did in the first place or, indeed, why he made it at all. So, too, we do not learn why God chose the people of Israel or, indeed, why he chose any people at all. All we learn, *a posteriori,* is what God wants to do with this people. "The secret things [*ha-nistarot*] are for the Lord our God; but the revealed things [*ve-ha-niglot*] are for us and our children forever: to practice all the commandments of this Torah" (Deut. 29:28).

However, on the human side of this relationship of election, it is not only Abraham who is to respond to election. Election is primarily generic and only secondarily individual. Abraham is elected as the progenitor of a people. Every member of this people is elected by God, and every member of this people is called upon to respond to his or her generic election. So, even if Abraham's individual reasons for accepting God's call could well be left alone as his own private and inscrutable business, speculation about his generic reasons for accepting it is our business as well inasmuch as his response is archetypal for all of us who follow after him.[4] For a communal response is a public matter, one whose reasons have to be rooted in continuing common experience before they can enter into personal reflection. This, then, calls for our reflection on our own human situation and what conditions in it enable us to respond to God's electing presence without caprice. Projecting our own reflection on the human conditions for election back to Abraham retrospectively is essential midrashic thinking.[5] Without it, we would lose our singular connection to the text of Scripture. It would become merely *a* datum among other data rather than *the* datum for us.

4. See Isa. 41:8-10; 51:1-2.
5. See Isaak Heinemann, *Darkhei Ha'Aggadah,* 2d ed. (Jerusalem: Hebrew University Press, 1954), pp. 21ff.

Of course, at the most original level, the prime reason for obeying God is that God is God. In Scripture, God's original presence is explicitly normative: his first contact with humans in the Garden is set forth in these words: "The Lord God commanded [*vayitsav*] the humans [*al ha'adam*]" (Gen. 2:16).[6] Norms are a necessity for human life because humans are beings who must consciously order the conflicting parts of their experience if they are to survive and cohere. That ordering requires a primary point of authority. (One can only be a moral relativist when looking at someone else's choices from afar, not when one is required to make his or her *own* choices at hand.) A human life without an ordering hierarchy of authority could only be that of an angel: an infallible life without conflict.[7] So it follows that any rejection of God's norms presupposes the substitution of God's authority by the authority of one who is not-God being made into God. The prime authority is always taken to be God. There can be no normative vacuum.[8] That is why the first temptation to disobey God is the temptation that "you will be like God" (Gen. 3:5). You, not God, will become the prime authority. Without absolute authority, the creator would no longer be the creator; he would be forced to abdicate, as it were.

The relationship with God the creator at this original level is essentially negative, however.[9] It only consists of prohibitions that function as divine limitations of human illusions of self-sufficiency and autonomous authority. So far there is nothing positive between humans and God. It is with Abraham's call that we begin to see the establishment of a substantive relationship of humans *with* God. And in order for any such positive relationship to be sustained, there must be the discovery of positive reasons by humans *within* themselves for them to want to accept and maintain this relationship. Thus, whereas resistance to the idolatrous temptation to substitute the authority of not-God (the world or the human person) for God involves the affirmation

6. See B. Sanhedrin 56b re Gen. 2:16 and Exod. 32:8 (and, esp., the view of R. Judah; see the view of R. Meir on B. Avodah Zarah 64b); also, Maimonides, *Mishneh Torah: Kings*, 9.1.

7. See *Shir Ha-Shirim Rabbah*, 8.13 re Lev. 15:25 and Num. 19:14; B. Kiddushin 54a and parallels. In rabbinic theology, angels are seen as monads with only one function to perform for which they are programmed by God (see *Bereshit Rabbah* 50.2). The primary human need for conscious ordering is coeval with the need for communicative community because that ordering finds its locus in the *public* nature of speech. See Gen. 2:18; B. Yevamot 63a re Gen. 2:23; B. Ta'anit 23a. Cf. Aristotle, *Politics*, 1254a20.

8. That is why God's most generic name is *elohim*, "authority," which is first divine and then human. See B. Sanhedrin 56b re Gen. 2:16 and Exod. 22:7; also, David Novak, "Before Revelation: The Rabbis, Paul, and Karl Barth," *Journal of Religion* 71 (1991): 58.

9. Thus the Noahide laws, stipulating the minimal relation of humankind to God, are essentially prohibitions. See B. Sanhedrin 58b-59a and Rashi, s.v. "ve-ha-dinin" re Lev. 19:15.

of truth, the response to the covenant involves the desire for good.[10] By obeying God, what good did Abraham desire? What did his response intend?

The covenant itself must be the object of human desire. This desire for it as good is an essential component of it. Hence in presenting the positive covenantal norms, Moses appeals to the desire of the people for what is their good.[11] "The Lord commanded us to practice [*la'asot*] all these statutes, to fear the Lord our God, which is good for us [*tov lanu*] all times for our vitality [*le-hayyotenu*] as it is today. And it will be right [*tsedaqah*] for us to be careful to do this whole commandment before the Lord our God as he has commanded us" (Deut. 6:25). And shortly before this passage, each one of the people is commanded to "love the Lord your God with all your heart, with all your life, and with all your might" (6:5). But can there be any love without desire? And is not desire experienced — inchoately, to be sure — even before its desideratum comes to it?[12] "For you, O Lord, is my whole desire [*kol ta'avati*]" (Ps. 38:10).[13] And does not desire entail hope, which is essentially an anticipation of something in itself unknown in the present? Moreover, can there be any desire that does not intend good for the one in whom it stirs?[14] Or, as the Psalmist puts it, "Who is there for me in heaven, and besides you I

10. See David Novak, *Jewish Social Ethics* (Oxford: Oxford University Press, 1992), pp. 14ff.

11. See Novak, *Jewish Social Ethics*, pp. 27ff.

12. There is an important debate about the role of *erōs* — i.e., desire — in the God-human relationship between Christian theologians that I venture to enter here because it helps one gain a better philosophical perspective on the role of desire in the biblical covenant itself (see M. Avot 4.1 re Ps. 119:99 and Maimonides, *Commentary on the Mishnah:* intro., trans. Y. Kafih, 3 vols. [Jerusalem, 1976], vol. 1, p. 247). The main protagonists are Augustine and Paul Tillich, who emphasize the erotic component, and Karl Barth and Anders Nygren, who deny it. I would say that without the factor of inherent human desire for God, the covenantal relationship between God and humans can only be seen as essentially one of God with himself rather than one between God and his nondivine covenantal partners. So it seems to me that Jewish covenantal theologians have more in common with Augustine and Tillich than they do with Barth and Nygren on this key point. See Augustine, *Confessions*, 7.10; Paul Tillich, *Systematic Theology* (Chicago: University of Chicago Press, 1951), vol. 1, p. 282; Karl Barth, *Church Dogmatics*, 2/2, sec. 37, pp. 555ff.; Anders Nygren, *Agape and Eros*, trans. P. Watson (Chicago: University of Chicago Press, 1982), pp. 160ff.; also, Novak, *Jewish Social Ethics*, pp. 5ff.

13. Following R. Judah Halevi, "Adonai Negdekha Kol Ta'vati," in *Selected Poems of Jehudah Halevi*, ed. H. Brody (Philadelphia: Jewish Publication Society, 1924), p. 87.

14. See Aristotle, *Nicomachean Ethics*, 1094a1; *Metaphysics*, 1072a25. For the recognition of the universal desire for God, see Mal. 1:11 and R. Solomon ibn Gabirol, "Keter Malkhut," in *Selected Religious Poems of Solomon ibn Gabirol*, ed. I. Davidson (Philadelphia: Jewish Publication Society, 1924), p. 86. The kabbalists called human *eros* for God *it'aruta dil-tata* ("awakening from below" — see *Zohar:* Vayetse, 1:164a). But without an adequate theology of revelation, the God so desired becomes trapped as an eternal object like the intransitive god of Aristotle (see *Metaphysics*, 1072a20ff.) or something similar to it.

desire [*lo hafatsti*] no one on earth. . . . As for me, the nearness of God, that is my good [*li tov*]. . ." (Ps. 73:25, 28). Is not God to be served by a "desiring soul" *(nefesh hafetsah)* (1 Chron. 28:9)?

It seems to me that the reasons for Abraham's answering the electing call of God, and thus the paradigm for all subsequent Jewish answering of it, can be seen in the promise made in the initial call itself that Abraham and his progeny will be the source of blessing for all of humankind. Accordingly, Abraham's relationship with God is correlative to his relationship with the world. And the precise presentation of that correlation is found in Abraham's dialogue with God over the judgment of the cities of Sodom and Gomorrah. God justifies including Abraham in this dialogue as follows:

> How can I conceal what I am doing from Abraham? And Abraham shall surely become a great and important [*atsum*] nation, in whom all the nations of the earth shall be blessed. For I know him, so that [*le-ma'an*] he will command his children and his household after him to keep the way of the Lord to do what is right [*tsedaqah*] and just [*mishpat*]. (Gen. 18: 17-19)

The question now is to determine the connection of the blessing of the nations of the earth to Abraham and his people keeping the way of the Lord to do what is right and just.

The first thing to note is that God's statement of his knowing does not seem to be a noetic prediction. The text does not say "I know that" but rather "I know him [*yed'ativ*]."[15] Abraham is the direct object of God's knowing, and the result of his being aware of God's knowing him will be that he will be able to keep the way of the Lord. Without God's knowing him and his being aware of it, Abraham would not be able to recognize the way of the Lord and keep it.[16]

---

15. For this epistemological distinction, see Bertrand Russell, "Knowledge by Acquaintance and Knowledge by Description," in *The Problems of Philosophy* (Oxford: Oxford University Press, 1959), pp. 46ff. Although there are significant differences between Russell's empiricism and my phenomenology, his essay is still useful for making my point here.

16. "He [R. Akibah] used to say that man [*ha'adam*] is beloved [*haviv*] being created in the image [*be-tselem*]; even more beloved in that it is made known to him that he is created in the image of God. . . . Israel is beloved being called children of God; even more beloved in that it is made known [*noda'at*] to them" (M. Avot re Gen. 9:6; Deut. 14:1). Thus human knowledge/awareness is subsequent to God's knowledge/care (in the sense of *Sorge* in German, meaning care/concern/attention/interest/involvement, etc.). Revelation, then, brings the truth of being elected to conscious mutual relationality. The creation of humans in the *imago Dei* is also election; hence the Torah is "the book of human history [*toledot ha'adam*]" (Gen. 5:1; see Nahmanides' comment thereon). It brings the meaning of being created in the image of God to

Here "knowing" is not a judgment of a state of affairs drawn from the objects of past experience and then projecting from them into the future. This knowing is, rather, a relationship of direct and intimate personal contact. It is presence. Thus in the Garden the "tree of the knowledge [ets ha-da'at] of good and bad" is a symbol for the direct contact with all the experience the world now has to offer and which the first human pair desire.[17] Since they were able "to judge favorably [va-tere] that [ki] the fruit of this tree is good to eat and delightful in appearance" (Gen. 3:6) even before they ate it, their judgment preceded their experience or "knowledge." Their judgment is in essence a prediction of what they think they will experience. This is why "knowledge" is used to designate the intimacy of sexual contact — "And the man knew [yada] Eve his wife and she conceived" (Gen. 4:1) — although it is not limited to sexual contact.[18] It is something that can be judged desirable based on one's desire of it in advance, but it can only be experienced directly in the present.

In connection with the election of Israel, the prophet Amos conveys to Israel God's announcement: "Only you have I known [raq etkhem yad'ati] of all the families of the earth" (Amos 3:2). Now, the prophet could not be saying that God is unaware of the other nations inasmuch as he himself has already been called to prophesy about them by God.[19] What the prophet is saying is that God shares a unique intimacy with Israel that is the basis for the unique claims he makes upon her. The claims are because God cares for Israel. Since these claims are made in the context of covenantal intimacy, the prophet then says in the very next verse, "Can two walk together if they have not met each other [no'adu]?"[20] Israel is intimately known by God and is to act based upon

---

human awareness and action. And the *tselem elohim* itself is the human capacity for a relationship with God (see David Novak, *Law and Theology in Judaism*, 2 vols. (New York: Ktav Publishing House, 1974, 1976], vol. 2, pp. 108ff.; *Halakhah in a Theological Dimension* [Chico, Calif.: Scholars Press, 1985]). It is not a quality humans have any more than the election of Israel is due to any quality she has. For a quality can be discovered through solitary introspection or inferred by ratiocination. Although felt inchoately by desire in advance, the meaning of this capacity only comes to knowledge/experience when her desideratum presently reveals itself to her. For the relation of humankind and Israel indicated in the above mishnah, see R. Israel Lipschütz, *Tif'eret Yisra'el (Bo'az)* thereon.

17. See Maimonides, *Guide of the Perplexed*, 1.2.

18. See Martin Buber, "The Election of Israel: A Biblical Inquiry," trans. M. A. Meyer in *On the Bible*, ed. N. N. Glatzer (New York: Schocken Books, 1968), pp. 80-81.

19. See Amos 1:3ff.

20. Whether the roots *yod daled ayin* and *yod ayin daled* are etymologically related or not, a literary relation between them seems to be made by this juxtaposition. (I thank my colleague Professor Gary Anderson for pointing this out to me.)

her intimate experience of that knowing. The relationship here is not a noetic relation of a subject and an object. It is the divine I reaching out to embrace a human thou who then chooses to be so embraced.[21] Thus at the very beginning of God's regeneration of the covenant with Israel in Egypt, Scripture states,

> And the children of Israel groaned from their toil and cried out, and their cry reached up to God from out of their toil. Then God took notice [*va-yizkor*] of his covenant with Abraham and Isaac and Jacob. And God looked with favor [*va-yar*] at the children of Israel and God cared [*va-yeda*]. (Exod. 2:23-25)[22]

As for Abraham's response to God's election, it is initially a response to being in intimate contact with God. That is what he desires. That intimacy is, as we shall soon see, the main characteristic of the covenantal life of the Jewish people in the present. Those commandments of the Torah that specifically celebrate the historical singularity of the covenantal events give that life its rich substance.

What we must now see is how the experience of being known by God leads Abraham and his progeny to practice the way of the Lord. That can be better understood if we remember that the act of election is first a promise. Thus the covenant itself is founded in a promise. But why does Abraham believe the promise of God? Is his response anything more than a "leap of faith"?

In terms of the sequence of the biblical text itself, it is important to remember that the promise of God to Abraham is not the first promise God has made. After the Flood God promises that "I shall uphold my covenant with you . . . and there will be no further deluge [*mabul*] to destroy the earth" (Gen. 9:11). The Rabbis were very astute in insisting that unconditional divine promises are made as oaths. Any oath made by God could not be annulled by God thereafter inasmuch as the annulment of an oath *(shevu'ah)* can only be done by a higher authority than that of the one who made it. But there could

---

21. See Abraham Joshua Heschel, *Man Is Not Alone* (New York: Farrar, Straus & Young, 1951), pp. 125ff.; *God in Search of Man* (New York: Farrar, Straus & Giroux, 1955), pp. 136ff.

22. Note how the Passover Haggadah connects this "knowing" with the sexual "knowing" of the people themselves, the essential connection between the two being the factor of intimacy. See M. M. Kasher, *Haggadah Shlemah*, 3rd ed. (Jerusalem: Torah Shelema Institute, 1967), pt. 2, p. 41. That is how R. Akibah could see the eroticism of Song of Songs as the holiest intentionality (see *Shir Ha-Shirim Rabbah*, 1.11). And whereas in Song of Songs human sexuality suggests God's love of Israel, here God's love of Israel suggests human sexuality. Along these lines, see Novak, *Jewish Social Ethics*, pp. 94ff.

be no higher authority than God to annul it. God must keep his own word, then; if not, his credibility would be totally undermined.[23] Moreover, the connection between the promise made to Noah and the promise made to Abraham is explicitly made by Deutero-Isaiah: "For this is to me like the waters of Noah: just as I promised [*nishba'ti*] that the waters of Noah would never again pass over the earth, so do I promise . . . that even if the mountains be moved and the hills be shaken, my kindness shall not be moved and my covenant of peace [*u-vriti shalom*] shall not be shaken — so says the Lord who loves you" (Isa. 54:9-10). Furthermore, we learn that God's relation to the world is the correlate of his relationship with Israel, and Israel's relationship with the world is the correlate of her relationship with God.

I think that one can see the inner connection of these two promises in the term used to characterize the "way of the Lord" that Abraham is to teach his progeny: "what is right and just" *(tsedaqah u-mishpat)*. But this requires that we look upon the two words in the term as denoting two separate but related acts. The usual interpretation of them sees them as denoting one single act — namely, correct justice, which is the standard whereby the distinction between the innocent and the guilty is consistently maintained in adjudication. This interpretation of the term is appropriate to the immediate context of the dialogue between God and Abraham in which Abraham indicates that consistency in judgment is the bare minimum to be expected from God, who has chosen to be "the judge of all the earth" (Gen. 18:25). This interpretation concentrates on the ethical issues in the text.[24] However, looking at the even deeper theological issues in the text, one can take *tsedaqah* as one term and *mishpat* as another. Along these lines, one can interpret *tsedaqah* as the transcendent aspect of God's relation to creation and *mishpat* as the immanent aspect of it. The elect people, then, are to imitate both the transcendent and the immanent aspects of God's relation to the world.

Tsedaqah is the transcendent aspect of God's relation to creation because it is something totally gracious. God's creation of the world is an act of grace; there is nothing that required that there be something created rather than nothing. And after the Flood, the renewal of creation in the covenant with the earth is even more gracious inasmuch as God's human creatures — made in his own image — were so ungrateful for the gift of their existence and that of the world.

God's *tsedaqah* is the ultimate explanation of the contingency of exis-

---

23. See, esp., B. Berakhot 10a re Exod. 32:13; also, Novak, *Halakhah in a Theological Dimension*, pp. 116ff.

24. So I too argued in *Jewish Social Ethics*, p. 41n.48.

tence. As such, it could only be expressed in a promise, which extends from the present into the future. For the past by itself never guarantees any continuity or permanence. Its immanent order is itself contingent.[25] So, to use a current metaphor, reliance on this order in itself might be nothing more than "arranging deck chairs on the *Titanic.*" But a primary promise in and of itself has no antecedents; indeed, if it did, it would be the process of making an inference and then a prediction based upon that inference. It would, then, designate a relation *within* the world already there. A primary promise, conversely, is infinitely more radical, infinitely more originating. Accordingly, it could not come from the world itself, whose real existence (rather than its abstract "Being") is no more necessary than real, mortal, human existence.[26] It could only come from the One who transcends both the world and humankind.

Yet despite its ultimate contingency, worldly existence has structure and continuity. The primal event of creation founds existence as an orderly process. That is because the divine promise is itself covenantal. The structure and continuity of existence, its essential character, is what is meant by *mishpat.* It is through *mishpat* that existence coheres. Minimally, that coherence is seen in the principle of contradiction, by which things maintain their net identities in relation to each other. Abraham's challenge to God that the judge must act justly and consistently distinguish between the innocent and the guilty is the biblical presentation of this basic principle of all reason. *Mishpat,* then, is the standard whereby the boundaries between things and between acts are maintained. *Mishpat* is violated when those boundaries are not respected. That is why *mishpat* is basically negative. It functions as a limit. Indeed, it is not inappropriate here to use Spinoza's formula: *determinatio negatio est.*[27] *Mishpat* is that fundamental *determinatio* that makes an ordered approach to existence possible. Nevertheless, *mishpat,* precisely because it is essentially negative, can never guarantee the facticity of existence; it always presupposes that existence is being maintained by God's *tsedaqah.* Expressions of *mishpat* are always ultimately conditional — namely, *if* there is a world, *then* it must have certain structures to cohere. As Jeremiah expresses it, "Without my covenant by day and by night, I would nave put the laws [*huqqot*] of heaven and

25. See David Hume, *A Treatise of Human Nature,* 3.1.2, ed. L. A. Selby-Bigge (Oxford: Clarendon, 1888), pp. 473ff.

26. See Novak, *Law and Theology in Judaism,* vol. 2, pp. 19ff.

27. *Epistola,* no. 50, in *Opera,* ed. J. van Vloten and J. P. N. Land (The Hague: M. Nijhoff, 1914), 3:173: "Haec ergo determinatio ad rem juxta suum esse non pertinet: sed contra est eius non esse . . . et determinatio negatio est."

earth in place [*lo samti*]" (Jer. 33:25).[28] Essence in biblical theology follows from existence, but existence is never derived from essence.[29]

That is why truth *(emet)* is God's faithfulness before it is external correspondence and before it is inner coherence. Truth is first God's faithful promise that created existence will abide. "He makes heaven and earth, the sea and all that is in them, keeping faith [*ha-shomer emet*] forever" (Ps. 146:6).[30] Only when nature is "your faithful seasons [*emunat itekha*]" (Isa. 33:6) can it function as a standard to which human judgment can truly correspond. And human judgment and action can only cohere fully, can only "do justly and seek fidelity [*emunah*]" (Jer. 5:1), when it is aware of the coherence of cosmic *mishpat*. That complete awareness only comes when the Torah functions as the "true witness [*ed emet*]" (Prov. 14:25) of creation and its order in both nature and history.

The world until the time of Abraham was certainly aware of cosmic *mishpat* and the necessity to practice it in society. Thus after the Flood and the reconstruction of human life on earth, the basic moral law prohibiting bloodshed and establishing its commensurate punishment — "one who sheds human blood shall have his blood shed by humans" (Gen. 9:6) — is directly preceded by the affirmation of the cosmic order: "For as long as the earth endures [*od*], there will be seedtime and harvest, cold and heat, summer and winter, day and night, they shall not cease" (Gen. 8:22). That cosmic order, in which both the human and the nonhuman participate, is its *mishpat*. Thus Jeremiah employs an analogy between human and nonhuman *mishpat* to make the following point: "Even the stork in the sky knows her seasons, and the turtledove, the swift, and the crane keep the time of their coming; but my people do not know the law [*mishpat*] of the Lord" (Jer. 8:7). Clearly, the "seasons" *(mo'adeha)* of the stork and the regular cycles *(et bo'anah)* of the other birds are their *mishpat*.

Mishpat, however, is known only as a negative, limiting force. Because of that, the violation of it is considered a denial of the fear of God, which is in effect restraint before the highest authority, the epitome of *mishpat*, the pinna-

---

28. In the Talmud, that covenant is seen as the covenant between God and Israel (B. Pesahim 68b; also *Ruth Rabbah*, Petihah, 1 re Ps. 75:4). Indeed, the divine *tsedaqah* that creates the world and maintains its existence is most immediately experienced in the covenant with Israel. See *Mishnat Rabbi Eliezer*, sec. 7, ed. Enelow, 1:138; R. Judah Halevi, *Kuzari*, 1.25 re Exod. 20:2.

29. See Heschel, *God in Search of Man*, p. 92.

30. For two important discussions of truth as faithfulness *(emet v'emunah)*, see Martin Buber, *The Knowledge of Man*, ed. M. Friedman (New York: Harper & Row, 1965), p. 120; and Eliezer Berkovits, *Man and God* (Detroit: Wayne State University Press, 1969), pp. 253ff.

cle of cosmic justice. Thus when Abraham assumes that there is no respect for the boundaries of the marital relation in the Philistine city of Gerar, specifically assuming that his wife Sarah will be abducted into the harem of the city's ruler, Abimelech, he justifies his lying about Sarah being his wife by saying, "Surely [*raq*] there is no fear of God [*yir'at elohim*] in this place" (Gen. 20:11). In other words, there is no *mishpat* there.[31]

What is not recognized, though, until the time of Abraham, is the reality who is the source of this cosmic order, this *mishpat,* the reality who created and sustains the cosmos in which *mishpat* is to be operative as its norm.[32] But the philosophical questions to be asked now are these. What difference does it make whether we know or do not know the source of this cosmic order? Indeed, why does it have to have a source at all to be appreciated theoretically and implemented practically by us? And, furthermore, why does this source have to reveal his presence to Abraham, which is simultaneously an act of election, as biblical revelation always is? And if there is such a cosmic source, why can't this source be discovered by ratiocination, which is universal in principle?

Only when the cosmic order is perceived by those who suffer enough philosophical unrest can the most basic existential question be asked authentically: What is my place in the world? That question lies at the heart of Abraham's desire for God's presence.

This question arises from our experience of the phenomenal order of things we immediately and regularly experience around us through our bodily senses. What we soon learn from this order is our own mortal vulnerability, our superfluity in the world. When we "eat of the tree of knowledge of good and bad" (Gen. 2:17) — which is the acquisition of worldly experience — we simultaneously discover the imminence of our own death.[33] "Dust you are and to dust you shall return" (Gen. 3:19). "All is futile [*havel*]. What advantage [*yitron*] is there for man in all his accomplishments [*amalo*] under the sun? One generation goes and another comes and the earth remains the same forever" (Eccles. 1:2-4). Therefore, throughout human history, perceptive persons have become aware that their place is not immanently available as an animal-like instinct. As a result of this existential predicament, the transcendent desire that goes beyond immanent need arises.[34]

31. See B. Baba Kama 92a. For the distinction between universal *mishpat* and local custom, cf. Gen. 29:26 and 34:7.

32. See Novak, *Jewish Social Ethics,* pp. 163-64.

33. See Nahmanides' comment thereon.

34. Along these lines, see Hannah Arendt, *Lectures on Kant's Political Philosophy,* ed. R. Beiner (Chicago: University of Chicago Press, 1982), pp. 12-13.

The first possibility is for us to discern with the intellect a higher noumenal order undergirding the phenomenal order initially perceived by the senses. Our motivation is to subordinate ourselves to this order. It alone offers us a transcendent end for our participation.[35] This is the attitude of scientific (understood as *scientia* or *Wissenschaft,* that is) *homo spectator.* The second possibility is for us to despair of ever finding the higher noumenal order "out there" and thus to look within our human selves for an order of our own device with which to use and control as much of the world as we can. This is the attitude of technological *homo faber.* The third possibility is for us to cry out for the person who stands behind this cosmic order to reveal himself to us; since the presence of persons can never be inferred from something nonpersonal, it must always be self-revelation.[36] This is the attitude of *homo revelationis,* the person of faith. For the Bible, Abraham is the first *homo revelationis.*[37]

In the biblical narrative preceding the emergence of Abraham, we find hints of both the first and the second possibilities and their attendant human attitudes. And both are seen as being in essence idolatry.

As for the first possibility, Scripture notes that during the time of Enosh, the grandson of the first couple, "the name [*shem*] of the Lord began [*huhal*] to be invoked" (Gen. 4:26). Rabbinic interpretation notes that the word for "begin" is etymologically similar to the word for "profane" (*hol*).[38] Thus it sees the time of Enosh as the beginning of idolatry, not the worship of the true God. The question here is this: If this interpretation is accepted, what did this idolatry consist of?

Maimonides, in introducing his comprehensive treatment of the specifics of Jewish tradition concerning idolatry, speculates that at this time human beings were so impressed with *what* they perceived — namely, the cosmic order, the highest manifestation of which is the astronomic order — that they forgot *who* so ordered it.[39] Their worship, then, was transferred from the creator to his most impressive creations. In an earlier discussion of the essence of idolatry, Maimonides speculates that the worship of the cosmic order itself inevitably leads to a situation where some people understand this order much

35. See Plato, *Republic,* 476bff.

36. See David Novak, "Are Philosophical Proofs of the Existence of God Theologically Meaningful?" in *God in the Teachings of Conservative Judaism,* ed. S. Siegel and E. B. Gertel (New York: Rabbinical Assembly, 1983), pp. 188ff.

37. See B. Berakhot 7b re Gen. 15:8.

38. *Bereshit Rabbah* 23.7.

39. Maimonides, MT: Idolatry, 1.1. See also T. Boman, *Hebrew Thought Compared with Greek,* trans. J. L. Moreau (Philadelphia: Westminster Press, 1960), p. 117.

better than others by virtue of their greater powers of discovery. As such, they translate their noetic power into political power by convincing the masses that they should be given absolute authority, being the effective conduits of that cosmic power. They alone can channel it for the public weal.[40] Here we have the rule of the philosophical guardian.[41] In Maimonides' reading of Scripture, tyranny is the practical result of theoretical idolatry.

As for the second possibility, Scripture is more explicit. During the time of the Tower of Babel, humankind despaired of ever discovering the cosmic order, much less making peace with it in order to live *within* its limits. The cosmic order is now the enemy to be conquered by technological means. "And each man said to his neighbor, 'Come, let us make bricks and fire them in a kiln . . . come let us build for ourselves a city, and a tower with its head into heaven, and we will make a name [*shem*] for ourselves, lest we be scattered over the face of all the earth'" (Gen. 11:3-4). In response to all this, the Lord says, "This they have begun [*hahillam*] to do, and now nothing they are plotting [*yazmu*] to do will be withheld from them" (Gen. 1:6). An important thing to note here is that in the preceding passage, dealing with what we might in modern terms call "heteronomous idolatry," the *name* sought is still something external to humans themselves. Here, however, dealing with what we might in modern terms call "autonomous idolatry," the *name* sought is one of human making.

The connection between this idolatry and political tyranny is even more obvious. Here we have the rule of the technocrat.[42] Here the exercise of power becomes an end in itself. There is no longer even the pretense of a higher justification and purpose for the exercise of human power. Thus in rabbinic interpretation, Nimrod is the true founder of Shinar, the place where the Tower of Babel was built.[43] About Nimrod it is said, "He began [*hehel*] to be a mighty man on earth. He was a mighty warrior [*gibor tsayid*] before the Lord" (Gen. 10:8-9). And in rabbinic tradition, Abraham's quest for God quickly challenged the tyranny of Nimrod and was taken as a mortal threat by Nimrod.[44] And, finally, since I am following rabbinic insights, it should be noted that in the case

---

40. Maimonides, *Commentary on the Mishnah*: Idolatry, 4.7; also, Maimonides, MT: Idolatry, 11.16.

41. See Karl Popper, *The Open Society and Its Enemies*, 2 vols. (Princeton: Princeton University Press, 1962), vol. 1, pp. 138ff.

42. See Jacques Ellul, *The Technological System*, trans. J. Neugroschel (New York: Continuum, 1980), pp. 145ff.

43. See Louis Ginzberg, *The Legends of the Jews*, 7 vols. (Philadelphia: Jewish Publication Society, 1909-38), vol. 5, pp. 199ff., nn.81ff.

44. See *Pirqei De-Rabbi Eliezer*, chap. 26.

of Enosh, in the case of the Tower of Babel, and in the case of Nimrod, the word that the Rabbis saw as connoting idolatry *(hallel)* is found.[45]

As for the third possibility, which is the cry for the person behind the cosmic order to reveal himself, we only have our speculation that God's call to Abraham is in truth a response to an existential question. And there is a long tradition of speculation about just what this question is. In this tradition, Abraham begins his career as a philosopher.[46] The error, however, of many in this tradition was to assume that Abraham *found* God through what is called "the argument from design" — namely, that the perception of order leads one to *conclude* that there is an orderer who brought it about.[47] But as many philosophers have argued, no such conclusion is necessary. One can take the order itself as ultimate.[48] And if there is such an orderer, then the most one can rationally conclude is that the orderer and the order are essentially identical, and that the orderer cannot be understood as transcending his order in any way, as in Spinoza's view of God as *causa sui.*[49] In other words, the orderer need not be taken as a person — that is, one consciously engaged in transitive acts, let alone mutual relationships.

Abraham's cry for the master of the universe to reveal himself, to follow the speculation of a well-known midrash, is not an exercise in inferential thinking.[50] Without the revelation whereby God personally elects him through a promise and establishes a perpetual covenant with him and his progeny — without that, Abraham's cry would have been the epitome of futility, an unheard cry in the dark, a dangerous gamble, an exercise in wishful thinking. The free choice of God, his liberty to be when he will be, where he will be, with whom he will be, cannot in any way be the necessary conclusion by any inference whatsoever.[51] The most Abraham or any human person can

45. See *Bereshit Rabbah* 23.7.

46. See Ginzberg, *The Legends of the Jews*, vol. 5, p. 210n.16; also, Maimonides, MT: Idolatry, 1.3, and *Guide of the Perplexed*, 3.29.

47. The first to make this argument was Josephus in *Antiquities*, 1.155-56. Cf. Novak, *Law and Theology in Judaism*, vol. 2, pp. 21-22.

48. See Plato, *Euthyphro*, 10e.

49. See Novak, *The Election of Israel: The Idea of the Chosen People* (Cambridge: Cambridge University Press, 1995), pp. 23-26; also, H. A. Wolfson, *The Philosophy of Spinoza*, 2 vols. (Cambridge, Mass.: Harvard University Press, 1934), vol. 2, p. 346, who sees the deity of Spinoza as a return to Aristotle's deity, "an eternal paralytic," in Wolfson's colorful words.

50. *Bereshit Rabbah* 39.1: "Abraham used to say, 'Could it be that the world has no leader [*manhig*]?' God peered out and said to him, 'I am the leader and the lord [*adon*] of all the world.'"

51. See Exod. 3:13 and the discussion of its philosophical career by David Novak, "Buber and Tillich," *Journal of Ecumenical Studies* 29 (1992): 16ff.

do is to prepare himself or herself for the possibility of revelation, to clear the ground for God, but without any immanent assurance that God will ever come.

One can speculate, from philosophical reflection on the human condition itself, that Abraham could not accept the first and second approaches to the cosmos (that of *homo spectator* and that of *homo faber*) because neither of them could establish the cosmos as the authentic dwelling-place for humans. Abraham the bedouin is looking for his home.[52]

To regard order itself as ultimate, as does *homo spectator,* is to regard humans as souls from another world, souls whose task is to "escape and become like God."[53] And in this view, God is eternal and immutable Being. But there is no relationship *with* Being; there is no mutuality between Being and anything less than itself. There is only a relation *to* Being. God dwells with himself alone. That is why in this view of things, the highest achievement of humans is to reach the level where they can only silently gaze on that which is eternal. The philosopher, like God, is ultimately beyond human community and beyond the world.[54] And to regard the cosmic order as mere potential, a resource for its own use, as does *homo faber,* something to be ultimately outsmarted, is to regard the cosmos as ultimately disposable. All being is engulfed *by* human *technē.* There is, then, no authentic being-at-home in the world.[55] One is in constant struggle *against* the world. Humans dwell with and among themselves alone, but that brings them no rest. For the struggle against the world is extended into their struggle with each other for mastery.[56] For *homo faber,* there is not enough trust of either the world or one's fellow humans for him to be able to enjoy the vulnerability of a Sabbath.

Only an authentic relationship with the creator God who made both world and humankind enables humans to accept the world as their dwelling place. Without that, the world becomes either our prison that we are to escape *from,* or our prison *against* whose walls we battle, striving to tear them down. "For so says the Lord, the creator of heaven, he is the God who formed the earth, who made it and established it, who did not create it to be a void

---

52. See Rashbam, *Commentary on the Torah* and Hizquni, *Commentary on the Torah:* Gen. 20:13.

53. Plato, *Theaetetus,* 176ab. See also *Republic,* 501b; *Timaeus,* 68e-69a; *Philebus,* 63e; *Laws,* 716c.

54. See Aristotle, *Nicomachean Ethics,* 1177b25ff. For Plato's struggle with this problem, see *Republic,* 516cff.; also, David Novak, *Suicide and Morality* (New York: Scholars Studies Press, 1975), pp. 21ff.

55. See Novak, *Jewish Social Ethics,* pp. 133ff.

56. See, e.g., Ginzberg, *The Legends of the Jews,* vol. 1, p. 179.

[*tohu*], but who formed it to be a dwelling [*la-shevet*]" (Isa. 45:18). "God brings the lonely homeward [*ha-baytah*]" (Ps. 68:7). All true dwelling-in is a dwelling-with more than ourselves. But it is only the case when we prepare the world from our singular place for God's descent into the world to dwell with us therein in covenantal intimacy. "They shall make for Me a holy place [*miqdash*] and I shall dwell in their midst" (Exod. 25:8). "Surely the Lord is here [*yesh*], in this place [*ba-maqom ha-zeh*] . . . it will be the house of God [*bet elohim*]" (Gen. 28:16, 22).⁵⁷

Here the propensity for tyranny we noticed in the first and second human approaches to the cosmos (that of scientific *homo spectator* and that of technological *homo faber*) is less. For here is where everyone in the covenant is to be directly and equally related to God. Even the quintessential modern apostate from Judaism, Baruch Spinoza, was impressed by this political aspect of the covenant.⁵⁸ Here is where the prophet can say, "O were it so [*mi yiten*] that all the people of the Lord would be prophets, that the Lord would place his spirit upon them" (Num. 11:29).⁵⁹

Thinking along these lines, one can see why Scripture requires the people of Israel, when they are at home in the land of Israel and satiated with an abundant harvest, to remember their bedouin origins by declaring about Abraham (and perhaps the other patriarchs too), "a wandering Aramean was my father" (Deut. 26:5).⁶⁰ Indeed, even in the land of Israel, which is since Abraham's election itself elected to be the homeland, the dwelling place of his people, this people is reminded in Scripture that "the land is Mine, that you are sojourning tenants [*gerim ve-toshavim*] with Me" (Lev. 25:23).⁶¹ Indeed, the purpose of a home is to be the location for persons to co-exist, a place for authentic *mitsein*. It is not a part of them, and they are not parts of it, as is the case with the first two attitudes we have detected above. Although God dwells with the people of Israel wherever they happen to be, the most complete dwelling-together of God and his people is only in

---

57. See B. Pesahim 88a and Rashi, s.v. "she-qara'o bayit."

58. See Novak, *The Election of Israel*, pp. 31-38.

59. Cf. Exod. 20:15-18. That is why, it seems to me, the Rabbis had to impugn the motives of Korah's rebellion against the authority of Moses (e.g., *Bemidbar Rabbah* 18.1ff.) — namely, the argument "You have taken too much for yourselves, for the entire assembly is holy and the Lord is in their midst. So why do you elevate yourselves above the congregation of the Lord?" (Num. 16:3). The premise of the argument is surely valid *prima facie*. Indeed, there is always a suspicion of too much human authority in the covenantal community (see, e.g., Judges 8:22-23; 1 Sam. 8:7ff.).

60. See the comments of Ibn Ezra and Rashbam thereon.

61. See Ps. 119:19; 1 Chron. 29:15.

the land of Israel.[62] The rest of the earth is created; the land of Israel, like the people of Israel, is elected in history. It is selected from among multiple possibilities.

On the basis of this theology, time and space are to be constituted as abstractions from event and place.[63] Time is ordered by the events in which Israel is elected and the covenant with her given its content. These events are the prime point of temporal reference; they are not in time, but all time is related to them. As Scripture puts it in the first creation narrative itself: "And God said, 'Let there be lights in the expanse of the sky to divide between day and night, and to be for signs and seasons [*le'otot u-le-mo'adim*], for days and for years'" (Gen. 1:14).[64] And space is ordered by its relation to the land of Israel. It is the *axis mundi,* the prime point of spatial reference.[65] It is not in space, but all space is related to it. As Scripture puts it just before the people of Israel entered the land of Israel, "When the Most High gave nations their homes [*be-hanhel*] and set the divisions of man, he fixed the boundaries [*gevulot*] of peoples in relation to the numbers [*le-mispar*] of the children of Israel" (Deut. 32:8).[66]

Getting back again to Abraham's keeping of "the way of the Lord to do what is right [*tsedaqah*] and just [*u-mishpat*]," we are now in a better position to discern the reason for his — and our — acceptance of God's election. It must be immediately recalled that Abraham's concern with *tsedaqah u-mishpat* is in connection with the nations of the world which are to be blessed through him. Indeed, his concern here is that justice be done to the people of Sodom and Gomorrah, whom Scripture shortly before described as "exceedingly wicked sinners [*ra'im ve-hat'im*] against the Lord" (Gen. 13:13). Abraham is concerned that justice be done to these people as the due process of law that even they deserve, whether the final verdict be guilt or innocence. His response to his being known-and-chosen by God is to want to imitate in microcosm the way God relates to the whole world in macrocosm. Both God and Abraham are now concerned with the earth and especially with all the peoples in it. Thus Abraham's concern is that *mishpat* be done. That in itself is an act of justice; he acts as their defense attorney seeking some merit in them.

---

62. See Nahmanides, *Commentary on the Torah:* Deut. 8:10; also, David Novak, *The Theology of Nahmanides Systematically Presented* (Atlanta: Scholars Press, 1992), pp. 89ff.

63. "And even as prayer is not in time but time in prayer, the sacrifice not in space but space in the sacrifice — and whoever reverses the relation annuls the reality" (Martin Buber, *I and Thou,* trans. W. Kaufmann [New York: Scribner, 1970], p. 59).

64. See Rashi's comment thereon.

65. See Nahmanides, *Commentary on the Torah:* Gen. 14:18; Deut. 16:20.

66. See *Targum Jonathan ben Uziel* thereon.

And the very fact that he involves himself in their case, when he owes them nothing, is an act of *tsedaqah*. Knowing that he is known by God, Abraham is now in a position to act truly as *imitator Dei*.[67] His being known by God is not only something he enjoys and can celebrate; it is something he can act on.

As *homo revelationis*, Abraham desires to dwell *with* God *in* and *for* the world. Conversely, the desire of *homo spectator* is for absorption *into* God *outside* the world; and the desire of *homo faber* is to be God *against* the world. Only the right relationship with God founds one's rightful place in the world. And only the acceptance of one's rightful human place in the world prevents one from intending either absorption into God or the replacement of God.

Finally, in the covenant, the relation of existential *tsedaqah* and essential *mishpat* is not only one of originating event and subsequent process. Sometimes, *tsedaqah* is subsequent to *mishpat* and not just the origin behind it. *Mishpat's* world is never so tightly constructed that *tsedaqah* cannot on occasion intrude into it. Indeed, the contingency of created existence would be eclipsed if even God's *mishpat* were to be taken as an impermeable total order, as a system perfect in itself. There always remains the possibility of miracle. *Tsedaqah* can be directly experienced at rare times in history/nature (time/space). For a miracle is the unpredictable exception to ordinary, normal order, and it is beneficial to those for whom it is performed. In fact, outside the singular experience of the faithful, illuminated by revelation, a miracle can soon be explained by more mundane categories.[68] Thus the splitting of the Red Sea for Israel was seen by them as the "great hand" (Exod. 14:31) of the Lord. But precluding the presence of God, one could see the act as that of "a strong east wind" (Exod. 14:21). Clearly Israel is redeemed from Egyptian slavery because "the Lord took us out of Egypt with a mighty hand" (Deut. 26:8). However, precluding the presence of God, one could see it as an escape by fugitives: "It was told to the king of Egypt that the people had escaped [*barah*]" (Exod. 14:5).

The election of Israel is assumed to be the greatest intrusion of divine *tsedaqah* into the usual order of nature and history:

> You have but to inquire about bygone ages that came before you, ever since God created humans [*adam*] on earth, from one end of the heavens to the other: has anything as great as this ever existed or has it ever been heard of? Has any people ever heard the voice of God speaking out of fire, and you

67. See B. Shabbat 133b re Exod. 15:2 and 34:7; Maimonides, *Guide of the Perplexed*, 3.54 re Jer. 9:23; and David Novak, "Maimonides' Concept of Practical Reason," in *Rashi 1040-1990: hommage à Ephraim E. Urbach*, ed. G. Sed-Rajna (Paris: Cerf, 1993), pp. 627ff.

68. See Nahmanides, *Commentary on the Torah*: Gen. 14:10.

have and are still alive? Or has God ever so miraculously [*hanissah*] come to take for himself one people out of another? (Deut. 4:32-34)

This notion of intrusive *tsedaqah* — miraculous grace — became the background for explaining how God can mercifully cancel the inevitable consequences of sin by forgiveness and atonement. For the Rabbis, the world could not be sustained if strict justice (*mishpat* as *din*) were always maintained consistently by God.[69] And the covenantal community could not be sustained without periodic infusions of grace by those in legal authority, at times ruling "deeper than the limit of the law [*lifnim me-shurat ha-din*]."[70] The theological import of all of this is enormous.

---

69. See, e.g., *Bereshit Rabbah* 12.15 re Gen. 2:4; B. Rosh Hashanah 17b; also, Ephraim E. Urbach, *Hazal* (Jerusalem: Magnes Press, 1971), pp. 400ff.

70. See T. Shekalim 2.3; B. Baba Metsia 30b. For the use of the term *lifnim me-shurat hadin* re God's merciful overriding of his own created *mishpat*, see B. Berakhot 7a; also Y. Makkot 2.6/31d re Ps. 25:8 and R. Moses Margolis, *Penei Mosheh* thereon. Cf. W. Eichrodt, *Theology of the Old Testament*, trans. J. A. Baker, 2 vols. (Philadelphia: Westminster Press, 1961), vol. 1, p. 244.

5 The Life of the Covenant (1995)

Whereas the origin of the covenant between God and Israel lies in *tsedaqah* as an act of God's grace, and whereas the most evident structure of the covenant is in the standards of *mishpat* as cosmic justice, the life of the covenant itself largely consists of an elaborate system of acts that we today would call "ritual." The word itself is hardly adequate to describe what Jewish tradition has designated as "what is between humans and God" *(bein adam le-maqom),* so it should be discarded after it has performed the most elementary task of introduction. Indeed, in our current parlance, *ritual* in its adjectival form, *ritualistic,* most often connotes an obsession with minutiae, something designed to divert our attention from reality. That, of course, is opposite to what the commandments as mitsvot are designed to accomplish, as we shall soon see.[1]

This system of acts comprises what most consistently gives the Jewish people its distinct character in its own eyes and in the eyes of the world. Because of this, however, it has been as vexing a problem for modernity as has been the doctrine of God's election of Israel itself. For us, retrieving its meaning philosophically is, therefore, essential for our philosophical retrieval of the doctrine itself. It lies at the heart of the traditional Jewish relationship with God.

Whereas in modernist versions of the covenant, the cultic realm had to be ultimately justified within the context of the moral-political realm, in the classical versions of the covenant, it is the exact opposite. That is, the moral-political realm is ultimately justified within the covenant. It is the relationship between God and Israel that gives ultimate meaning to the relationships

1. For the admonition not to "ritualize" the commandments, see M. Avot 2.13.

66

between humans themselves. Without covenantal intimacy, morality loses its ultimate justification.[2] Life together with God minimally requires respect of the order of his creation, which is most immediately required in the proper order of human society. Thus in the Decalogue itself, the first tablet deals with what is to obtain between God and his people, and only thereafter, in the second tablet, do we learn what is to obtain between the people themselves. The first tablet begins with "I am to be the Lord your God" (Exod. 20:2), and only after the relationship with God is given substance in the commandment "Remember the Sabbath to sanctify it" (Exod. 20:8) do we hear "You shall not murder" (Exod. 20:13), which begins the second tablet.[3] So, too, all crimes between humans themselves are ultimately seen as sins against God, requiring reconciliation first with the wronged human party and, finally, with the wronged divine party. "When a person sins and offends [*teheta u-ma'alah ma'al*] the Lord by cheating his fellow [*ve-khihesh ba'amito*]. . . he shall pay it to the owner when he becomes aware of his guilt [*be-yom ashmato*]. Then he shall bring his guilt offering [*ashamo*] to the Lord" (Lev. 5:21, 24-25).[4] Along these lines, it should be recalled that Joseph justifies to Potiphar's wife his refusal to make love to her, first because it would betray Potiphar's trust in him, and second because "How can I do this great evil and sin against God [*ve-hat'ati l'elohim*]?" (Gen. 39:9). Also, Joseph's brothers' sense of guilt over their selling him into slavery is first seen as something humanly evil. "We are guilty [*ashemim*] over our brother" (Gen. 42:21). And immediately thereafter it is said that "his blood too will surely be avenged [*nidrash*]." This vengeance undoubtedly refers to God's promise to avenge all innocent human blood that has been shed and not been avenged by human justice. "Surely, your lifeblood I [God] will avenge [*edrosh*]" (Gen. 9:5).

When this centrality of the life of the covenant that is essentially celebrated in cultic acts is appreciated, it becomes clear that the numerous prophetic statements that are critical of the sacrificial cult, and indeed of worship in general, are not rejecting them in principle.[5] What is being condemned is the human tendency to isolate the cult from considerations of human justice *(mishpat)*. Without these considerations, the cult deteriorates into a human invention designed to control God rather than a divinely ordained institution

2. See R. Joseph Albo, *Sefer Ha'Iqqarim,* trans. I. Husik (Philadelphia: Jewish Publication Society, 1929), 3.28; also, R. Meir Leibush Malbim, *Commentary on the Torah,* 2 vols. (New York: n.p., 1956): Deut. 6:25.

3. See *Midrash Leqah Tov:* Yitro, ed. Buber (Vilna: n.p., 1884), 69b; *Zohar:* Yitro, 2:90ab.

4. See *Sifra:* Vayiqra, 27d; M. Yoma 8.8 and B. Yoma 87a re 1 Sam. 2:25; also, Jon D. Levenson, *Sinai and Zion* (Minneapolis: Winston, 1985), pp. 49ff.

5. See G. Ashby, *Sacrifice: Its Nature and Purpose* (London: Macmillan, 1969), p. 45.

designed to bring the whole covenantal community, all of whom have been elected by God, into a more intimate relationship with God their elector. For without considerations of human justice — that is, justice *for* humans *by* humans coming *from* God — the cult becomes a means of human exploitation: those in hierarchal power at the cult shrine (priests, king, and plutocracy) use the cult as an endorsement of their own power. Thus Jeremiah rebukes the people of Israel:

> Improve your ways and your actions and I will let you dwell in this place. Do not trust the lying words: "the Temple of the Lord, the Temple of the Lord, the Temple of the Lord are these precincts *(hemah)*" . . . . Only if you do justice *(mishpat)* between a man and his neighbor . . . and you do not go after other gods to do evil for yourselves . . . then will I let you dwell in this place. (Jer. 7:3-7)

What is seen from this most explicit prophetic rebuke is that the ultimate *telos* for mundane *mishpat* is the cultic center, the Temple. Justice is to be practiced *in order that* the people can dwell *with* the true God in covenantal intimacy in *his* sanctuary, and not enshrine there a god of their own making. The sanctuary is the center of the covenantal life of the people, to be sure, but that life is not confined to the sanctuary.[6] Thus the proper ordering of the extracultic relationships *between* the members of the covenantal community themselves must be consistent with the will of the Dweller within the sanctuary, he who is the Lord of all creation, all mundane existence too. Hence all immorality is related to idolatry — the primarily cultic sin of worshiping other gods — because both are lies and both entail bad, not good, for Israel wherever.

Bible scholars both ancient and modern have pointed out that the Temple is an earthly microcosm of the created cosmos itself.[7] The emphasis on the human need for *mishpat* reminds the worshipers of Israel, especially when they are deeply involved in the singularities of their cultically centered life, that the Lord is the creator God of the whole world. And this is directly connected to election. For only a God who is over the whole world has the options to elect or not to elect, and to elect this people rather than that people. Since the world cannot contain him, his entrance into the world is on his

---

6. That is why the Temple is seen as the desideratum of Jewish religious life but not its *sine qua non*. See A. Büchler, *Studies in Sin and Atonement in the Rabbinic Literature of the First Century* (New York: Ktav Publishing House, 1967), p. 353.

7. See B. Ta'anit 27b; *Midrash Aggadah: Pequdei*, 189; also, Levenson, *Sinai and Zion*, pp. 111ff.

terms alone, not those of the world.[8] God's special interest in the sanctuary — "You shall make for me a sanctuary and I will dwell therein [*betokham*]" (Exod. 25:8) — does not nullify his interest in the whole life of his people. And God's interest in the life of his people is not confined to the singularities of their life exemplified by their cult. God is still just as interested in those aspects of their life that pertain to *mishpat,* the order of the cosmos and humankind in general. In fact, when the people of Israel assume that the Lord is bound to them by a natural bond *aside from* the world, a bond over which they have equal control and therefore equal liberty, the Lord reminds them that as God he has not ceased to be involved with his other creatures as well, even with other nations. "To me, O Israelites, you are just like the Ethiopians, says the Lord. True, I brought Israel up from the land of Egypt, but also the Philistines from Caphtor and the Arameans from Kir" (Amos 9:7). God's relationship with Israel is indeed special. Thus the prophet continues, "I will restore my people [*ammi*] Israel" (Amos 9:14). But that relationship is not that of an only child. Being "holy unto the Lord, his first [*re'shit*] produce" (Jer. 2:3) implies that there are others for God too. Israel's relationship with God is unique but not symbiotic.

The substance of the life of the covenant is the practice of those commandments known as "testimonies" *(edot)*. They testify to the mighty acts of God's grace for Israel. First and foremost among these acts is the Exodus from Egypt, to which the celebration of Passover is the prescribed response. As the paradigm for all Jewish commemorative celebration, the celebration of Passover is the key to our understanding of the life of the covenant at its most direct level. Thus the Torah states,

> When in time to come your son will ask you, "What mean the testimonies [*edot*], rules and regulations [*ve-ha-huqqim ve-ha-mishpatim*] that the Lord our God commanded you?" you tell him, "We were slaves unto Pharaoh in Egypt, but the Lord brought us forth from Egypt with a strong hand. . . . Then the Lord commanded us to practice all these rules, to fear the Lord our God for our good [*le-tov lanu*]." (Deut. 6:20-21, 24)

The Passover event, then, is the reason given for practicing all the commandments. But how does it function as a reason? The answer to this question is determined by how we see the relation of the past and the present in the life of the covenant.

One could easily see the reason for practicing the commandments as be-

8. See 1 Kings 8:27-30; Isa. 66:1-2; 2 Chron. 2:4-5.

ing gratitude. In view of the great good the Lord did for Israel in redeeming her from Egyptian bondage, it seems only fair that Israel owes the Lord a positive expression of gratitude in return.[9] In this view, the present owes a debt to the past. The problem with this view, however, is that it is based on *quid pro quo* logic: God did good for Israel, so Israel must now do good for God. But debts are eventually paid off. When, then, is Israel's debt to God paid off? And if a debt is to be paid *off*, then it would seem that the purpose of the covenant is finally to terminate itself. Moreover, since the Holocaust especially (although not originally), we might ask the question with great poignancy: What is our relationship with God, based on the *quid pro quo* model, when by all humanly known standards there are times when God has been bad and not good to Israel? Are there not times when "the Lord has become like an enemy" (Lam. 2:5)? Finally, if Israel is to do good to God in return, that means that God and Israel have commensurate needs. We know what Israel's needs are. Certainly the need to be free from human bondage is such a need. But what are God's needs? Indeed, if God has needs by nature as humans have needs by nature, then does that not imply that nature is a reality in which both God and humans are participants and to which, therefore, they are both subordinate?[10] All of these theologically troubling problems follow when we probe the gratitude model carefully.

But, on the other hand, what if we assume that the past is for the sake of the present in the covenant? So, let us interpret the relation between the Passover event in the past and its celebration in the present as follows:

The experience of what is good for us can only be in the present. If one is miserable in the present, remembering past good is not only not compensatory in any way, but actually makes matters worse by reminding the now miserable person what he or she has lost.[11] A past good can only be appreciated when one is experiencing good in the present. One then wants to relate the past good to the present good, as well as project future good from the present good, so that the present good is not to be taken as peripheral or ephemeral.

---

9. For the notion of repayment of a debt *(hov)* as the basis of the obligation of children to honor their parents (Exod. 20:12), see Y. Kiddushin 1.7/61b.

10. See Walther Eichrodt, *Theology of the Old Testament* (Philadelphia: Westminster Press, 1961), vol. 1, pp. 42ff.

11. In Aristotle, *Nicomachean Ethics*, 1100aff., the famous maxim of Solon, "Look to the end," is presented as a paradox — namely, only after one is dead does one know whether or not he or she was happy. One of the implications of this paradox is that even if one lived a happy life for the majority of his or her years, misery in the last years is not alleviated by pleasant memories. Quite the contrary: the misery of the present is exacerbated by remembering how different the good of the past is from the misery of the present.

"Be thankful [*hodu*] to the Lord, for that is good, for his mercy endures forever" (Ps. 118:1). According to the Torah's teaching, the prime good experienced in the present is active, not passive. More than what God has done for us, the good is what God enables us to do with him here and now — namely, practice the commandments. Thus it is not that Jews are to observe the commandments in return for what God did when he "took us out of the land of Egypt, out of the house of slavery" (Exod. 20:2), but rather God's taking Israel out of Egypt is the beginning of the good we now experience in keeping his commandments.[12] Unlike a debt, the commandments are to be observed for their own sake, not for their elimination.[13]

Remembering the events of the past, in which God's saving power manifested itself to Israel, indicates to us what first occasioned the commandments to be kept. The event is for the sake of the practice, not vice versa. This can be seen in the interpretation of the following verse discussing the observance of Passover: "You shall remember that you were a slave in Egypt and the Lord freed you from there; therefore [*al ken*] I command you to practice this commandment" (Deut. 24:18). The eleventh-century French commentator Rashi stresses that this is the logic of the verse: "For the sake of this [*al menat ken*] I freed you, in order to keep my laws, even if there is cost involved."[14] In other words, past redemption is celebrated because it has enabled present observance. And an essential part of this present good is that it can only be experienced by free beings, those who chose to be redeemed, whatever the cost. Thus the Passover Haggadah notes that the one who considers the observance of Passover to be a burden rather than a boon in the present would not have been redeemed had he been in Egypt. "If he had been there [*ilu hayah sha*], he would not have been redeemed." It is only those who regard themselves "as if" (*k'ilu*) they went out from Egypt themselves in the present who fulfill the commandment of "telling" (*haggadah*) the Passover event.[15] Moreover, it is

12. See *Sifre: Devarim*, no. 33 re Deut. 6:6, ed. Louis Finkelstein (New York: Jewish Theological Seminary of America, 1969), p. 59; also, Levenson, *Sinai and Zion*, p. 43.

13. See Aristotle, *Nicomachean Ethics*, 1094a1-5 for the distinction between integral and instrumental teleology. While not denying that the commandments have their good consequences, the emphasis of rabbinic teaching is that they are ends in themselves as responses to God's commanding presence (see M. Avot 1.3; *Avot De-Rabbi Nathan*, A, chap. 5, ed. S. Schechter [New York, 1967], 13b).

14. Nahmanides' comment thereon, however, stresses remembrance itself as the reason of the commandment. For Nahmanides, the *edot* are participations in the archetypal events of the past. See David Novak, *The Theology of Nahmanides Systematically Presented* (Atlanta: Scholars Press, 1992), pp. 8ff., 116ff.

15. See Menachem Kasher, *Haggadah Shlemah*, 3rd ed. (Jerusalem: Torah Shelema Institute, 1967), pt. 2, pp. 23-24, 63-64 re Exod. 13:8.

important to recall that the first Passover was observed in anticipation of re-demption, not because of it.[16] In other words, redemption is retroactive from the present back into the past or projective from the present into the future. Passover is as much a celebration of the past as it is an anticipation of the fu-ture. As such, its meaning is essentially present before it is either past or fu-ture. This too might be the reason why the elements of Passover observance have symbolic significance in the present but are not fundamentally represen-tational of the past. They are not re-enactments. Not every detail of the past is to be repeated in the present.[17] In this way, the remembered past makes room for the lived present, providing points of reference for it but not subsuming it by making it a clone.

This explains the joy that traditional Jews have known in the observance of the commandments, especially the commemorative commandments, whose main points of reference are so experiential. Even though we are fully aware of the fact that we will frequently sin — "There is no human who only does good and does not sin" (Eccles. 7:20) — that is a chance worth taking for the good of being able to observe the commandments and live the life of the covenant. "Even a live dog is better than a dead lion" (Eccles. 9:4) is inter-preted by the Rabbis as follows: "*The live dog* is the wicked person still alive in this world; if he repents God accepts him. But the righteous person [*the wicked lion*] once dead can never again increase benefit [*zekhut*] for himself anymore."[18] The earlier rabbinic text in the Mishnah that inspired this inter-pretation is the statement of the sage Hillel: "If not now [*im lo akshav*], when?"[19]

16. See Exod. 12:11-14.
17. See M. Pesahim 9:5; B. Pesahim 96ab.
18. *Avot de-Rabbi Natan,* A, chap. 27, p. 27b.
19. M. Avot 1:14.

6 The Role of Dogma in Judaism (1988)

The greatest Jewish theologian of this century, to my mind, was the late Franz Rosenzweig, who always had the gift of uttering *multa in parvu*. He once noted that Judaism has dogmas but no dogmatics.[1] What he meant was that although Judaism certainly affirms a number of truths — what one would call official doctrines or dogmas — these affirmations are not ordered in their own independent system which itself has the collective authority of its parts. Of course, various Jewish theologians, usually under the influence of some philosophical system, have tried to construct a dogmatics of Judaism.[2] But none of these "dogmatics" would be termed a *Summa Theologiae Iudaicae or Die Synagogliche Dogmatik* in the sense that similar terms have been used in the history of Christian theology. All of these efforts, as impressive as some of them have been, could be essentially characterized as individual schematizations of traditional Jewish teaching, nothing more.[3]

---

1. Rosenzweig, *Kleinere Schriften* (Berlin: Schocken Books, 1937), p. 31: "Das Judentum hat namlich Dogmen, aber keine Dogmatik." See Paul Ricoeur, *History and Truth*, trans. C. A. Kebeley (Evanston, Ill.: Northwestern University Press, 1965), p. 179.

2. See M. M. Kellner, *Dogma in Medieval Jewish Thought* (Oxford: Oxford University Press, 1986); also, Solomon Schechter, *Studies in Judaism* (Philadelphia: Jewish Publication Society, 1896), pp. 146ff.

3. These efforts are precisely what Karl Barth termed "systematic theology," in distinction from *Kirchliche Dogmatik* — that is, "an edifice of thought, constructed on certain fundamental conceptions which are selected in accordance with a certain philosophy by a method which corresponds to these conceptions." See *Dogmatics in Outline* (New York: Harper, 1959), p. 5.

I

Rosenzweig's remark, which I believe is correct, is a rejection of two other views of the role of dogma and dogmatics in Judaism. On the one hand, it rejects a view shared by some Orthodox and many secular Jews (ironically enough) that Judaism is only a system of behavior, "revealed legislation" in the famous phrase of the Enlightenment Jewish philosopher Moses Mendelssohn.[4] They do differ, nevertheless, on the specific question of how much behavior is necessarily Jewish (the Orthodox insisting on both ritual and ethics; the secularists emphasizing ethics and subordinating ritual to it, if not virtually eliminating it altogether).[5] My late revered teacher, Abraham Joshua Heschel, dubbed this approach "religious behaviorism," the term being chosen both for its denotation and for its pejorative connotation.[6] On the other hand, Rosenzweig is rejecting a view held by most liberal Jews — namely, that Judaism as a system is to be found in its "teaching" (Lehre) rather than in its law. Indeed, Rosenzweig's essay was written as a critique of "apologetic thinking," specifically as found in Leo Baeck's influential statement of liberal theology, Das Wesen des Judentums.[7]

Clearly, dogmas are not just propositions but laws, in the sense that they are propositions-to-be-affirmed. Rosenzweig's prime example is the Jewish prayerbook, the Siddur, the liturgical order, whose structure and content are dealt with by halakhah (Jewish law) with the same meticulous care taken in dealing with the keeping of the Sabbath or the payment of debts or any other area of human action. Following Rosenzweig, it would seem that the liberal error is to attempt to construct a Jewish dogmatics outside the Law; and the error of the Orthodox and secularist "behaviorists" is to attempt to construct a Jewish dogmatics without dogmas.

One might conclude that Judaism does have a systematic structure or "dogmatics," since the halakhah is a structure of the commandments and the awareness that the Law requires certain truths to be affirmed as dogmas and

---

4. Mendelssohn, Jerusalem, trans. A. Arkush (Hanover, N.H.: University Press of New England, 1983), p. 97.

5. For a secularist treatment of the primacy of ethics in Jewish teaching (to be distinguished from the liberal assertion of the same point, made on theological grounds), see Ahad Ha'Am, Selected Essays (Philadelphia: Jewish Publication Society, 1912), pp. 125ff.

6. Heschel, God in Search of Man (New York: Farrar, Straus & Giroux, 1955), pp. 320ff.

7. Rosenzweig's essay was written in 1923. The final and greatly expanded version of Baeck's work came out in 1922. The original version came out in 1905 as a Jewish response to Adolf von Harnack's Das Wesen des Christentums. See The Essence of Judaism (London: Macmillan, 1936), esp. pp. 59ff., 261ff.

their denials to be rejected as heresies. This would seem to suggest, therefore, that dogmas are a subset of halakhah. To be sure, Maimonides did begin his great code of the Law, *Mishneh Torah,* with a major dogmatic treatise, *Hilkhot Yesodei Ha-Torah* ("the laws pertaining to the foundations of the Torah"). But even Maimonides' dogmatics never achieved the authoritative force that the more practical aspects of his halakhic magnum opus did. Moreover, none of his halakhic successors resumed or initiated any such grand dogmatic project.

Most of the great masters of halakhah after Maimonides were not dogmaticians or even theologians in the strict sense. They confined their intellectual attention to writing *responsa* or commentaries. Their occasional forays into theology were usually homiletical. This does not mean that theological issues did not interest them or enter into their work of responding and commenting, but they were dealt with more as an accompaniment to the business of the Law than as an independent discipline.[8] The greatest project of Jewish theology after Maimonides was the Kabbalah, especially the *Zohar* and the works it inspired. But it was developed for the most part by thinkers who were not distinguished as masters of the Law. And even when masters of the Law were also kabbalistic theologians, they managed to keep the two disciplines separate and distinct.[9] Furthermore, Kabbalah, like the theological system of Maimonides, never achieved the status of classical — that is, rabbinic — dogma. Indeed, there have been pro- and anti-kabbalists to this very day, both of whom have been considered very much legitimate members of the traditional Jewish community but subordinate to the Law.[10] The same, *mutatis mutandis,* could be said of pro- and anti-Maimonists.[11]

Traditionalist Jewish thinkers would regard this as both a correct assessment of Judaism and a good thing about Judaism as well. For it means that Judaism regulates action more strictly than it does the formulation and expression of thought. Action is the immediate subject of communal norms, whereas thought, although formulated in a common language, is still more in the domain of individual insight. This does not mean that one can affirm or deny anything one chooses and still remain part of the traditional Jewish community. But the limitations are more negative limits *(perata)* than first

---

8. See Louis Jacobs, *Theology in the Responsa* (London and Boston: Routledge & Kegan Paul, 1975).

9. See R. J. Z. Werblowsky, *Joseph Karo: Lawyer and Mystic* (Philadelphia: Jewish Publication Society, 1980), pp. 289ff.

10. For the anti-mystical views of the founder of modern neo-orthodoxy, see Rabbi Samson Raphael Hirsch, *The Nineteen Letters of Ben Uziel* (New York: Bloch, 1942), p. 187.

11. For a contemporary anti-Maimonidean Orthodox theology, see Michael Wyschogrod, *The Body of Faith: Judaism as Corporeal Election* (New York: Seabury Press, 1983), esp. pp. xiv-xv.

principles *(archai)* in the Aristotelian sense.[12] Thus, for example, Baruch Spinoza, the most famous Jewish heretic in the modern sense of "nonbeliever," was excommunicated by the rabbinical authorities of Amsterdam because his expressed thoughts explicitly denied traditional Jewish practice. This was practically manifested by the fact that Spinoza himself had abandoned that very religious practice to such an extent that he no longer even lived among Jews when he was finally excommunicated. Had Spinoza remained in the Jewish community and been more pious (at least in public), and had he not so directly challenged the dogmas mandated by the Law, the Rabbis of Amsterdam could have probably tolerated him as a member of the normative community.[13]

The emphasis on action over thought is one that finds instant sympathy in the modern world in which even traditionalist theologians must speak and write. It seems to be consistent with democratic notions about freedom of opinion. It also finds similar sympathy with those desiring the political climate most conducive to a philosophically receptive culture, a desire going back to the archetypal philosopher Socrates. It will be recalled that Socrates was willing to accept communal authority in the practical realm while at the same time insisting upon freedom in the theoretical realm.[14]

The question before us is not *how* Judaism formulates dogmas. The dogmas mandated by the halakhah — such as the transcendence of God, divine creativity, providence, judgment, human freedom of choice, the election of Israel, the revelation of the Torah, and the eschatology of the advent of the Messiah and the resurrection of the dead and the world-to-come — all have already been formulated in the classical rabbinic sources and canonized in the traditional liturgy. That they require continued explication and that this explication has wide latitude, few would deny. But there does not seem to be room for any genuine innovation here in traditional Judaism. At this level, radical innovation would fundamentally sever the *traditio* of the Tradition.[15]

12. Note Aristotle, *Metaphysics,* 1022a10: "The principle [*archē*] is a sort of limit [*peras*], but not every limit is a principle." For the notion that a positive assertion of a dogma about God in Scripture or tradition functions negatively for theology, see Maimonides, *Guide of the Perplexed,* 1.58; also, Thomas Aquinas, *Summa Theologiae,* 1, q. 3, prol.

13. Spinoza's own existential removal from the Jewish community is, no doubt, expressed in his definition of religion as *quod viri privati officium est* (*Tractatus Politicus,* 3.10). See Leo Strauss, *Spinoza's Critique of Religion* (New York: Schocken Books, 1965), pp. 164-65.

14. See Socrates, *Apology,* 29d, and *Crito,* 54c. For the rejection of this political freedom in Plato's political philosophy, see Karl Popper, *The Open Society and Its Enemies,* 5th ed., rev. (Princeton: Princeton University Press, 1966), vol. 1, pp. 86ff.

15. For a fundamental re-interpretation of the rabbinic dogma of the resurrection of the

The real question is how the authoritative structure of the halakhah can be correlated with theological speculation. And they are indeed correlated, if for no other reason than that we are commanded by the Torah to love the Lord God with all our powers: practical, emotional, and intellectual.[16] Furthermore, this is demonstrated by the fact that in the formative rabbinic period, the greatest masters of the Law were also great masters of theological speculation, aggadah, and that each pursuit informed the other on many key issues.[17]

At the present time, there appear to be three correlations of halakhah and theology in the traditionalist Jewish world, a world defined by acceptance of the full authority of the Law, irrespective of political groupings in Jewry. Let us briefly outline the first two, stipulate why they seem inadequate, and then explicate more fully the third correlation.

II

The first correlation is that of undoubtedly the most influential traditionalist theologian today, Rabbi Joseph B. Soloveitchik. In his seminal 1944 essay *Halakhic Man* (only recently translated from the original Hebrew into English), Soloveitchik posits a thesis in which *halakhah is Jewish theology* when properly understood as a unified system.[18] For Soloveitchik, halakhah is what God reveals as the true structure of the world *sub specie aeternitatis*. The theoretical task is to grasp the intelligibility inherent in this eternal view of the world, in the sense of pure mathematics. The practical task is to direct this intelligibility to the problems of the world at hand, in the sense of applied mathematics. Soloveitchik's great appeal to many thoughtful traditionalist Jews is largely the result of the clarity and consistency of his basic thesis, the philosophical sophistication he seems to employ, and the fruitful hermeneutic it has given him in explicating many classical Jewish texts in his long career

dead, see Maimonides, *Mishneh Torah:* Repentance, 3.6. Cf. M. Sanhedrin 10.1 and B. Sanhedrin 90b.

16. In Hellenistic Jewish tradition, *be-khol m'odekha* ("with all your might" — Deut. 6:5) is sometimes seen as *dianoia* (LXX according to Codex Vaticanus; see Philo, *De Opificio Mundi,* 60.146; Mark 12:30 and parallels). In rabbinic tradition, *amor Dei intellectualis* is included in the heart. See M. Berakhot 9.5 and B. Berakhot 5a.

17. See David Novak, *Law and Theology in Judaism,* vol. 1 (New York: Ktav Publishing House, 1974).

18. Soloveitchik, *Halakhic Man,* trans. L. Kaplan (Philadelphia: Jewish Publication Society, 1983). See pp. 55ff.

as a most compelling teacher. The Achilles' heel of this approach, however, is history. Not only is it ahistorical in the sense that many premodern theologies were ahistorical or "prehistorical"; it is antihistorical. As such, it can be seriously faulted by both internal and external criteria.

In terms of internal criteria — namely, halakhah itself — the facts show a decidedly nonmathematical type of system, far more akin to one of precedent, like English Common Law, than the legal systems of the Roman codes, which strove to be deductively constructed *more geometrico*.[19] In other words, the recognition of historical development is one which halakhah itself makes; it is not the imposition of modern critical scholars, although external conditions certainly made the explication of the historicity of Judaism a more pressing need.[20]

In terms of external criteria, one must theologize within a wider cultural context if one is to speak to Jews who have been exposed to it and who inevitably speak its language. Soloveitchik clearly recognizes his extensive use of neo-Kantian philosophy, especially its philosophy of science and mathematics. And it is worth noting that those Orthodox Jews who have rejected all contact with non-Jewish thought as heresy-breeding have rejected Soloveitchik with particular vehemence.[21]

If one acknowledges the wider cultural context in which one theologizes, one cannot select one part of it and reject others without giving theology a decidedly arbitrary cast. Soloveitchik, who has indeed dismissed (disingenuously, I believe) attempts to deal with halakhah and the rest of Judaism historically, seems to be, on the one hand, adopting a modern language (taken in the Wittgensteinian sense of a "language game") and, on the other hand, arbitrarily eliminating some of its most basic vocabulary and conceptuality. Such elimination *a priori* is a very different procedure from theologically critical reworking and appropriating material from the external culture.[22] All of this creates a major credibility problem for Soloveitchik's theology.[23]

19. It is interesting to note that one of the greatest medieval halakhists, Nahmanides, whom Soloveitchik himself often quotes, cautions that "everyone who studies our Talmud knows that in this type of wisdom there is no clear proof as in geometric calculations." Quoted in I. Twersky, *Introduction to the Code of Maimonides (Mishneh Torah)* (New Haven: Yale University Press, 1980), p. 168n.204.

20. See David Novak, *Halakhah in a Theological Dimension* (Chico, Calif.: Scholars Press, 1985).

21. See D. Singer and M. Sokol, "Joseph Soloveitchik: Lonely Man of Faith," *Modern Judaism* 2, no. 3 (October 1982): 228.

22. See Paul Tillich, *Theology of Culture* (Oxford: Oxford University Press, 1959), pp. 40ff.

23. See "Lonely Man of Faith," *Tradition* 7, no. 2 (Summer 1965): 9.

The same antihistorical tendency, although here it is more implicit, characterizes the approach of Rabbi Adin Steinsaltz, one of the most committed kabbalists today (as distinguished from historians of Kabbalah like the late Gershom Scholem). Steinsaltz, best known as a modern commentator on the Talmud, has also presented a modern restatement of kabbalistic theology, *The Thirteen-Petalled Rose*.[24] In this work, he has attempted to reformulate the basic kabbalistic doctrine that the Torah is an elaborate and systematic *corpus symbolicum* of the divine life itself, even in those passages where the Torah seems to be concerned with rather mundane matters.[25] In other words, whereas for Soloveitchik *theology is halakhah*, for Steinsaltz *halakhah is theology*, if essentially conceived of as *Gotteslehre* (namely, *theo-logy* in its original sense). Like Soloveitchik, Steinsaltz skillfully uses the language of modern science and mathematics, in his case the language of atomic physics. Needless to say, history *qua* development and change *a posteriori* cannot play any role in this theology — and it does not. Along these lines, I do not think it at all accidental that when the modern Jewish historical approach known as *die Wissenschaft des Judentums* was being formulated and applied in the nineteenth century, its most vehement opponents were the Hasidic masters of Eastern Europe, whose theology was so heavily kabbalistic.[26]

There seems little doubt that no Jewish theology can eliminate the component of historical development and still speak in any modern language. Nevertheless, without some limitation of the role of historical descriptiveness in Jewish discourse, it would seem that all we have left is historicism, whose inherent relativism is deadly for theology (and for the Law). It is deadly because theology must deal with *truths-to-be-affirmed*.[27] If history is concerned with truth *wie es eigentlich gewesen* (or, better, *wie es eigentlich geworden*),[28] theology is concerned with truth as normative, or as we might say, continuing the German nomenclature, *wie es eigentlich sein soll*. In other words, theology

24. Steinsaltz, *The Thirteen-Petalled Rose*, trans. Y. Hanegbi (New York: Basic Books, 1980), esp. pp. 87ff.

25. See Gershom Scholem, *On the Kabbalah and Its Symbolism* (New York: Schocken Books, 1969), pp. 32ff.

26. See R. Mahler, *Hasidism and the Jewish Enlightenment* (Philadelphia: Jewish Publication Society, 1985), pp. 47-53.

27. See W. F. Albright, *From the Stone Age to Christianity*, 2d ed. (Garden City, N.Y.: Doubleday, 1957), pp. 82ff. See Y. H. Yerushalmi, *Zakhor: Jewish History and Jewish Memory* (Seattle: University of Washington Press, 1982), pp. 87ff., for a reflection on the inadequacy of historicism for Jewish existence by a leading contemporary Jewish historian.

28. The implicit imperative in the gerund form is used in the sense that Thomas Aquinas used it in defining the first principle of practical reason as *bonum est faciendum* (*Summa Theologiae*, 1-2, q. 94, a. 2).

must in some way speak with some conviction about the word of God. That normative affirmation itself presupposes finitude in the sense that a finite number of truths are to be affirmed and all other competing affirmations are to be denied as false.[29] Since theology is normative, not just empirical, its choice of affirmations is not tentative in the sense of being refutable by as yet unknown data. This does not mean that theological statements are not correctable. Theologians are not prophets.[30] Correctability is based on reinterpretation, not experimentation.

History, conversely, when striving to approximate what is believed to be the certitude of the natural sciences by becoming a "social science," seems to presuppose infinity. There seems to be an infinite number of possible historical data on the horizon. As such, all historical affirmations are only tentative empirical descriptions, subject to immediate revision based on any new data not yet known or not yet properly considered. When a historical approach to theology is adopted, we seem to have the following scenario. A theologian says, "Judaism affirms w," whereupon a historian counters, "But at time x, y affirmed z [z being the opposite of w]." The historian's counterpoint seems to entail the assumption that the only authoritative statements in theology must be statable in the universal propositions of deductive logic — that is, "all a is b." Of course, one is precluded from making any such statement because it can only be proposed *a priori* and historians (*pace* Spengler, Toynbee, et al.) can only speak *a posteriori*. Following this view, theology is impossible because one cannot even speak of "Judaism" as a coherent essence but only of "Judaisms."

This type of historicist reasoning strove to approximate the certitude of the natural sciences and assumed that its criterion of truth is verifiability.[31] In this view of science, propositions *depict* empirically accessible reality either correctly or incorrectly. It is the empiricist reworking of the old medieval formula, *veritas est adaequatio intellectus ad rem.*[32] An experiment is supposed to prove — that is, demonstrate — whether any such scientific depiction is correct or incorrect. It is correct if it covers all the data; it is incorrect if it does

---

29. See Martin Heidegger, *Kant and the Problem of Metaphysics* (Bloomington and London: Indiana University Press, 1962), p. 223.

30. For the difference between rabbinic and prophetic authority, see Maimonides, MT: Rebels, 1.3.

31. For the failure of the historicist attempt to approximate natural science, see Alasdair MacIntyre, *After Virtue* (Notre Dame: University of Notre Dame Press, 1981), pp. 83ff.

32. See Wittgenstein, *Tractatus Logico-Philosophicus,* 2.1, 2.12. Cf. Martin Heidegger, "On the Essence of Truth," in *Heidegger: Basic Writings,* ed. D. Krell (New York: Harper & Row, 1977), pp. 118-22.

not. Logically, if not chronologically, the theory always generalizes *from* the data; thus verifiability and inductive reasoning are two sides of the same intellectual coin. The data include the theory and can instantly destroy it in the same way the infinite includes the finite and obliterates it in Hegelian *Aufhebung*.[33] It is, thus, understandable why this view of truth, best known as logical positivism, could not tolerate metaphysics, ethics, or theology because the truth they purport to express is clearly not verifiable in this narrowly empiricist sense. Like all positivisms, this one too claimed to be employing Ockham's razor. It is one thing when that razor cuts off redundant cultural bulk; it is quite another when it severs the cultural jugular vein, leaving us to bleed a nihilistic death.[34]

III

When one looks at the work of Karl Popper in the philosophy of science, it becomes apparent, as he himself has not tired of emphasizing in always polemically charged writings, that this view of truth is greatly flawed. It simply is not what the scientific community does in its work, work which, it must be admitted (however grudgingly by theologians and all other non-scientists), is the most impressive intellectual achievement of the modern world. As Popper has convincingly pointed out, the criterion of scientific truth is not verifiability but falsifiability. The difference is crucial.

Scientific theories are not verifiable in the sense of direct correspondence to data *per se*. This means that a scientific model is not a generalization, not even a generalization by anticipation. It is, rather, an intellectual construct (hence, mathematically conceived) *a priori*, which attempts to solve a problem or group of problems facing the community of scientific discourse. Naturally, the model must pertain *to* the data that are involved in the particular discursive problem at hand. The model would be inadequate as a solution to the problem at hand if it could not do as much as constitute the data in its conceptuality. And if the very data so constituted by the model *a priori* turn out to contradict what the model necessarily asserts, then the model has been thereby falsified.[35] Verifiability presupposes an infinite range of data on the horizon, whereas falsifiability presupposes a finite, temporally bound, se-

33. See *Phenomenology of Spirit* (Oxford: Oxford University Press, 1977), pp. 100-102.

34. See Leo Strauss, *Natural Right and History* (Chicago: University of Chicago Press, 1953).

35. *Popper Selections*, ed. D. Miller (Princeton: Princeton University Press, 1985), esp. pp. 133ff. See also W. V. Quine, *From a Logical Point of View*, 2d rev. ed. (New York: Harper & Row, 1961), pp. 37ff.

lected range of data at hand. And that finitude is due to the necessarily selective nature of any range of human discourse within time. It can only effectively handle those questions which bother it.[36] This discursive, social element is the crucial mediating factor here between the model proposed by the individual scientist and the data he or she is attempting to explain. Finally, since logical positivism and historicism are linked by their common reliance on the verifiability theory of truth, Popper rejected the latter with the same vehemence that he rejected the former (actually with more vehemence, since he saw historicism at the heart of a number of modern political evils).[37]

Following Popper's lead, Thomas Kuhn has shown how the change in basic scientific orientations ("paradigms," as he calls them) is due less to external empirical factors than to internal discursive factors.[38] Thus, there is now a three-point relation between the scientist, the community of scientific discourse, and the data at hand. For positivists and idealists, conversely, there is only a two-point relation. For positivists, the mind of the thinker essentially follows the infinite external world; for idealists, the external world is projected from the infinite mind of the thinker.[39] And both have a marked tendency to see the world of social discourse as being essentially epiphenomenal. Furthermore, if history aspires to the intelligence of the natural sciences, and if the current philosophical estimation of the natural sciences now recognizes their true context to be in purposive (that is, problem-solving) human discourse, then history becomes more of an appreciation of still-developing human discourse, in Michael Polanyi's sense of being "personal knowledge."[40]

It would seem that Dilthey's uniquely nineteenth-century demarcation between the methods of *Naturwissenschaften* and *Geisteswissenschaften* is no longer valid. Therefore, history and even the natural sciences are now closer to what theology has always been — namely, the study of the discourse of a particular living community in the present, moving into the future, and appropriating as much of its past as the problematics of this movement require. They are distinguished more by their respective subject matters and less by their respective methodologies. All of them have a normative thrust, although theology's normative thrust is much more explicit. And it is this more explic-

---

36. Popper writes that "science starts from problems and not from observations" (*Popper Selections*, p. 179).

37. See *Popper Selections*, pp. 289ff.

38. See his *The Structure of Scientific Revolutions* (Chicago: University of Chicago Press, 1962), esp. p. 108; see also Wittgenstein, *Philosophical Investigations* (New York: Macmillan, 1967), pp. 5, 11, 99.

39. See *Popper Selections*, pp. 135ff.

40. See his *The Study of Man* (Chicago: University of Chicago Press, 1959), pp. 78ff.

itly normative thrust which enables theology to include history in its project in a way that history cannot include theology *per se* — that is, constructive theology as opposed to historical theology (the latter being essentially a historical and not a theological enterprise).

IV

Theology's agenda is one which deals with the problems the community of faith faces here and now, problems with which it must adequately deal, if not actually overcome, if it is to maintain both its authority and its credibility in the modern world. If the community's intellectual leaders shirk their responsibilities here and now, the people will be forced to seek other authority to deal with these inescapable problems. In this sense, history is needed for precedents (and the critical study of history broadens and deepens the range of these precedents), but the function of judgment, which can only be that of present authority, is itself not historical *per se*. It is not simply the consequent of past antecedents. Rather, it includes the past ("prehending" it in Whitehead's sense), an inclusion not just subjectively eclectic, but one bound by objective canons. History is thus included in the theological circle in much the same way as the material cause *(hylē)* is included in the final cause *(telos)* in Aristotelian philosophy.[41]

It is important to comprehend, moreover, that the recognition of the essential finitude involved in this process of making temporally conditioned normative judgments is itself an issue of faith. It saves theology from arrogant triumphalism, from the oftimes blasphemous impression that its voice is God's last word. When theology does that, attempting to permanently subsume the transcendent within its own immanent utterances, it thereby denies its own doctrines of redemption. If the final word is to be God's, then all human utterances must be tentative before the final redemption is with us. As a famous rabbinic dictum puts it:

> Rabbi Tarfon said that the time is short, the work far greater, the workers incompetent, the reward is much, and the master of the house presses us on. . . . It is not for you to complete the work, but you are not permitted to desist from it either.[42]

41. See Aristotle, *Physics*, 195a15ff.; *Metaphysics*, 983a25-30. Cf. A. N. Whitehead, *Process and Reality* (New York: Macmillan, 1929), pp. 66, 259-60; also, H. G. Gadamer, *Truth and Method* (New York: Crossroad, 1982), pp. 274ff.

42. M. Avot 2.18-19.

The problems facing the Jewish religious community are twofold: practical and theoretical. Practical questions, which are the more evident issues of halakhah, are more specific in that they entail matters which require immediate judgment and which affect a larger number of the members of the community. An example of such a practical problem today would be how to determine the point of death of a brain-diminished patient attached to a respirator and other life-sustaining (or death-prolonging) equipment. Past precedents can be invoked, but authoritative judgment in the present must do a great deal more than simply deduce conclusions from them. Modern medical technology has literally thrown too many new factors into the situation at hand. Hence, for traditionalist Jews, these questions have opened up a whole new area for halakhic judgment.[43] These judgments show halakhah to be a developing yet orderly process.[44]

Theoretical questions, on the other hand, are more general and less evident in the lives of most of the members of the faith community. They call for a broader dialectical effort on the part of theologians, requiring them to show how aspects of various non-Jewish philosophies, ideologies, and theologies are compatible with traditional doctrine, and to show how others are not, either partially or totally, especially when they explicitly or even implicitly deny the legitimacy of Judaism. That denial can either be by means of outright condemnation or by the relegation of Judaism to the status of a historical relic. In this latter dialectical function, theology must show how these external points of view are inadequate in terms of their own claims and criteria of meaning and truth, over and above showing how they do not understand Judaism at all. In other words, it must employ the method of philosophical dialectic, going back to Socrates. For example, one could show how Freud's theory of human sexuality is compatible with Judaism, even illuminating many traditional discussions about human sexuality. As for Freud's atheism, however, it would have to be shown, among other things, that it is not necessarily entailed by Freud's psychology.[45] If theology shirks this dialectical responsibility, it leaves the faithful with a two-truth epistemology with all its absurdities.

Looking at the practical perspective as one pole and the theoretical perspective as the other pole, one might characterize Judaism as containing a field of normativity delimited by these two poles. The practical pole is halakhah; the theoretical pole, theology. How they are related in dealing with

---

43. See Novak, *Law and Theology in Judaism,* vol. 2, pp. 98ff.

44. See Novak, *Halakhah in a Theological Dimension,* chaps. 1, 7.

45. See M. Ostow, *Judaism and Psychoanalysis* (New York: Ktav Publishing House, 1982), pp. 20ff.

the Jewish problematic can be best seen by looking to the most important classical source of Jewish normativity, the Babylonian Talmud.[46]

V

In the Babylonian Talmud, much more often than not, issues of concern are presented in the form of a dispute between the ancient authorities. The subject matter of the particular dispute will determine the type of methodological question to be asked. If one begins with a situation where two different practices are being advocated, then the question to be raised is the difference in theory *(be-ma'y qe-mipalgey)*.[47] Conversely, if one begins with a situation where two different theories are being advocated, then the question to be raised is the practical difference *(ma'y beynihu)*.[48]

In many practical cases, the answer to the question about theoretical distinctions is to offer a juridical principle, which itself is not theological. Nevertheless, although such juridical principles might not be immediately theological, they can be seen as leading to a broader theological principle in their background. Along these lines, Maimonides (to the mind of many, the greatest halakhist and theologian in the history of Judaism) defined *talmud* as a method (rather than its more usual denotation as a specific literature) to understand the immediately practical and ultimately theoretical meaning of revelation and tradition. For him, it is "to understand and discern the end of something from its beginning and to infer one thing from another. . . to compare one thing to another . . . . it includes those subjects called *pardes*."[49]

Pardes, a vague rabbinic term that probably originally meant something like theosophy, for Maimonides includes *ma'aseh bereshit* (speculation about divine creation of the universe) and *ma'aseh merkavah* (speculation about the vision recorded in Ezekiel, chapter 1, connoting metaphysics).[50] It indicates Maimonides' reworking of basic rabbinic terms along the lines of Aristotelian/neo-Platonic philosophy. Thus, we see how legal reasoning does lead to the ontological concerns of theology, if examined deeply enough.

In utilizing the work of Popper and Kuhn in the philosophy of science

---

46. For the centrality of the Babylonian Talmud in Jewish law and theology, see B. Sanhedrin 24a and Tos., s.v. "belulah."

47. See, e.g., B. Kiddushin 47ab.

48. See, e.g., B. Baba Metsia 15b-16a.

49. Maimonides, MT: Torah Study, 1.11-12.

50. See Maimonides, MT: Foundations, 4.13, and *Guide of the Perplexed*, 1, intro. Cf. B. Hagigah 14b.

(similar to Maimonides' critical and selective use of the work of Plato, Aristotle, Ibn Sina, and Alfarabi) for purposes of Jewish theology, I propose that although halakhah cannot verify every or even most theological statements in that these statements are often far more than rationales for specific commandments *(ta'amei ha-mitzvot)*, it can falsify them. By this I mean that a theology, in order to be adequate — let alone sufficient — for Judaism, cannot fail to properly constitute *a priori* an aspect of Judaism as persistent and indispensable as halakhah. It cannot do so any more than a scientific hypothesis can dismiss *a priori* or inadequately constitute data which have been persistent in the discourse of the scientists' own community, the community whom they are to primarily address, and still claim to be speaking the same language.

An *a priori* dismissal of this kind can be done in one of three ways. First, it can act as if the data never existed. In our case, that would be tantamount to absurdly asserting that Judaism has no law and never did have one. Second, it can refer to the data in such a way as to destroy their essence. That was epitomized by the remark of the liberal Jewish thinker Mordecai Kaplan, about the law having "a vote but not a veto."[51] However, since halakhah is operative law, and operative law by definition has authority — that is, a veto — this is tantamount to saying that Jewish law is not law. In other words, this approach violates the very phenomenological integrity of the law. Finally, *a priori* dismissal can be by means of abrogation and making a new law to replace the old law. This is what the church did when it changed the traditional Jewish practice of conversion as recorded in Acts 15. This was both a practical decision and a theoretical judgment, the latter being a radical reconception of what the election of the people of God is to be.

When this happens, the field of Jewish normativity has in truth been broken. The realm of common Jewish discourse is rent asunder. And, although we see this most immediately at the practical end of the field, its ramifications extend to the farthest reaches of the theoretical end of the field. The Jewish-Christian schism, which we have all inherited, it seems to me, can only be understood within this twofold perspective. Without it, the schism seems either too abstract when viewed from the practical side alone, or too mundane when viewed from the theoretical side alone.

The schism did not occur because Judaism affirmed the Law and Christianity denied it, but rather because Christianity put forth its own new law as

---

51. Kaplan, *Not So Random Thoughts* (New York: Reconstructionist Press, 1966), p. 263. For the fuller expression of his anti-traditionalist views of the Law, see *Judaism as a Civilization* (New York: Macmillan, 1934), pp. 424-25, 469-70.

part of its new covenant. And understanding dogma as a subset of halakhah rather than as a set of independent propositions directly descriptive of an immediately experienced external reality (even if metaphysical rather than physical) would seem to be almost as true about Christianity as it is about Judaism, if one follows the argument recently put forth by George Lindbeck in his widely discussed book *The Nature of Doctrine*. Is not Lindbeck asserting that Christian doctrine is necessarily correlated with Christian halakhah? He writes:

> I shall briefly compare regulative and propositional approaches and suggest that the former has advantages, not only because it can give a more plausible account than can the alternatives, of the permanence of doctrine amid historical change, but also for the traditional and yet modern-sounding reason that makes church doctrines more effectively normative by relating them more closely to praxis.[52]

Judaism has norms, and these norms have a structure called halakhah, and Judaism is never to be less than it. Thus, if a speculative theological statement either directly denies a halakhically constituted dogma of Judaism, or undergirds a rejection or distortion of halakhah in part or wholly, then it has been thereby falsified. Hence, regarding any theology, one might say that halakhah is a necessary condition but not *the* sufficient condition for its validity in traditional Judaism.

---

52. Lindbeck, *The Nature of Doctrine* (Philadelphia: Westminster Press, 1984), p. 91. See also pp. 17-18, 74.

7 Is There a Concept of Individual Rights in Jewish Law? (1994)

The Interest in *Mishpat Ivri*

The growth and vitality of the Jewish Law Association must be seen within the larger context of the growth and vitality of the relatively new discipline of *mishpat ivri* (literally "Hebrew jurisprudence"). Although *mishpat ivri* deals with the same sources as does the ancient discipline of halakhah, its scope and its methods distinguish it from halakhah. First, whereas halakhah is concerned with all human activities, both those pertaining to the relationship between man and God *(bein adam lemaqom)* and the relationship between humans themselves *(bein adam lehavero)*, *mishpat ivri* is only concerned with the interhuman realm, and only with that aspect of the interhuman realm which is the subject of other modern secular systems of law.[1] Thus its scope is narrower. Second, whereas halakhah is always studied as normative and at least potentially prescriptive,[2] *mishpat ivri* is studied in a more academic fashion; its methods are far more descriptive. The reason for this latter distinction is that halakhah still governs the lives of many Jews, but *mishpat ivri* governs no one's life. It is neither the law of the Jewish state of Israel nor the law of any segment of the Jewish people anywhere. For this reason the methods of *mishpat ivri* are largely those of the discipline of historical jurisprudence. The end pursued seems to be information, not regulation.

Despite these distinctions between *mishpat ivri* and halakhah, however, I

1. See Menachem Elon, *Hamishpat Ha'Ivri*, 2d rev. ed. (Jerusalem: Magnes, 1978), vol. 1, pp. 146ff.; also, Asher Gulak, *Yesodei Hamishpat Ha'Ivri* (Berlin: Devir, 1922), vol. 1, pp. 6ff.

2. Thus even speculation about what the law is pertaining to the Temple (which had not been in existence since 70 C.E.) is considered to have prescriptive potential to be actualized when the Temple is rebuilt. See, e.g., B. Zevahim 45a and Rashi, s.v. "hilkhata lemeshiha."

think one can further distinguish between two types of interest in *mishpat ivri,* one farther removed from halakhah and the other closer to it.

Farther removed from halakhah is the study of *mishpat ivri* for the sake of information *per se.* Here the methods employed are exclusively those of historical jurisprudence. As in all such historical scholarship, the end sought is to understand a phenomenon *wie es eigentlich gewesen.* One can see this approach beginning in the nineteenth century when West European Jewish scholars adopted the methods of the surrounding culture and then invented the new discipline of *Wissenschaft des Judentums.* Here is where the academic study of "Jewish law," such as it was, began long before the term *mishpat ivri* was coined.[3]

Nevertheless, it is no accident, it seems to me, that *mishpat ivri* is a term coined in modern Hebrew, even before there was such a thing as "Israeli law" *(mishpat ha-medinah).*[4] The connection of this term to the Zionist project is quite evident. Just as the Hebrew language was being made into a language capable of functioning in the modern secular world, so was Jewish law being studied so that it too could function in this world. But legal function is by definition normative. In this sense, then, *mishpat ivri* is much more than an academic pursuit; its project is itself normative. Unlike historical jurisprudence, where a spectator views an external object, in this type of *mishpat ivri* the researcher identifies with the object of research, at least nationalistically, if not religiously.[5] However, unlike language that only needs a hospitable culture in which to function and develop, law (in the secular sense) requires a state that accepts it as its own criterion of governance. Thus, whereas the Hebrew language has become the *lingua franca* of the culture of the land of Israel, *mishpat ivri* has not — or has not yet — become the criterion of governance for the Jewish state of Israel. The question for some Jews is how the legal situation could be otherwise. The answers to this question can be formulated politically, historically, or philosophically.

For those Jews who refuse to distinguish between halakhah and *mishpat ivri,* seeing the latter only as a subset of the former, Jewish law could only govern a Jewish state if that state were to become an explicitly religious state. For

---

3. See Gulak, *Yesodei Hamishpat Ha'Ivri;* see also Louis Ginzberg, "Jewish Thought as Reflected in the Halakah," in *Students, Scholars, and Saints* (Philadelphia: Jewish Publication Society, 1928), pp. 110ff. For a discussion of some of these early modern studies in Jewish law, see my late revered teacher Boaz Cohen, *Jewish and Roman Law* (New York: Jewish Theological Seminary of America, 1966), vol. 1, pp. 8ff.

4. For the distinction between these two disciplines, see Elon, *Hamishpat Ha'Ivri,* vol. 1, p. 151n.49.

5. See Hans-Georg Gadamer, *Truth and Method* (New York: Crossroad, 1982), pp. 274ff.

them, the only way this could happen would be through a total political revolution. Short of this happening, the sanctity of halakhah is best protected by keeping it as far from the grasp of the current secular state as possible.[6] The opponents of this approach, on the other hand, usually see the face of Khomeini behind the beards of those who advocate it. That is, in their eyes, the establishment of a religious state seems to entail a dictatorship of clerics. And the advocates of this approach have done very little to allay this fear of their opponents.

For those Jews who are able to distinguish between halakhah and *mishpat ivri*, at least formally, it is possible to see a larger governing role for *mishpat ivri* in a Jewish secular state in a more historically developmental sense. For them, the development of Jewish law is to be seen as more closely analogous to English common law than to the more deductively constructed systems of law that adopted Roman law as their model.[7] As such, just as English common law is based more on *a posteriori* precedents than on *a priori* principles, so can the content of traditional halakhah be gradually introduced into Israeli jurisprudence as precedents without requiring the acceptance of the principles that were given as its justification in the original sources, principles ultimately theological. Clearly the political implications of this approach are far more conservative than the political implications of the more radically religious approach discussed above.

It might well be the case, however, that both of these approaches to the question of *mishpat ivri* as normative misconstrue the actual relation between principles and rules (and their application in precedents) in Jewish law. The first approach seems to overestimate the role of principles; the second approach seems to underestimate it. The first approach seems to employ a deductive model for this relation — that is, rules are derived from principles; hence the rules cannot cogently function without the prior acceptance of the principles from which they are derived. The second approach seems to assume that precedents can be transposed into new legal contexts informed by principles foreign to Judaism and still retain their normative force without any consideration of the principles that informed their own historical development.

If the relation of principles and rules in Jewish law is one of association rather than the literal derivation of the latter from the former, one need not then require prior acceptance of the classical principles in order for the rules

---

6. See I. Englard, "The Problem of Jewish Law in a Jewish State," in *Jewish Law in Ancient and Modern Israel*, ed. Haim H. Cohn (New York: Ktav Publishing House, 1971), pp. 143ff.

7. See E. N. Dorff and A. Rosett, *A Living Tree: The Roots and Growth of Jewish Law* (Albany: State University of New York Press, 1988), p. 435.

to cogently function.[8] Yet, to be sure, legal judgment inevitably involves various philosophical assumptions about principles, especially when novel situations make whatever analogies that can be made to earlier precedents quite tenuous.[9] Without the eventual introduction of at least the most immediately relevant principles involved in the precedents cited, most of the precedents drawn from the traditional Jewish legal literature will often appear redundantly obscure, and thus become a source of needless distraction in the process of rendering justice as quickly and efficiently as possible. Indeed, the very location and choice of precedents are inevitably guided by the principles that inspired their research to begin with.[10]

The Necessity of Individual Rights in a Modern State

The interest in *mishpat ivri* has come about, we have seen, as part of the fairly recent (at least as regards Jewish history) Jewish attempt to constitute the Jewish nation as a modern state. The great political-philosophical question is just what sort of modern state the Jewish nation is to become.

Although the Jewish nation, at least until very recent times, has considered herself to be under the rule of the Creator God, who has made a unique and everlasting covenant with her, the political forms that her corporate life has assumed have often been borrowed to a large extent from their historical surroundings. Thus, for example, when the Jewish nation became a monarchy, the motivation behind the choice of this form of government was the people's desire for "a king to judge us like all the nations . . . to go out before us and fight our wars" (1 Sam. 8:6, 20). During much of the history of the monarchy in Israel, the task for Jewish thought was how to ground this institution, not at all uniquely Jewish, in the uniquely Jewish idea of covenantal theocracy.[11]

In the ancient world the Jewish nation had the choice of being either a monarchy or a tribal confederation. In the modern world the Jewish nation has the choice of being either a democracy or some type of tyranny, secular or religious. Just as the ancient world basically offered two political options, so

8. See David Novak, *Jewish Social Ethics* (New York: Oxford University Press, 1992), pp. 232ff.

9. See Novak, *Jewish Social Ethics*, pp. 4-5, 161, 189ff.

10. See Hermann Cohen, *Religion of Reason Out of the Sources of Judaism*, trans. S. Kaplan (New York: F. Ungar, 1972), p. 4.

11. See Yehezkel Kaufmann, *The Religion of Israel*, trans. M. Greenberg (Chicago: University of Chicago Press, 1960), p. 266.

does the modern world. And just as the ancient Jewish nation clearly opted for monarchy, so has the modern Jewish nation clearly opted for democracy, both in the state of Israel itself and throughout the diaspora. Not only have modern Jews best thrived in modern democracies, but they have invariably been great victims of the worst modern forms of tyranny, especially Fascism and Communism. The positive experience of democracy and the negative experience of tyranny have affected modern Jewish consciousness and Jewish conscience in indelible ways.[12] The real challenge for contemporary Jewish thought is how to ground democracy, which is not at all a uniquely Jewish institution, in the uniquely Jewish idea of covenantal theocracy.[13]

Democracy is not just the rule of the majority as opposed to that of an oligarchy. If that were all democracy is, then Iran — or, for that matter, Nazi Germany — would qualify as a democracy. In both societies the governing powers clearly have or had the support of the vast majority of the citizens. Instead, democracy combines majority rule with the protection of individual rights, even the rights of individuals who are in conflict with the interests and policies of the society, as long as they do not pose a clear and immediate danger to the society. As one prominent Anglo-American legal philosopher has put it, the presence of the institution of individual rights is what prevents a society and its legal system from becoming "ordered brutality."[14] For today's Jews this insight is anything but arcane. The question is whether or not the concept of individual rights can be found in the traditional sources of Jewish law. Those who desire a closer connection between the legal heritage of the Jewish people and their current political situation ought to be especially motivated to find this concept and elaborate on its philosophical implications.

Naboth's Vineyard

The question of individual rights must be seen in the context of rights in general. Rights might be defined as justified claims of a first party upon a second party, to which the second party must respond. These claims often but not always require the response of a third party to be properly enforced. The rights

---

12. For an example of how contemporary experience in the world affects Jewish self-understanding, see, e.g., Y. Berakhot 7.3/11c.

13. One of the most important reflections on the relation of theocracy and democracy is that of Simon Federbush, *Mishpat Hamelukhah Beyisrael*, 2d rev. ed. (Jerusalem: Mosad ha-Rav Kook, 1973), esp. pp. 26ff.

14. Ronald Dworkin, *Taking Rights Seriously* (Cambridge, Mass.: Harvard University Press, 1978), p. 205.

of the first party are sometimes optional and thus may be waived; other times they are mandated and may not be waived.[15] In the latter case, rights are also duties — that is, justified claims of the law itself that one exercise his or her claims on some other party.[16] The responses of the second and third parties to the justified claims of the first party are always mandated and are therefore always duties. Thus the word for "duties" and the word for "debts" is essentially the same: *hovot*.[17] Duties are what one party owes another.

Since the traditional Jewish covenantal system involves three parties — God, the Jewish community, and the individual Jew — one can see each party being justified to make claims upon the others.

The most prior claims belong to God as Creator even before there is a covenant with the world, let alone before there is a covenant with Israel. Indeed, God's first words to his human creatures — that is, those creatures capable of responding *to* God's word and not just proceeding *from* it — are a commandment: "And the Lord God commanded [*vayitsav*] the human being [*al ha'adam*] saying, 'From any of the trees of the garden you may surely eat, but from the tree of the knowledge of good and bad you may not eat from it, for the day you eat from it you shall surely die'" (Gen. 2:16-17).[18] Commandments *(mitsvot)*, then, are connected to the Creator's power of granting life or death, even though that power goes far beyond God's rights that call for human response. "I am the one who grants death and life; I wound and I heal" (Deut. 32:39). When that power does function as a right calling for a human response, that corresponding response is a duty. As Creator, God has rights that create human duties. To assume any other foundation for human duties, be they collective or individual, is to assume that either man or human society is God, which is the primal lie. "Our fathers inherited lies [*sheqer*], what is worthless and useless. Can one make for himself God?!" (Jer. 16:19-20).[19] For this reason, human duties to God always encompass more than human rights in relation to anyone else.[20]

---

15. See B. Kiddushin 32a-b.

16. See B. Sotah 35a and 41b, and Tos., s.v. "mitsvah."

17. See Y. Kiddushin 1.7/61b re Deut. 5:16, where the *mitsvah* of honoring parents is also seen as paying one's debt to them for his or her upbringing *(kefriyat hov)*.

18. This verse is taken by the Talmud to be the scriptural allusion *(asmakhta)* to the Seven Noahide Laws. See B. Sanhedrin 56b; also, R. Judah Halevi, *Kuzari*, 3.7; David Novak, *The Image of the Non-Jew in Judaism: An Historical and Constructive Study of the Noahide Laws* (New York and Toronto: Edwin Mellen, 1983), pp. 4ff.

19. See David Novak, "Before Revelation: The Rabbis, Paul, and Karl Barth," *Journal of Religion* 71 (1991): 57-58.

20. See David Novak, "Maimonides and the Science of the Law," *Jewish Law Association Studies* 4 (1990): 101n.6.

Usually it is assumed that God himself enforces his own rights, but there are times when the community or an individual is authorized to enforce God's claims upon someone else as, for example, when capital punishment is mandated. "Whoever sheds the blood of a human being by another human being [ba'adam] shall his blood be shed, for in the image of God did He make human beings [ha'adam]" (Gen. 9:6).[21] Finally, in the relationship of God and humans as Creator and creatures, the creature has no claims at all on the Creator; he or she has no rights to be enforced. Thus God answers the complaints of Job with the words "Where were you when I laid the foundations of the earth?" (Job 38:4), to which Job ultimately concludes, "I know that You can do everything, that nothing You propose is impossible for You. . . . Therefore, I abhor my words and repent, being but dust and ashes" (Job 42:2, 6).[22]

The great innovation of the covenant with Israel is that both the community and the individual are granted the power to make claims upon God. This is because in the covenant God obligates himself by making promises. Based on faith in these promises, Israel's claims upon God are addressed to God in petitionary prayer (baqashah).[23] Nevertheless, one cannot truly expect that these promises will be fully fulfilled in this world (according to one rabbinic opinion), or fulfilled here at all (according to another rabbinic opinion).[24] Needless to say, human covenantal claims upon God cannot be enforced by any third party, much less by the people of Israel themselves.

Thereafter, the next most complete set of rights are those claims of the community upon the individual.[25] Usually, these rights of the community are

---

21. M. Makkot 1.10; T. Yevamot 8.7 and B. Yevamot 63b re Gen. 9:6 for uneasiness with human enforcement of this divine claim. See Novak, *Jewish Social Ethics,* pp. 174-75.

22. Even Abraham, who because of the covenant is permitted by God to question God's justice (Gen. 18:17-19), still reiterates his basic nothingness in relation to God: "Behold now I dare to speak to my Lord, even though I am but dust and ashes" (Gen. 18:27). See Ibn Ezra *ad loc.* a la Gen. 3:19, and Rabbenu Bahya ben Asher *ad loc.,* who follows Ibn Ezra's interpretation and cites Job 42:6. For that reason too, outside of the covenant any disobedience of God's law is seen as deserving death. See B. Sanhedrin 10a and Rashi, s.v. "malkot" (also Tosafot, s.v. "malkot" re B. Sanhedrin 58b).

23. See B. Berakhot 32a re Exod. 32:13; also, David Novak, *Halakhah in a Theological Dimension* (Chico, Calif.: Scholars Press, 1985), pp. 124ff.

24. B. Kiddushin 39b and Tos., s.v. "matnitin"; B. Hullin 142a.

25. See, e.g., B. Baba Batra 8b and *Mordecai: Baba Batra,* no. 480. For the community's right to waive its claims on an individual's property, see, e.g., B. Baba Batra 23a and Tosafot, s.v. "aholei." Interestingly enough, the basic principle ultimately used to authorize the court to cancel private property privileges on occasion *(hefker bet din hefker)* is not invoked in the Talmud to justify seizure of private property for public use *per se,* but rather to justify the court's redistribution of property from one individual party to another when the rights of one of them unjustly limits the rights of the other according to criteria of general justice. See B. Yevamot 89b re

enforced by the community itself, but there are rare occasions when an individual is authorized to act *ex post facto* on behalf of the community for its sake without actually being designated as its agent.[26] Also, the community regularly requests God in prayer to vindicate their claims that have been defied by recalcitrant individuals.[27]

Following this set of rights come the claims of one individual upon another individual. Unlike the rights of the community against an individual, which are usually enforced by the community, it is only on rare occasions that an individual is permitted to exercise his or her own claim upon another individual as, for example, in cases of self-defense of one's own life or property.[28] In the absence of the power of either the community or the individual to enforce his or her own rights against another individual, God is invoked as one's protector and vindicator.[29]

The classical sources of Jewish law are replete with examples of the first three sets of rights: God's claims upon both the community and the individual, the community's claims upon the individual, and the claims of one individual upon another. The literature of *mishpat ivri* has devoted its attention to the second and third set of rights with a number of informative and insightful studies. However, the issue of the rights of the individual against those of the community is an area where strenuous research must be conducted if anything relevant is to be found at all. And yet, as we have seen, the very constitution of a state that is both Jewish and democratic requires that this research be conducted with a sense of normative urgency, for many who are immersed in the classical sources of halakhah, upon which *mishpat ivri* must draw, openly deny that there is anything democratic at all in them.[30] The political overtones of these assertions and counterassertions are obvious at this juncture of Jewish history.

If one looks to the very beginnings of Jewish law, in Scripture itself, one notices that the original prohibition of robbery *(gezel)* is presented in this context: "You shall not exploit your neighbor and you shall not rob [*lo tigzol*];

Ezra 10:8 and parallels; *Encyclopedia Talmudit*, vol. 10, pp. 95ff.; also, see Maimonides, *Mishneh Torah:* Marriage, 14.17.

26. See B. Sanhedrin 82a.

27. Hence the additional nineteenth section *(birkat haminim)* in the *Shemoneh Esreh* requesting God to eliminate informers and others dangerous to the community. See *Authorized Daily Prayer Book,* rev. ed. (London: Eyre & Spottiswoode, 1962), p. 50.

28. See B. Sanhedrin 72a; B. Baba Kama 27b; B. Baba Batra 34b; and *Responsa Haro'sh,* 77.1.

29. This theme is found throughout Scripture, especially in the Psalms. See, e.g., Ps. 3:7-9.

30. See E. Don-Yehiya, "The Negation of Galut in Religious Zionism," *Modern Judaism* 12 (1992): 151.

you shall not let the hired laborer's pay remain overnight with you until morning" (Lev. 19:13). Note that the juxtaposed prohibitions are all concerned with both individual subjects and individual objects. The "you" who is not to exploit, rob, or delay the payment of wages is in singular form. "Your neighbor" *(re'akha)* does not refer to any collective object.[31] Here we have the claims of one individual upon another. There is also a prohibition of the individual appropriating the community's sacred property connected with the Temple without appropriate compensation.[32] But we have no explicit source for the prohibition *(azharah)* of or the punishment *(onesh)* for the community appropriating the property of an individual. We have no explicit source for individual rights against those of the community in the Pentateuch.

When we look to the Prophets, however, we come across one of the best-known and most dramatic incidents in Scripture, the incident of the vineyard of Naboth being appropriated by King Ahab:

> And it came to pass after these events: there was a vineyard in Jezreel next to the palace of Ahab king of Samaria belonging to Naboth the Jezreelite. The king spoke to Naboth saying, "Give me your vineyard to become a vegetable garden for me, since it is near my house, and I will give you in its stead a better vineyard, or if you please its price in money." But Naboth said, "It is forbidden to me from the Lord himself to give my ancestral inheritance [*nahalat avotai*] to you." (1 Kings 21:1-3)

As the story continues, Ahab, in his frustration over Naboth's refusal to sell or exchange what the king wants, relates the problem to his wife Jezebel. She then takes it upon herself to have Naboth framed on charges of blasphemy, for which he is quickly stoned to death by the elders of his city, who are the queen's accomplices. The queen then tells the king that he can now take possession of Naboth's vineyard because Naboth is now permanently out of the way. The king follows his wife's bidding as usual. In response to this shocking abuse of power, the prophet Elijah is sent by God to warn Ahab and Jezebel that they will pay for this crime with their lives, dying a particularly ignominious death.[33]

It would seem from a *prima facie* look at this fascinating story that we have some sort of precedent for the concept of individual rights.[34] The con-

---

31. See M. Baba Kama 4.3; T. Baba Kama 4.1, 3; B. Baba Kama 37b re Exod. 21:35.

32. Lev. 5:15-16. See *Sifra*, ed. Weiss, 25b.

33. See 1 Kings 21:17ff.

34. It is interesting that in his by now classic study of natural right, Leo Strauss quotes this passage as a biblical inscription to introduce his book. See *Natural Right and History* (Chicago: University of Chicago Press, 1953).

flict seems to be between Naboth as an individual and society in the persons of the king, the queen, and the elders of Jezreel. Nevertheless, this almost obviously modern approach to the story is not reflected in rabbinic treatments of it. This comes out in discussion of what the rights of the king are in relation to those of his individual subjects.

The prophet Samuel had stated that if the people of Israel chose a king for themselves, "this will be the practice of the king who will rule over you. . . . Your best fields and vineyards and olive groves he will take and give them to his servants" (1 Sam. 7:11, 14). The word translated "practice" — *mishpat* — can have either a descriptive or a prescriptive meaning.[35] Thus one rabbinic opinion takes the term in its descriptive sense and interprets the passage to be a warning designed to frighten the people about what is likely to happen, even though it is not what is to be done by the king lawfully. But an opposing rabbinic opinion takes the term in its prescriptive sense and thus interprets the passage as stating an actual norm: what is to be done by the king *(melekh muttar bo)*.[36] At this point a medieval gloss on the Talmudic text raises the case of Naboth and Ahab.[37] How can this be the actual norm? If it were, then why would Ahab's appropriation of Naboth's field be considered a crime? Why did Jezebel have to resort to the crime of framing Naboth for the crime of blasphemy in order for Ahab to take what was lawfully his to take anyway? Several answers are proposed, and they are illuminating not only for what they say but also for what they infer.

One answer argues that Ahab's crime was that he took Naboth's vineyard for his own personal use, but if he had taken it for public use (the public being "his servants" mentioned in 1 Sam. 7:14), he would have been justified in so doing.[38] Another answer argues that Ahab engaged in *noblesse oblige* by asking Naboth (1 Kings 21:2) to *give* him his vineyard, thereby himself creating Naboth's right *(reshut)* of refusal, but if he had just taken it outright, there would have been no crime.[39] Yet another answer argues that Ahab would have

---

35. For a discussion of the meanings of *mishpat*, see Novak, *Jewish Social Ethics*, pp. 30-31.

36. T. Sanhedrin 4.5; B. Sanhedrin 10b.

37. San. 20b, Tos., s.v. "melekh." For further examples of royal rights, see T. Sanhedrin 4.6 and B. Sanhedrin 48b; B. Kiddushin 43a.

38. The law is that the king has the right to appropriate land for public use (M. Sanhedrin 2.4; also, M. Baba Bahra 6.7; see B. Baba Batra 100b and Rashbam, s.v. "shelemelekh porets"). For discussion of any limits to that right, see B. Baba Kama 60b and Tos., s.v. "mahu." See also R. Zvi Hirsch Chajes, *Torat Hanevi'im*, chap. 7 in *Kol Kitvei Maharats Chajes* (Bnei Brak: Divre Hakhamim, 1958), p. 47.

39. Modern biblical scholarship has shown this to be the procedure of suzerainty treaties in the ancient Near East — that is, where a king allows vassals to give their consent to his rule, even

had the right to take Naboth's field if it had been his property through ordinary commerce *(sdeh mikneh)*, but the crime was that Ahab wanted to take a field that Naboth had inherited as his ancestral portion and which was therefore something he was not entitled to dispose of.[40] This answer reflects the tensions described in Scripture between the earlier form of tribal government and intertribal confederation and the newer centralized authority of the monarchy.[41] In other words, Naboth is not an individual whose rights have been violated by the king and the political forces of society he controls, but rather a representative of the older tribal rights in conflict with the newer monarchial rights. Finally, the last answer proposed is that Ahab did not have monarchial rights to begin with, since he was not chosen by God and did not rule over both Israel and Judah. The implication here is that if he were of the divinely chosen Davidic line, he would have been able to take Naboth's vineyard with impunity.[42] In summary, one cannot derive from any of these answers the concept of individual rights. Naboth only has a claim upon the king and society because of a prior *social* claim on them. The king is only a criminal because he was not acting as the true leader of society.

The upshot of all these answers is that the case of Naboth's vineyard is an exception to the ordinary rule that society as a whole has unlimited rights over any individual, rights limited only by its own conscience, but not by any real legal rights of individuals.[43] The case of Naboth's vineyard is only a case of individual rights if we see it as the clash between the individual rights of Naboth and the individual rights of Ahab, either Ahab acting illegitimately in his own private interest instead of the public interest, or Ahab reducing himself to the level of an individual citizen through an act of *noblesse oblige*, or Ahab as an illegitimate king and thus legally no more than an individual citizen himself.

---

though it is not really necessary. See D. R. Hillers, *Covenant: The History of a Biblical Idea* (Baltimore: Johns Hopkins University Press, 1969).

40. See Lev. 25:23; Ezek. 46:16-18; also, B. Baba Metsia 79a; Y. Kiddushin 1.5/60c.

41. See, e.g., Judg. 8:22-23; 9:8ff.; 1 Sam. 10:17ff.; 1 Kings 4:7.

42. The Rabbis' concern with non-Davidic kings clearly reflects the problems their Pharisaic predecessors had with the Hasmonean monarchs, who often regarded themselves as above Jewish law. See, e.g., B. Kiddushin 66a; B. Sanhedrin 19ab; also, Novak, *The Image of the Non-Jew in Judaism*, pp. 180-81.

43. Maimonides especially emphasized how conscience should guide those having political and legal power, making them ever aspire to the highest ends of the Torah. See MT: Sanhedrin, 24.10; MT: Kings, 4.10; *Guide of the Perplexed*, 2.40; also, Novak, *Jewish Social Ethics*, pp. 193ff.

The Right of Eminent Domain

The right of eminent domain is usually defined as the justified claim of society upon private property if it is needed for the common good. The questions associated with this right are these: (1) Is the consent of the individual owner of the property required in advance of the appropriation of his or her property?; and (2) Does the individual owner have to be compensated, as would be the case in a transaction with another individual?

The Mishnah states that "whoever has a public road [*derekh harabim*] passing through his field and he appropriated it and gave them another road off to a side: what he gave the public is considered given, and he may not take possession of what was meant to be his own [*shelo lo higi'o*]."[44] Here we have a case of the interests of the community against the interests of an individual property owner. The question is, why should he be penalized for what amounts to an even exchange? The Gemara answers in the name of R. Zevid in the name of Rava that this is a rabbinic decree *(gezerah)* designed to discourage this sort of practice because inevitably the individual owner will appropriate public property which is more convenient for everyone and substitute for it property which is inconvenient for most people.[45] Earlier the Gemara reasoned that this Mishnaic ruling also implies that the individual owner may not protect his own property from public use even if public use of it entails monetary loss *(psayda)* for him.[46]

As is so often done in amoraic analysis of an anonymous statement *(stam)* in the Mishnah, there is an attempt in the Gemara to discover just who uttered the statement. Such identification will, hopefully, cast further light on the meaning of the passage in the Mishnah by placing it in the context of the legal thinking of a particular tannaitic authority, thinking that is assumed to be inherently consistent. This is done by identifying the logic of the anonymous statement with the logic of a statement explicitly attributed to a particular tannaitic authority. In the case at hand, the Gemara tries to show that the author of the anonymous statement in the Mishnah is really R. Eliezer ben Hyrcanus, who is quoted in an extra-Mishnaic statement *(baraita)* as saying, "When the public [*rabim*] chose a road for themselves, what they chose is considered lawfully chosen [*mah shebireru bireru*]."[47]

The Gemara is shocked by this seemingly total disregard for individual

44. M. Baba Batra 6.7.

45. B. Baba Batra 99b. Nahmanides reasons that only public authority can prevent anyone from inconveniencing the public at will *(Hidushei Haramban ad loc.)*.

46. B. Baba Batra 99b; cf. B. Baba Kama 27b.

47. B. Baba Batra 100a.

property rights of any kind when the adversary is the public, and it exclaims, "According to R. Eliezer, are the public allowed to be robbers [*gazlanim*]?!"[48] In order to dispel this conclusion, the Gemara contextualizes R. Eliezer's dictum by having it refer to a case where the true location of the public road had been lost sight of, so the public may use a private road temporarily until the true location of the public road has been found again.[49] Nevertheless, even this qualification of the statement of R. Eliezer is seen as leading to a conclusion more radical than that involved in the original ruling in the Mishnah. Hence the Gemara specifically states in the name of Rabah bar R. Huna in the name of Rav that the law does not follow the opinion of R. Eliezer. Instead, the Mishnah's ruling is seen as being based on the broader rule in the name of the *amora* R. Judah that "it is forbidden to upset [*asur lekakalo*] a field adjoining [*metsar*] private property that the public has taken possession of [*shehehziku bo rabim*]." In the Gemara's reworking of the tannaitic sources, the overall aim seems to be to refute the inference that the public can simply seize private property for themselves. The difference between the view of R. Eliezer and that of the anonymous sage of the mishnah at hand is that R. Eliezer holds that the public may take possession of private property temporarily simply by walking on it.[50] The other opinion, which is taken to be the normative one, holds that the public may only take possession of private property if (a) they make actual improvements in it, and (b) the original owners do not protest what has been done.[51] This latter condition is acquiescence tantamount to explicit consent, a tacit contract, as it were.[52]

---

48. B. Baba Batra 100a. Nahmanides *ad loc.* in his critique of Rashbam and Rabbenu Tam argues that R. Eliezer's original position is totally unconcerned with the problem of public robbery. He then concludes that this position has been rejected by the Rabbis because it is irrational (*v'ein ta'am badavar*). Thus we can see why the Gemara on B. Baba Kama 28a does not even mention R. Eliezer's ruling when discussing the question of public appropriation of private property. For similar shock with another opinion of R. Eliezer, see B. Baba Kama 84a and cf. *Mekhilta: Mishpatim,* ed. Horovitz-Rabin, 277n.8 *ad loc.*

49. However, even here Rashbam (s.v. "mah") infers from the text, "even though they did not get permission [*shelo natlu reshut*] from the owner of the field."

50. See Tos., s.v. "Rabbi Eliezer."

51. For the background of the legal institution of *hazakah*, see M. Baba Batra 3.1ff.; B. and Y. *ad loc.*; also, *Encyclopedia Talmudit*, vol. 13, pp. 453ff.; Cohen, *Jewish and Roman Law*, vol. 2, pp. 465ff.

52. See B. Yevamot 87b. As in all cases of *hazakah*, if the original owner claims he never gave his permission to others to take possession of his property, the burden of proof is on him. See R. Jehiel M. Epstein, *Arokh Hashulhan: Hoshen Mishpat*, 377.3; also, B. Baba Batra 166b and Rashbam, s.v. "teiku."

The Talmudic text itself does not answer the underlying question, which is this: What right does the individual property owner have against the right of the public to take possession of his or her land? The surprise expressed over the view of R. Eliezer, which seems to permit public robbery of private property, is not fully answered in principle. In other words, why is the view of R. Eliezer unacceptable? Is its rejection rather arbitrary, perhaps the result of the extreme ostracism by the Rabbis that R. Eliezer suffered at the end of his career because of his refusal to accept their legal authority when it conflicted with his own legal opinions, which he seemed to have regarded as authentic and even divinely sanctioned?[53]

The principle underlying the ruling of R. Eliezer seems to be that the public interest is always to be protected over against the private interest. This principle is enunciated and justified by the twelfth-century French exegete R. Samuel ben Meir, known as Rashbam, and his younger brother R. Jacob ben Meir, known as Rabbenu Tam, even though they could not of course accept the specific ruling of R. Eliezer because of its undisputed rejection in the Talmud. This principle is justified by them as follows: The Rabbis were much more concerned with protecting the public interest than with protecting the private interest.[54] An individual may not sue the public because the public is like the court itself *(rabim kevet din damu)*. As such, how could the public adjudicate a case in which it was one of the litigants?[55] The necessary separation of interest from judgment, which is presupposed by impartial justice, is here precluded.[56] Therefore, we are left with two problems in any attempt to constitute a principle of individual rights: (1) Where do we find the prohibition of public robbery of private property? and (2) Even if there is assumed to be such a prohibition, how could the rights of the individual property owner be protected if the court system is identical with society itself? Whom could he or she sue? Is it not in effect an empty right?

The second question is easier to answer than the first. What this answer requires is a refutation of the assumption of Rashbam especially, that the court is identical with the public about whom the Talmudic texts at hand are concerned. This comes out in the treatment of both the Talmudic texts and

53. See B. Baba Metsia 59b; B. Shabbat 130b; B. Niddah 7b.

54. B. Baba Batra 99b, s.v. "gezerah."

55. B. Baba Batra 100a, s.v. "kesh'avdah." The text of Rashbam literally states, "But the public are like a *bet din* inasmuch as any one of them could subpoena the owner [*mazmin lehai ledina*]." In other words, any one of the defendants could be the agent of the court *(shaliah bet din)*. See B. Baba Kama 112b and Rashi, s.v. "shaliah derabanan."

56. See B. Ketubot 105b and Tosafot, s.v. "la." Cf. Maimonides, MT: Sanhedrin, 23.3, and R. Joseph Karo, *Kesef Mishneh ad loc.*

the French interpretation of them by the Spanish exegetes, beginning with Nahmanides, who was the first Spanish exegete who critically entertained the views of the French exegetes (Rashi and the tosafists).

The key point of difference between the two schools, it seems to me, is over the question of the inability of an individual to sue the public who have appropriated his or her property. Rashbam had stated that the individual "is not able to sue the public in court [eino yakhol leha'amid rabim badin]."[57] The "ability" here seems to be legal capacity. "Not able" refers to the individual's lack of legal power when faced with the issue of public appropriation of his or her property. However, in criticizing Rabbenu Tam, whose views were apparently identical with those of his brother Rashbam, Nahmanides argues that the inability of the individual to sue the public is because "the public" here is in effect a mob and "he cannot summon each one of them to court."[58] In other words, the inability here is physical, not legal. Thus Nahmanides assumes that the mention of self-defenses of one's private property from the public at the beginning of the Gemara here is being endorsed, not rejected, in a case where an individual had no recourse to protection by the public authorities from what was in effect a lawless mob.

The underlying assumption of Nahmanides' criticism of the French position is that there is a distinction to be made between the public and the judicial system. Only an independent judiciary could possibly adjudicate between the rights of an individual and the rights of the public. Thus R. Solomon ibn Adret, known as Rashba, the most prominent disciple of Nahmanides, in a case involving the claim of an individual that the community had unfairly taxed him, stated in his responsum that "the argument that the community has the right to make [unfair] laws and rulings in this matter seems to me to be nothing but robbery [gezel], and they do not have the right [v'ein yekholin] to make stipulations [lehatnot] that are robbery [al hagezelot]."[59] From this important responsum we see that there are three parties, not two, involved in a dispute between an individual and society: the individual, society, and the judiciary. The judiciary here is in effect a rabbinate not under the control of the community and, therefore, able to objectively adjudicate between the interests of individuals and those of the community. Of course, in most cases the interests of the community will take precedence. Bonum commune should take precedence over bonum sibi, certainly in a social realm constituted by a

57. B. Baba Batra 99b, s.v. "am'ai."

58. Hidushei Haramban: Baba Batra 99b-100a. See also B. Baba Kama 28a, Tosafot, s.v. "velinkot"; Hidushei Harashba: B. Baba Batra 99b-100a; Rabbenu Nissim (Ran) on Alfasi: Baba Batra, ed. Vilna, 49a; R. Yom Tov Lippmann Heller, Tosfot Yom Tov: M. Baba Batra 6.7.

59. Responsa Harashba, 1, no. 178; see also 1, no. 788; Elon, Hamishpat Ha'Ivri, pp. 617ff.

covenant, both between God and the people and between the people themselves.[60] Nevertheless, an independent judiciary does make possible the defense of the rights of the individual against the rights of the community, when the rights of the individual do not interfere with the common good.[61] For Rashba, this was certainly to be the case when the rights of the community were based on an arbitrary and unfair favoritism, respecting one party over another.

Along these lines, a somewhat later Spanish authority, R. Isaac bar Sheshet Parfat, known as Ribash, stated that "the community had no right [*ein yekholin*] to make any law or enactment discriminating against any individual from the community [*shum yahid min hakahal*] not according to law."[62] Although he explicitly bases his view on the earlier one of Rashba, Ribash's argument adds a new point. That is, he argues that the community has moral restrictions on its rights against individuals even though stipulations can be made in monetary matters *(ten'ai shebemamon)* that are not according to the strict letter of the law.[63] In other words, more general standards of justice should prevail even in situations where the innovative power of the community is very broad.[64]

The institutionalization of the real distinction between the public and the judiciary can be seen in the institution of the "Seven Trustees of the City" *(shiva tovei ha'ir)*. Although we do not know very much about the origins of this institution, it seems to have been a secular one, not in the sense of being autonomously independent of the governance of the Torah itself, but in the sense of being separate from the institution of the rabbinical judiciary.[65] Thus

60. See Federbush, *Mishpat Hamelukhah Beyisrael,* pp. 88ff.; Novak, *Jewish Social Ethics,* p. 15. For the similar problem of *bonum commune* and *bonum sibi* as it pertains to eminent domain in American law, see W. M. Treanor, "The Origins and Original Significance of the Just Compensation Clause in the Fifth Ammendment," *Yale Law Journal* 94 (1985): 694ff. (I thank Professor Michael A. Wolf for this reference.)

61. Thus (R. Menahem) Meiri (13th c.) argues that private property may only be appropriated by the public either by legal right (*badin,* implying both pressing public need and fair compensation to the individual owner) or with the consent of the individual owner. He furthermore argues that if a private property owner substituted another road for the public, one just as convenient as the first one was, such an exchange is valid. See *Bet Habehirah:* Baba Batra 99b-100a, ed. Menat, 321.

62. *Responsa Ribash,* no. 477.

63. See B. Kiddushin 19b. For the wide power of the court to adapt Jewish civil law to changing economic realities, see Novak, *Jewish Social Ethics,* pp. 212ff.

64. See B. Baba Kama 99b-100a re Exod. 18:20; B. Baba Metsia 83a re Prov. 2:19.

65. See B. Megillah 26ab; Y. Megillah 3.2/74a; also, T. Megillah 2.16. For the distinction between *tovei ha'ir* and the rabbinate, see R. Solomon ibn Adret, *Responsa Harashba,* vol. 1, no. 617; cf., however, Maimonides, *Responsa Harambam,* ed. Blau, vol. 2, no. 271. See also *Encyclopedia*

even the Torah system itself has room for secular (without being "secularist") authority. This non-secularist secularity, if you will, is recognized by the sixteenth-century Polish authority R. Moses Isserles, known as Rema. In a responsum he writes,

> It is evident [pashut] that the trustees of the city do not have the legal power [ein koah] to enact anything that is not according to law and justice [al pi hadin vehamishpat] to behave with tyrannical force [behazakah] with individuals. . . . They only have the right to enact enactments by right of the law and not do whatever suits their fancy [mah sheta'aleh al ruham].[66]

Aggadic Insights

Perhaps the reason why there is no explicit prohibition of the public robbing private individuals is that it is seen under a rubric other than that of robbery (gezel) per se. Thus when the Gemara is shocked that R. Eliezer would allow the public to be "robbers" (gazlanim), it may have been thinking of a crime at least specifically different from robbery in the usual sense, and a crime not specifically proscribed in the halakhah.

The crime of public robbery may well be that of "violence" (hamas), which was considered to be the crime of the Generation of the Flood, the crime for which God almost completely destroyed the inhabited world. This sin was considered grave because it was collective rather than individual. In speculating about this crime, the Gemara presents the following rabbinic dicta:

> R. Yohanan said, "Come and see how serious the crime of violence is. The Generation of the Flood committed every transgression, but judgment against them was not sealed until they extended their hands into robbery, as it is said, for 'the earth is filled with violence because of them, and I shall destroy them along with the earth' (Genesis 6:13). . . . It was taught in the

---

Talmudit, vol. 19, pp. 72ff.; S. W. Baron, The Jewish Community (Philadelphia: Jewish Publication Society, 1945), vol. 2, p. 55; vol. 3, p. 27n.19; vol. 3, pp. 120-21n.4; and my late revered teacher Louis Finkelstein, Jewish Self-Government in the Middle Ages, 2d ed. (New York: Feldheim, 1964), pp. 52-53.

66. Responsa Harema, ed. Ziv (Jerusalem: Feldheim, 1970), no. 308. Considering the development of the law up to this point, the view of the seventeenth-century Polish commentator R. Joshua Falk is somewhat strange. For he argues that the Seven Trustees of the City are able to exchange any property they want "because no one can prevent them from doing so" (Melrat. Eineiyim on Shulhan Arukh: Hoshen Mishpat, 377).

School of R. Ishmael that even Noah was included in their judgment, only he found favor in the eyes of the Lord, as it is said, 'I regret that I made them; and Noah found favor in the eyes of the Lord'" (Genesis 6:7-8).[67]

The crime of violence is explicitly identified as public robbery of an individual in a midrashic treatment of the sins of the Generation of the Flood. There it is related that when a person came along with a basket of nuts, each one of the people stole a negligible amount so that none of them would be liable individually for the crime of robbery.[68] In other words, they justified to themselves collectively what they could not justify to themselves individually.[69]

Nahmanides, following the Midrash and Rashi, saw the crime of the Generation of the Flood as being led by the officials and judges of the society, whom no one restrained. He considered the crime to be contrary to reason *(inyan muskal)* and therefore not needing a specifically revealed prohibition *(einenu tsarikh latorah)*.[70] In a related comment he argues that this rational commandment *(mitsvah muskelet)* did not need to be prohibited through prophetic revelation, and that it is "something evil both towards God and man" *(ra lashamayim velaberiyot)*.[71] Here we see an explicitly natural-law type argument.

The question is this: Why is the reason for the sin of violence more obvious than the reason for the sin of individual robbery? I would venture the following answer. In presenting the reason for the prohibition of robbery by individuals of each other, the author of *Sefer Hahinukh*, a popular treatise on the *mitsvot* and their reasons, argues as follows:

---

67. B. Sanhedrin 108a. The sense of the interpretation of Gen. 6:7-8 is this: "I regret I made *them and Noah*." See R. Samuel Edels (Maharsha), *Hidushei Agadot ad loc.*

68. *Bereshit Rabbah* 31.5. (See ed. Theodor-Albeck, p. 279nn.7-8 for the textual variants, especially re *gezel* or *hamas.*) For the rule that one is not liable in a human court for robbing someone of less than a *perutah*'s worth, see B. Sanhedrin 57a and Rashi, s.v. "tsa'ara" re Lev. 5:23. Cf. B. Yevamot 47b. In Y. Baba Metsia 4.2/9c this sin of the Generation of the Flood is brought into a discussion about the Mishnah where the moral, but not legally punishable, sin of backing out of a business transaction before the full exchange has been concluded *(mi she par'a)* is treated (M. Baba Metsia 4.2). There also the sin of the Sodomites is considered to be the same as this sin of the Generation of the Flood. For the notion of the Sodomites committing moral sins technically within the limits of the law, see M. Avot 5.10; also, B. Baba Batra 12b for the designation of such activity, *mutatis mutandis,* as *midat Sodom.*

69. For another discussion of public crime, see B. Shabbat 33a.

70. *Ramban* ad Gen. 6:2, ed. Chavel (Jerusalem: n.p., 1963), vol. 1, p. 48. For the role of natural law in Nahmanides' theology, see David Novak, *The Theology of Nahmanides Systematically Presented* (Atlanta: Scholars Press, 1992), chap. 7.

71. *Ramban* ad Gen. 6:11, p. 52.

The root [*shoresh*] of the commandment is evident [*yad'ua*] since it is something required by reason, something from which it keeps us far away, and it *is* right [*ra'ui*] that we be kept far away from it. For the one who robs someone weaker than himself knows that someone stronger than himself will come upon him and that he too will be robbed. This would be the cause of the destruction of civilized life [*hurban hayishuv*].[72]

In order for this reason to be cogent, one must turn the prohibition of robbery into what Kant designated as the first formulation of the categorical imperative — namely, one should universalize his or her act by asking, What if *everyone* did what I am tempted to do now?[73] Of course, the inner contradiction then becomes apparent. If everyone did what I am tempted to do now, then the institution of private property would become obsolete, and it is for the sake of increasing my own private property that I am tempted to rob in the first place.[74] However, even if the individual tempted to rob another individual can see what the social consequences of his or her act *would be if universalized*, it is quite easy, at least for this person, to rationalize that his or her *own particular act* is an exceptional case rather than an example for a universal maxim. In other words, appreciation of the social significance of robbery is something that presupposes a considerable personal identification with the interests of society in general. That cannot be realistically expected of most robbers, who are usually very much alienated from society to begin with. This, then, may be the reason why the Torah has to address the commandment "You shall not rob" (Lev. 19:13) to the individual directly and does not assume on the mediation of abstract universality as does the categorical imperative. Thus in the verse after the one in which this prohibition is presented, the Torah states in the singular, "You shall fear [*veyar'eta*] your God [*Elohekha*]; I am the Lord" (Lev. 19:14).[75] In other words, it is a crime that God himself will punish even if there is no harm to society as a whole, either permanent or even temporary, because of it.

In the case of public violence against individuals, on the other hand, the evident reason for the prohibition is immediate to every individual. For here one need not speculate about *what would be if* robbery were the norm for all of society. In this case it is not *what would be* but *what already is*. Robbery has in reality, not just by a projection of universalizing reason, become the norm

72. *Sefer Hahinukh*, neg. no. 229.

73. See Kant, *Groundwork of the Metaphysics of Morals*, trans. H. J. Paton (New York: Harper & Row, 1964), pp. 88-89.

74. See Kant, *Groundwork of the Metaphysics of Morals*, p. 90.

75. See Rashi ad Lev. 19:16.

of the society. Public robbery of individuals means that the most minimal reason for anyone's allegiance to his or her society — namely, the reasonable expectation of protection from violence — is absent. It is now how Hobbes described the presocial "state of nature": *bellum omnium contra omnes.*[76]

Participation by individuals in a criminal group enables each individual member of the group to think that he or she is exempt from any personal responsibility. Certainly, in this bloody century especially, we have seen how the greatest crimes, which led to the wholesale destruction of millions of human lives and much authentic human sociality, have been committed not by lone individuals but by human collectives in which individual persons have been reduced to functioning as merely dispensible individual parts.[77] When society is not respectful of the rights of individual persons, when it ceases to be a true communion of free, rational persons whose personhood is to be respected, then these persons inevitably lose respect for and allegiance to their society.[78] For they sooner or later realize how immediately vulnerable *each and every one of them* truly is.

Finally, following Nahmanides' second reason for the general prohibition of violence — namely, it is "something evil both towards God and man" — we must ask in what sense it is an evil toward God. The question can be addressed with two answers, it seems to me. Both answers involve natural-law type reasoning inasmuch as the Rabbis themselves, when they were shocked that R. Eliezer would allow the public to rob with impunity, never to my knowledge designated the specific prohibition of this act in either the Written Torah or the Oral Tradition, or in positive rabbinic legislation. The question presupposes the more fundamental question of the relation between God and natural law.

76. See Hobbes, *Leviathan,* chaps. 13-14.

77. No modern thinker explored this in greater depth than Reinhold Niebuhr. See his *Moral Man and Immoral Society* (New York: Scribner's, 1932), esp. chap. 1.

78. Thus Plato argues that even a group of thieves, in order to be successful, must be able to assure each other that they will not rob each other (*Republic,* 351c). Of course, the members of such groups usually turn against each other, since their allegiance to even this standard of "justice" is only immediately utilitarian. As soon as they see a quicker way of gaining wealth than that required by loyalty to their present comrades, they exploit them just as they have been exploiting their victims. Therefore, for there to be any permanent loyalty to a society, that society has to affirm individual human rights *per se.* Regarding the distinction between a state under law and a state as a band of robbers, see Maimonides, MT: Robbery, 5.18 re B. Baba Batra 54b. For the idea of society as a communion of unique persons rather than a mere collective of individual parts, see Jacques Maritain, *The Person and the Common God,* trans. J. J. Fitzgerald (Notre Dame: University of Notre Dame Press, 1966), pp. 31ff., and *Man and the State* (Chicago: University of Chicago Press, 1951), pp. 12ff.

On the one hand, one can see two types of divine law: the more specific law of the Torah itself directly revealed by God in history, and the more general Noahide law indirectly revealed by God through nature. The direct law of God is to be accepted by covenantal confirmation; the less direct law of God is to be discovered by ratiocination.[79] In this sense of natural law, human reason, especially as it pertains to human sociality, attempts to locate itself within the cosmic order. Thus justice is not only a matter of social utility; it is much more deeply a participation, however fallible, in the divinely ordained order of the universe.[80] Hence an affront to human justice, such as we have seen in the case of public robbery of private property without just cause and without being decided by due process of law, is ultimately an assault on God's just universal order.

On the other hand, natural-law thinking, at least since Grotius in the seventeenth century, has tended to follow his argument that there could be a natural law "even if we assume there is no God" (etiamsi daremus non esse Deum).[81] This point has led to two different trends.

First, it has led to the type of natural-law reasoning based on the idea of autonomy, a type of thinking most cogently developed by Kant and those who came to be Kantians of one sort or another.[82] Despite the gigantic efforts of a Jewish thinker of the philosophical profundity of Hermann Cohen, most traditionalist Jewish thinkers have rejected this type of reasoning altogether as being essentially incompatible with the doctrine of divine law — Torah min hashamayim.[83] But because of the power and influence of Cohen's thought, they have assumed (quite wrongly, I believe) that any natural-law thinking ultimately requires the foundation of human autonomy, which itself entails, if it does not actually presuppose, the atheistic idea that man, not God, is the measure of all things.[84]

Second, however, one need not assume that Grotius was saying anything more than what Nahmanides said when he pointed out that the prohibition of

---

79. See, e.g., R. Israel Lipschuetz, Tiferet Yisra'el (Bo'az) on M. Avot 3.14.

80. See Novak, Jewish Social Ethics, pp. 163-64.

81. Grotius, De Belli ac Pacis, prol., ii.

82. See Groundwork of the Metaphysics of Morals, pp. 98ff. For the most influential contemporary version of Kantian-type autonomy, see John Rawls, A Theory of Justice (Cambridge, Mass.: Harvard University Press, 1971), esp. p. 516.

83. See Novak, The Image of the Non-Jew in Judaism, pp. 399-400; and Jewish-Christian Dialogue: A Jewish Justification (New York: Oxford University Press, 1989), pp. 148ff.

84. For recent Jewish rejections of natural law theory along these theological lines, see E. E. Urbach, Hazal: Emunot Vede'ot (Jerusalem: Magnes, 1971), pp. 283ff.; Y. Leibowitz, Yahadut, Am Yehudi Umedinat Yisrael (Jerusalem: Schocken Books, 1976), pp. 26-27.

violence does not need a specific command from God. Neither Nahmanides nor Grotius was an atheist. (Indeed, even a casual reading of Grotius's great work, *De Belli ac Pacis,* indicates he was a religious believer, a Protestant heavily influenced by the Hebrew Bible and Maimonides, among others.[85] And Nahmanides' work can only be described as "God-intoxicated."[86]) Along these lines, it might be helpful to constitute a second relation between God and natural law distinct from the first one that is constituted as natural law *stemming from* the affirmation of God's *orderly creation* of the universe. This second relation is constituted by seeing that human sociality *points to* more than the institution of human society *per se,* and that when that intentionality is denied, human society ceases to be a true communion of persons.[87] Individual rights, as I have defined them in this essay, are inherently connected with this intentionality.

The question of individual rights is the question of balancing the claims of individuals and the claims of society. On the *prima facie* level, the claims of society do always take precedence inasmuch as society as an institution can certainly survive without any ordinary individual, but hardly any ordinary individual can survive without society.[88] Accordingly, it is quite easy to see how in many cultures individual persons really have no independent identity at all. Nevertheless, at least in the West, we have come to regard individual identity and thus individual rights as absolutely indispensable. (The fall of both European Fascism and Communism might well be seen to be the result of the refusal of a large majority of Europeans and others to give up the idea of individual rights for the sake of absolute collectivism.) This regard for individual rights has great religious significance.

One can see individual rights as a limit on the power of society because the life of the human person itself seems to point to a transcendent dimension beyond the grasp and thus beyond the authority of society. Indeed, without the acknowledgment of that dimension society presents its own power as the power of God by presenting its own claims as absolute. Even without a positive affirmation of the reality of God, let alone the positive relationship with that God in the covenant, one can still deny the unlimited power and au-

85. See Grotius, *De Belli ac Pacis,* 1:10ff.; also, Anton-Hermann Chroust, "Hugo Grotius and the Scholastic Natural Law Tradition," *The New Scholasticism* 17 (1943): 126ff.

86. See Novak, *The Theology of Nahmanides Systematically Presented,* chap. 2.

87. See David Novak, *Law and Theology in Judaism* (New York: Ktav Publishing House, 1976), vol. 2, pp. 15ff.

88. See B. Ta'anit 23a; Aristotle, *Nicomachean Ethics,* 1169b5ff.; *Politics,* 1253a1ff. Aside from the fact that a person who eschewed society would be living a life without humanizing discourse, his or her physical survival would still depend on skills learned from earlier social experience.

thority of any human society as being a radical lie. This can first be done by the affirmation of individual human rights and the admission of at least the possibility that they come from a source other than the individual himself or herself (autonomy) or from society itself (heteronomy).[89]

If there is to be a true *mishpat ivri,* based on inherently Jewish principles and not just a sop to nationalistic pride, then those who teach it and seek its governance must be able to convincingly show the vast majority of the Jewish people — indeed, the world — that the society they propose at least points to a transcendent authority essentially beyond its and *their* power, that it is limited by both individual rights from inside and God's rights from above, just as individual rights are limited by society's rights from outside and God's rights from above.

---

89. This third source can be constituted, at least theologically, as "theonomy." See Novak, *Jewish Social Ethics,* chap. 2.

THE PRECONDITION FOR THE PHENOMENA: NOAHIDE LAW AS NATURAL LAW

8   Noahide Law: A Foundation
for Jewish Philosophy (1979)

Jewish Philosophy and the Limits of Judaism

Judaism, even as lived by its most devout adherents, has definite limits in both time and space. Its history begins at a point within human history; its extension stops at a point within humanity. It cannot be regarded as originating with the creation of man or as encompassing all of humanity. Thus a reflection on the essential structures of Judaism — that is, one which regards it as an original intelligible object, irreducible to something else — ought to begin by defining the limits or boundaries of Judaism. The most important methodological question any such reflection must answer is this: When do I begin and when do I stop? Any reflection which has not taken this as its first question cannot be considered systematic.

Scripture, the most original point of reference in Judaism, begins its narrative by asserting that before the emergence of Israel, the covenanted people of God, there is *adam* — man. Man is a concrete entity having a definite personality, engaged in a number of relationships and capable of self-understanding. "And the Lord God said: 'Surely man has become one [*ehad*] like us, knowing good and bad'" (Gen. 3:22).[1] Furthermore, for Judaism *adam* is more than the personification of its prehistory. His independence has not been absorbed by the historical emergence of Israel; rather, he has survived

---

1. This translation is based on Rashi's comment thereto — namely, that human *uniqueness* is analogous to God's, not that God and man are members of the same class, which includes other members as well, especially angels. (Cf. Ibn Ezra and Sforno to Gen. 1:26.) For a philosophical interpretation of *ehad* as "unique," see Hermann Cohen, "Einheit oder Einzigkeit Gottes," *Jüdische Schriften* (Berlin: C. A. Schwetzke, 1924), vol. 1, pp. 87ff.; and *Religion der Vernunft aus den Quellen des Judentums* (Darmstadt: J. Melzer, 1966), chap. 1.

independently and confronts the Jew with his real presence. Halakhah, the most evident structure of Judaism — that is, its manifestation as law — acknowledges this fact. In halakhah *adam* is designated *ben Noah* — "Noahide." A Noahide is by definition a human person. This human person is recognized as the subject of a special category of law: Noahide commandments *(mitsvot bnei Noah)*.

This essential connection between the biblical *adam* and the rabbinic *ben Noah* is brought out by a crucial terminological fact. The term *ben Noah* has a double denotation: it signifies both the non-Jew who confronts the Jew in the present and also the non-Jew who preceded the Jew in history. *Ben Noah* designates, then, both pre-Judaic man *(adam)* and co-Judaic man *(nokhri)*.[2] The limit or boundary of Judaism both in the past and in the present is, therefore, the Noahide. A study of the Noahide, the subject of Noahide law, is necessary for understanding both the origin and the horizon of Judaism. In other words, Noahide law contains the correlation of a historical standard for judging the present and a practical model for judging the past. Any analysis of it, then, would be incomplete if it did not take this necessary correlation into immediate consideration.

The Noahide is the starting point for Jewish philosophy as a reflection on Judaism. Philosophical reflection is the systematic inquiry into the essential structures of an object, those intelligible conditions which make the existence of the object possible.[3] Essential structures begin by delimiting the object; they enclose it within a boundary. It is this initial enclosure of the object unto itself that allows it to be a consistent entity capable of penetration by the inquiring subject. Something either infinite or structureless is incomprehensible. Therefore, philosophical reflection on Judaism ought to begin at its outer boundaries and systematically proceed inward. Descartes's problem of the starting point of reflection is the first problem for any philosophy. Jewish philosophy is no exception.

If essentially to understand something is to understand it as bound and limited, then one must first understand what stands at the boundary. Since Judaism's beginning lies within humanity, an essential reflection on it ought to begin with the Noahide. He seems to be the sentry at the gate of Judaism in both time and space. It is the Noahide who provides us with our first introduction to the treasures of the palace within. The concept of the Noahide is the limiting concept *(Grenzbegriff)* of Judaism, to use Kant's important

---

2. See *Encyclopedia Talmudit*, vol. 3, p. 348; also, T. Hullin 7.8; B. Hullin 100b.

3. For the distinctions between law, theology, and philosophy in Judaism, see my *Law and Theology in Judaism* (New York: Ktav Publishing House, 1974-76), vol. 1, pp. 1-4.

term.[4] The Noahide is the point of interrelation between the palace within and the wilderness outside. And limits are only meaningful when we know what is present on both sides, as Wittgenstein so astutely pointed out.[5]

However, this entire approach might be rejected by students of Jewish philosophy. They might well suspect the propriety of beginning a reflection on Judaism at its periphery with Noahide law. Might not reflection more appropriately begin with doctrines more central to Judaism itself, such as the existence of God, the creation of the world, the election of Israel, and the revelation of the Torah? Why not proceed to the center rather than tarry at the border? No one could very well deny that Noahide law is an authentic element in Judaism, but one could very well question its primacy and argue that it hardly merits the dignity of being chosen as the starting point for an essential reflection on Judaism. If it is so crucial, then why did not medieval Jewish philosophers such as Saadia, Halevi, Maimonides, and Crescas begin their reflections with Noahide law? In modern times one could ask the same question about Hermann Cohen, Franz Rosenzweig, and Abraham J. Heschel.

It would seem that Noahide law, which lies at the very periphery of Judaism, is the proper subject matter for apologetics rather than philosophy. Apologetics is a translation or paraphrase of something specifically Jewish into something more universal, so that those who do not live in the palace can get some small glimpse of the treasures inside. Apologetics is like a museum tour: one may look at the objects on display from behind a rail, but one may not touch them or use them, for a museum is but a lifeless replica for the masses. The palace itself, however, is the splendid home of the King and his court. Why should those who desire to live in the real palace pretend to be tourists? Perhaps dwelling with the peripheral Noahide too long might thwart the goal of penetrating the core of Judaism and foster the illusion that the replica of the palace is the palace itself.

The dangerous distraction of an apologetic approach to Noahide law, an approach which did manifest itself in the history of Judaism, is that it distorts the true value of Noahide law for the essential understanding of Judaism. Apologetics is a distortion because it turns a problematical starting point into a final conclusion. Apologetics lacks the self-consciousness required for authentic insight, as Franz Rosenzweig saw in his critique of two great German Jewish apologists early in this century — Max Brod and the young Leo Baeck.[6] Apologetics is not philosophy.

---

4. Kant, *Critique of Pure Reason*, B295, B311-312.

5. Wittgenstein, *Tractatus Logico-Philosophicus,* 5.61.

6. Rosenzweig, "Apologetische Denken," *Kleinere Schriften* (Berlin: Schocken Books, 1937),

Jewish philosophy must begin its systematic inquiry at the very periphery with Noahide law for two reasons.

First, any philosophy must not only consider the boundaries of its object in determining its starting point, but must also consider the situation of those reflecting on it. In fact, the very choice of an object for reflection must parallel the situation of the inquiring subject if full penetration is to be achieved. In other words, the object and the subject must have something essential in common — in our case, a common frontier. As Aristotle well pointed out, it is only the ethical person who can intellectually penetrate ethics; or as Husserl pointed out, the subject's act of knowing *(noesis)* parallels its known object *(noema)* in any systematic reflection.[7] Therefore, the *full* projection of Jewish philosophy into Judaism requires as its inquiring subject the Jew who has already committed himself to live and die within the historical community of Israel. An initial commitment must precede a full philosophical integration into Judaism.

Judaism must be of primary concern to the philosopher attempting to penetrate its core. And only what demands both life and death is worthy of such a lifelong endeavor. Judaism has always demanded both.[8] Only a fool would bother to dedicate his life to anything less serious.[9] Thus, if Judaism is not of primary concern, the philosopher, who is by definition not a fool, will have eventually to subordinate Judaism to that object which is in fact his authentic primary concern. The history of Jewish philosophy, especially in modern times, is replete with examples of philosophical reflections on Judaism where Judaism is eventually reduced to a manifestation of something more primary in the concern of the particular philosopher.[10] A philosophical

---

pp. 41-42. In his first work, *Der Wesen des Judenthums* (1905), Baeck was surely an apologist. However, beginning with his work after the rise of the Nazis, I think his apologetics ceased. Cf. D. Neumark, *Toldot Ha-filosofia be-yisrael* (New York: A. Y. Shtibl, 1921), vol. 1, pp. 5-6.

7. Aristotle, *Nicomachean Ethics,* 1095a1-10; Edmund Husserl, *Cartesian Meditations,* 11.14, trans. D. Cairns (The Hague: M. Nijhoff, 1960), pp. 31-32. Cf. Plato, *Seventh Letter,* 344A.

8. Judaism demands life: see Deut. 30:19. Judaism demands death: see B. Berakhot 61b commenting on Deut. 6:5 and B. Sanhedrin 74a.

9. Thus Socrates admits to Parmenides that his philosophy of ideas is only of sustained interest *(pragmateumenos diatribō)* when concerned with the just, the beautiful, and the good *(Parmenides,* 130bd). It should be recalled that Socrates willingly died rather than abandon the object of his philosophy *(Apology,* 29d). Also, Heidegger pointed out that Husserl's phenomenology only qualified as philosophy in the true sense if it were taken ontologically — i.e., concerned with nothing less than Being. See *Sein und Zeit,* 8th ed. (Tübingen: Niemeyer, 1957), p. 37.

10. See Nathan Rotenstreich, *Jewish Philosophy in Modern Times: From Mendelssohn to Rosenzweig* (New York: Holt, Rinehart & Winston, 1968), esp. pp. 6-29, 106-48; Novak, *Law and Theology in Judaism,* vol. 2, pp. xiii-xvi, 77-79.

reflection on Judaism is essentially doomed if Judaism is epiphenomenal rather than the *Urphänomenon*, the primary datum.

On the other hand, the subject and the object are certainly not identical. A degree of detachment is necessary for philosophical reflection lest the respective characters of the subject and the object be distorted. Yet much Jewish theology which is not philosophically critical often speaks in the name of Judaism as if the theologian were an oracle. True concern, however, includes objectivity. True objectivity includes concern. In short, it might be said: Detachment without concern destroys the primacy of the object; concern without detachment destroys the independence of the object. As the contemporary philosopher Paul Ricoeur has noted,

> . . . it is always in the midst of contingency that rational sequences must be detected. Anyone who wished to escape this contingency of historical encounters and stand apart from the fame in the name of a nonsituated "objectivity" would at the most know everything, but would understand nothing. In truth, he would seek nothing, not being motivated by concern about any question.[11]

Our inquiring subject is the Jew of today who, no matter how committed, is, however, a peripheral Jew living on the boundaries of Judaism. His journey must begin at the periphery where he is situated. The Jew of today is probably closer in spirit to the Noahide than he has been at any other time in his history. This is so because the long process of spiritual absorption into the non-Jewish world begun in the eighteenth century has affected every Jew. Some may applaud it; others may bemoan it. Its value is highly debatable; its facticity, however, is something too obvious for debate. Even those Jews who take a stand of most rigid non-compromise with the non-Jewish world reveal by their very reaction how much they are part of it, how well they know its ways. For this reason the Jew who wishes to penetrate Judaism, not so much to escape the external world as to discover more than it alone, must begin where he is situated. He closely resembles his Noahide cousin who stands at the outer gate of the palace.

The second reason why Jewish philosophy must begin at the periphery is because of the structure of Judaism itself as an object. Inquiries can be of two types: either they proceed out from the core toward the periphery, or they begin at the periphery and proceed inward to the core. Aristotle distinguishes

---

11. Ricoeur, *The Symbolism of Evil*, trans. E. Buchanan (New York: Harper & Row, 1967), p. 24. For the necessity of both concern and detachment in any philosophical theology, see Paul Tillich, *Systematic Theology* (Chicago: University of Chicago Press, 1951), pp. 8-15.

between discourse from first principles *(apō tōn archōn)* and discourse toward first principles *(epi tas archas)*. In what we would later term the "cultural disciplines" *(Geisteswissenschaften)*, he advises the second method of inquiry because they do not deal with objects "known in themselves" *(haplōs)* — that is, immediately intelligible at the core *(ratio per se)*.[12] Method of inquiry is not only determined by the historical situation of the subject but even more so by the very structure of the object itself. For only an object which is constituted as a deductive model admits of a method of inquiry where one proceeds from first principles to conclusions. As for Judaism, such a process of understanding would only be possible if Judaism were constituted dogmatically — that is, if at its core we found certain elementary propositions from which everything subsequent is then systematically deduced. Leaving the much-debated question of the role of dogma in Judaism aside, no one could successfully maintain that the core of Judaism is dogmatic. If it were, then why has dogmatics never developed into a specific discipline within the history of Judaism?[13]

One evident example ought to suffice to prove this point. If one were to ask what is the most systematic exposition of Judaism ever written, he would have to answer that it is Maimonides' *Mishneh Torah*. It is a work designed to systematize halakhah, the most evident structure of Judaism. Nevertheless, its system is not deductive. Even though it begins with such dogmas as the existence of God and the revelation of the Torah, it does not deductively proceed from these central dogmas to more specific questions. These dogmas are taken as general assumptions, but the various laws of the *Mishneh Torah* are not presented as further specifications of these general principles in any deductive way.[14]

Therefore, Judaism itself requires a process of understanding which penetrates inward rather than deducing outward if its intelligibility is to be grasped. This process of beginning at the periphery, then, is not just a technique for marginal Jews who are alienated from Judaism. It is, rather, the way that any Jew, no matter how immersed he is in Judaism, must proceed in a philosophical reflection on Judaism.

Of course in some quarters philosophical reflection on Judaism is seen as intellectual arrogance. It is accused of being a high-handed attempt to know more than our nonphilosophical ancestors.[15] It is seen as an attempt to sub-

---

12. Aristotle, *Nicomachean Ethics*, 1095a30-1095b10. Cf. 1094b10-25 and Plato, *Republic*, 510b; also, Wilhelm Dilthey, *Gesammelte Schriften* (Leipzig: Teubner, 1914), vol. 7, pp. 79-88.

13. See Novak, *Law and Theology in Judaism*, vol. 1, p. 155n.2.

14. See Maimonides, *Mishneh Torah*, intro. following B. Berakhot 5a.

15. See the note of R. Abraham ben David of Posquières (Rabad) to Maimonides, MT: Re-

sume Judaism into the categories of something basically foreign if not antithetical to it. Therefore, if Judaism and philosophy have difficulty in making contact, it is seen as proof of the basic futility of the whole project. The difficulty is seen as the just desert for such arrogant presumption. There have been attempts to eliminate Jewish philosophy by halakhic means. The most famous example of this was the partial *herem* (ban) on the study of philosophy issued by the rabbinate of Barcelona in 1305, led by the eminent halakhist R. Solomon ibn Adret (Rashba), who argued that one who was devoted to "the books of the Greeks makes them the root [*iqqar*] and uproots [*oqer*] the Torah of the Lord."[16]

If Jewish philosophy is to be an acceptable Jewish discipline, it must find its justification in the most evident structure of Judaism: halakhah. This was done for us, I believe, by Maimonides.

The Talmud states:

> Rab Safra said in the name of Rabbi Joshua ben Hananyah . . . that one should divide his years of study into a third of the time for Scripture, a third for Mishnah, a third for Talmud.[17]

In codifying this prescription, Maimonides writes:

> One ought to divide his study time into three parts: one third for the Written Torah, one third for the Oral Tradition, and one third for understanding and comprehending a subject from beginning to end and inferring one thing from another and comparing one thing with another and understanding the principles by which the Torah is interpreted so that he knows the essence of these principles. . . . This is what is called *Gemara* . . . and those subjects called *Pardes* (that is, physics and metaphysics) . . . [18]

---

pentance, 3.7, and I. Twersky, *Rabad of Posquières* (Cambridge, Mass.: Harvard University Press, 1962), pp. 282ff. For an excellent discussion of philosophy's essential humility, see Josef Pieper, *Leisure: The Basis of Culture* (New York: New American Library, 1963), pp. 107ff.

16. *Responsa Rashba* (n.p.: B'nai B'rak, 1958), no. 414, vol. 1, p. 150. See J. Sarachek, *Faith and Reason: The Conflict over the Rationalism of Maimonides* (New York: Hermon, 1935), pp. 199ff. Cf. D. J. Silver, *Maimonidean Criticism and the Maimonidean Controversy* (Leiden: Brill, 1965), pp. 148ff.

17. B. Kiddushin 30a.

18. Maimonides, MT: Torah Study, 1.11-12. See also B. Shabbat 31a (bot.) and Rashi, s.v. "hebanta." For an analysis of the antecedents and consequents of this text, see I. Twersky, "Some Non-Halakhic Aspects of the *Mishneh Torah*," in *Jewish Medieval and Renaissance Studies*, ed. A. Altmann (Cambridge, Mass.: Harvard University Press, 1967), pp. 106ff. On the other hand, J. Faur in his book *Iyunim be-Mishneh Torah le-ha-Rambam* (Jerusalem: Mossad ha-Rav Kook, 1978), p. 53, insists that Maimonides only means "legal thought" *(ha-mahshavah ha-mishpatanit)*, à la the use of *gemara* in B. Baba Metsia 33a. However, he neglects to quote the crucial inclusion of

For Maimonides, *Talmud* or *Gemara* is primarily a *method of inquiry,* and all method is ultimately a *philosophy* of its subject matter. If Talmud is method, then it can be extended beyond its previous explication in a particular body of literature, for method is necessarily less explicit than data.[19] This understanding of *Talmud* as method in the deepest sense is the greatest Jewish justification of philosophical reflection I have ever seen.[20]

If philosophy is understood as method, then I believe it is not difficult to refute charges that it is either arrogant, un-Jewish, or both. As a method of inquiry, rather than a competing source of wisdom, it at all times respects the independent integrity of the object of its concern.[21] It begins at the border with the humble sentry and humbles itself in order to understand the peripheral Noahide, rather than boldly marching into the throne room of the King and immediately attempting to read his mind and deduce his decrees. And like all authentic humility, it is compassionate. It recognizes the situation of those Jews who stand at the boundary of the palace longing to penetrate its delights, yet who are confused by its labyrinth of passages. It takes its stand with them, even if more knowing of the palace and more familiar with its halls, because the Jewish philosopher realizes that every Jew is detached from the core of Judaism, that when we glimpse the inner court, we do so as guests of the King. The right to treat the palace as a habitation is the privilege of the King alone. Indeed, it is this detachment, recognizing as it does our transitory situation, that enables us to appreciate in proper awe the sanctity of the palace.[22]

---

pardes in *talmud.* For other Maimonidean sources dealing with the order of studies, see *Hakdamot Perush le-Mishnah,* ed. Rabinowitz (Jerusalem: Mossad ha-Rav Kook, 1961), pp. 79ff.; *Commentary to the Mishnah:* Hagigah 2.1; Maimonides, MT: Foundations, 4.13; Maimonides, *Guide of the Perplexed,* intro. and 3.51.

19. For those who are not philosophically inclined, however, *Talmud* or *Gemara* is ultimately the particular body of literature which subsequently came to bear this name. See B. Kiddushin 30a, Tos., s.v. "lo" based on B. Sanhedrin 24a.

20. Note: "Die erste und grundlegende Aufgabe der mittelälterlichen Philosophie ist die gesetzliche Begründung der Philosophie, d.i., vor allem der Nachweiß, daß die zum philosophieren geigneten Menschen durch das offenbarte Gesetz zum philosophieren verpflichtet und also ermachtigt sind." See Leo Strauss, *Philosophie und Gesetz* (Berlin: Schocken, 1935), p. 48. Cf. his *Persecution and the Art of Writing* (Glencoe, Ill.: Free Press, 1952), pp. 88-89.

21. Thus S. D. Luzzatto (Shadal, d. 1865) distinguished between philosophy beginning from premises antithetical to Judaism (especially "Greek" metaphysics) and "true" philosophy which is in harmony with Judaism. He claims that this latter philosophy has not yet been written. See his commentary to Deut. 6:5. Cf. B. Lonergan, *Method in Theology* (New York: Herder & Herder, 1972), pp. 24-25; A. Nygren, *Meaning and Method,* trans. P. S. Watson (Philadelphia: Fortress Press, 1972), pp. 359-60.

22. This image is based on Maimonides, *Guide of the Perplexed,* 3.47. See B. Hagigah 7a interpreting Prov. 25:17.

This detachment, so clearly manifest in the alienation of our age, can strongly stimulate an essential reflection on Judaism if correctly understood. Perhaps our very situation today, so alienated and yet so full of longing, calls for Jewish philosophy as both a systematically cogent approach to the essential structures of Judaism, and a humble and compassionate approach to the essential structures of today's Jews. By beginning at the boundary with the Noahide, we see the necessary nexus between the intelligent subject and the intelligible object.

The success of Jewish philosophy ultimately depends on the ability of the particular Jewish philosopher. Some attempts have been brilliant successes; others dismal failures. However, I believe that Judaism itself admits of philosophical reflection as a legitimate method of inquiry. Philosophy is possible for Judaism. As such, Judaism is an authentic challenge for any committed Jew who is stirred by philosophical *eros* to discover the essential structures of the object of his primary concern.[23] As Plato taught, philosophical *eros* is first aroused by paradox.[24] The paradox here is that I am conscious of being both human and Jewish. Logic indicates that the species "Jew" is a subset of the genus "humanity." Jewish tradition, on the other hand, often indicates that the Jew is *sui generis,* someone apart from humanity.[25] This paradox, then, manifests itself in a fundamental feeling of ambivalence. Philosophical *eros* is the philosopher's desire to resolve his ambivalence. I do not think Judaism precludes this desire by making its resolution impossible.

23. See Maimonides, *Commentary to the Mishnah,* Berakhot, end. The term "primary concern" is consciously based on the notion of "ultimate concern" of the late Protestant theologian Paul Tillich (d. 1965). See *Systematic Theology,* 1.11ff., and *Dynamics of Faith* (New York: Harper, 1957), pp. 1ff. I agree with Tillich that God alone is worthy of our ultimate concern. However, for us, revelation, whereby God makes himself manifest, is first experienced as a cultural datum with which we are *primarily concerned.* See Novak, *Law and Theology in Judaism,* vol. 1, pp. 144-45, and vol. 2, pp. 35-36.

24. See *Symposium* 202e, where philosophical *eros* is experienced as the "ambivalence" *(metaxu)* of immortal and mortal; *Republic* 523c, where "paradoxical" experience *(to enantion)* "calls" *(parakalounta)* the mind to "reflection" *(episkepsasthai); Theaetetus* 155cd, where "wonder" *(to thaumazein),* the beginning of philosophy, results from the experience of "contradiction" *(paradexometha).* Cf. Jean-Paul Sartre's critique of the lack of motivation in Husserl's phenomenology in *The Transcendence of the Ego,* trans. F. Williams and R. Kirkpatrick (New York: Noonday, 1957), pp. 102-3.

25. Cf. Aristotle, *Topics,* 109b5; B. Yevamot 61; and Tos., s.v. "ve-eyn." Note: "Aber dieser selbst enthaelt einen Doppelsinn in sich, insofern er ein Sohn Adams und ein Sohn Abrahams ist." Cohen, *Religion der Vernunft aus den Quellen des Judentums,* p. 133.

Jewish Philosophy and the Structure of Judaism

Noahide law is within the realm of halakhah and is developed by its legal dialectic. On the other hand, the concept of the Noahide is within the realm of aggadah and is developed by its theological speculation. The concept of the Noahide is, however, unintelligible without Noahide law, the *mitsvot bnei Noah*. The understanding of the Noahide is fundamentally legal before it is theological, and certainly before it is historical or sociological. Therefore, Jewish philosophy begins at the boundary of Judaism with a fundamentally legal datum.

The question now arises: Does halakhah admit of philosophical reflection?

The surprising fact is that most philosophical reflections on Judaism have not only avoided Noahide law as a starting point, but have avoided halakhah in general. Why is this the case if the most evident structure of Judaism is halakhah? I believe this is because of two basic misunderstandings in Jewish philosophy. If they can be cleared away, I can better employ the method outlined in this introduction.

The first misunderstanding has already been discussed. It is the assumption that the only systematic structure admitting philosophical analysis is one evidently deductive. Since halakhah is not a process where first principles are set down and thereafter specified, it seems to elude philosophical analysis. It seems unstructured in comparison with the impressive dogmatic edifices of some other religions. Halakhah can scarcely be conceived by means of a mathematical model.[26] For this reason much of Jewish philosophy has been begun elsewhere because of the basically non-architectonic character of halakhah. Nevertheless, this approach is based on a misunderstanding of philosophical method — namely, it does not appreciate philosophy as a process of discovery. In a process of discovery, one begins with seemingly disjoined data and only *subsequently* glimpses the essential structures. Therefore, philosophy can begin *wherever* the particular philosopher's interest is primarily located, as Socrates demonstrated. Indeed, a dogmatic structure actually hampers the critical function of philosophy, as the history of European philosophy beginning with Socrates has shown repeatedly.

The second misunderstanding of halakhah's philosophical significance concerns the ontological grounds of halakhah. These grounds are themselves non-halakhic — that is, halakhah does not manifest itself as self-sufficient. Its grounds are not immanent but transcendent. Halakhah justifies itself as an

---

26. Cf. J. B. Soloveitchik, "Ish Ha-Halakhah," *Talpiyot,* 1:3-4 (1944): 665, who compares the halakhist with the mathematician.

expression of God's will directly revealed in Scripture and indirectly revealed in Jewish tradition. Therefore, it would seem that halakhah's grounds are theological, and that aggadah is more fundamental than halakhah. Hence it seems to follow that Jewish philosophy ought to begin with aggadah.

Does aggadah, then, admit of primary philosophical reflection?

Aggadah is not a system but rather a collection of (1) individual descriptions of Jewish religious experience, (b) individual speculations about halakhah, and (c) individual speculations about the ways of God. However, in all three types of aggadah an indispensable halakhic factor is present.

In the area of individual descriptions of Jewish religious experience, a halakhic limit is present. No religious experience, no matter how exalted, can be interpreted so that its practical meaning contradicts halakhah.[27]

In the area of individual speculations about halakhah, we might simply recall the classic definition of truth as being contingent on external reality for its fundamental criterion.[28] In this case the external reality, the object, is halakhah.

As for individual speculations about the ways of God, although here aggadah has had historically the widest freedom of expression, nevertheless, these speculations are initially stimulated by some religious experience, and here again the halakhic limit appears. Moreover, speculations about the ways of God have dogmatic limits which themselves are halakhically presented.[29]

This relation between halakhah and aggadah by no means implies a dismissal of the importance of aggadah either as a genre of rabbinic literature or as a theological enterprise. For it is aggadah which makes halakhah philosophically interesting. Without aggadah, halakhah can easily be reduced to the particularities of the various historical periods wherein it made itself manifest. When this is the case, when halakhah has been totally historicized, then it can no longer be of primary concern to anyone who philosophically longs for ultimate truth. As I pointed out earlier, only a datum of primary concern admits of philosophical reflection. Aggadah ensures halakhah's being of primary concern by positing that halakhah is the expression of the will of the transcendent God, and continually developing that position. Halakhah, thanks to aggadah, is more than positive law, more than "revealed legislation," as Moses Mendelssohn wrongly assumed.[30]

27. Maimonides, MT: Foundations, 8.1-3; Nahmanides, "Vikuah Ha-Ramban," para. 39 in *Kitvei Ramban,* ed. C. B. Chavel (Jerusalem: Mossad ha-Rav Kook, 1963), vol. 1, pp. 308-9.

28. See Aristotle, *Categories,* 14b15-20; *Metaphysics,* 1051b5; Thomas Aquinas, *De Veritate,* q. 1, a. l.

29. See M. Sanhedrin 10.1 and Maimonides, *Commentary on the Mishnah:* Sanhedrin, end.

30. "I believe Judaism knows nothing of a *revealed* religion. . . . The Israelites possess a *divine legislation* — laws, commandments, statutes . . . but not dogmas, propositions concerning

Furthermore, aggadah provides us with partners in discourse, an indispensable factor in any intelligent human enterprise. The aggadah contains a tradition of theological discourse. It does not, however, provide us with a starting point for philosophical reflection. Aggadah occupies a chamber deeper within the palace of the King. Beginning with halakhah does not mean we will end with halakhah alone.

In terms of this inquiry, then, we must reflect on Noahide law before we reflect on the theological concept of the Noahide. Halakhah is the general starting point for Jewish philosophy; Noahide law the specific starting point.

At this point of contact, the requirements of Judaism as an intelligible object, and the requirements of philosophy as an intelligent method of inquiry, are satisfied. Noahide law is their first point of real contact. Now let us examine how that contact developed in the history of Judaism.

The Law of Adjudication

As clearly pointed out in the introduction, Noahide law has a double jurisdiction. On the one hand, it is the system of law to which non-Jews *are* universally obligated. On the other hand, it is the system of law to which Jews *were* obligated before the full revelation of the 613 commandments of the Torah from Sinai. The correlation between these two jurisdictions is that Jews began as Noahides. Before the Sinaitic covenant, all men were bound by the Noahide law. Since the Sinaitic revelation, however, Jews are now bound by the 613 commandments, whereas the non-Jewish obligation remains at the Noahide level. In other words, their obligation remains unchanged. Thus it would seem that Noahide law is *currently* relevant for non-Jews and only *historically* relevant for Jews. The following Talmudic text seems to express this understanding of the legal application of Noahide law:

> A baraita taught: Just as Jews are commanded to establish [*le-hoshiv*] courts of law [*battey din*] in every district and in every city, so are Noahides commanded to establish courts of law in every district and in every city.[31]

---

salvation, or self-evident principles of reason." See Moses Mendelssohn, *Jerusalem,* trans. A. Jospe (New York: Schocken Books, 1969), p. 61. For Mendelssohn, the propositions Judaism does *not* have, natural reason *does* have. Therefore, "self-evident principles of reason" are superior to Judaism as is necessary to contingent truth. See *Schriften,* Jubilee ed. (Berlin: Akademie-Verlag, 1929-1932), pp. 43-44. For Mendelssohn, Judaism is essentially beneath philosophy. See A. J. Heschel, *God in Search of Man* (New York: Farrar, Straus & Giroux, 1955), pp. 321-22, 332-33.

31. B. Sanhedrin 56b.

The question which underlies the treatment of Noahide adjudication is that of enforcement. Who enforces the Noahide legal system?

Do Jews enforce Noahide law among non-Jews, or do non-Jews enforce it themselves? If it is ultimately a matter of Jewish enforcement, then Noahide law is essentially a specific extension of Jewish law for non-Jews — that is, it is a form of legal suzerainty. If, conversely, it is essentially a non-Jewish responsibility, then Noahide law is something Jews *recognize* as obligatory for non-Jews, but something Jews themselves are not obliged to enforce. The former view implies a legally constituted imperialism. Its intent is clearly external. The latter view, on the other hand, seems to imply that lawfulness is not essentially something which Jews impose on non-Jews but is, rather, something inherent in humanity itself. Furthermore, since Jews began as Noahides, human lawfulness is seen as a necessary prerequisite for the very emergence of Judaism.

From the perspective of the former view, Jewish interest in Noahide law is essentially prescriptive. Ultimately, as a matter of Jewish enforcement, it presupposes the legal constitution of the Jewish community. From the perspective of the latter view, however, the Jewish interest in Noahide law is descriptive. It presupposes a state of affairs outside the legal constitution of the Jewish community. The motivation for Jewish interest according to the prescriptive view is clear: a part of Jewish law for whose enforcement Jews are ultimately responsible has universal scope. The motivation for the descriptive view seems to be to discover a point in common between Jews and the non-Jewish world, a world which both precedes them and confronts them.

This difference in judgment as to the essential meaning of the doctrine of Noahide law can be seen in the following dispute between Maimonides and Nahmanides.

In prescribing the Noahide commandment regarding *dinim* (adjudication), Maimonides employs a scriptural example to emphasize and illustrate the point he is making:

> How are they commanded concerning the *dinim?* They are obligated to install judges [*dayyanim*] and legal authorities [*shoftim*] in every district and to judge according to these six commandments and to warn [*1e-hazhir*] the people. And a Noahide who transgressed any of these seven commandments is executed by decapitation [*yehareg be-sayyif*]. Because of this all of the Shechemites deserved death, for Shechem deserved death by commiting abduction [*gazal*] and they saw it and did not judge it [*ve-lo danuh*].[32]

32. Maimonides, MT: Kings, 9.14.

Maimonides is referring to the abduction and rape of Jacob's daughter Dinah by Shechem, a Canaanite prince (Gen. 34). The brothers of Dinah, Simon and Levi, executed the male Shechemites after concluding a treaty with them, however. Thus they were seemingly guilty of both bloodshed and deception. Nevertheless, Maimonides exonerates them from any culpability, inasmuch as they were Jews enforcing Noahide law among non-Jews. Noahide law required the people of Shechem to execute their prince for his abduction and rape of Dinah. By neglecting to do so, they gave their tacit approval to his act. The sons of Israel were justified, therefore, in executing Shechem for his crime and the Shechemites for the crime of neglecting to adjudicate this matter. Thus Maimonides sees this case as a paradigm for the right, even the obligation, of Jews to enforce Noahide law among the gentiles when they will not or cannot do it for themselves. "And so did Moses our teacher command us by divine authority [mi-pi ha-gevurah] to force [le-kof] all humanity to accept the commandments of the sons of Noah; and whoever does not accept them is to be executed."[33]

However, the question is this: Does the text of Scripture really exonerate Simon and Levi? If not, then this case is not a paradigm for Jewish enforcement of Noahide law but, instead, it is a paradigm for Jewish noninvolvement in the legal affairs of gentiles. It should be remembered that Jacob disapproved of the actions of his sons (Gen. 34:30; 49:5-7). This is exactly the point Nahmanides makes in his comment to Genesis 34:13, criticizing both Maimonides' exegesis and his legal theory as well:

> This view is incorrect in my opinion because if it were so our father Jacob would then have been obligated to be the first to merit executing them. . . . Why was he angry with his sons?[34] . . . In my opinion the commandment of dinim which was specified [she-manu] for Noahides not only includes adjudication but, also, such things as the prohibitions of stealing, cheating, etc. . . . like the concept of laws [k'inyan ha-dinim] for which Jews are commanded. . . . However, they are not executed for failing to fulfill the positive

33. Maimonides, MT: Kings, 8.10. Note Maimonides, MT: Kings, 10.11: "The Jewish court is obligated to appoint judges for these resident-aliens to adjudicate for them on the basis of these laws in order that society not be destroyed. If the court deems it proper [ra'u] that they appoint their own judges, let them appoint them. And if they deem it proper to appoint Jewish judges for them, let them do so." See the comment of Radbaz (d. 1573) thereto, who emphasizes that Jewish judges are appointed if qualified non-Jewish judges are unavailable. The only difference between the ger toshav and the ben Noah in terms of obligation for the Noahide laws is that the former accepts them voluntarily, the latter involuntarily. See Maimonides, MT: Kings, 8.11.

34. See B. Megillah 9a for the attempt to soften Jacob's curse in Gen. 49:5-7. Cf. LXX and Targum Onkelos thereto.

commandment of adjudication. . . . In their law not acting is not punishable by death.[35]

Nahmanides' contemporary R. Jacob Anatoli saw *dinim* as essentially the obligation of non-Jews to obey the laws of their own society.[36]

This difference of interpretation is based on a fundamental theoretical difference about the essence of Noahide law. If one holds that Noahide law is ultimately a Jewish responsibility, then it is essentially positive law. It presupposes external authority. If, on the other hand, Noahide law is ultimately a human responsibility, both universal and perpetual, then it is essentially a law inherently binding on mankind. Thus its authority is internal — namely, moral.

The first point of view sees Noahide law as a prime topic on the messianic agenda, for Jews did not have non-Jews (slaves aside) under their political and legal control. One can discuss the content of Noahide law now, but its essential meaning, like that of all positive law, depends upon the character of the external authority who enforces it.[37] For Jews, without full religious and political sovereignty, this meaning depended on the character of the authority who *will* enforce this law. Thus pre-messianic Jewish interest in Noahide law *now* is basically a specification of the general messianic hope that

> In the end of days the mountain of the house of the Lord will be secure at the head of the mountains . . . and many nations shall come saying, "Come and let us go up to the mountain of the Lord, to the house of the God of Jacob, and He will instruct us of His ways, and we will walk in His paths," for from Zion shall go forth Torah and the word of the Lord from Jerusalem. (Isa. 2:2-3)

According to the second view, however, Jewish interest in Noahide law seems to be of greater significance in the present. It sets up a model for the interrelation between a revealed system of law and a non-revealed system of law. By constituting Noahide law as essentially independent, the second view forces Judaism to understand itself in relation to something outside its actual or even potential legal control. As such, the concept of *dinim* becomes the legal "border concept" *(Grenzbegriff)* between Judaism and the outside world.

35. See his comment to Gen. 26:5. Nahmanides interprets B. Sanhedrin 58b, "the death penalty is their warning," as only applying to an act where restraint *(meni'ah)* should have been exercised. See Schreiber, *Hatam Sofer* (Vienna: J. Schlesinger), vol. 2, p. 14.

36. *Melamed ha-Talmidim* (Lyck: R. Siebert, 1866), Noah, 12b. See Mishpatim, 72a, and M. M. Kasher, *Torah Shlemah* (Jerusalem: Torah Shlemah Institute, 1967), vol. 17, p. 218.

37. For Maimonides' essentially political view of the Messiah, see MT: Kings, chaps. 11-12, based on B. Berakhot 34b.

A border by definition is where two sides make contact. *Dinim* functions as a point of essential contact between Judaism and the non-Jewish world. Thus Nahmanides, who, we have seen, had argued for the independence of *dinim* among gentiles, sees this independent phenomenon as a comparative standard for Jewish law. Consistency with universal standards of justice is seen as a *conditio sine qua non* of Judaism. "As the judgments of civilized society [*mishpatei yishuv ha-medinot*]. . . the laws [*ha-din*] are right and good as all who see them will recognize."[38] In another context he designates the prohibition of violence *(hamas)*, the very opposite of the rule of law, as something rational *(inyan muskal)* not requiring revelation *(eino tzarikh la-torah)*.[39]

Noahide Law and Sinaitic Revelation

The question of the relation of Noahide law, especially Noahide *dinim*, to the Torah revealed at Sinai can be seen in the dispute between the amoraim R. Yochanan and R. Isaac as to which word in Genesis 2:16 refers to the Noahide commandment of adjudication.[40] R. Yochanan derives it from the words "He commanded" *(vayitzav)*, whereas R. Isaac derives it from "God" *(Elohim)*. According to the astute insight of R. Moses Isserles, this dispute is not just a matter of exegetical technique but indicates a fundamental difference as to how one views the essence of law for Noahides:

> It is clear as the noonday sun that R. Johanan . . . thinks that a Noahide is only commanded to observe the juridical procedure of society [*ha-minhag ha-medini*] and to adjudicate between persons equitably [*mishpat yosher*], but not in the way of the Jewish laws that Moses gave us from Sinai, but only by the rule of law [*hoq nimusi*]. . . . Jewish law is one thing and Noahide law is something else.[41]

Thus the view of R. Yochanan is that Jewish interest in Noahide law is essentially descriptive. R. Isaac, on the other hand, is seen as advancing the pre-

38. Comment to Deut. 6:20. See Halevi, *Sefer ha-Hinukh* (Jerusalem: Mossad ha-Rav Kook, 1966), nos. 49, 58; R. Meir Simhah of Dvinsk, *Meshekh Hokhmah*, ed. A. Abraham (Jerusalem: A. Abraham, 1972), Mishpatim (Exod. 24:3), 133; R. Yehiel M. Epstein, *Arukh Ha-shulhan he'atid* (Jerusalem: Mossad ha-Rav Kook, 1973), 79.15, p. 93.

39. Comment to Gen. 6:2. See his comment to Gen. 6:11; also, Faur, *Iyunim be-Mishneh Torah le-ha-Rambam*, p. 143.

40. B. Sanhedrin 56b.

41. *Responsa Ramo*, ed. Ziv (Jerusalem: Feldheim, 1970), no. 10, pp. 45-46. See *Encyclopedia Talmudit*, vol. 3, p. 355.

scriptive view that Noahide law is a part of Jewish law. Surely it could not be known, much less enforced, without direct Jewish involvement:

> R. Isaac is of a different mind . . . and thinks that Noahide laws are the same as the laws the Jews were commanded at Sinai and, therefore, derives them from a verse (Exodus 22:7) said at Sinai . . . except where there is direct evidence [*yadayim nokhihot*] of a difference.[42]

Although Isserles sees the view of R. Isaac as authoritative, the much earlier Geonic work, *Sheiltot de-Rav Ahai Gaon,* sees the view of R. Yochanan as authoritative.[43] As an immediate rule of law *(halakhah le-ma'aseh),* the issue is not of much import. But as a theological issue it is crucial — namely, does law presuppose revelation, or does revelation presuppose law?

For R. Isaac it would seem that the ultimate responsibility for the enforcement of Noahide law is Jewish. Thus if the non-Jews do not administer justice, Jews are obligated to do so for them, because Noahide law is essentially a special branch of Jewish law. For R. Yochanan, on the other hand, it would seem that both the immediate and the ultimate responsibility for the enforcement of Noahide law is non-Jewish: Jews are not obligated to enforce Noahide law — indeed, they may even be prohibited from enforcing it among non-Jews: Noahide law both antedates and continues to exist independent of the law revealed to Israel at Sinai.

The question of whether *dinim* are something essentially universal and so accepted as a moral criterion by Judaism itself, or whether *dinim* are an essentially Jewish concept applicable to mankind as a whole underlies the following rabbinic dispute:

> "And Jethro Moses' father-in-law heard" (Exodus 18:1). What did he hear and then come? — He heard about the war against Amalek which is described in the preceding section [*she-hi ketubah be-tsido*] and then came — in the opinion of R. Joshua. R. Eleazar of Modi'im said that he heard about the giving of the Torah and came.[44]

At the exegetical level this dispute seems to be based on two differing views of the literary structure of the Torah. R. Joshua seems to base himself on the

---

42. *Responsa Ramo,* no. 10, pp. 45-46. See Bereshit Rabbah 34.7 commenting on Deut. 18:12; also, Finkelstein, "Some Examples of the Maccabean Halaka," in *Pharisaism in the Making* (New York: Ktav Publishing House, 1972), pp. 223-24n.4.

43. *Sheiltot de-Rav Ahai Gaon,* ed. Kenig (Jerusalem: Erets Yisrael, 1940), vol. 2, p. 6b.

44. *Mekhilta,* Yitro, ed. Horovitz and Rabin (Jerusalem: Bamberger & Wahrmann, 1960), p. 188. See n. 1 thereto for the parallel passages.

principle of juxtaposition *(smukhim)* — namely, that the order of presentation in the Torah is not haphazard, that passages are juxtaposed in order that
they might be seen in intelligible sequence.[45] Thus the fact that Jethro's ar-
rival in the Israelite camp is directly preceded by the account of the war
against the Amalekites indicates that his hearing of this event motivated him
to reunite with his son-in-law, Moses. R. Eleazar of Modi'im, on the other
hand, seems to base himself on the principle that the order of presentation of
events in the Torah is not strictly sequential *(ein muqdam u-me'uhar ba-
torah)*, that passages should be interpreted in terms of their conceptual context rather than in terms of strict literary juxtaposition.[46]

Now, at the exegetical level, the view that Jethro arrived in the camp before the giving of the Torah *(qodem mattan torah)* seems to be more plausible, for Jethro expresses his motivation for coming as wonder at the military
feats of God on behalf of the Israelites (Exod. 18:10). If this is so, then why
does R. Eleazar insist that Jethro came after the giving of the Torah *(ahar
mattan torah)?* Indeed, in the version of this debate in the Babylonian Talmud, the amoraim R. Hiyya and R. Joshua ben Levi see the crucial point as
being whether Jethro came before or after the revelation of the Torah.[47] Why
should one want to change the plain meaning of Scripture, which places the
Jethro story before the revelation at Sinai? The answer to this question seems
to me to be that if one holds that *dinim* are essentially Jewish and only universal through enforced Jewish application, how can Jethro's juridical advice
have been acceptable except if it were an expansion and application of the
Torah *already* revealed?[48] Jethro sets forth a system of adjudication for the
people of Israel (Exod. 18:17-26). What law is presupposed by this system of
adjudication? If, however, one holds that *dinim* are essentially universal and
not a purely Jewish doctrine, then one can see Jethro as laying down the normative conditions making the social acceptance of the revealed law possi-

45. See B. Berakhot 21b and parallels; also, Abarbanel's comment to Num. 16:1.

46. See B. Pesahim 6ab and parallels, and Sforno's comment to Num. 9:1. For the rabbinic
transfer of scriptural verses from one context to another, see B. Kiddushin 43a. For discussion of
the theology behind these exegetical principles, see A. J. Heschel, *Torah min-ha-shamayim*
(London: Shontsin, 1962), vol. 1, pp. 199ff.

47. B. Zebahim 116a. Note B. Abodah Zarah 24b, Tos., s.v. "Yitro," which attempts to resolve
this dispute by stating that Jethro arrived before the giving of the Torah but did not give his juridical advice until after the giving of the Torah. Dr. C. B. Chavel notes in his edition of
Nahmanides' Torah commentary (Jerusalem: n.p., 1959), 1.374-75, that this is the basis of
Nahmanides' view. However, nowhere does Nahmanides explicitly state this. In fact, he explicitly accepts the view of R. Joshua. Also, see Rashbam to Exod. 18:1; he argues on purely literary
grounds that Jethro came after the giving of the Torah.

48. See *Yalqut Shim'oni*, Yitro, p. 273; Abrabanel to Exod. 18:1ff., q. 5.

ble.[49] Thus Nahmanides in his comment to Exodus 18:1 endorses the view of R. Joshua as the most plausible — namely, Jethro came before the giving of the Torah: he does so on exegetical grounds. However, since we have just seen that Nahmanides, in contrast to Maimonides, acknowledges that *dinim* are not essentially Jewish, it is not unwarranted, I believe, to see Nahmanides' interpretation of the meaning of the Jethro story as being influenced by this very acknowledgment.

The view, however, that gentile normativity is subsequent to the revelation of the Torah to Israel at Sinai finds expression in this motif developed in the aggadah:

> R. Judah says that they wrote the Torah on the outside of the altar. They said to him, "How did the nations of the world learn the Torah?" He said to them, "God put the desire in their hearts and they sent scribes [*notarii*] and they copied the script from the stones in seventy languages. At that time the judgment [*gazar dinan*] of the nations of the world was sealed in hell."[50]

According to the elaboration of this text from the Tosefta in the Palestinian Talmud, the gentile scribes took their copies of the Torah home with them, obviously to share with their respective peoples.[51] In the elaboration of this text in the Babylonian Talmud, the gentile neglect of the law they had received was the cause for their doom — namely, "they should have learned but they did not" [*she-hayah lahen lilmod ve-lo lamdu*].[52] This seems to refer to the Septuagint translation of the Torah, which made its teachings available to the entire Hellenistic world, where there was widespread interest in Judaism.[53]

The important point in this entire aggadic motif is that the gentiles were not obligated to observe the laws which pertained to them until the Jews *published* these laws for them from out of the Mosaic Torah. Indeed, the Jews themselves were not obligated to the commandments of the Torah until they

---

49. See B. Sanhedrin 15b, Rashi, s.v. "mah"; Tos., s. v. "shor." Cf., however, *Pesikta de-Rav Kahana*, Bahodesh, ed. Mandelbaum (New York: Jewish Theological Seminary, 1962), p. 211; Novak, *Law and Theology in Judaism*, vol. 2, pp. 24-27.

50. T. Sotah 8.6, ed. Lieberman (New York: Jewish Theological Seminary, 1955-), p. 205, following Ms. Erfurt.

51. Y. Sotah 7.5. See *Bamidbar Rabbah* 14.35 for the notion that the Noahides had prophets who taught them their law.

52. B. Sotah 35b. For the use of this principle for a pre-Sinaitic situation when it could not have been referring to Jewish law, see B. Baba Kama 92a and B. Makkot 9b.

53. See *Letter of Aristeas*, sec. 65; Philo, *De Vita Mosis* 11.7, 37-39; B. Megillah 9a and M. Soferim 1.8.

had been published.[54] My teacher, Professor Saul Lieberman, has well illustrated the Greco-Roman background of this type of theological reasoning:

> The Rabbi argued according to the legal practice of the Roman govern-
> ment. An edict had to be displayed in a public place; until then the people
> were not punishable for its transgression. . . . In the opinion of the Rabbi it
> is portions of international law that were published by Joshua on the
> blocks of stone which he set up.[55]

According to this aggadic motif, then, revelation is the actual ground
(conditio per quam) of normativity. The latter presupposes the former.

The Elimination of the Double Standard

Although it does not seem likely that Jews had direct political control over
any groups of non-Jews during the rabbinic period, they certainly had legal
contacts with individual non-Jews. The question arose as to whether Jews
were to attempt to use Jewish law against them in Jewish self-interest, or
whether non-Jewish normativity had to be both recognized in theory and
honored in practice. This point of difference comes out in the following text:

> When a Jew and a Canaanite come to a legal dispute: if you can declare the
> Jew innocent [le-zakkehu] by Jewish law then do so and say that this is our
> law [dinenu]; if by Canaanite law then do so and say this is your law
> [dinkhem]. And if this is impossible practice deceit [akifin]. This is
> R. Ishmael's view. . . . Since when is it permitted to rob a gentile? . . . R. Jo-
> seph said that there is no contradiction. The former view refers to a
> Canaanite; the latter to a resident alien [ger toshav].[56]

Now the term Canaanite is only found in the later printed texts of the
Talmud. The earlier printed texts and the manuscripts simply distinguish between a gentile (nokhri) and a resident alien (ger toshav).[57] Despite the fact

---

54. Shir Ha-Shirim Rabbah 2.11; Vayikra Rabbah 1.10.

55. Lieberman, Hellenism in Jewish Palestine, 2d imp. ed. (New York: Jewish Theological
Seminary, 1962), pp. 200-202.

56. B. Baba Kama 113ab. Note: ". . . a ger toshav . . . is always judged by their law."
Maimonides, MT: Kings, 10.12.

57. See R. N. N. Rabbinovicz, Dikdukei Soferim, Baba Kama, p. 56b. Note the conceptual
justification for such a later emendation given by Meiri, Bet Ha-Behirah, ed. Schlesinger (Jerusalem: n.p., 1961), p. 330.

that Christian censorship undoubtedly led to the choice of the archaicism *Canaanite* (it could not be misconstrued as anti-Christian), it nevertheless helps emphasize the difference between law-abiding gentiles and lawless ones. Just as the Canaanites of biblical times were seen as being the very epitome of lawlessness and therefore were denied the protection of Jewish law,[58] so lawlessness leads to similar results in later times with any gentiles with whom Jews happen to come into contact. In other words, the later use of the term *Canaanite* is by analogy. There were no Canaanites in the Talmudic period.[59] Furthermore, the term *ger toshav* as a designation of law-abiding gentiles is also by analogy. Technically there were also no "resident aliens" in Talmudic times.[60] The recognition of gentile normativity, then, requires a single standard in Jewish civil law. No longer can there be a double standard when normativity is assumed on the part of both Jews and law-abiding gentiles. Equal rights are thus determined by the moral character of the weaker party rather than by the will of the stronger. This recognition led to considerable adjustments in Jewish law, as we shall see. It functions as a moral *sine qua non* for a system of revealed law.

The following text indicates how such a moral standard of equality functioned in the development of Jewish law: "The ox of a Jew who gored the ox of a gentile is exempt [*patur*], but the ox of a gentile whether docile [*tam*] or vicious [*mu'ad*] who gored the ox of a Jew pays full damages."[61] Surely this is the most glaring example of a legal double standard possible. The Talmud's discussion of this text includes the following historical background of the problems caused by the text.

> Our rabbis taught that the Roman government sent two officials [*stradiyotot*] to the sages of Israel saying, "Teach us your Torah." They read it two and three times. At the time of their departure they said to them, "We have examined your Torah and it is true except for this matter concerning the ox of a Jew who gored the ox of a gentile . . . but we will not make this matter known to the government."[62]

58. *Sifre al Devarim*, ed. Finkelstein (New York: Jewish Theological Seminary, 1969), no. 202, p. 238; Y. Shevi'it 6.1; B. Sotah 35-36a and Tos., s.v. "le-rabbot"; B. Avodah Zarah 26b and Tos., s.v. "ve-lo."

59. See Maimonides, *Sefer ha-Mitzvot*, pos. no. 187.

60. Note how Maimonides carefully terms a gentile accepting Noahide law as "*ke*-ger toshav" (MT: Circumcision, 1.6). See also my "The Origin of the Noahide Laws," in *Perspectives on Jews and Judaism: Essays in Honor of Wolfe Kelman* (New York: Rabbinical Assembly, 1978), pp. 301ff.

61. M. Baba Kama 4.3.

62. B. Baba Kama 38a.

Whether or not this exact incident happened is not crucial. What is important is that such would very likely be the reaction of a contemporary Roman jurisconsult to a rule denying legal redress to an alien.[63] And, although Rashi emphasizes that it would have been dangerous to reveal the background of this distinction to the Roman officials, the Gemara itself searches for an answer as to the reason for such inequity in Jewish law.

The Gemara questions the very logic of such a distinction. If the law only applies to Jews, then the gentiles should be exempt; if the law applies to everyone, then Jews should be liable. The following exegetical reason is presented as an explanation for the seeming disregard of moral reasoning in the Mishnah:

> R. Abbahu said that when Scripture states, "He stood and measured the land; He saw and uprooted nations" (Hab. 3:6), it means: He saw the seven commandments which the Noahides had accepted upon themselves, and because they did not uphold [she-lo qiyyamu] them He stood up and permitted their property to Jews.[64]

This, however, leaves us with the moral problem of contemporary people being legally penalized for the misconduct of their ancestors. "Will the fathers eat sour grapes and the teeth of the children be set on edge?" (Ezek. 18:2).[65] Furthermore, it assumes there is no gentile normativity, a point belied by the legal objections of the two Roman officials. Their objections would be most typical of those committed to the system of Roman law.

The version in the Palestinian Talmud quotes two other rabbis arguing as R. Abbahu is reported to have argued in the Babylonian Talmud. However, here R. Abbahu himself is quoted as giving a more cogent explanation for the double standard in Jewish law:

> R. Abbahu said in the name of R. Yochanan that this is according to their law [ke-dinayhen]. . . namely, a gentile's ox who gored another gentile's ox, even if he agreed to be judged according to Jewish law — whether the ox was docile or vicious, he pays full damages . . . according to their law.[66]

63. B. Cohen, *Jewish and Roman Law* (New York: Jewish Theological Seminary, 1966), vol. 1, p. 25.

64. B. Baba Kama 38a. See B. Avodah Zarah 2a.

65. For the attempt to determine moral culpability on an individual basis, see B. Berakhot 7a. It need hardly be pointed out how the concept of inherited guilt was used against Jews throughout history. See *The High Holyday Prayerbook*, trans. and arr. B. Bokser (New York: Hebrew Publishing Co., 1959), pp. 430ff. *(eleh ezkerah).*

66. Y. Baba Kama 4.3.

However, if "their" law makes them responsible for the damages of their animals to *anyone else's*, why does "our" law make us responsible for the damages our animals cause to the animals of *other Jews only*, but makes us exempt from the damages our animals cause to the animals of non-Jews? R. Abbahu's reasoning only accentuates the double standard of the Mishnah, for "their" law by its very consistency appears more just than "our" law with its insurmountable inconsistency.

Maimonides, in codifying the law, took another line of interpretation. He states that since gentile law does not hold one liable for damages committed by his animals, it is clearly unjust; therefore, gentiles are fined *(qanas)* by Jewish law so as to lessen irresponsibility and financial loss to humanity *(ha-beriyot)*.[67] Here again we see that Maimonides affirms the need of gentiles to be ruled by Jewish law. Nevertheless, Maimonides' logic contains a flaw. For if exemption from payment for the damages of one's animals made for general irresponsibility among gentiles, would not similar exemption make for similar irresponsibility among Jews?[68]

Moreover, the text in the Palestinian Talmud indicates that the Roman officials also found two other laws morally objectionable — namely, (1) that a Jewish woman may deliver a non-Jewish child, but a non-Jewish woman may not deliver a Jewish child,[69] and (2) a gentile is prohibited from stealing from a Jew but not vice versa.[70] It is reported that Rabban Gamliel II ruled that it is forbidden for a Jew to steal from a non-Jew because of the defamation of the Name of the Lord *(hillul ha-Shem)* — namely, it makes Judaism appear morally inferior.[71] Concerning the law of the goring ox, however, he simply advises keeping the matter secret. The version in the *Sifre*, on the other hand, only mentions the law permitting robbing gentiles and its abrogation.[72] Furthermore, the reason given for Rabban Gamliel's change of the law is not fear of the Roman government, as in the case of the goring ox, but rather leaving the law as it had been would imply the moral inferiority of Judaism. Therefore, the acceptance of a moral standard among the gentiles, acknowledged by Judaism, had internal implications for the development of Jewish law. Once

---

67. Maimonides, MT: Property Damage, 8.5. For the originality of this argument, see De Bouton, *Lehem Mishneh* thereto. Cf. B. Nedarim 28a and Ran, s.v. "be-mokes."

68. Cf. *Bereshit Rabbah* 41.7; *Seder Eliyahu Rabba*, chap. 28.

69. M. Avodah Zarah 3.3; B. Abodah Zarah 26a. However, see Y. Abodah Zarah 2.1 and Meiri, *Bet Ha-Behirah*, ed. Sofer (Jerusalem: n.p., 1964), p. 58 for the attempt to qualify this law.

70. B. Baba Kama 113b.

71. T. Baba Kama 10.15. For Jewish arguments contra charges of misanthropy, see Josephus, *Antiquities*, 16.30, 42-43.

72. *Sifre al Devarim*, no. 344, pp. 400-401.

again the current printed text of the Babylonian Talmud refers to the lawless gentiles as "Canaanites" — a clear attempt to use a historically recognizable term of distinction between lawful and lawless gentiles. This is based on the explanation of R. Menahem Meiri that the case of the goring ox in the Talmud is now atypical:

> This only [davka] applies to those nations not bound [she-eynam megudarim] by the ways of the revealed religions [datot] and morality [nimusim] . . . but anytime the law obligates them for the seven Noahide laws their case before us is like our case before us. We do not favor ourselves in the case. Thus it goes without saying that such applies to the nations bound by the ways of the revealed religions and morality.[73]

Now Meiri had earlier explained the double standard in a way similar to that of Maimonides, whom he often follows — namely, gentiles do not accept responsibility for the damages caused *by* their animals, hence they are not entitled to claim legal redress for damages *to* their animals.[74] At this level one could criticize the same flaw in his moral reasoning as was criticized in Maimonides' — namely, exemption from responsibility will lead to irresponsibility, no matter who is exempt. However, the matter does not remain here at this point because Meiri places all of this in the past. Revealed religion and its moral standards have changed the status of those gentiles — namely, Christians and Muslims, who are bound by them. Thus Meiri does not have to offer a categorical justification for the double standard of the Mishnah because it is no longer applicable. Thus what Rabban Gamliel II partially accomplished by legislation, Meiri completely accomplished by interpretation.

Non-Jewish Participation in Jewish Law

We have now seen how Jewish interest in independent non-Jewish law is for the sake of constituting a moral standard to be used in regulating Jewish law itself. Such interest, it seems to me, led to a gradual acceptance of the validity of certain universal non-Jewish legal practices and institutions for Jewish litigation. In the area of *dinim* the question arose as to whether non-Jewish adju-

---

73. *Bet Ha'Behirah*, Baba Kama, p. 122. No doubt Meiri's reasoning as brought by Ashkenazi, *Shitah me-qubetzet* (Baba Kama 38a), influenced the subsequent printed reading of "Canaanite." Cf. *Seder Eliyahu Rabba*, chap. 15.

74. *Bet Ha-Behirah*, Ketubot (15b), ed. Sofer (Jerusalem: n.p., 1946), pp. 67-68. See also J. Katz, *Exclusiveness and Tolerance* (Oxford: Oxford University Press, 1961), pp. 114ff.

dication as an independent legal procedure was in any way valid in Jewish cases:

> R. Eleazar ben Azaryah said that if the gentile law is like Jewish law, may I conclude that their law [*dineyhem*] is valid? — Scripture states, "And these are the ordinances [*mishpatim*] you shall place before *them*" — *you* judge *their* cases, but they do not judge yours.[75]

Here we have an example of the principal of legal suzerainty — namely, Jews have the right, even the obligation, to enforce the rule of law among the gentiles. The Mekhilta then sees this principle as the basis for the following law found in the Mishnah:

> A bill of divorce ordered [*get me'useh*] by Jewish authorities is valid [*kasher*], but by gentile authorities is invalid [*pasul*]. But, if the gentiles beat the husband and say, "Do as the Jewish authorities tell you" — it is valid.[76]

In other words, gentile law is only valid for Jews as an extension of Jewish enforcement; but Jewish law is valid wherever it applies to them, and the Jews have the power to enforce it.[77]

However, in the Mishnah we also find a tacit recognition that Jewish law and non-Jewish law have enough *in common* to allow non-Jewish jurisdiction to have validity in some cases involving Jews:

> All documents deposited in the gentile courts [*arka'ot she-la-goyim*], even though their sealing is witnessed by gentiles, are valid [*kesherin*] — except bills of divorce and manumission of slaves.[78]

The simplest and most constricted interpretation of the text is given by R. Mordecai ben Hillel, a thirteenth-century authority. He states that this is a specific rabbinic decree concerning documents. The reason he gives is that gentiles are very careful *(maqpidin)* about the signatures on documents registered in their courts.[79] He undoubtedly based this on the fact that the ques-

---

75. For the sake of clarity I have combined the readings of the *Mekhilta,* Mishpatim, from ed. Horovitz-Rabin, p. 246, and ed. Lauterbach (Philadelphia: Jewish Publication Society, 1933), vol. 3, p. 2.

76. M. Gittin 9.8.

77. See B. Gittin 88b and Tos., s.v. "u-ba-akum"; Maimonides, MT: Sanhedrin, end.

78. M. Gittin 1.5. See Novak, *Law and Theology in Judaism,* vol. 1, pp. 128-29.

79. *Mordecai:* Gittin, no. 324. See *Shulhan Arukh,* Hoshen Mishpat, 66.6-7.

tion of witnesses for documents is a matter of rabbinic law where much flexibility is allowed.[80] Hence this is simply a specific concession in Jewish law. The later codes, no doubt reflecting fears of the even further erosion of Jewish autonomy in the Middle Ages, follow Mordecai in restricting non-Jewish legitimacy in Jewish legal affairs as much as possible.[81]

However, the Gemara proper to this Mishnah bases the ruling on the much more comprehensive principle of the third-century Babylonian amora Samuel, "the law of the kingdom is the law" *(dina de-malkhuta dina)*. R. Samuel ben Meir (Rashbam, d. 1174) elsewhere explains this principle as follows:

> All the levies and taxes and procedures regularly enacted by kings in their kingdoms are binding as law [*dina*]. For all the subjects of the kingdom freely accept [*mirtsonam*] the statutes of the king and his enactments.[82]

This principle, as explained by Rashbam, sees the legal authority of the state to make laws for its subjects — including Jewish subjects — as grounded in popular consent and acceptance of external authority. In later political thought this type of reasoning was called the theory of the "social contract." Nevertheless, this principle in and of itself in no way presents any standard of judgment for determining whether these laws are themselves right or wrong.

Finally, commenting on a passage in the Gemara where our Mishnah is cited, Rashi presents the broadest and deepest basis for the specific ruling of the Mishnah:

> Although sacramental matters [*kritut*] do not concern gentiles, nor matters of Jewish divorce and marriage [*gittin ve-qiddushin*], they are, nevertheless, commanded concerning the rule of law [*dinin*].[83]

This explanation indicates that a non-Jewish society — in nonritual cases, of course — can be the context for Jewish legal action, provided that that society's legal and political order is in basic conformity with the Noahide commandments. This is not only a *de facto* recognition of Jews being subject to a non-Jewish regime; it is a *de jure* recognition that the state's right to rule is grounded in a law directed to the conscience of man. In other words, we now have a moral grounding for the positive law of the non-Jewish state. This goes

80. See B. Gittin 9b, s.v. "af al pi."

81. See *Shulhan Arukh*, Hoshen Mishpat, 26.1-4; 68.1. For permission to use the *arka'ot* of the gentiles for specific Jewish self-interest, see B. Avodah Zarah 13a.

82. B. Baba Batra 54b, s.v. "dina." See Maimonides, MT: Robbery, 5.13 and 18 and *Maggid Mishneh* thereto. See also *Digest* (from the Justinian Code) 1.4.1.

83. B. Gittin 9b, s.v. "huts."

far beyond a principle of consent. For a social contract theory itself provides no standard for judging which of the ruler's laws are morally binding[84] — indeed, which of the laws the ruler himself has the moral right to enact. Consent alone can be either moral or immoral. It is even found among thieves.[85]

The recognition and affirmation of the presence of *dinim* among the gentiles provided a theoretical model for determining the necessary minimum moral standards to which Jewish law must adhere. It also provided a morally acceptable system of civil law for Jews when lack of political independence made their own system of civil law practically inoperable. It enabled non-Jewish civil law at times to be morally obligatory for Jews, not just politically expedient. Thus we will see that Rashi's designation of gentile jurisdiction as morally binding because of their adherence to Noahide *dinim* not only explains the law concerning documents deposited in gentile courts; it also became the ultimate moral justification for the most comprehensive principle in this area — namely, *dina de-malkhuta dina,* "the law of the kingdom is the law."

We have already seen how this general principle was used by the Gemara to explain why Jewish civil documents deposited in gentile courts are valid. Nevertheless, the principle itself requires justification. Rashbam, as we have seen, justifies it on the basis of consent — namely, Jews have the right to contract the loss of civil independence in return for a degree of political sufferance. Civil rights, according to the Talmud, can be waived by stipulation.[86] In the *locus classicus* of this principle in the Gemara, it is presented as contradicting another statement recorded in the name of Samuel — namely, "the possessions of gentiles are like the wilderness [*ka-midbar*], whoever takes hold of them acquires them."[87] Maimonides explains that this other statement only applies in the absence of explicit political authority governing gentiles and Jews. The presence of such authority, on the other hand, with its advantages of law and order, removes this right from Jews.[88] Thus both Rashbam and Maimonides use social-contract type reasoning to explain this radical principle.[89]

The Jewish version of the social contract theory escaped one of the main

---

84. For the moral inadequacies of the social contract theory, see Levi Strauss, *Natural Right and History* (Chicago: University of Chicago Press, 1953), p. 119.

85. Prov. 1:13-14; Halevi, *Kuzari,* 2.48 and Ibn Daud, *Ha-Emunah Ha-Ramah,* ed. Weil (Berlin: Lamm, 1919), p. 75, following Plato, *Republic,* 351d.

86. See B. Yevamot 89b; B. Kiddushin 19b.

87. B. Baba Batra 54b.

88. Maimonides, MT: Acquisition and Gift, 1.14-15.

89. See Thomas Hobbes, *Leviathan,* chaps. 14-24.

criticisms of the theory in later philosophy. It was argued by more historically minded thinkers that such a contract could not be the absolute beginning of society because a contract presupposes the existence of society, not vice versa.[90] However, the Jewish version of this theory did not use it to explain the origins of society but merely to justify the right of Jews as a minority to contract for their political sufferance by relinquishing their civil autonomy. The theory thus enabled Jews to live in a society not grounded in the Sinaitic covenant and its law.

Nevertheless, the principle does not offer a criterion for determining which non-Jewish systems of law are not only politically expedient but morally binding on the Jewish conscience. If obedience to the laws of the state is simply political expediency, then the Jewish community has indeed not only lost its civil independence but some of its moral integrity as well. This point was brought out by the great Spanish halakhist R. Solomon ibn Adret (Rashba):

> I say that whoever relies on this to say that something is forbidden because "the law of the kingdom is the law," he is in error and a robber . . . and in the category of one who uproots all of the laws of the perfect Torah. What need would we have of all the holy books . . . ? They might as well teach their children the laws of the gentiles! Concerning this principle . . . I have greatly agonized [*yagati harbeh*].[91]

However, on the other hand, if one can see something basic in common between Jewish and non-Jewish society as a universal *sine qua non*, then the acceptance of the temporal authority of non-Jewish law does not involve a loss of Jewish moral integrity. The Noahide commandment of *dinim*, which we may interpret as *due process of law*, is the *sine qua non* for any society hav-

---

90. For the most insightful critiques of constituting society on the basis of a contract, see Max Scheler, *Formalism in Ethics*, trans. M. S. Frings and R. L. Funk (Evanston, Ill.: Northwestern University Press, 1973), pp. 528-31; and Reinhold Niebuhr, *The Self and the Dramas of History* (New York: Scribner, 1955), p. 165. Earlier the German social philosopher Ferdinand Tönnies developed the thesis that contractual society *(Gesellschaft)* was subsequent to traditional society *(Gemeinschaft)*. See *Community and Society*, trans. C. P. Loomis (East Lansing: Michigan State University Press, 1957), esp. pp. 65ff. Also, see C. J. Friedrich, *The Philosophy of Law in Historical Perspective*, 2d rev. ed. (Chicago: University of Chicago Press, 1963), pp. 138ff.

91. *Responsa Rashba* VI, ed. Pietrkov, no. 254. See Karo, *Bet Joseph*, Hoshen Mishpat 26, end; and Isserles' note to *Shulhan Arukh*, Hoshen Mishpat 369, end. Along the lines of this type of concern, see R. Isaac Lampronti, *Pahad Yitzhak*, s.v. "pesulin min ha-Torah"; he rejects *dat ha-teva (ius naturale)* as a halakhic criterion. Also, see L. Landman, "Law and Conscience," *Judaism* 18.1 (Winter 1969): 27-28. Cf. J. Z. Lauterbach, *Rabbinic Essays* (Cincinnati: Hebrew Union College Press, 1951), pp. 130-34.

ing a moral claim upon its citizens.[92] If it is present, it has an immediate moral claim upon whoever lives in that society, including Jews. This is brought out by the modern halakhist R. Hayyim Hirschensohn:

> Because they are obligated for law they are obligated for the prescriptions of the state [*be-nimusey ha-malkhut*]. . . not because of the power of the king but because of the legal obligation [*hiyuv dinim*] for which Noahides are obligated. If so their state is able to enact decrees [*le-taken takkanot*] and methods of acquisition which are also effective [*mo'ilim*] between one Jew and another.[93]

Indeed, Samuel's very choice of the term *dina* might indicate that he defined non-Jewish law as valid by virtue of its adherence to the Noahide *dinim*.[94]

The acknowledgment that non-Jewish law may be authoritative for Jews in the absence of enough Jewish political independence to enforce Jewish civil law is ultimately based on an acceptance of gentile normativity. Thus a famous passage in the Mishnah states,

> R. Hanina the vice-High Priest says that one should pray for the wellbeing of the government [*shlomah shel malkhut*], for were it not for the fear of it [*mora'ah*] a man would swallow his neighbor alive.[95]

For Jews, acknowledgment of this type was like the principle in Roman law, *dura lex sed lex* — namely, a "hard" (that is, imperfect) law is better than no law at all. In fact, Jews were admonished not only for disobeying their own law but for abandoning law in general:

> R. Joshua ben Levi saw a contradiction between two verses in Ezekiel: "And you did *not* act according to the laws of the nations which surround you"

92. "Die sieben Gebote der Söhne Noahs bilden dieses sittliche Fundament. Das erste dieser sieben Gebote bildet demgemäß die Gerichtsverfassung. Das Recht ist die Grundlage der menschlichen Sittlichkeit . . . das formuliert das Recht für die allgemeine menschliche Sittlichkeit." Cohen, *Religion der Vernunft aus den Quellen des Judentums*, p. 381. See *Jüdische Schriften*, vol. 3, p. 86.

93. *Malki Ba-qodesh*, vol. 2, no. 2, pt. 2, quoted in S. Shilo, *Dina De-Malkhuta Dina* (Jerusalem: Jerusalem Academic Press, 1974), p. 83n.103. Also, see I. Z. Meltzer, *Even Ha-Ezel*, re Maimonides, MT: Property Damage, 8.5.

94. The noun *din* comes from the verb *dun*, "to judge," which has both a logical and a legal denotation. See, e.g., B. Sanhedrin 54a. For the relation between law and logic, see Cohen, *Religion der Vernunft aus den Quellen des Judentums*, pp. 12, 32.

95. M. Avot 3.2. See B. Abodah Zarah 4a and esp. B. Berakhot 58a commenting on 1 Chron. 29:11.

(5:7) — "You *did* act according to the laws of the nations which surround you" (11:12). He resolved it by saying: You did not act according to their good laws [*metuqanim*]; their bad laws [*mequlqalim*], you did act according to them.[96]

Obviously the only criterion to determine which non-Jewish laws are good or not is Noahide law. If these laws are good *per se,* then they are good for all men, Jews included.

This does not involve the permanent abandonment of Jewish civil law. The rule of law is only the necessary condition for society to have moral authority; it is not the sufficient ground for a historical community. The identity of the people of Israel is grounded in God's revelation of the Torah *(conditio per quam).*[97] Surely the hope of this covenanted community is that every aspect of human life, individual and collective, be illuminated by the light of the Torah and the particular historical experience of the Jewish people. Although it is acknowledged that certain areas of interhuman relationships, specifically civil law, can function independently of the revealed law of the Torah, such independence reflects a historical alienation, an unhappy situation where the Jewish people cannot exercise the full hegemony of the Torah over their communal life. The recognition of the universality of *dinim,* however, enables Jews to see the lack of full Torah hegemony as a political privation rather than a moral compromise. Moreover, by seeing the rule of law as a universal social requirement, it becomes a necessary condition for Jewish life as well, a necessary condition but never its sufficient ground. This concept of *dinim,* when properly understood, does not allow the revealed law of the Torah to be reduced to an immanent moral universalism.

Differences between Jewish and Non-Jewish Law

The Jewish interest in non-Jewish law is an attempt to see the necessary conditions for Jewish law as universal, because before the Sinaitic covenant, Jews were bound by these very same universal standards. This being the case, the specific revelation of the laws of the Torah presupposes human normativity in general. In this sense non-Jewish law functions as a positive criterion of comparison. However, non-Jewish law is used as a negative standard of comparison in those cases where Jewish law demands a greater legal obligation.

96. B. Sanhedrin 39b.
97. Novak, *Law and Theology in Judaism,* vol. 2, pp. 22-27.

Non-Jewish law as a *conditio sine qua non* only provides a minimal standard of similarity. Above this minimal level, however, Jewish law is dissimilar. Without this distinction one will fall into the error, especially characteristic of nineteenth-century interpreters, of reducing Jewish law to merely universal standards. Universal standards are necessary for Jewish law but not sufficient. This is brought out in the following Talmudic discussion of usury. Usury is something prohibited between Jews, but permitted between gentiles and between Jews and gentiles:[98]

> R. Safra said that anything which in their law [*be-dineyhem*] is transferred from borrower to lender, in our law [*be-dineynu*] is returned from the lender to the borrower. Anything which in their law is not transferred from the borrower to the lender, in our law is not returned from the lender to the borrower.[99]

The discussion in the Gemara limits the difference between "our" law and "their" law to stipulated interest *(ribbit ketsutsah)*. However, since unstipulated prepayments and unstipulated supplements are not legal matters in the gentile system, they need not be so in our law.[100] The reason here is probably because such practices are too informal to be effectively controlled by strict legal enforcement. But in the case of stipulated interest, we see the difference between a covenanted community and a non-covenanted community. Clearly the personal interdependence required in the former type of community must be greater than that required in the latter type. Nevertheless, the fundamental point in common is that the debt must be paid. This is something which the Torah need not legislate because a debt *by definition* is money lent in order to be repaid.[101]

The Talmud later attempted to conceptualize the entire relation between Jewish and non-Jewish law in this principle: "There is nothing permitted to

---

98. For attempts to morally discourage usury with gentiles, see B. Makkot 24a commenting on Ps. 15:5 and Meiri (ed. Strelitz [Jerusalem: n.p., 1937], p. 116) thereto; B. Baba Metsia 70b-71a, Tos., s.v. "tashikh," and Maharsha thereto. R. Joseph Albo (*Ikkarim* 111.25) limits the right to take interest only from idolators without religion, but prohibits taking interest from Noahides who are like *gerei toshav*. R. Isaac Abrabanel in his comment to Deut. 23:20 attempts to answer Christian charges that the permission for Jews to take interest from gentiles indicates the moral inferiority of Judaism. Along these lines see B. Nelson, *The Idea of Usury,* 2d ed. (Chicago: University of Chicago Press, 1969). Maimonides, on the other hand, rules that taking interest from a gentile is mandatory. See Maimonides, MT: Creditor and Debtor, 5.1, and Rabad thereto.

99. B. Baba Metsia 62ab.

100. M. Baba Metsia 5.10.

101. See B. Kiddushin 13b, Tos., s.v. "malveh"; B. Sanhedrin 10a, Tos., s.v. "mishum" (end).

Jews [*shry*] which is prohibited [*asur*] to gentiles."[102] In the case of lending money, the principle would apply as follows: Since gentiles are required to pay their debts, so are Jews; but gentiles being permitted both to take and to pay interest does not determine what Jews are to do in this area. In other words, gentile moral standards are the minimum but not the maximum in Jewish law. Although exceptions are found to this principle, it was adhered to with remarkable consistency. It provided an ethical criterion for Jewish jurisprudence, a philosophical starting point that prevented Judaism from being reduced to a religious monad (fundamentalism) or to a variety of universalism.

---

102. B. Sanhedrin 59a. Cf. ". . . quod civile, non idem continuo gentium; quod autem gentium, idem civile esse debet." Cicero, *De Officiis*, 111.69. See B. Yevamot 22a; Maimonides, MT: Sale, 13.7.

9 Persons in the Image of God (1998)

From all that we have been considering so far, one cannot say that Jewish natural-law thinking in and of itself produces any independent norms. It functions at the level of principles, not at the level of specific rules themselves. Actual law is always positive law at work with authority in a specific, concrete human community in history.[1] What natural law does is to provide certain general criteria in the form of a *conditio sine qua non* for the formulation of this positive law so that it can have truth value in the world. Thus it is the limit of the law, not its content and not its *telos*.[2] That is why I have been insisting that what is being presented here is a *minimal* natural-law theory.

This would seem to imply that we are not at all interested in the question of teleology. However, that would be unacceptable, inasmuch as natural law pertains to rational human action as distinct from mere behavior. The distinction between the two is that only rational action requires the acting person to be ever aware of its end when choosing to act or not to act in any specific situation. Thus the limits on human action proposed by natural law must have some connection to the ends proposed by positive law. If not, there is no way of telling whether the content of the positive law will destroy the limits natural law has placed upon it. In other words, to use Hegelian language, natural law must not be *aufgehoben* by positive law. It must not be so transformed by it that it eventually loses its former identity altogether.[3]

1. Along these lines, see Jacques Ellul, *The Theological Foundation of Law,* trans. M. Wieser (Garden City, N.Y.: Doubleday, 1960), p. 21.

2. See David Novak, *Jewish Social Ethics* (Oxford: Oxford University Press, 1992), pp. 74ff.

3. See B. Yevamot 22a.

So, it seems to me that the best mediating concept for this interrelation is a concept of human personhood inasmuch as human persons are the subject of both natural law and positive law. To assume that positive law, specifically the positive law of revelation, makes its addressees a new species (rather than members of a new culture) would make any notion of natural law irrelevant to a tradition like Judaism that bases itself on such a revelation. Thus the mediating concept must be a concept of human personhood in which the subject of natural law and the subject of positive law, even positive divine law, retain enough in common to still be considered human persons in a real sense — that is, members of the same species. And that is to be the case despite whatever differences subsequently intervene between Israel and the nations of the world in history. Accordingly, history presupposes nature; it does not consume it, however.

The questions now before us in our inquiry into natural law in Judaism are as follows: (1) How does a Jewish idea of human personhood become a matter of teleology? and (2) How does a Jewish idea of human personhood intend revelation without being strictly derived from it, a point which alone could make it relevant to natural law and for all those concerned with it?

When we understand the term *end* or *telos* as that which is intended (and thus it is more than a mere spatial or temporal limit), it can have two very different meanings. On the one hand, it can mean a state of being, as when Aristotle says that the end of human life is happiness *(eudaimonia),* which he explains to mean a state of present human activity that requires no external justification.[4] On the other hand, *end* can mean a person, as when Kant says that morality is treating other persons as ends-in-themselves *(Zweck an sick selbst),* which is to say that a person is not to be treated as a means to *something* else. That would be the case, though, in any activity in which the personal dignity of any man or woman as a rational, self-legislating being is violated or even ignored.[5]

Here we learn something extremely helpful from Kant, who after all has always been the favorite philosopher of the most modern Jewish thinkers. This requires further inquiry into what it means to identify the human person as an end of our action.

There is, of course, the need to reject Kant's ethical theory on theological grounds because of its insistence that the rational human subject is the source of its own law *(autonomy).* For that basically contradicts natural law and re-

---

4. Aristotle, *Nicomachean Ethics,* 1102a1-4.

5. Kant, *Groundwork of the Metaphysics of Morals,* trans. H. J. Paton (New York: Harper & Row, 1964), p. 101.

vealed law, both of which speak of a real, trans-human grounding of the law.[6] Nevertheless, if we shift his specific denotation of person as end-in-itself from the human *subject* of moral action to the human *object* of moral action, something quite helpful emerges for us theologically.

In Kant's own view, the other person who is the object of my moral action is constituted *after* I have constituted myself as a moral subject *a priori.* This other person, then, is essentially an analogue of my own fully conscious moral personhood.[7] Thus our commonality is our mutual autonomies subsequently interacting. Authentic human community, what Kant called a "kingdom of ends" *(Reich der Zwecke),* is simply the projection of what each of us has now going into the future, where we plan to exercise it more fully together.[8] It is in many ways an ontological constitution of the "social contract."[9]

But what if, by a phenomenological constitution of the moral realm (here following some of the insights of Martin Buber and, especially, Emmanuel Levinas), I discover that the object of my moral concern presents himself or herself to me *before* I have constituted myself as a moral subject?[10] We then have a very different idea of human mutuality and interaction. For here both the source and the end of my action are one and the same by the very act of the other person *presenting* himself or herself to me, without my prior permission, as it were.

This other person's very existence (qua source) is attractive (qua end) to me. My existence is the same to him or to her. Our mutuality is not something that each of us already has; rather, it is something new and unexpected, wherein we co-exist, going together into a largely unpredictable future. Each of us, then, to a certain extent, is a revelation to the other. Furthermore, my constitution of myself as a moral person is not initially based on my inner self-projection but, rather, it is my response to the presence of that other person. Minimally, as we shall see, it is my preparation for such a possible personal presentation. Moral action is reaction; it is essentially response. It is making oneself answerable, a truth well expressed by the German phrase *verantwortlich sein.*

6. See A. P. d'Entrèves, *Natural Law* (New York: Harper & Row, 1965), p. 101.

7. See Kant, *Groundwork of the Metaphysics of Morals,* pp. 105-6; cf. Aristotle, *Nicomachean Ethics,* 1166a30ff.

8. Kant, *Groundwork of the Metaphysics of Morals,* pp. 105-6.

9. See David Novak, *Natural Law in Judaism* (Cambridge: Cambridge University Press, 1998), pp. 1-26.

10. See Buber, *I and Thou,* trans. W. Kaufmann (New York: Scribner, 1970), pp. 124ff.; Levinas, *Totality and Infinity,* trans. A. Lingis (Pittsburgh: Duquesne University Press, 1969), pp. 289ff.

*   *   *

What is it about the other person that I am to find attractive, which minimally entails that I refrain from harming him or her in any way? What is it about the other person that teaches me the most elementary moral law, which is the most basic human right: "Do not harm me"? Are there not many other persons who are decidedly unattractive, not only aesthetically but morally as well? Can that other person's attractiveness be anything more than his or her good character that I perceive before me? Can the range of existential attraction be more than the objects of my *eros* or those who are deemed to be potential friends *(philoi)* of mine? How can it be extended so as to include those who do not act well for me or for anyone else, and even those who cannot act at all for anyone else, even themselves? None of these questions can be answered satisfactorily by any ethics that attempts to constitute an ontology or philosophical anthropology out of its own operations. It inevitably reduces human existence to the level of the immanent action of the world and thereby obscures the transcendent dimension of human existence in the world and the action that intends its truth.[11]

These questions, it seems to me, are better answered by an ontology and theological anthropology that emerge from the doctrine of creation, specifically the creation of the human person as the *image of God.* Human dignity, which is sufficient to ground the minimal right to life and safety of every descendant of the first humans, means that human beings *are* more than they can ever *do* or *make* of themselves. To understand this, though, requires some philosophical commentary on what is actually meant by asserting "man — male and female — is made in the image of God" (Gen. 5:1).

I think that one can conceive of the image of God both positively and negatively. Each conception of it must be carefully nuanced so that wrong implications are not drawn from either of them.

There has been a whole trend in the history of Western theology (both Jewish and Christian, where the *tselem elohim* or *imago Dei* doctrine is explicit) to positively conceive of the image of God as consisting of some quality humans share with God by virtue of a divine transfer at the moment of creation. Going back at least as far as Philo in the first century, many theologians have identified the image of God with reason.[12] Just as God is the rational power in the macrocosmos, so man is the rational power in the microcosmos.

---

11. See Novak, *Jewish Social Ethics,* pp. 14ff.

12. See Philo, *Legum Allegoria,* 3.31-132.96; *De Opificio Mundi,* 69; also, David Novak, *Halakhah in a Theological Dimension* (Chico, Calif.: Scholars Press, 1985), pp. 94ff.

Creation in the image of God means, then, that reason is what distinguishes humans from the rest of creation by enabling humans to have something substantial in common with God. This view nicely dovetails with philosophical notions, going back at least as far as Plato, and most widely discussed by the Stoics, that reason is what unites humankind and the gods, and that reason is therefore what separates humankind from the animals.[13]

However, in Jewish tradition humankind includes all those born of human parents.[14] Accordingly, this Platonic ontology and its philosophical anthropology are insufficient to ground an ethics that embraces all of humankind so defined. For this anthropology essentially identifies humanity *in se* with reason as opposed to more modestly seeing reason as an excellence to be developed by humans whenever they can and as much as they can. It provides no way of designating those of humankind who are without this property as essentially participating in human community. In our day especially, when essential humanness is denied by some to those at the edges of human life — the unborn, the permanently and severely retarded, the irrevocably comatose — such an ontology and its anthropology are inconsistent with the whole thrust of the Jewish tradition on the issue of human personhood. The issue now is anything but academic, as it once might have been. Maximally, this anthropology must be rejected because it has been invoked as grounds for dehumanizing those at the edges of human life in order to kill them. Minimally, this anthropology must be rejected because even when its adherents avoid drawing immoral conclusions from it in practice, they are still unable to reject with adequate reason such conclusions when they are drawn by others.[15]

Positively, one can also conceive of the image of God as being the human capacity for relationship with God grounded in revelation. This positive definition avoids the identification of a capacity with any specific quality. A capacity is a participant in a relation, only having meaning when viewed from within that relation. As such, it cannot realize itself; it requires the other participant or participants in that relation for its realization. A quality, by contrast, is a property within a substantial entity, a potential that can have meaning even before it is actualized. Indeed, that is the case because it essentially actualizes itself.[16] Nevertheless, it is hard to make a natural-law argument

---

13. See Plato, *Phaedrus,* 248a; *Theatetus,* 176ab; Aristotle, *Nicomachean Ethics,* 1177b25-1178a8; Epictetus, *Discourses,* 1.9; Cicero, *De Legibus,* 1.7.23.

14. See, e.g., M. Niddah 5.3.

15. See David Novak, *Law and Theology in Judaism* (New York: Ktav Publishing House, 1974-76), vol. 2, pp. 108ff.

16. See David Novak, *Jewish-Christian Dialogue* (New York: Oxford University Press, 1989), pp. 129ff.

based on this positive concept of the image of God, what might be called "covenantal possibility," inasmuch as it requires some sort of positive affirmation of revelation on the part of those to whom the argument is being addressed. Its constitution of human nature can only be made retroactively from revelation; as such, its logic is like that of a Kantian *a priori*.[17] At best, it works well in Jewish-Christian dialogue, where a covenantal affirmation can be assumed on both sides of the dialogue.[18] But natural-law discourse must be able to include nonbelievers as well. That is why it might be better, for purposes of a natural-law argument, to conceive of the idea of the image of God negatively.

To conceive of the idea of the image of God negatively is quite akin to the tradition of *via negativa*, which attempts to determine what God is *not* in order to move up to a knowledge of what God *is*.[19] In our case at hand, the *via negativa* helps us to determine what humankind is not, thereby preparing us to know what humankind is. That positive knowledge, at least for Jews and Christians, can only come from God's revelation — namely, where human identity in relationship *with* God is concretely realized. This *via negativa* can be better appreciated when we look at the etymology of the Hebrew term for the "image of God," which is *tselem elohim*. A plausible etymology of the word *tselem* is that it might come from the noun *tsel*, which means a "shadow." Now whereas an "image" (Greek *eikōn*; Latin *imago*) positively reflects *what* is being "imaged," a shadow only indicates that something lies behind the blank form that is cast.[20] A shadow is more primitive than an image since it is more inchoate. Unlike an image that gives us positive knowledge of form *(eidos)*, a shadow only gives us negative knowledge. It is a bare outline that simply tells us that something is there *(Dasein)*, but not what it is.[21] It is akin to what Spinoza meant by his identification of *determinatio* and *negatio*.[22] Minimally, a shadow only indicates that something lies behind it.

This understanding of shadow prevents us from making two erroneous

17. Thus Kant writes, "In the order of time [*Der Zeit nach*], therefore, we have no knowledge antecedent [*vorher*] to experience, and with experience all our knowledge begins [*fängt alle an*]. But though all our knowledge begins [*anhebt*] with experience, it does not follow that all arises out of [*aus*] experience." *Critique of Pure Reason*, B1.

18. See Novak, *Jewish-Christian Dialogue*, pp. 141ff.

19. See Maimonides, *Guide of the Perplexed*, 1.58.

20. For example, "Man walks about as a mere shadow [*be-tselem*]" (Ps. 39:7).

21. Cf. Philo, *Legum Allegoria*, 3.31.96, who employs the etymology of "shadow" *(skia)*, but then identifies it with a positive "image" *(eikōn)*. Cf. Heb. 10:1 for the emphasis of *eikōn* as positively transcending *skia*.

22. Spinoza, *Epistola*, no. 50, in *Opera*, ed. J. van Vloten and J. P. N. Land (The Hague: Martinus Nijhoff, 1914), vol. 3, p. 173.

assumptions about human persons. First, it prevents us from assuming that what is there comes from ourselves. It thus reminds us that everything we can possibly say about the shadow is only tentative until the real presence behind it makes itself known. To learn from Karl Jaspers, human existence intends transcendence, and to deny that is to confine human existence to a prison of its own making, to confine it to the epitome of what is unnatural for it.[23] Second, this understanding of shadow prevents us from appropriating the shadow into any of our own schemes. The shadow itself is *nothing* without its connection to what lies behind it. As a shadow of something *else*, it limits what use we can make of the space that it occupies. One can thus see the relation of the shadow to its source as limiting our pretension, both theoretical and practical. It is quite similar in its logic to the way Kant constitutes the relation of phenomena to the mysterious *Ding an sich*, the "thing-in-itself" that lies behind them and is never subsumed in them.[24]

Translating this into a philosophical anthropology, which is the proper juncture of ontology and natural law ethics, is to present a theory of human nature. This enables us to better see how such a *via negativa* works in terms of a minimal — hence most immediately universal — notion of the image of God. For if the human person is the "shadow of God," then even before God presents himself to us in revelation, we still have some apprehension of why the human person cannot be definitely categorized by any category by which we determine the nature of the things of the world. Any such categorization, including the category of *animal rationale*, reduces the human person to a merely worldly entity. It is thus a distortion of humankind's true being, especially when put into human practice. The things of the world, humans can name; their own name, however, can only come from beyond.[25] No matter how much humans might share with the other creatures in the world, they are always *in* the world, but never truly *of* it. Any attempt to reduce human persons to some worldly category is a distortion of truth, and it inevitably leads to acts of great injustice against humans as well.

The force of this negative anthropology, as it were, comes out in the great insight of the first-century Sage Akibah ben Joseph:

> Rabbi Akibah used to say that man [*adam*] is beloved being created in the image [*be-tselem*]. It is an additional act of love [*hibbah*] that it is made

---

23. See Jaspers, *Philosophy,* vol. 3, trans. E. B. Ashton (Chicago and London: University of Chicago Press, 1971), p. 164.

24. See Kant, *Critique of Pure Reason,* B311.

25. See *Tanhuma:* Pequdei (Jerusalem: Levin-Epstein, 1964), no. 3 re Eccles. 6:10. Cf. *Bereshit Rabbah* 17.4 re Gen. 2:20.

known to him that he is created in the image as Scripture states, "in the image of God [*be-tselem elohim*] He made man" (Genesis 9:6).[26]

Following Rabbi Akibah's line of thought, we could say that even before revelation, humans have some inchoate notion of their special status, and that it is beyond anything one could get from the world. But only in revelation do humans learn the truth from the One who is the source of that worth, which is that these humans are loved by this God. And through positive commandments that give the covenant concrete content, humans are enabled to respond to that love as their desired end.[27] But all of this is preceded by a ground-clearing, as it were, a *via negativa*. This is the necessary precondition for being able to receive the positive truth of revelation. Nevertheless, even without revelation, which in Jewish tradition always *precedes* revelation, one can take this essential limitation of human pretense as knowledge that can well inform human action. Only when human finitude has been properly accepted can God's light shine through into the world.

Ultimately, we affirm the worth of every human person because we believe somehow or other that we are all the objects of God's concern. To apprehend that concern and Who is so concerned for us is the desire of all desires. That desire is so powerful, so urgent, that we cannot suppress it to wait for confirmation of the reality of its goal, to wait for the truth of the Subject of that concern to be revealed to us. It is, indeed, the greatest proof of our own unique existence as humans. One could well say, "I desire, therefore I am" *(cupio ergo sum)*. Without that desire, I am something much less, a disposable thing of the world. It is that desire which enables me to pray even without any real assurance that my prayer is heard. "Towards you [*negdekha*] O Lord is my whole desire [*kol ta'avati*]; let not my cry be hidden from you" (Ps. 38:10).[28]

This desire of all desires is our craving to be known more than it is our aspiration to know. Hence our apprehension of the goal, or this desire must always outstrip our comprehension of it. Our existence intends more transcendence than our action does or could do. That is so whether our action be thought or deed. Moreover, to regard any human person as anything less than the object of God's concern is to fundamentally deny the true intention of his or her existence — and our own, even if the goal of that intention is only to be found in our desire of it. "Whoever belittles [*lo'eg*] the poorest one blas-

---

26. M. Avot 3.14.

27. See Y. Berakhot 9.5/14d.

28. This follows the interpretation of R. Judah Halevi. See *Selected Poems of Jehudah Halevi*, trans. N. Salaman (Philadelphia: Jewish Publication Society, 1924), p. 87. Cf. Augustine, *Confessions*, 1.1.

phemes his Maker" (Prov. 17:5).[29] No one can desire God's concern for himself or herself alone without denying the very meaning of that concern. Its very operation can only be apprehended as being for more than one existence. It is the very opposite of the narcissism of wanting "not universal love but to be loved alone," as the poet W. H. Auden once put it.[30] Thus our desire to apprehend this concern is the epitome of our existence as communal beings. Our desire can only be answered in the company of those whose desire is for it with us.

Only in human community can we properly wait for God. That is why natural law is manifest to us as moral law, which orders our interhuman relationships. That is what connects it to the law of God.

29. See B. Kiddushin 33a; also, Nahmanides, *Torat Ha'adam*, in *Kitvei Ramban II*, ed. C. B. Chavel (Jerusalem: Mossad ha-Rav Kook, 1963), p. 128.

30. "September 1, 1939," in *Seven Centuries of Verse*, ed. A. J. M. Smith (New York: Scribner, 1957), p. 687.

10 Natural Law, Universalism, and Multiculturalism (1998)

There are two ways of engaging in natural-law thinking. One way, which is epitomized by Saadia and Maimonides, is to speculate teleologically — namely, to reflect on what the ends of law are and how natural-law precepts are the proper means to fulfill them.[1] The "nature" in *natural* law in this way of thinking is an all-encompassing whole, each of whose parts is a good attracting intelligent human action. The other way is to reflect on the inherent negative limits of the human condition and to see law as the way of practically affirming the truth of that limitation of a finite creature, a limitation apprehended by its intelligence. The "nature" in *natural* law in this way of thinking is internal structure — that is, what limits personal and communal pretensions.[2]

The actual content of the law comes from specific positive law-making. It is the ordering of the singular substance of a historical culture for the sake of those ends the authorities in that culture see as good and as thus truly worthy of its members, ends about which the members of the community can be persuaded. In Judaism, those ends are covenantal. Natural law is a contributing factor in that law-making, but it is never the only factor. Hence natural law does not function as the normative whole of which positive law is the applied part thereof. Positive law is not deduced from natural law, but is only explained and guided by it. Its function, then, is essentially heuristic. Accordingly, even when natural law is invoked as the teleological justification for

---

1. David Novak, *Natural Law in Judaism* (Cambridge: Cambridge University Press, 1998), pp. 125ff.

2. Thus natural law is a limit *(peras)*, but not a *telos*. Borrowing from Aristotle: every *telos* is a *peras*, but not every *peras* is a *telos*. See *Metaphysics*, 1022a14.

some positive legislation, as in cases of the invocation of the principle of the common good, that invocation is penultimate.[3] That is, the common good is instrumental; it is for the sake of the real ultimate ends of *that* community.[4] Neither negative limits nor positive means are those ultimate ends. And the difference between them is that the negative limits are more general than the positive means; hence they are more abstract and so more easily recognizable as natural law.

The relation of negative form and positive content might be illumined if we recall how Aristotle constituted the relation of justice *(dikaiosynē)* and friendship *(philia)*. Justice is the overall minimal structure required for any interhuman relationship worthy of its human members.[5] Friendship is the actual content of such relationships at the direct personal level. But, whereas the most basic forms of justice might be taken as universal, the highest form of friendship, which for Aristotle is when two persons share qualities they both regard as good, depends to a large extent on what their own culture specifically values as good.[6] Whatever law could contribute to this positive state of human affairs would have to be based on the lawgiver's vision of the specific goals of the culture in which he or she lives.[7]

In the first way of thinking, the locus of concern in natural-law theory is with the question of *good* — that is, the positive state of affairs for which humans are to ultimately act. In the second way of thinking, however, the locus of concern is with the question of *truth*, which, in its critical function, is primarily a negation of the arrogant pretensions of humans acting as if they

3. Thus invocation of the principle of *tiqqun olam,* which is the rabbinic equivalent of *bonum commune,* always turns out to be for the ultimate sake of covenantal ends. See, e.g., M. Gittin 4.1ff.; B. Ketubot 56b; also, David Novak, *Jewish Social Ethics* (New York: Oxford University Press, 1992), pp. 206ff.

4. For the difference between instrumental/penultimate ends and noninstrumental/ultimate ends, see Aristotle, *Nicomachean Ethics,* 1094a1ff.

5. Aristotle, *Nicomachean Ethics,* 1155a25ff. That is why Aristotle admits the possibility of at least some universal standards of justice (*Nicomachean Ethics,* 1134b20ff.).

6. See Aristotle, *Nicomachean Ethics,* 1156b8ff.; also, *Politics,* 1280a25ff. Following this last reference, one could say that if for Aristotle "friendship is the highest form of justice" (*Nicomachean Ethics,* 1155a28), then that justice is the more specific distributive justice rather than the more general rectifying justice (see *Nicomachean Ethics,* 1130b30).

7. See Aristotle, *Nicomachean Ethics,* 1155a22, where Aristotle recognizes the universality of the need for friendship *(philia),* but then, more specifically, concentrates on the lawgivers of the *polis.* But their criteria of *philia* would certainly be different from that of the lawgivers of other societies and cultures, who have other values. Let it be remembered that the *polis* is a uniquely Greek form of polity. Aristotle's constitution of *philia* presupposes the reality of the *polis.* See Alasdair MacIntyre, *Whose Justice? Which Rationality?* (Notre Dame: University of Notre Dame Press, 1988), pp. 103ff.

themselves were infinite. Therefore, it stands to reason that the first, more positive view of natural law will assign a more maximal role to it in Judaism, whereas the second, more negative view will assign a more minimal role to it.

Although teleology is necessarily connected to natural-law theory, the more minimal view of natural law that I propose requires that we first look at the more negative rather than the more positive character of Noahide law. And here I think that the data from the rabbinic sources are more supportive of this view than of the more teleological views. Also, this view seems to have more in common with modern "rights talk" than does more metaphysically constituted natural-law theory. That is important because this commonality enables Jewish insights into law and morality to be more easily introduced into current normative discourse, in which the language of rights seems to supply some of its most indispensable vocabulary.[8] That is, unless, of course, dogmatic secularism and the atheism it presupposes are also required for one's views to receive a hearing in the secular sphere.[9]

As even a cursory presentation of the Noahide laws indicates, six are negative and only one positive. Moreover, the positive one — namely, the requirement to establish a judicial system — is actually for the sake of the adjudication of cases involving the other six, negative precepts. In other words, it is a procedure that functions as a means to the actual social enforcement of the six others.[10] Therefore, it is reasonable to inquire into the essentially negative character of this whole doctrine. And this has a close connection to one of the main features of modern rights-talk.

*　　　*　　　*

Perhaps the greatest vulnerability of natural-law theory, both in ancient and in modern times, is its seeming obliviousness to and disrespect of cultural diversity, especially in normative matters. Natural law is taken as what is to be universal. But from where does one begin to constitute this universe? Those who take their natural-law inspiration from Plato and Aristotle must also become aware of the fact that they were speaking Greek to Greeks. It would seem that they mostly followed the assumption of their culture that non-Greeks, or at least non-Greek speakers, are really subhuman "barbarians."[11] Consequently, they were, in effect, attempting to conceptualize what was regarded in their

8. See Charles Taylor, *Sources of the Self* (Cambridge, Mass.: Harvard University Press, 1989), pp. 11ff.

9. Novak, *Natural Law in Judaism*, pp. 12ff.

10. See H. L. A. Hart, *The Concept of Law* (Oxford: Oxford University Press, 1961), pp. 94ff.

11. See Aristotle, *Politics*, 1252b5-15; also Plato, *Republic*, 469bc.

own culture as optimal human standards, when being "Greek" and being "human" were taken to be identical. (The Greek conquests of large numbers of barbarians during the time of Alexander the Great were an attempt to Hellenize their captives both physically and culturally.[12]) Moreover, the Roman concept of the "law of nations" *(ius gentium),* without which their concept of *ius naturale* cannot be understood, was originally an institution of Roman imperialism conceived for the rule over certain non-Romans living under Rome. And natural law as most famously conceived by Roman Catholic theorists is part of the teaching of a church that explicitly attempts to include all humankind within herself. Jews too must admit that much of what could be termed "Jewish universalism" is the hope of a kind of "judaizing" of the world, as it were.[13] All of this leads to a considerable credibility problem for a "universality" that is not, in effect, a reduction of the many particularities to one particularity, which only becomes universal by a process of elimination.[14]

The problem is not only the moral one raised above; there is also an epistemological problem. Universal thinking by very particularly formed persons seems to be an imaginative attempt to constitute a world that *would be the case if I were not part of the singular culture in which I now have been living concretely.* But does this world actually correspond to anything we have really experienced? Any attempt to locate some universal moral phenomena is so vaguely general as to be normatively useless. Such attempts to transcend cultural particularity remind me of a judge instructing a jury to "disregard the statement you have just heard," when a lawyer or a witness says something ruled out of order in court. Of course, such a judicial pronouncement is effective in preventing the introduction of such statements from explicitly becoming official points of reference during the actual deliberations of the jury. But it cannot be forgotten (and that is usually why it was made anyway, often with full awareness that a competent judge would most certainly rule it out of order in the trial). It will implicitly influence the thinking of the jurors who heard it, like it or not. Our imagination can tentatively abstract us from our own cultures from time to time, but we cannot transcend them by some nonculturally conceived Archimedean fulcrum in order to escape them, destroy them, or re-create them.

Instead of an attempt to find some universal phenomenon to ground natural law, it seems more authentic and more useful to see it as the constitu-

---

12. See 1 Macc., ch. 1.

13. See Novak, *Jewish-Christian Dialogue* (Oxford: Oxford University Press, 1989), pp. 57ff.

14. See Hegel, *Lectures on the Philosophy of Religion,* ed. P. C. Hodgson, trans. R. F. Brown et al. (Berkeley and Los Angeles: University of California Press, 1988), pp. 202, 371ff.

tion of a universal horizon by a thinker *in* a particular culture *for* his or her own culture. Here is where the doctrine of creation comes in because it does not allow any member of the covenanted community to ignore the world beyond the community facing her. It must be taken with utmost seriousness. (The minimization of that political reality very much correlates with a weak or nonexistent theology of creation.[15]) As we have seen already, that imaginative project is one where one conceives just what sort of a world revelation (the founding event of the culture) requires in order for the One who speaks to present himself in it. The coherence of that imaginative construction makes it plausible. The "construction" here is of the approach to the reality; it is not the reality itself that is constructed. It is like making a telescope, assuming there is something "out there" to be discovered, but which is unlike any object that could be seen by the naked eye. The object to be discovered must be believed to exist, even if there is no other way to see it except through the telescope. (Quantum Theory argues that such "telescopes" themselves are inseparable from the objects they telescope. That is a most useful analogue for natural-law theory.) Only that belief, functioning as a regulative principle, saves this type of natural-law thinking from becoming, in effect, an elaborate and unconvincing rationalization for a body of positive law (human or revealed) that is better presented authoritatively rather than by argument.

*   *   *

The coherent plausiblity of natural-law theory, when it is theoretically good, is complemented by work in comparative law and ethics. The fact is that there are commonalities *between* the universal normative constructions of a number of different cultures. That is especially the case when one looks at Jewish, Christian, Islamic, Greek, and Roman ways of thinking about natural law. These commonalities certainly do not verify natural law. They are themselves too general to do that, and their abstract speculation can never reach the level of universal morality.[16] They do not themselves directly correspond to a reality readily apprehended. But they do have correspondences among themselves, what some have called "overlappings."

Despite the minimal character of these overlappings, they do admit of further development, especially in a multicultural context, where enough people want it to be intercultural as well. (That is without, however, the pro-

<hr/>

15. See David Novak, *The Election of Israel* (Cambridge: Cambridge University Press, 1995), pp. 16ff.

16. Cf. Kant, *Critique of Practical Reason*, preface.

posal that it must become supercultural, which means one culture swallowing up all the rest.) And if this represents a desire on the part of people and communities to discover criteria for living together in mutual justice and peace, then perhaps this type of natural-law theory will have some sort of correspondence with the lives of the human subjects of natural law. In order for this type of correspondence to be valid, however, the test of its universality will be the extent to which it is able to be interculturally inclusive. Perhaps natural-law thinking can save "multiculturalism" from the moral dead end of relativism; and perhaps multiculturalism can save natural-law thinking from its all-too-frequent myopia.

II TRADITION IN THE PUBLIC SQUARE

Judaism and Multicultural Politics

11   Law: Religious or Secular? (2000)

Law: Ordinary and Extraordinary

All great legal debates are not about what the law is, but about why the law is to be. Such debates are extraordinary, not because they concern what is more unusual or even more bizarre than the subject matter of ordinary legal debates, but because they directly question the foundations of the law in a way these foundations are not ordinarily questioned. A legal conclusion in such extraordinary debates will not be soon relegated to the historical sidelines as something peripheral. Such a legal conclusion will quickly become the center of much future discussion and deliberation. When such debates actually reach the courts, we call the way they have been decided "landmark" decisions.

It is the business of ordinary legal debate to decide under which specific rule of law a particular case is subsumed. In ordinary legal debate, such reasoning simply takes what seems to be the proper specification *prima facie* and applies it so as to make the conclusion of the law the conclusion of the case. The underlying moral premises of this law, let alone law itself, need not be considered. In fact, much of the ordinary business of law requires this simple type of syllogistic reasoning in which the premises of the deduction are not critically examined. Judgment here is specific, not generic. In most cases, the stability of the legal system itself needs what is readily at hand, either law on the books or easily cited precedent. Ordinarily, questions of the foundations of the law need to be bracketed for reasons of efficiency. Indeed, that is the moral premise of ordinary legal decision-making — namely, that we invoke no principles deeper than what the case before us calls for so as to avoid seemingly endless philosophical discussion. In ordinary cases, such protracted discussion would unduly delay the delivery of justice.[1]

Conversely, it is the business of extraordinary legal debate to decide why a specific law is sufficient to bring justice to a particular case, or why that specific law is insufficient to do so. More often than not, such extraordinary judgment is exercised when a decision of a lower court is sent to a higher court on appeal. In such extraordinary debate, two types of extraordinary judgment are called for. When the higher court confirms the ruling of a lower court, the judges must give a new and better reason for the law first applied to the case in the lower court. When the higher court overturns the decision of a lower court on a point of law rather than on a point of fact, the judges need to show why this is so — that is, why another rule of law is more appropriate to the case before them. That too involves giving a new and better reason for the law now deemed more appropriate. On this level, surely something philosophical is required of our jurists, those who are called upon to decide such cases in our highest courts. Whether we get good or bad law from them depends on their philosophical ability as well as on their commitment to justice. However, avoiding the deep judgment required in landmark cases by refusing to recognize their extraordinary character threatens to leave the system of law without rational foundations at all. Surely these foundations need to be shown when the justice of the system itself is called into question on these rare, truly significant occasions.

Religion in the Law

There is no debate in our society today that is more important than the debate over the role of religion in a constitutional democracy. Religion has become a matter of extraordinary legal debate indeed. Like all great moral questions, it has inevitably come before both the courts and the legislatures. In both places, though, questions pertaining to religion have proven to be uncomfortably difficult to simply subsume under ordinary legal rules or to make the subject of new, intelligent rules. Thus the record of both the courts and the legislatures concerning religious matters is quite erratic because most of our judges and most of our legislators (and their clerks and aides) do not

---

1. The rabbinic admonition to judges to "be deliberate [*metunim*] in judgment" (M. Avot 1.1) can mean determining whether a case calls for ordinary, concise legal debate or extraordinary, prolonged legal debate. See T. Hagigah 2.9 and T. Sanhedrin 7.1. The rabbinic admonition about "delaying judgment [*innui ha-din*]" (M. Avot 5.8) applies to the needless prolongation of ordinary legal debate. See B. Shabbat 33a and Rashi, s.v. "innui ha-din."

seem to be philosophically reflective enough to deal with the moral issues that are unavoidable whenever religion is at the center of a serious discussion. Also, many of them have very little factual knowledge about religions.

In a democracy, when judges and legislators are not well-informed on an issue, they should seek the counsel of citizens who are better informed to help them make rational decisions in such matters. In fact, one could see it as both the democratic right and the democratic duty of those citizens who have some counsel to give those in authority to offer it, whether solicited or not, if for no other reason than that as citizens they too will be affected by jurisprudence or legislation in this area, either for good or for ill. In this lecture, here in the Law School of the University of Virginia, which past experience has taught us is a place where a number of our future judges and legislators are being educated, I am exercising that right and duty as my own in the form of the remarks that are to follow. I assume that is why I have been honored to deliver this Meador Lecture on Law and Religion today, not being a judge (or even a lawyer) or a holder of any government office, legislative or administrative (where law-like judgment may be required at times).

Too often the issue of law and religion has been limited to questions of the practice of religious rituals in public. We are used to debates about uttering prayers at public events, or the display of religious scenes on public property, or the offering of public aid to parochial schools, or the wearing of religious costumes by men and women in the military, or exempting from certain public duties those with prior religious duties. In these cases the question seems to revolve around the issue of whether the legal permission of such religious activity in the public square implies the public endorsement of one religion at the expense of all the others, and at the expense of those who have no religion at all and who do not want one.

Although the legal importance of such questions should not be underestimated, they do not really deal with the essential philosophical issue of religion in the law of our Western democracies. That question is not how law deals with religious institutions and practices within a realm already secular. The question is much more fundamental: Can anyone represent religion to be the basis of the rule of law in a constitutional democracy that defines itself as a secular polity? It is clear that in a secular polity, where a specific religious affiliation cannot be a prerequisite of full citizenship, one could not make a public argument to every citizen that the legitimacy of the state and its law is based on the authority of one's own historical religion, with its full set of institutions and practices. That is because historical religion is rooted in a unique revelation and developed in the tradition of a community who has accepted that revelation forever. But not everyone in the society is a member of that community or wants to be a member. Hence, acceding to any such specific religious argument would require religious conversion as its logical conclusion. Nevertheless, does that also rule out, *ab initio*, cogently deriving the law's secular legitimacy from a religious commitment that sees itself as being distinct from the acceptance of the full set of institutions and practices of a specific, historical religion? In other words, must the legitimization of a secular — that is, nonsectarian — polity be made from purely secularist grounds? Must the legitimization of the polity itself necessarily require atheism *de facto* if not *de jure?* Can one have religious reasons for the legitimacy of the secular polity that do not presuppose conversion to (or reconfirmation of) a traditional religious community? And where does this question most acutely arise politically?

The great moral issues, being of such political import that they quickly find their way into legal debate — such questions as abortion, capital punishment, euthanasia, and who may enter civil marriage, among others — are of far greater political import than questions of public displays of religion by private citizens. They are questions that are directly involved in what Professor James Davison Hunter of the University of Virginia has called "culture wars" (an English version of the older German term *Kulturkampf*).[2] The opposing sides in these culture wars are not to be described by the usual differentiations between "liberals" and "conservatives." They go far deeper than that, often crisscrossing over these rather simplistic demarcations. I submit that all of these great questions at the center of our legal-political-moral debates, if not yet our wars, can be reduced to one great question: *Does a person's moral adherence to a body of law require a god or not?* Could there be a source of the law itself (the *Grundnorm*, to use Hans Kelsen's important term) other than a god?[3] In one way or another, how a person answers this great question will determine how he or she answers all the great moral questions that are debated both in public forums and before the courts and the legislatures. Since all great moral questions are questions of justice, and since justice is the political norm *per se*, as Aristotle insisted, it is inevitable that great moral questions have immediate legal significance.[4]

The moral/legal debate over religion is deeper than just the question of the practical co-existence of religious practices and secularity, since most religious people are now democratic enough to reject any notion of governmen-

2. Hunter, *Culture Wars* (New York: Basic Books, 1991), esp. chap. 4.

3. See Kelsen, *The Pure Theory of Law,* trans. M. Knight (Gloucester, Mass.: Peter Smith, 1989), pp. 8-10, 193-95.

4. See Aristotle, *Nicomachean Ethics*, 1129b26.

tal coercion in the area of religious affiliation and practice (what we would now call "theocracy").[5] As such, they can tolerate those who are "secularists," those without any religion, just as they can tolerate those having a religion different from their own. And most secularists are still democratic enough not to advocate outlawing religion (as has been done under communist regimes). As such, they can tolerate those who are religious. After all, if democracy means recognizing the religious rights of minorities, certainly it means recognizing the religious rights of the majority. Most immediately, that means the right to practice one's religion in public. (The fact is that the majority of citizens in the United States and Canada have some public religious affiliation, and even more publicly profess belief in some god.[6])

Nevertheless, there is more to one's religion than that; it also has a body of moral teachings. Hence, does a person have the right to base adherence to the laws of the polity on his or her religious/moral principles?[7] Unlike the right to openly practice one's own religious rites, which can easily be tolerated as part of one's right to an individual "lifestyle," basing one's public moral stance on religious grounds seems to make a claim on everyone in the society. When the question of religion reaches this necessarily public level, even many secularists who are usually tolerant of religion become quite fearful because religion seems to be making a requirement of them, and without their consent. This fear is most often expressed by such words as "Who are you to impose your religious morality on society?" More crudely, it is most often expressed in such words as "Who are you to shove your religion down my throat?" As Kant best taught us, the logic of any moral argument must be capable of being universalizable — that is, directed to everyone without exception.[8]

At this philosophical level, which is not just a question of theory but which is also embedded in extraordinary legal questions, we finally get to what might well be the most important question any human being ever

5. The term *theocracy* was first coined by the first-century C.E. Jewish historian Josephus, and it meant a society totally governed by divinely revealed law. See Flavius Josephus, *Contra Apionem*, trans. H. St. John Mackeray (Cambridge, Mass.: Harvard University Press, 1926), 2.164-67. In later Judaism, that idea became a messianic desideratum. See Maimonides, *Mishneh Torah*: Kings, 11.1. Today, alas, it usually means, in the eyes of both its upholders and its detractors, a dictatorship of clerics, usually coming as the result of a coup d'état in a previously secular state.

6. See Stephen L. Carter, *The Culture of Disbelief* (New York: Basic Books, 1993), p. 4.

7. See Carter, *The Culture of Disbelief*, for a sustained cultural polemic against the type of doctrinaire secularism that would dismiss the democratic validity of any approach to public morality coming from a religious commitment.

8. See Immanuel Kant, *Groundwork of the Metaphysics of Morals*, trans. H. J. Paton (New York: Harper & Row, 1964), pp. 69-71.

asked: Is there God *(quod sit deus)?* Here the options seem to be mutually exclusive. Despite the attempt to create a neutral position called "agnosticism," one can show that agnostics are actually timid atheists, those who have not yet taken moral responsibility for their contrary stance regarding God. Thus I am reminded of the time I asked the president of a leading society of atheists what the difference between an atheist and an agnostic is, and he said "guts."

Since the connection between God and laws has been constant throughout most of human history, the question of God has inevitably become the question of what is one's basis of moral authority. It is hard to imagine a god who does not command. A normatively neutral god would be functioning at a level of human concern too shallow for people to take upon themselves the type of existential vulnerability necessarily involved in invoking such a weighty name as "God."[9] Even nonbelievers will still use the name "God" for superlative reasons, such as questioning someone's moral authority by asking, "Who do you think you are — God?" (Indeed, the most general name for "God" in the Bible is *elohim,* which means "authority": first divine, then human. We shall return to this point later.) The type of atheism that undergirds authentic secularism, by its inevitably vehement denial of any god, is just as concerned with the connection of religion and morality as are religious people. Authentic secularists know very well where the essential question lies, and why the stakes are so high in anyone's answer to it.

The answer to the question of whether your adherence to a body of law requires a god is not something where tolerance of principle can be cogently argued, however civil one might want to act toward those holding different principles. There are very good moral reasons for such tolerance of opinion when this argument takes place in a democracy, but at the level of principle, more decisive commitment is called for. Discursive pluralism need not lead to epistemological pluralism, let alone ontological pluralism. Truth is a greater issue than prudence. Indeed, the cause of truth itself requires that there be enough social pluralism to enable prudential persuasion rather than coercion to be one's modus operandi in public discourse. Anything more than that, however, presupposes the epistemological dead-end of relativism and the ontological dead-end of nihilism.

At the most theoretical level, on the one hand, we have the recent proposal of a member of the parliament of Canada that the name "God," mentioned in the first sentence of the Canadian constitution, be eliminated, and on the other hand, the occasional demand by some Americans that the United States be designated a "Christian" nation. These are the most obvious

---

9. See Plato, *Laws,* 885cd.

examples of the cultural debate over religion and law, but they are not the most important historically. There is little likelihood that even most secularist Canadians, in the interest of constitutional stability, would want to tamper with the opening words of their hard-won written constitution. And there is little likelihood that most American Christians, even if they are in the majority, would want to make all the non-Christians in the United States mere sojourners in somebody else's house. After all, even if America were to be officially defined as a Christian nation, deciding whose Christianity makes America Christian would probably lead to the type of violence and political disruption that Europe saw in the sixteenth and seventeenth centuries in the wars between Catholics and Protestants, or even to the way Jews and Muslims were treated for a much longer period of time in Christian Europe. Surely most Christians would want to avoid that happening again here. So the most important cases are not where religion itself is the immediate subject of the debate, but rather where religion underlies the debate, and where one's religious stance is the basic determining factor in moral decisions of great consequence in the lives of many citizens. A belief in the essential need for a god behind the law, or a denial of it, makes a real difference in cases that are (or are likely to be) landmark cases, thus affecting the development of the whole legal system and impacting many lives.

Needless to say, I cannot specifically deal here and now with these great moral questions in which belief or nonbelief in a god makes the difference in one's normative stance. Suffice it to say, however, that one can see the basic outlines of the connection between theology (or anti-theology) and great moral questions when one detects whether or not the term *sacred* is invoked in the analysis and judgment of these questions. (For example: Human life is "sacred." Marriage is "sacred.") Instead, I want to deal with the question of how one can see a god as either present or absent at the foundation of law itself.

Grotius, the Stoics, and Plato on Natural Law

Although there are some ancient precedents, the notion that law can be totally secular — without a founding god — is usually taken to be a distinct feature of modernity.[10] Many locate its beginnings in a famous statement by Hugo Grotius, the early seventeenth-century Dutch Calvinist jurist, regarded

---

10. Plato, *Laws*, 889e-890a. See also J. W. Gough, *The Social Contract: A Critical Study of Its Development* (Oxford: Clarendon, 1957), pp. 11-15.

as the founder of modern international law. He writes, "And what we have said would still have great weight, even if we were to grant [*etiamsi daremus*], what we cannot grant without wickedness, that there is no God [*non esse Deum*], or that he bestows no regard on human affairs."[11] Shortly thereafter he continues, "But even that Natural Law [*naturale jus*] . . . although it do proceed from the internal principles of man, may yet be rightly ascribed to God; because it was by His will that such principles came to exist in us. And in this sense, Chrysippus and the Stoics said that the origin of *Jus* . . . was . . . to be sought in . . . Jove himself. . . ."[12] This statement of Grotius can be interpreted in one of three ways. We shall examine the two more obvious ways now, and the third, least obvious way later.

First, the most common interpretation is that given both by religious opponents of natural law and by natural-law opponents of religion. For them, Grotius is saying quite clearly that there is a body of law adequate for the basic normative needs of any human society. This body of law is independent of any divine command, being accessible to human reason. So, *even if* (*etiamsi*, to recall Grotius's hypothetical term) it is *also* a matter of divine command in biblical revelation, that is essentially superfluous to the intelligibility and practice of this law itself.[13]

As for Grotius's disclaimer of any atheism on his own part, that could be taken as a simple concession to the political power of popular piety, which even a philosopher dare not explicitly antagonize.[14] Or we might say more cautiously that even if Grotius the Protestant believer needs God, Grotius the legal theorist does not. Thus the God Grotius invokes is much like the God of the English Deists some two centuries later — that is, a God who creates a world that is self-sufficient thereafter and who, therefore, steps out of the world picture permanently. But doesn't Grotius's God — at least along the lines of this interpretation — turn out to be a premise that the coherent explanation of the phenomenon of law does not require? Consequently, isn't this God dispensable from within the legal order by Ockham's razor in much the same way that Kant eliminated God as first cause from within the natural order?[15]

11. Grotius, *De Jure Belli et Pacis*, trans. William Whewell (Cambridge: Cambridge University Press, 1953), p. xlvi.

12. Grotius, *De Jure Belli et Pacis*, pp. xlvi-xlvii.

13. This can be inferred from Grotius's statement that "the Mother of Right, that is, of Natural Law, is Human Nature." *De Jure Belli et Pacis*, p. xlix.

14. Along the lines of this type of speculation, see Leo Strauss, *Persecution and the Art of Writing* (Glencoe, Ill.: Free Press, 1952), pp. 22-37.

15. Kant, *Critique of Pure Reason*, B637.

Second, this secularist interpretation would be a lot more plausible were it not for Grotius's invocation of "Chrysippus and the Stoics." The Stoics clearly did not eliminate God from their thinking about anything, least of all from their thinking about law. And a good scholarly case can be made that the origins of Stoic teaching go back to Plato. Thus, as the Talmud puts it rhetorically, "When we have the words of the master and the words of the disciple, to whom do we listen?"[16] Let us look, then, to Plato on the question of God and law for our interpretation of Grotius's suggestive statement. In so doing, we might very well discover that it is only the God of the Bible, and not "the God of the philosophers" (Pascal's famous distinction), who is dispensable for Grotius's natural-law theory, or at least for the type of natural-law theory he seems to be connecting himself to.

Plato raises this question in one of his earliest dialogues, the *Euthyphro*, this way: "Is the holy [*to hosion*] loved by the gods because it is holy [*hoti hosion*], or is it holy because it is loved by the gods?"[17] Then Plato has Socrates get his interlocutor, the pious Euthyphro, to agree that the holy is "a part of the just."[18] What emerges from this is that, for Plato, the gods are not absolute, but their authority comes from their participation in an ultimate order, which is here called "the just" *(to dikaion)*.[19] This order is what justifies the religious claims of the gods on humans the same way it justifies the moral claims of humans on other humans. Developing this notion in the *Republic*, Plato designates "the Good" *(t'agathon)* as the summit of this order of eternal, intelligible forms.[20] They are "ideas," not in the modern sense of being produced by human minds, but in the ancient sense of being realities which are capable of being thought by human minds in acts of truly intelligent discovery.

However, what is of vital importance to remember is that this higher order is itself divine. It is divine because it is immortal; hence, as Antigone reminded the tyrant Creon, although he can kill human beings, he cannot kill these divine principles. They will still be there after he is long dead.[21] They are not subject to the control of kings, philosophical or otherwise. That is why natural law is much more than what is postulated by human reason, which could just as easily take it away as give it. Human reason *per se* is the finite capacity of mortal beings. Human reason intends this divine order; this order

16. B. Kiddushin 42a and parallels.
17. Plato, *Euthyphro*, 10a.
18. Plato, *Euthyphro*, 12d.
19. Plato, *Euthyphro*, 12d.
20. Plato, *Republic*, 509b.
21. See Sophocles, *Antigone*, ll. 59-65, 173-74, 449-57.

does not presuppose human reason. It is discovered, not invented. It alone is autonomous. It is certainly more than procedural.[22] Being immortal, it is ultimate; hence it makes claims on humans by virtue of its irresistible attraction to all intelligences, human and godly. The truly rational human being, one whose desire is what Plato called philosophical *eros,* is one who aspires to be like the gods, who themselves participate in divinity eternally.[23] Philosophy, including philosophical law-giving, is the attempt to transcend our earthly, human mortality. Anything less than that cannot truly command rational human beings.

This divine principle, unlike the God of the Bible, does not itself make the laws. But just laws, even when made by human lawgivers, must find their ultimate justification in this living principle, which Aristotle, Plato's star student, saw as the supreme activity of intelligence *(noesis)* contemplating its own intelligibility. And Aristotle calls this reality both "the divine" *(to theion)* and "the God" *(ho theos).*[24] Common to Plato, Aristotle, and the Stoics, "nature" *(physis)* is divine, not as the sum of all entities but rather as the intelligible order of the universe by which all entities are governed. In the case of the human world, this is the order by which it is to be governed by those intelligent enough to be able to access it and translate it into human-made laws *(nomos).* Indeed, by so doing, these human lawgivers themselves partake of divinity. Law-giving is very much an act of *imitatio dei.*[25]

Since human rationality and human sociality are two sides of the same coin, this access to the cosmic order is of immediate political significance. Only a society whose law is based on nature is worthy of the moral allegiance of any rational person. Since this natural order is divine, it is different in kind from anything made by human beings by their own authority.[26] But those who are godly mediate between the immortal divine realm and the mortal

---

22. The problem with a merely procedural notion of natural law, like that proposed in Lon L. Fuller, *The Morality of Law* (New Haven: Yale University Press, 1969), pp. 96-106, is that it only provides a criterion of inner coherence for a legal system — that is, *how* to operate it well. But it does not provide a criterion of *why* the legal system could claim the moral loyalty of those whom it governs — that is, *why* it is to be trusted and obeyed.

23. See Plato, *Laws,* 899d; *Phaedrus,* 248a; *Symposium,* 202e; *Theaetetus,* 176ab; *Timaeus,* 68e-69a.

24. Aristotle, *Metaphysics,* 1072b20-30, 1074b1-4.

25. See Plato, *Timaeus,* 29e-30d; cf. *Republic,* 500cd and *Laws,* 624a, 713c.

26. The quintessential expression of non-divine, purely human authority is the dictum of the ancient sophist Protagoras that "man is the measure of all things useful [*tōn chrematōn*]." See Plato, *Theaetetus,* 152a. The term *useful* comes from the Greek for *hand (cheir)* — namely, what can be manipulated for humanly constructed goals *(technē).* See Aristotle, *Nicomachean Ethics,* 1140a1-20.

human realm.[27] One sees something like this vision — minus the metaphysics, of course — when Professor Ronald Dworkin becomes almost rhapsodic when talking about the role of judges in higher courts as "princes."[28]

Covenantal Theology

In common with the Platonic/Stoic natural-law theory, we cannot settle for any natural law without a god behind it because the immortality of a god is the only power that can possibly contain the human violence that would destroy the law itself. And only a god is superior enough in power and in wisdom to all humans for any human to listen to its commands without being able to say, Who are you to tell me what to do?[29] But is Platonic/Stoic natural law theory the only alternative to the type of legal theory that would give one group of humans (the rulers) absolute authority over the lives of another group of humans (the ruled)?

At this point, let us return to Grotius's statement about the possibility of law "even if we say there is no God." We have seen how Grotius's invocation of

27. Thus one can even see Kant's notion of autonomy along these same Platonic lines. When he speaks of "the Idea *of the will of every rational being as a will which makes universal law*" (Kant, *Groundwork of the Metaphysics of Morals,* p. 98), he is speaking of the self-sufficiency of the moral law itself (what Plato might have called *nomos kath'autos*), which is then promulgated by the rational being who knows it and thus wills it to be instantiated in the world. See Kant, *Critique of Pure Reason,* B843. In fact, in one place Kant explicitly calls the morally thinking/acting person one who "must make himself such a God [*einen Gott machen*] according to moral concepts . . . he must first of all compare his representation [*Vorstellung*] with his ideal in order to judge whether he is entitled to regard it and honor it as a divinity [*für eine Gottheit*]." See Kant, *Religion within the Limits of Reason Alone,* trans. T. M. Greene and H. H. Hudson (New York: Harper & Row, 1960), p. 157n. All of this follows from Kant's distinction between "commands of God" *(Gebote Gottes)* and "divine commands" *(göttliche Gebote)* in Kant, *Critique of Pure Reason,* B847. For Kant's admitted Platonism, see *Critique of Pure Reason,* B374-75.

28. Ronald Dworkin, *Law's Empire* (Cambridge, Mass.: Belknap Press, 1986), p. 407: "The courts are the capitals of law's empire, and judges are its princes, but not its seers and prophets. It falls to philosophers, if they are willing, to work out law's ambitions for itself, the purer form of law within and beyond the law we have." Cf. Plato, *Republic,* 473d.

29. Thus Pharaoh, whose self-acknowledgment of his own divine status was recognized by the Bible (e.g., Ezek. 29:9), challenges the divine authority of the God of Israel to command him to release this God's people from slavery to him: "Who is YHWH that I should listen to his voice?" (Exod. 5:2). The assumption inherent in this very plausible challenge is that Pharaoh would only obey someone generically different from and higher than himself. A major point of the Exodus narrative is that the God of Israel forces him to accept just that (see Exod. 8:6; 12:12) in spite of his "hardness of heart" (see Exod. 7:14; 8:15).

the Stoics could lead us to believe that he is substituting the god of Plato for the God of the Bible, which means placing God under the rule of the law's ultimate paradigm. Nevertheless, we should also remember that Grotius quotes the Bible to illustrate his points about the foundations of law. And considering the fact that he was a Calvinist Christian, the burden of proof is on those who would judge him to be a crypto-atheist, and even on those who would see his invocation of the Stoics as being more significant theologically than his invocation of the God of the Bible. Perhaps it is best to see Grotius's statement in the light of the biblical theology that was so dominant in the Netherlands (and elsewhere) both before, during, and long after Grotius's time. In so doing, we might discover a biblically authorized natural law, one that is consistent with biblical theology, but one whose precepts and whose theory need not be derived by the exegesis of specific biblical passages, especially not from explicit biblical precepts.[30]

If a natural-law theory without some kind of god soon becomes incoherent, then Grotius's statement might well be saying that even without the invocation of a certain mode of God's action, we can still have natural law. We have seen how that interpretation works in the Platonic sense of a divine realm above the function of the individual gods. In biblical theology, we of course cannot posit a divine realm above the individual gods since there is only one God. It makes no sense to posit a separate divine realm from the person of God when there is only one member of such a realm. Only a plurality of members of a class prevents any one of them from becoming identical with the class itself. Thus for the ancient Jewish theologian Philo, the realm of the forms becomes the primordial world God creates *(logos)*.[31] Unlike Plato, for whom the forms are what-is-there-already-to-be-thought, for Philo, the forms are the ideas or words made by the mind of God. They are projects from God, not what is already there for God. They are "ideas" in our modern sense of what is made by the mind, which can be seen as the modern attempt to supplant the creativity of God with the creativity of humans. That *is,* though, an underestimation of God and an overestimation of humans. Returning truly original ideas to the mind of God makes much more sense.

The way to interpret Grotius's statement in a way that preserves an idea of natural law and is faithful to the God of the Bible worshiped by Jews and

30. See David Novak, *Natural Law in Judaism* (Cambridge: Cambridge University Press, 1998), pp. 27-61.

31. See Philo, *De Opificio Mundi,* trans. F. H. Colson and G. H. Whitaker (Cambridge, Mass.: Harvard University Press, 1929), 5.20; and H. A. Wolfson, *Philo: Foundations of Religious Philosophy in Judaism, Christianity, and Islam* (Cambridge, Mass.: Harvard University Press, 1947), pp. 226-52.

Christians is to look to the ways the Bible names God. Despite the essential difference between biblical monotheism and Platonic polytheism, there is, nevertheless, more than one name of God in the Bible. That means that the one God manifests himself in more than one way. The two most frequently used names of God in the Bible are *elohim,* usually translated as "God" (*theos* in Greek; *Deus* in Latin), and the ineffable tetragrammaton YHWH, for which the name of "the Lord" is always substituted (*adonai* in Hebrew; *kyrios* in Greek; *Dominus* in Latin). A good case can be made that frequently enough "God" *(elohim)* is used to designate God as creator of the world and the One who sustains the world by engendering a permanent order within it.[32]

Unlike Platonic nature, this order of creation does not transcend what it orders; hence its presence does not signify the eternity of the world. It simply means that as long as the world exists, its order, its essential structure, will be coeval with it. Nevertheless, this order does transcend all the powers within the world. The whole is greater than any one of *its* parts, but not greater than all of them in concert. The cosmic order permeates its parts, and like them it too is created.[33] The internality of the cosmos is its inherent order, its *mishpat* in biblical terms, which is "justice" in the widest possible sense.[34] The tetragrammaton, on the other hand, designates the God who has elected Israel and is continually involved with Israel in a special covenantal relationship. "God" is the master of created nature; "the Lord" is, in addition to God's natural role, the master of historical revelation and historical redemption. "God" names the more universal but less intense acts of God; "the Lord" names the more intense but less universal (at least here and now) acts of God.[35] Could we not say that Grotius is expressing a theological tradition that says that some of God's law can be known without a direct revelation from God? In other words, we could say that "no God" *(non esse Deum)* here means "no revealed God," what Luther called *Deus absconditus.*[36]

Let us see how the particular name of God we invoke gives ontological foundation to the natural law we see ourselves duty-bound to obey. That requires seeing the political context of the law.

---

32. See *Bereshit Rabbah* 33.3 for this generalization as a staple of rabbinic theology; see also A. Marmorstein, *The Old Rabbinic Doctrine of God* (London: Oxford University Press, 1927), pp. 43-53.

33. See B. Pesahim 87b re Prov. 8:22; Maimonides, *Guide of the Perplexed,* 1.65.

34. See David Novak, *Jewish Social Ethics* (Oxford: Oxford University Press, 1992), pp. 29-33.

35. See *Exodus Rabbah* 3.6.

36. See Paul Althaus, *The Ethics of Martin Luther,* trans. R. C. Shultz (Minneapolis: Fortress Press, 1972), pp. 45-48.

The key political term in the Bible is *berit*, what is usually translated as "covenant." It denotes the ultimate context of all worldly relationships. We tend to confuse a "covenant" with a "contract," and so use the words interchangeably. That is unfortunate, since a covenant is much more than a contract. Indeed, as we shall see later, a contract is actually a diminished covenant, and one whose integrity gets lost when the covenantal connection is severed. Accordingly, whereas the idea of contract can be derived from the idea of covenant, a covenant cannot be seen as merely a glorified contract without distorting the idea of both relationships. A covenant is a relationship between two persons initiated and renewed in promises of fidelity made by each one to the other.

The first covenant God makes is with creation after human violence almost destroys humankind, and the earthly order along with them, at the time of the Flood. In this covenant, God promises the perpetuity of the natural order to Noah and all humankind after him. "As long [*od*] as there is seedtime and harvest, the cold and the hot, summer and winter, the days of the earth shall not cease [*lo yishbbotu*]" (Gen. 8:22). And directly following this, the minimal tasks of humans in the world are ordered. These tasks are to procreate and thus carve out of the larger wilderness a world fit for continued human dwelling, and to control violence so that this human dwelling not be destroyed as it nearly was when Cain murdered his brother Abel and when nature was perverted at the time of the Flood.[37] The reason for both of these primary tasks seems to be the same, being expressed as follows: "Whosoever sheds the blood of a human, by humans his own blood shall be shed, because in the image of God [*be-tselem elohim*] God made humans [*ha'adam*]" (Gen. 9:6).

The fact that God promises to let created nature in general endure establishes enough of an atmosphere for human nature specifically to endure. The duration of nature is a tangible result of God's faithfulness *(emunah)*. Truth *(emet)*, then, is the internal coherence of the natural order, a sign that it is endurable because of God's faithfulness to it. That is why our words can coherently correspond to it. It holds together so that we can say something consistent about it.[38] Human nature is that part of the natural order closest to our

---

37. In the Bible, Cain, the first murderer, is the founder of the first city, which might be a way of teaching that the purpose of human sociality, structured by law that is applied in a political order, is to sublimate violence into civilization and thus to protect humans from each other and from themselves. See Gen. 4:17. Genesis 4:13-14 implies the possibility of suicide. See B. Baba Kama 91b re Gen. 9:5.

38. See David Novak, *The Election of Israel* (Cambridge: Cambridge University Press, 1995), pp. 126-27.

own concern. Hence our faithful response to God's faithfulness to creation and its inseparable order is demonstrated in how faithful we are to the legitimate needs of our fellow human beings, both individual and communal. In a biblical sense, that is what could well be called "natural law." It is where our fidelity to the world and God's fidelity to the world coincide. It is what the Bible calls "the way of all the earth" *(derekh kol ha'arets),* and what the ancient Rabbis called *derekh erets,* which might be translated as "the proper way to conduct oneself within the world."[39] Since this *derekh erets* is described rather than specifically prescribed, one could also infer that it is something learned from the world. It is not derived from the voice of God directly speaking to us in revelation; instead, it is the echo of the voice of God that reverberates from our experience with our human sisters and brothers in our joint task to make the world a dwelling and not a cemetery. God speaks *through* their just claims.[40]

The main motif of biblical moral teaching is covenantal faithfulness. It is considered to be in the nature of human beings to make various covenants with each other, and all of these covenants look to the covenant at the time of Noah as their basic form. Furthermore, the covenantal character of biblical morality indicates a more dynamic quality to a society that looks to biblical morality as its political model than one finds in a society that looks to Platonic/Stoic natural-law ethics as its political model. The reason for this difference is that in Platonic/Stoic ethics — what Leo Strauss liked to call "classic natural right" — natural law is taken as the maximum general standard of all human relationships.[41] In more Platonic conceptuality, one can see the events of human histories as either being instantiations of the known form of justice or denials of it. One has to know the whole before knowing the parts therein.[42] But in biblical morality, whose basic principles, we have seen, need not be derived from explicit biblical norms, those basic principles do not function as a genus with everything that follows being its subordinate specification. There is always the possibility of new relationships that could not be deduced from the basic moral principles or norms of the law. The most that is asked of the formulation of these new relationships is that they not contradict the law already in place.

39. In the Bible, *derekh erets* refers to human mortality. See Josh. 23:14; 1 Kings 2:2. For the Rabbis, the term means how mortal humans in general are to conduct themselves without self-destruction. See, e.g., M. Avot 3.17; *Leviticus Rabbah* 9.3 re Gen. 3:24.

40. See Novak, *Covenantal Rights* (Princeton: Princeton University Press, 2000), pp. 142-52.

41. Strauss, *Natural Right and History* (Chicago: University of Chicago Press, 1953), pp. 120-64.

42. Plato, *Republic,* 501bc.

This feature of biblical morality has been a very important source for the main mode of political arrangement in our Western, liberal democracies: social contract. The question is whether social contract, or any contract, can be totally severed from its covenantal roots. If it can be so severed, then we can locate the point in history when the notion of a totally secular law really took hold. But if it cannot be so severed, then either we are forced back to these covenantal roots or we wind up with an insufficient idea of social contract altogether.

Social Contract

As noted earlier, Hugo Grotius is considered to be the founder of modern natural-right theory as well as the founder of modern international law. Indeed, these two roles can be closely correlated. The point of correlation is the centrality of contract. International law, especially the law of the seas, was something vital to the interests of Grotius's nation, the Netherlands, a small but highly ambitious trading nation at the time. The political security required for sustained and successful international trade can only be based on contract, since the parties to international trade have been separated by nature or history or both. They must, therefore, create their relationship by mutual agreement. The Calvinism of Grotius's Netherlands prepared him and the whole society he served, in an official as well as a theoretical capacity, for this new challenge because of its immense preoccupation with the biblical idea of covenant. A contract is derivative of covenant. Both have a temporal beginning, a *terminus a quo;* unlike a covenant, though, a contract can also have a temporal end, a *terminus ad quem.*[43]

The English Puritans of the seventeenth century closely followed the biblically based political theology of their Calvinist brethren in the Netherlands, especially the emphasis on covenant. We see this well expressed by the Puritan divine William Perkins, who in 1624 wrote, "We are by nature covenant creatures, bound together by covenants innumerable and together bound by covenant to our God. Such is our human condition. Such is this earthly life. Such is God's good creation. Blest be the ties that bind us."[44]

43. Thus, although marriage is taken to be a covenant (see Mal. 2:13-15), the written marriage agreement *(ketubah),* stipulating the various (mostly monetary) obligations of the parties, provides for settlement in the event of the termination of the marital relationship by divorce. See B. Yevamot 89a and parallels; Novak, *Law and Theology in Judaism* (New York: Ktav Publishing House, 1974-76), vol. 1, pp. 1-14.

44. John Witte Jr., "Blest Be the Ties That Bind: Covenant and Community in Puritan

The emphasis on contracts, both between private parties and between individual nations, was quite prominent in the Netherlands, and in its commercial and political rival, England. The fact that both were Protestant nations, with a renewed interest in distinctly biblical theology (paralleling Luther's *sola Scriptura*), no doubt gave a theological impetus for this otherwise mundane preoccupation.[45] Following this interest in the very phenomenon of contract, it is understandable how the idea of contract became prominent in the great debates that took place in both countries about the foundations of polity itself. Could the very foundation of a society, its political and legal legitimacy, be seen as a contract between the individual members of the society and their state? Could the *res publica* themselves be seen as contractual in essence? Could the state be founded in a *social contract*? And for some who were eager to explore that theoretical route, it seemed that there could indeed be a basis for society found neither in nature nor revelation — that is, neither in the god of Plato nor in the God of the Bible. If so, could we at long last interpret — or re-interpret — Grotius's "even if we say there is no God" in the most radical way possible — namely, *etiamsi daremus non esse deum in toto*? These questions bring us straight to the portals of Thomas Hobbes.

The key difference between Hobbes's natural-law theory on the one hand, and Platonic natural-law theory and the covenantal theology of the Bible on the other hand, is whether the location of our earthly nature is a dwelling we can care for or an inferno we can only protect ourselves from. That inferno is what Hobbes saw as natural right *(ius naturale)* — namely, "the liberty each man hath, to use his own power, as he will himself, for the preservation of his own nature; that is to say, of his own life."[46] That natural liberty is an entirely individual matter as, for instance, when a thief says, "It is my nature to take whatever I want whenever I want it." At this elementary level, there is no trust whatsoever between persons, who are competing for what are always scarce resources, other than the most ephemeral utility, what Plato saw as being like the temporary agreements of a band of thieves. It is everyone for himself or herself *(bellum omnia contra omnes)*.[47] There is a total absence of the kind of sustained and sustainable trust a genuine human community presupposes.[48]

Thought," *Emory Law Journal* 36 (1987): 579, quoting A. Kuyper Jr., *Die Vastigheid Des Verbonds* (Amsterdam: Kirchner, 1913), p. 104.

45. See Althaus, *The Ethics of Martin Luther*, pp. 43-66.

46. Hobbes, *Leviathan*, ed. Michael Oakeshott (New York: Collier, 1962), p. 103.

47. See Hobbes, *The Elements of Law: Natural and Politic*, ed. J. C. A. Gaskin (Oxford: Oxford University Press, 1994), pp. 77-81.

48. See Gough, *The Social Contract*, pp. 110-13.

Hobbes is acutely aware that no society can be based on this type of terri-fying anarchy. But how can we get people to keep their word to others — that is, to engage in the type of contract-making that is so necessary for any soci-ety, and especially for a commercially ambitious society, to endure? The an-swer is that at this level (this "state" or *status*), persons are so terrified of the loss of their lives and property at the hands of others that they are willing to sacrifice all their natural liberty to a superhuman creation who will protect them all for the price of their obedience. Whatever liberty they have left after this irrevocable bargain is what is too unimportant for the state to bother to regulate, which means what the state in effect gives back to them is a sort of revocable entitlement.[49] Hobbes continues the argument by telling us why this new bondage is better than the old uncertainty. Hobbes recognized that the ordinary business of society, especially in a society where the greater equality among the rising commercial class was fast replacing the greater in-equality of the old feudal order with its more fixed status levels, was becom-ing increasingly characterized by more flexible contractual arrangements. The main question he had to answer was, therefore: Why should people be faithful to their contracts? Why should people keep the promises that initiate these contractual relationships?

Hobbes's answer about the power of the state to enforce contracts, first and foremost the social contract between the state and its citizens, is based on the absolute priority of the power of the state. Like the myth of Gyges' ring in Plato's *Republic,* Hobbes assumes that human beings left to their own devices, which would be the case if they were invisible to public scrutiny, would not be capable of the self-sacrifice required for anyone to keep his or her word to an-other person.[50] Everyone would be everyone else's enemy *(homo homini lupus)* or, at best, everyone else's "fair-weather friend," which might be worse, inas-much as one can be more certain of an enemy than a supposed friend. Con-sidering how basically self-serving human beings are, no promise would be possible if the matter were left to simple trust *ab initio.* Fear of harmful conse-quences, then, is the greatest manifestation of that self-interest. As Hobbes puts it, "There must be some coercive power, to compel men equally to the performance of their covenants, by the terror of some punishment, greater than the benefit they expect by the breach of their covenant. . . ."[51] And at this point, Hobbes reveals the divine character of this "coercive power." It is "that

49. See Hobbes, *A Dialogue between a Philosopher and a Student of the Common Laws of England,* ed. Joseph Cropsey (Chicago: University of Chicago Press, 1971), p. 73.

50. See Plato, *Republic,* 359c-360d.

51. Hobbes, *Leviathan,* p. 113.

great Leviathan, or rather, to speak more reverently, that *mortal* god, to which we owe under the *immortal God,* our peace and defence."[52]

Following this, one could ask whether or not the power of this "mortal god" is consistent with the power of the "immortal God," who for Hobbes's readers, no doubt, is the God of the Bible. After all, isn't Hobbes's notion of contract quite similar to biblical notions of covenant? Doesn't the Bible threaten God's punishment if the covenant between God and his people is broken? The people are told, "You shall keep the words of this covenant [*ha-berit ha-z'ot*] and do them in order that you might succeed" (Deut. 29:8), and anyone who violates it is threatened with "all the curses of the covenant [*kekhol alot ha-berit*] written in this book of the Torah" (Deut. 29:20). And as the Talmud tells it in a theologically charged vision, God held Mount Sinai over Israel's head and told them, in effect, "accept the Torah or else."[53]

Nevertheless, the failure of the English (and American) Puritans to develop a biblically based political theology, cogent enough to truly counter either the Hobbesian version of the absolute state or the royalist version of the divine right of kings, might well be due to their greater concern with divine punishment as a consequence of breach of the covenant than with the divine faithfulness that is the antecedent, the ground of the covenant itself.[54]

To do better than the Puritans, biblical believers today who are committed to a democratic form of polity need a phenomenology of human agreement itself. This involves asking the most basic question: Why should I believe your commitment to me to do what you promise to do with me? In other words, why should I accept you as my partner? We have already seen one answer to this question: You can believe my commitment to you in what I promise to do with you because I fear the legal consequences of breach of contract. But that does not involve trust, and most of us see trust as an essential element in our human agreements. Many of us would not enter into an agreement with a person we regarded as untrustworthy, even if we were assured that we would not suffer loss by the breach of contract this untrustworthy person would probably commit. (We can always hire a good lawyer for that.) Breach-of-contract provisions in the law are like a life insurance policy: We want to know it's there, but we act as if it weren't there. In other words, we make provisions in the event of death, but we act now as if we are to live for-

---

52. Hobbes, *Leviathan,* p. 132. See also Hobbes, *The Elements of Law,* p. 162.

53. B. Shabbat 88a re Exod. 19:17.

54. For strengths and weaknesses of Puritan political/covenantal theology, see John Dykstra Eusden, *Puritans, Lawyers, and Politics in Early Seventeenth-Century England* (New Haven: Yale University Press, 1958), pp. 121-25; Perry Miller, *Errand into the Wilderness* (Cambridge, Mass.: Belknap Press, 1956), pp. 60-68.

ever. Death is a hidden horizon we prepare for, but it is not the purpose of our action here and now. So too it is with fear of punishment.

The primacy of trust itself is brought out quite well by a contemporary legal theorist, Professor Charles Fried, in his book on the foundations of contract law. He writes, "So remarkable a tool is trust that in the end we pursue it for its own sake; we prefer doing things cooperatively when we might have relied on fear or interest or worked alone."[55] That is a powerful insight, one designed to turn our thinking away from making contracts simply the instruments of our selfish interests. And so he implies that contracts must be seen as a specific manifestation of a deeper mode of interrelationship between persons. Could it perhaps be a sign of a covenantal desire on our part? Nevertheless, Professor Fried does not ask the obvious question: Why should I trust you? Why should I want to enter a covenant with you? All of us learn quite early in life that there are some people we can trust and others we cannot trust. What makes one person trustworthy and another person undeserving of my trust?

So, why should I trust you? It would seem that my trust depends on some knowledge of your character, of the type of person that experience teaches that you have been in the past and are likely to remain in the future. Surely we trust someone either who we know or who is reputed to be law-abiding. *He or she is someone who will not change his or her word to me because he or she is committed to an unchanging word.* The promise to me, then, must be part of that larger, more lasting commitment. Since humans in and of themselves are mortal, subject to death, the greatest of all changes, their commitment has to be to an immortal word, one not subject to death in the world. In biblical language: "The grass withers and the flower fades, but the word of our God [*dvar eloheinu*] endures forever [*l'olam*]."[56] For biblical believers, God's faithfulness (*emunah*) to creation and its veridical order (*emet*) is to be imitated by human fidelity to it, especially the rational discovery of the rights inherent in human nature.[57]

What does that mean? It means that I can trust you to keep your word to me because you are personally committed to a law or standard not of your own making. You will not be disloyal to your word to me because you are loyal to the word laid upon you by a power higher than yourself or by any other mortal human like yourself. That is why I can trust you and thus desire

55. Fried, *Contract as Promise: A Theory of Contractual Obligation* (Cambridge, Mass.: Harvard University Press, 1981), p. 8.

56. Isa. 40:8. For a rabbinic treatment of the theme that God's word sustains the world as its essential order, see B. Pesahim 68b and B. Nedarim 32a re Jer. 33:25.

57. See Gen. 18:17-25.

to develop a social relationship with you and all others like you. Because you are committed to truth in the way it has been shown to you, I can be reasonably sure that you will not deceive me. Minimally, a commitment to truth involves my saying what I mean and doing what I say. My commitment to truth begins in my abhorrence of liars and hypocrites. Liars construct the truth to suit their own whims; similarly, hypocrites distort the truth.

Does this mean, then, that the social contract can only be affirmed in good faith (in the original sense of *bona fides*) by those who have a god? In other words, can an atheist be trusted? This question is always thrown up to religious people by those who are quick to point out that there are virtuous atheists and religious scoundrels. An overly hasty answer to this question puts religious people into the position of having to affirm a religious test for citizenship in a democracy, and that is just as undemocratic as those doctrinaire secularists who seem determined to outlaw religion incrementally, step by step. The answer to the question hinges on what one means by atheism. The classic rabbinic answer was to identify an atheist as one who followed the Hellenistic philosopher Epicurus; hence they were called in Hebrew *apiqorsim.*[58] Epicurus and his followers did not deny the possibility that there are gods in the sense of superhuman cosmic causes — a possibility that cannot be proven to be impossible. What the Epicureans believed was that even if these gods do exist somewhere, they have no interest in human affairs, let alone any interest in judging human affairs.[59] Thus the Rabbis said such a person is one who denies that there is a law and that there is a judge *(leyt din ve-leyt dayyan).*[60] Certainly an adherent of Platonic/Stoic natural law is not such a person. (Indeed, here we see the basis of a moral alliance between Athens and Jerusalem.) But is there any such person at all?

In private, no doubt, there are such persons. For example, the type of princes for whom Machiavelli wrote are those persons who see the fulfillment of their desires for power as being their primary motivation.[61] But it is a mistake, I think, for religious people to quickly conclude that such egotists or libertines have a god in that which they desire. Since these egotists or libertines so identify themselves with their desires, there is not enough externality here to warrant calling the objects of these desires "gods." Be-

---

58. The Rabbis saw the Epicureans as those whom the faithful should "know how to answer" (M. Avot 2.14). See also Maimonides, *Guide of the Perplexed,* 3.17 re Jer. 5:12.

59. See Epicurus, fragments nos. 57-58 in *The Stoic and Epicurean Philosophers,* ed. Whitney J. Oates (New York: Random House, 1940), p. 50. See also Cicero, *De Finibus,* 1.28.

60. See *Leviticus Rabbah* 28.1; *Ecclesiastes Rabbah* 1.4 re Eccles. 1:3; *Targum Jonathan ben Uzziel* to Gen. 4:8.

61. See Niccolo Machiavelli, *The Prince,* chap. 8.

cause our desires themselves do not manifest themselves to us in lawlike fashion — that is, as *nomos* — it is a mistake to render our unencumbered fulfillment of them "autonomy." The gods come into the picture when persons seek public approval of their own desires. Thus the "morally debased person [*naval*] who says in his heart 'there is no God' [*eyn elohim*; Ps. 53:2]" only says that in private.[62] In public, this same person must acknowledge some judging authority *(elohim)* who, if not a god, must function like one, so that other people will want to do business with him or her and not lock their doors every time he or she approaches.

In public, everyone must invoke some god or other because there everyone has to speak normatively. One cannot participate in any public activity without acknowledging the need for law. The best example of that is speech itself, which requires laws of grammar in order to be intelligible, laws which no one speaker of a language could arbitrarily make for himself or herself alone.[63] Thus grammar commands a speaker how to speak correctly. Hence, just as a speaker desirous of promoting his or her point of view requires the prior guarantee of grammar to get his or her point of view across to others, so any person participating in society requires the prior guarantee of law to be there in order to fulfill his or her personal desires. And, surely, the fulfillment of these personal desires involves relations with other persons already there with us in society. (The primacy of *eros* as the archetype of all desire makes this point most strongly.) But if law is to intelligently order our interpersonal desires in such a way that the common good is properly served, how could that law be the product of the desires of any of those who need to be governed by it? Thus it must come from the will of someone not governed by it. Once there is an externally imposed law on our desires, here is a god of some sort or other. It would seem that we only want to obey someone generically different from and superior to ourselves. Thus, for example, once we discover our parents are generically similar to ourselves, that they are mortal like us and we like them, we have already divested them of the godlike status they had in our infancy. We now honor and respect them because of the command of the everlasting God, who is different in kind both from us and from them and thus prior to their claims on us.[64] The question, then, is not a god or no-god. The question is *whose god*.

---

62. The usual English translation — namely, "The fool says in his heart, 'There is no God'" — follows the Vulgate *(dicit insipiens in corde sua non est Deus)*. Nevertheless, the Hebrew *naval* denotes willful moral fault, not just intellectual obtuseness *(in-sapiens)*. See, e.g., 1 Sam. 25:25.

63. See Ludwig Wittgenstein, *Tractatus Logico-Philosophicus*, 5.4731, 5.552, 5.6-62, 6.13, 6.3, 6.373.

64. See B. Yevamot 6a re Lev. 19:3.

When it comes to a worshiper of the god of Hobbes, it is hard to find any good reason for trust. Such a person can only be held to agreements that have been legally formalized — that is, agreements that have been concluded in a written document subject to the law of contracts, agreements whose violation can result in court proceedings to rectify the wrong. However, this assumes that there is no natural communality between persons wherein trust can be established.[65] When there is such communality, written contracts are only necessary either for the sake of clarity in complicated transactions or where the parties are total strangers one to the other. Without such communality, we need "the fear [*mora'ah*] of the government, without which one person would swallow up another," as an ancient Jewish maxim put it.[66]

Even more profoundly, the Hobbesian situation is one where friendship is impossible. Yet as Aristotle pointed out, who would want to live without friends, even if he or she had everything else in life?[67] Along the same lines, an ancient sage is reported in the Talmud to have said, "Either friendship [*haveruta*] or death."[68] Friendship cannot endure where there is no trust, and how can there be trust if there is no standard to which persons are answerable both to themselves and to others? These standards "stand to reason," and they have long traditions which indicate agreement about them that cannot be isolated into a mere historical episode.

That is why, even though I might have to enter into a contractual agreement with such a person, one for whom nothing normative stands between him or her and the humanly instituted state, it is not something I would seek. In fact, I might well want to avoid it as much as possible. Even if I could be assured that the law would protect my interests that have been guaranteed by a written contract, such a person is not someone I would trust under any other circumstances. In other words, such a person is not someone I would want to be my friend. And even though only a very small percentage of the people I do business with in society are my friends, it would seem that if the vast majority of those who are not my friends could not be my friends under any circumstances, then such a society is a rather frightening place, no matter how many laws are on the books or no matter how well-armed the police are.[69]

---

65. Thus in John Locke's version of the social contract, even in the pre-societal "state of nature," there is still enough natural community so that "no one ought to harm another . . . for men being all the workmanship of one omnipotent, and infinitely wise Maker. . . ." See Locke, *The Second Treatise of Civil Government*, 2.6 and 2.9. Cf. Y. Nedarim 9.4/41c re Gen. 5:1.

66. M. Avot 3.2. See also B. Avodah Zarah 4a.

67. See Aristotle, *Nicomachean Ethics*, 1155a5.

68. B. Ta'anit 23a.

69. See Aristotle, *Nicomachean Ethics*, 1155a20-29, 1167b1-4; Aristotle, *Politics*, 1292b25.

One might well say that the reason our polities in Britain, the United States, and Canada (and others that have a connection to the biblically and philosophically informed morality epitomized by English common law) have not become Hobbesian-type tyrannies is because the majority of the citizens believe themselves obligated by a prior, divine morality, despite the fact that most of them are unable to argue for it theoretically. That is the job of philosophers and theologians morally committed to our form of government. Only such prior obligation can make our human rights natural rights and thus limit the power of the humanly created state, making it our servant, not our master.

Without such prior obligation and its protections, our rights as humans cannot trump the power of the state because they are derived from that very power which, without true covenant, can easily take away what it has given.[70] So those who would interpret Grotius's dictum literally, that we can have law "even without God" (etiamsi non sit Deus), and who claim that de facto atheism is the only cogent basis for commitment to a democratic polity, have no basis for rationally challenging the unjust exercise of state authority, which is the very antithesis of constitutional democracy. Ironically, those whose god is neither the cosmic order nor the orderer of the cosmos have their human rights protected for them by the democratic commitments of those who have a moral religion or a religious morality. But how, then, can our doctrinaire secularists attempt to exclude their very protectors from the conversation any democracy needs to justify its own life and future?

70. Cf. Ronald Dworkin, *Taking Rights Seriously* (Cambridge, Mass.: Harvard University Press, 1978), pp. xi, 198.

12 What Is Jewish about Jews
and Judaism in America? (1993)

American Jews or Jewish Americans?

It is certainly the prerogative — indeed, the responsibility — of the editor of a volume to determine its topic. The condition for acceptance of participants in any such volume is that they agree to address themselves to the topic which has been so determined. In the case of this volume, or, to be more precise, what our editor Professor Raphael has called a "consultation," we participants have agreed to address ourselves to the topic he has determined: "What is American about Jews and Judaism in America?" That is certainly in order. Furthermore, the quality of our consultation promises to be high not only because of the quality of the invited participants, but more importantly because the very topic itself is so intriguing. It definitely calls for hard thinking. Nevertheless, I hope I am not taking undue liberty when I deconstruct the chosen topic — to be sure, only for myself — and reverse the relation of its key terms. Instead of asking "What is American about Jews and Judaism in America?" I want to ask "What is Jewish about Jews and Judaism in America?" This I do for two reasons.

One, although I am a fifth-generation American, I am no expert on "America," not being a historian, or a sociologist, or a constitutional scholar. I am, however, a student of Judaism, specializing in Jewish law and theology. That is my personal reason. And two, my interpersonal reason is that I think my deconstruction of our assigned topic is appropriate because Jews and Judaism are far older than America. Jews have been Jews by virtue of Judaism far longer than some of them have also been Americans by virtue of America. It seems only right, therefore, to look at what is younger and more circumscribed from the perspective of what is older and more pervasive. Accordingly, the topic of my own essay is not extraneous to the general topic (if so, that would indeed be inappropriate); rather, it asks a prior question. Prior questions always have something to contribute to the discussion of subsequent questions. Hopefully, my reflections on this prior question will contribute something to this consultation on the subsequent question. For when this subsequent question is taken to be prior, which has been the case for many American Jews for many years now, it assumes that the perspective of the younger and the more circumscribed is adequate to understand the older and the more pervasive. That sets the ground, however, for major misunderstandings which, I believe, have characterized too much American Jewish self-understanding for too long.

Along these lines, I do not know of any better statement of the foregoing assumption than the words of a distinguished thinker about America, the late Jesuit theologian and philosopher John Courtney Murray. In 1960, the very year in which a Catholic candidate for the office of president of the United States was being publicly questioned about what was American about his Catholicism, Murray had the courage to write this:

> [A] Catholic . . . knows that the principles of Catholic faith and morality stand superior to, and in control of, the whole order of civil life. The question is sometimes raised, whether Catholicism is compatible with American democracy. The question is invalid as well as impertinent; for the manner of its position inverts the order of values. It must, of course, be turned around to read, whether American democracy is compatible with Catholicism.[1]

Mutatis mutandis, I think Murray's question can and should be asked by American Jews — namely, whether American democracy is compatible with Judaism. Or, to be more specific: What in Judaism justifies American Jews identifying themselves as "Americans"? Is the designation "American" in "American Jews" anything more essential than a merely accidental geographical location of some Jews during a certain period in history?

The Current Constitutional Debate

The question I am raising is logically the same question that the members of any religious community in America must ask themselves. Thus my quote

---

1. Murray, *We Hold These Truths: Catholic Reflections on the American Proposition* (New York: Sheed & Ward, 1960), pp. ix-x.

from Murray is for its logic and obviously not for its real content (which can only be the question of a Catholic). But the logical question is not just being asked, or to be asked, by members of religious communities; it is also the question being addressed by constitutional experts during the very bicentennial of the Bill of Rights. It concerns the relationship between religious communities and the state, the so-called church-state question. The question centers on how we are to read the two parts of the Religion Clause of the First Amendment to the Constitution.

The Religion Clause states, "Congress shall make no law respecting an establishment of religion, or prohibiting the free exercise thereof." The question of textual interpretation, which of course is the locus of a basic conceptual dispute, as we shall soon see, concerns the relation between the two provisions of the clause that contain merely sixteen words in all. The question is this: Does the first provision determine the meaning of the second provision, or does the second provision determine the meaning of the first provision? (Students of rabbinic exegesis will be well prepared for this question inasmuch as rabbinic literature is replete with questions about the proper relation between two juxtaposed statements either in the Bible or in the Mishnah.[2]) Here it is being asked: Does the free exercise of religion presuppose the disestablishment of religion by Congress, or does the disestablishment of religion presuppose its free exercise? Or, to put it in other words: Does the practice of religion outside governmental control follow from the government relinquishing such control, or does this relinquishment of control by the government follow from the priority of the practice of religion? Some of the most fascinating and learned discussions among constitutional scholars today are over this very question.[3]

I leave the question of actual textual interpretation to constitutional scholars and American historians. (The question of how to read a text is at the heart of much discussion about literature in general in our culture; and as we are all becoming quite aware, the way an authoritative text is read is always politically significant.) I do want to take up, however, the underlying philosophical question. To me it seems to be as follows: Does the state have to grant religious liberty, or does the state have to respect religious liberty? In other words: Is the state authoritatively prior to the exercise of religion, or is the ex-

---

2. Regarding the logical relation of juxtaposed phrases in the Bible, see, e.g., M. Berakhot 9.5 regarding Ps. 119:126 and Y. Berakhot 9.5/14cd. Regarding the logical relation of juxtaposed phrases in the Mishnah, see, e.g., B. Hullin 94b.

3. See Michael W. McConnell, "The Origins and Historical Understanding of the Free Exercise of Religion," *Harvard Law Review* 103 (1990): 1410ff.; Mary Ann Glendon and Raul F. Yanes, "Structural Free Exercise," *Michigan Law Review* 90 (1991): 477ff.

ercise of religion authoritatively prior to the state? I can think of no more important question for us to ask at this juncture of our common life.

Until very recently, the public voice of American Jewry seemed to be virtually unanimous on the side of the dispute that sees the first part of the Religion Clause as primary and the second part as secondary logically as well as textually.[4] The major issue is the necessary disestablishment of state-supported religion; the minor issue is the free exercise or the optional practice of religion by whoever wants to do so.

This is quite understandable historically. In those societies where there had been an established state religion, Jews — certainly at the time of the institution of the Bill of Rights — had always been second-class citizens at best, and more often than not, literal aliens. The memories of Jewish political vulnerability in European Christendom were all too fresh. The disestablishment of state-sponsored religion in America meant a new and exhilarating containment of Christian power over Jews. An essentially secular society, at the time a historical *novum,* seemed to give Jews a breathing space they had not had since losing their own national sovereignty. From the perspective of political liberty, secular America seemed to be at least just one notch below the full return to Zion itself. I do not think it is an accident that the most prominent Jewish jurist ever to serve in America, Mr. Justice Brandeis, himself a highly secularized Jew, argued that the most basic right Americans have is "the right to be let alone."[5]

As for the practice of religion, for Jews that being Judaism, it was to be a *Privatsache,* following the whole tendency of the European Enlightenment.[6] However, that philosophical judgment is now being exposed to increasing criticism, not only from non-Jewish sources, but from Jewish sources as well. The criticism has been on a number of important points.

First, this relation between religion and the state seems to be historically inaccurate. To relegate religion to the realm of the private, especially in the context of the republican thinking of the founders of this *res-publica,* would have meant the essential replacement of the authority of religion by the authority of the state in the lives of its citizens. The public held clear priority over the private, and religion was most definitely a public matter.[7] Indeed, in the Declara-

---

4. See Anson Phelps Stokes and Leo Pfeffer, *Church and State in the United States,* rev. ed. (New York: Harper & Row, 1964), pp. 100ff.

5. *Olmstead v. United States,* 277 U.S. 438, 478 (1928) (Brandeis, J., dissenting).

6. See Moses Mendelssohn, *Jerusalem,* trans. A. Arkush (Hanover, N.H.: University of New England Press, 1983), sec. 1.

7. See Glendon and Yanes, "Structural Free Exercise," pp. 501ff.; also, Michael Sandel, "Freedom of Conscience or Freedom of Choice?" in *Articles of Faith, Articles of Peace: The Religious Liberty Clauses and the American Public Philosophy,* ed. James D. Hunter and Os Guinness

tion of Independence, which many have seen as the real preamble to the Constitution for all intents and purposes, the very authority of the state is seen as being warranted and thereby limited by the relationship between man and "Nature's God," for whose citizens this God is "their Creator." The public character of ubiquitous nature took precedence over the public character of any particular human society. The very priority of this relationship made it something too precious to be determined by the state. Religion was already to be freely exercised by human persons; that was precisely why it should not be the business of the state in her relationship with those same persons as her citizens. To assume otherwise is to ignore the pervasive role of religion in the life of those times.

Secondly, this relation between religion and the state seems to be sociologically inaccurate about the life of our own times. The large majority of Americans consider themselves religious in one way or another. Religion is the basis of their moral judgments. One of their most important moral judgments is that the polity of the United States is worthy of their loyalty — even to be defended with their lives. Accordingly, their fundamental relationship with the state is justified religiously.[8]

To assume, therefore, that the state is to be above religion is to place Jews at odds with the vast majority of their fellow Americans. To those who would say that that is the danger of being a small minority, I would answer as follows. It is one thing to fight against those who would restrict the right of Jews to be Jewish in public, be it wearing a yarmulke at work or not attending school on Passover, let us say. Not to fight against that type of discrimination could only be justified by assimilationists, those who want Jews to be Jewish in the closet only, if at all. However, to fight against public displays of religion by the majority, who regard those displays as part of the religious matrix of their civil commitment, *and who are willing to allow Jews (and other non-Christians) the same right,* is politically stupid. I have great differences with the Lubavitcher Rebbe on many halakhic and theological issues, but I think his followers are far more politically astute by putting up Hanukkah menorahs in public places than those Jewish constitutional purists who spend much of their own time and Jewish communal money in the courts fighting members of the Christian majority who want to put up Christmas crèches in those same public places. Most Americans do not want to live in what my colleague and friend Richard John Neuhaus has called "the naked public square"

(Washington, D.C.: Brookings, 1990), pp. 72ff.; Michael W. McConnell, "Free Exercise Revisionism and the Smith Decision," *University of Chicago Law Review* 57 (1990): 1109ff.

8. See Richard John Neuhaus, *The Naked Public Square* (Grand Rapids: Wm. B. Eerdmans, 1984), pp. 94ff.

— that is, a totally secularized arena of our common life.[9] There is no reason, either American or Jewish, for us Jews to be in the forefront of such unpopular resistance to that sociological fact. It is unhealthy both for our own self-image and for our public persona to be seen by many of our fellow citizens as the leading proponents of secularism and secularization. In the light of this sociology, we ought to learn to read the Constitution in the context of current American culture — indeed, in the context of the profound religious tendency of American history. What Alexis de Tocqueville wrote about America in the 1830s is just as true today — namely, "It must never be forgotten that religion gave birth to Anglo-American society. In the United States religion is therefore commingled with all the habits of the nation and all the feelings of patriotism; whence it derives a peculiar force."[10]

Finally, to read the disestablishment provision as prior to the free exercise provision is, I submit, un-Jewish. For it assumes that the practice of Judaism in America depends on the largesse of the secular state to let us alone. In other words, we have to justify our Judaism by American standards. Jewish self-respect, however, would seem to indicate that the opposite should obtain — that is, only when we are already freely exercising our duty to practice and understand Judaism can we appreciate how it is prior to our participation in any polity willing to respect that duty as a fundamental political right. Therefore, the question is this: How do we justify the political right to practice Judaism in America by our prior moral duty to live by the law of the Torah?

Whence Jewish Duty to Be Loyal to a Non-Jewish Polity?

Ironically enough, the classical rabbinic sources are clearer in constituting the duty of Jews to obey non-Jewish authorities than the duty of Jews to obey Jewish authorities. Scripture mandates that Jews obey their Aaronide priests (Lev. 13:3ff.), their king (Deut. 17:15), their prophets (Deut. 18:15), and their legislative judicial body (Deut. 17:11). However, none of these institutions has functioned politically since pre-rabbinic times.[11] In fact, the only one of these

9. See Neuhaus, *The Naked Public Square*, pp. 78ff.

10. Tocqueville, *Democracy in America*, trans. H. Reeve (New York: Appleton, 1904), p. 488.

11. Regarding the cessation of royal authority, see Maimonides, *Mishneh Torah:* Kings, 1.3 (cf. Kings 11.3-4). Regarding the cessation of prophecy, see B. Baba Batra 12ab. Regarding the cessation of the Sanhedrin, see B. Sanhedrin 37b and parallels; also, S. B. Hoenig, *The Great Sanhedrin* (New York: Bloch, 1953), pp. 109ff. For a discussion of the general problem of the religious grounds for the re-establishment of Jewish political authority, see R. Isaac Halevi Herzog, *Tehuqah Le-Yisrael Al-Pi Ha-Torah* (Jerusalem: Mossad ha-Rav Kook, 1989), esp. vol. 1, pp. 134ff.

institutions still operating at all is that of the Aaronide priesthood *(kehunah)*, and its operation is purely in the realm of certain ceremonial privileges.[12] The most likely institution to be re-established politically is the legislative-judiciary body, the Sanhedrin. But we do not really know how its political authority was constituted — that is, how one became a member of the Sanhedrin when there were conflicting candidates for membership. This is surely the essential reason why the attempt of the late Rabbi Judah Leib Maimon to revive the Sanhedrin in the early days of the State of Israel got so little support even from his fellow religionists, let alone from secularists.[13] That is why, it seems to me, even the political authority of the State of Israel — the *Jewish State* — still lacks an essentially Judaic foundation, even though it has clearly assumed the role of a Jewish political necessity in the world today. But for now and for the foreseeable future, it cannot locate its authority in any of the Judaic institutions mentioned above. The historical hiatus between the loss of sovereignty in ancient times and its being regained in modern times has not yet been satisfactorily bridged, even by those who would like to see it bridged.

On the other hand, though, there has been no such hiatus between the participation of Jews in non-Jewish polities in ancient (and medieval) and modern times. Here experience and law have kept pace with each other. Here the ruling principle has been that of the third-century C.E. Babylonian Jewish sage and leader Mar Samuel: "The law of the state is the law" *(dina de-malkhuta dina).*[14] But how is such a radical principle Jewishly justified? That, of course, requires an analysis of the fundamental authority of the type of state to which Jews can be loyal and whose law they can in good conscience obey, and, conversely, the type of state to which Jews cannot be loyal and whose law they cannot in good conscience obey.

The first word of the principle, *dina,* implies that Jews are bound to obey the rules of a society where there is a system of law, or where there is what we now call *due process* of law. Maimonides points out that there is an essential difference between a coherent system of law where individual rights are impartially protected and a system of state robbery conducted at the whim of

<hr/>

12. See M. Gittin 5.8 and B. Gittin 59b; also, *Tur:* Yoreh De'ah 61 (and *Bet Yosef* ad loc.), pp. 309, 322, 331, 333.

13. For Maimon's argument, see his *Hiddush Ha-Sanhedrin Be-Medinatenu Ha-Mehudeshet* (Jerusalem: Mossad ha-Rav Kook, 1951). Cf. S. Federbusch, *Mishpat Ha-Melukhah Be-Yisrael,* rev. ed. (Jerusalem: Mossad ha-Rav Kook, 1973), pp. 92ff.

14. B. Baba Batra 54b and parallels. For the most comprehensive study of this principle, see S. Shilo, *Dina De-Malkhuta Dina* (Jerusalem: Jerusalem Academic Press, 1974). See also L. Landman, *Jewish Law in the Diaspora: Confrontation and Accommodation* (Philadelphia: Dropsie College, 1968).

those in power.[15] The contemporary legal philosopher Ronald Dworkin has similarly argued that this is the real difference between law and "organized brutality."[16] Of course, there have been numerous times in history when Jews have had to live in societies where there was no true rule of law, but such domicile could only be justified on the grounds of immediate physical necessity, not any sort of conscientious choice.[17]

The second word of the principle, *malkhuta,* is more problematic because it literally means "kingdom." Indeed, many ancient and medieval discussions of the principle assume that governmental authority is essentially the right of a sovereign to rule over his subjects and impose laws upon them, as long as these laws are not arbitrary or capricious. Kingship was considered to be the most pervasive and, in fact, the best form of government for both Jews and gentiles, so much so that the right of gentile kings to rule over even their Jewish subjects was derived by some from the right of Jewish kings to rule over their Jewish subjects.[18] Thus in the absence of Jewish sovereignty — that is, a Jewish king — the rule of a gentile king in civil and criminal matters was better than no rule at all. Here we see the logic of *dura lex sed lex.*[19]

Whereas conscientious Jewish participation in the American polity can be justified by the first word of the principle *(dina),* it can hardly be based on the second word *(malkhuta),* for the very foundation of this polity stems from the rejection of the royal prerogative in principle.[20] Nevertheless, this would only apply to those forms of kingship where the sovereign grants rights to his subjects *ab initio.* Even in the Middle Ages, though, there were views of limited monarchy where the monarch's right to rule is based on the prior consent of the ruled. Along these lines, the eleventh-century French commentator Rabbi Samuel ben Meir (Rashbam) interpreted the foundation of the principle as follows:

> All the taxes and levies and legal procedures that the kings regularly enforce in their kingdom have the status of law [*dina*]. This is because all the

15. Maimonides, MT: Robbery, 5.18. See also Nahmanides, *Hiddushei Ha-Ramban* to B. Baba Batra 54b.

16. Dworkin, *Taking Rights Seriously* (Cambridge, Mass.: Harvard University Press, 1978), p. 205.

17. See, e.g., Maimonides, *Commentary to the Mishnah:* Avodah Zarah 1.5.

18. See Meiri, *Ber Ha-Behirah:* Baba Kama 113a, ed. Schlesinger, 3rd rev. ed. (Jerusalem: n.p., 1967), p. 329; also, Shilo, *Dina De-Malkhuta Dina,* pp. 77ff.

19. See B. Sanhedrin 39b regarding Ezek. 5:7 and 11:12.

20. As the Declaration of Independence states, ". . .governments are instituted among men, deriving their just powers from the consent of the governed. That whenever any form of government becomes destructive of these ends, it is the right of the people to alter or to abolish it and to institute new government."

subjects of the kingdom [*benai ha-malkhut*] willingly accept for themselves [*meqablim alehem mirtsonam*] the statutes and ordinances of the king. Therefore, it is complete law [*din gamur hu*]. Accordingly, anyone who takes possession of his fellow subject's property when authorized to do so by the king's law [*hoq ha-melekh*] enforced in the municipality is not guilty of robbery [*gezel*].[21]

The assumption here is that in principle Jews too are among those who have agreed to the rule of the king. And in this theory, the king is only an example of a freely chosen authority.

Of course, at the time of the writing of this justification, Jewish participation in the body politic was different from that of the other subjects of the king. Jews were regarded as an alien corporate body within the body politic, an alien body whose very presence was based on an explicit contract with the sovereign.[22] The relationship between the sovereign and his Christian subjects, however, was based on a more original tacit agreement between them, one generally regarded as far less conditional — indeed, one divinely ordained. (Such was the case until the English revolution in the seventeenth century, and even more so until the American and French revolutions in the eighteenth century.[23])

If one looks at the political philosophy of Locke, which had such a profound influence on the founders of the American republic a century later, and compares it with Rashbam's theory of kingship (which was not original to him, but typical of his time and place), one sees an important point in common concerning the consent of the governed. The difference between them, however, is that the type of contract Rashbam describes, which is without direct divine ordination of rulership, in his day really only applied to the relationship between the monarch and *aliens* like the Jews. But by the time of Locke, it was meant to apply to the relationship of *every citizen* with his government.[24] What happened as the result of the American Revolution is that this theory of government became a political reality. This concept of the essentially secular foundation of the political realm would seem to Judaically justify Jewish advocacy of a consistent secularism in American political and legal discourse. It would seem to justify the notion that the foun-

21. *Talmud Commentary:* B. Baba Batra 54b, s.v. "ve-he-amar Shmuel."

22. See Salo W. Baron, *A Social and Religious History of the Jews* (New York: Columbia University Press, 1966), vol. 9, pp. 3ff.

23. See F. Kern, *Kingship and Law in the Middle Ages,* trans. S. B. Chrimes (Oxford: Blackwell, 1939), pp. 5ff.

24. See Locke, *Second Treatise of Government* (1690), chap. 7.

dation of the polity is one of explicit contract between human beings themselves alone, what has become known as "the social contract." But in the remainder of this essay I shall attempt to show that this conclusion is in truth myopic.

Natural Law

Despite his use of contract language in explaining the principle "The law of the state is the law," Rashbam — or any traditional Jewish thinker, for that matter — certainly did not regard the presence of polity *per se* in human life to be founded in contract. Instead, it is part of the very cosmic order created by God. That is why (at about the same time as Rashbam) Maimonides can express the principle of Aristotle that "Man is a political life by nature" as being totally in harmony with the teaching of the Torah.[25] As such, it is not that contracts make society possible, but that society makes contracts possible. Contracts already presuppose that human beings are living a basically common life together. Thus the norm that contracts are to be kept *(pacta sunt servanda)* assumes that those contracting with each other already have a sense of what it means to be obligated by a norm. Clearly Rashbam (who probably never read Aristotle) did not mean that the contractual relationship between the king and his subjects was the primary political reality. Instead, it is simply a specific modification of a more primary political reality. What is that more primary political reality?

An answer to this question begins to emerge when we look at the third word in the principle, *dina*, meaning "law" — namely, "The law of the state is the law." What is the referent of this repetition of the word *dina?* Certainly it is not a tautology. It seems, therefore, to refer either to Jewish law or to law in general. If it refers to Jewish law, then we are left with the position of Rashbam — namely, Jews are participants in the state and are bound to obey its law by virtue of the right to contract given them by their own unique law.[26] Hence their participation in any such state is rather peripheral to their basic Jewish concern with the Torah itself.

If, however, this second use of the word *dina* refers to law in general, then Jews are participants in the state by virtue of law itself, which is a necessary condition even of their own unique law, the Torah. In most lists of the Noahide laws, which are the basic laws the Rabbis saw as binding all human-

---

25. Maimonides, *Guide of the Perplexed,* 2.40.
26. See T. Kiddushin 3.8; B. Ketubot 56a and parallels.

kind, the rule of law itself *(dinim)* is the very first norm.[27] According to Maimonides, the full law of the Torah completes what began in the Noahide law.[28] Or, as the Talmud put it earlier, "Nothing prohibited to the gentiles is permitted to Israel."[29] This, as I have long argued in many places, is the Jewish version of the idea of natural law.[30]

Indeed, the very word *din* in rabbinic Hebrew means that which stands to reason, what is *ratio per se,* as when the Rabbis say about the basic Noahide laws that "reason would have required that they be written [*din hu she-yikatevu*]" even if they had not been revealed in the Torah.[31] Along these lines it should be noted that the great commentator Rashi, the grandfather and teacher of Rashbam, when commenting on a text seen by the Talmud as a precedent for the principle "The law of the state is the law [*dina*]," notes that Noahides are commanded about proper adjudication *(al ha-dinin).*[32] Here we have the most exact connection of *dina* with *din* — that is, with the idea of law *per se.*

Jewish opponents of the idea of natural law (not unlike non-Jewish religious opponents of it) have generally based their opposition to it on the fact that it seems to essentially compromise the fundamental authority of divine commandments in human life.[33] From their point of view, then, seeing *dina* as natural law rather than contracted law would not make it any less peripheral to basic Jewish concerns. Since both seem equally secular in their meaning, contract is probably to be preferred simply because it is easier to argue for than natural law, with all the controversies surrounding the latter.

Although natural law began to assume this secular meaning in the seventeenth century in the writings of Hugo Grotius, and was already taken for granted in the nineteenth century in the writings of Hermann Cohen, in its more classical versions natural law was clearly a religious doctrine.[34] It was based on the doctrine that even though God's law is more specifically known

27. See David Novak, *The Image of the Non-Jew in Judaism: An Historical and Constructive Study of the Noahide Laws* (New York and Toronto: Edwin Mellen, 1983), esp. chap. 2.

28. Maimonides, MT: Kings, 9.1.

29. B. Sanhedrin 59a.

30. See, e.g., David Novak, "Natural Law, Halakhah, and the Covenant," *Jewish Law Annual* 7 (1988): 43ff.

31. B. Yoma 67b.

32. *Talmud Commentary:* B. Gittin 9a, s.v. "huts." See also R. Simon ben Zemah Duran, *Sefer Tashbets* (Lemberg: Salat, 1891), vol. 1, no. 78.

33. See, e.g., Marvin Fox, "Maimonides and Aquinas on Natural Law," *Dine Israel* 3 (1972): vff.

34. See Novak, *The Image of the Non-Jew in Judaism,* esp. pp. 407ff. Cf. Hugo Grotius, *De Jure Belli ac Pacis,* 1.1.10, 1.1.15; also, E. Bloch, *Naturrecht and Menschliche Würde* (Frankfurt: Suhrkamp, 1961), pp. 63ff. Cf. Hermann Cohen, "Die Nächstenliebe im Talmud," *Jüdische Schriften* (Berlin: C. A. Schwetske, 1924), vol. 1, pp. 159-60.

through historical revelation, its more general requirements are discernable in the created order of nature. The word by which God created the world and humankind therein was assumed to be evident to some extent even before the word he spoke directly to Israel at Mount Sinai. Indeed, without first being aware of this more general divine law, Israel would have found the directly revealed law of the Torah either unintelligible or unacceptable.[35] This was the version of natural law to which many more philosophically inclined Jews, Christians, and Muslims ascribed. Although formulated with the help of Aristotelian philosophy, it was not a doctrine found in the works of Aristotle himself. In Aristotelian thought, *nomos* is the human attempt to approximate the order of nature; but nature itself is no law in the literal sense of being a commanding voice.[36]

In the case of the Jewish relationship of American Jews to the American polity, understanding the idea of natural law in the light of the traditional Jewish doctrine of creation, and seeing that idea as the meaning of the predicate of the principle "The law of the state *is the law*," now enables us to constitute that relationship as something much less peripheral to fundamental Jewish concerns than mere contract. Following this line of thought, the question now is how this relationship, grounded as it is in the general natural law of God, can be seen as something more religiously significant than a social contract? How is the specific law *(dina)* of this American polity *(de-malkhuta hadayn)* related to law *per se (dina)*, which is the rule of the creator God?

Two Types of Covenant

In Scripture itself there does not seem to be anything corresponding exactly to our idea of contract — that is, a purely interhuman agreement basically governing itself through mutual consent alone. Interhuman agreements are covenants *(beritot* or *amanot)*. Covenants are not contracts because they require an oath invoking God's presence as the foundation of the agreement.[37] Thus they do not govern themselves, but rather place themselves in a higher order by relating what has been agreed upon on earth to the reality of heaven.

35. Maimonides, MT: Kings, 9.1.

36. Thus Aristotle speaks of "a universal law which is according to nature [*kata physin*]" at *Rhetoric*, 1373b6 — i.e., what is humanly formulated based on natural/universal considerations. But clearly for him there is no universal lawgiver *per se* from whom the law comes. Nature functions not as an efficient cause but rather as a limit *(peras)* and an exemplary end *(telos)*. See *Metaphysics*, 994b10.

37. See B. Shevu'ot 39a re Deut. 29:13.

In Scripture there are essentially two types of covenant. The first and most important type of covenant is often designated as the covenant *(ha-berit)*, as in "Not only with our ancestors did the Lord make this covenant [*ha-berit ha-z'ot*] but with us, all of us who are alive here today" (Deut. 5:3). This covenant is the perpetual relationship between God and Israel, initiated by God and to be accepted by Israel. It is the relationship which the Torah in all its details governs.[38] For Judaism, this is the prime normative reality.

The second type of covenant is one concluded between human parties *before* God. This type of covenant is that sort of human endeavor which, although not directly derived from the divine covenant *per se,* is taken to be consistent with it and thus worthy of being confirmed by an oath *(shevu'ah)* to God.[39] Most often it seems to be an agreement between two members of the people of Israel — as, for example, in the case of David and Jonathan: "Jonathan and David made a covenant" (1 Sam. 18:3); "And Jonathan said to David, 'Go in peace, and may that which we two have sworn [*nishba'nu*] in the name of the Lord be between me and you and between my descendants and yours for all time'" (1 Sam. 20:42).

Sometimes, though, a covenant can be established between an Israelite and a gentile. But this can only be done when the same God is invoked by both parties as the foundation of the covenant between them. When this cannot be done, any such covenant is then proscribed. For example, the Israelites are commanded not "to make a covenant" with the Canaanite peoples because that will necessarily entail their "making offerings to their gods" (Exod. 34:15). However, when such idolatry is not entailed, a covenant is not therefore proscribed but may indeed be concluded in good faith. Thus we read "Laban answered and said to Jacob . . . 'Come now, let us make a covenant me and you, and may there be a witness between me and you. . . . May the Lord watch between you and me, even when we are out of each other's sight'" (Gen. 31:43-44, 49). Note that Jacob, the patriarch Israel, can make a covenant with the idolator Laban because Laban has invoked the God of Israel, who is the universal God, as the foundation of this covenant; indeed, Laban is the initiator of the covenant with Jacob.[40]

The Rabbis, however, were stricter in connection with a covenant between a Jew and a gentile. Thus the Talmud rules, "It is prohibited for one to enter into a partnership [*shuttfut*] with a gentile lest an oath be required and

---

38. See my late revered teacher Abraham Joshua Heschel, *The Prophets* (New York: Harper & Row), pp. 229ff.

39. For the necessity of interhuman covenants being consistent with the divine covenant, see M. Shevu'ot 3.8.

40. See *Bereshit Rabbah* 74.16.

the gentile will swear by his god. This violates the Torah's command that [the name of any other god] 'shall not be heard in your mouth' (Exod. 23:13)." This is interpreted to mean that one might not even indirectly cause *(ligrom)* a gentile to invoke the name of another god.[41] In other words, although the gentile does not invoke his god initially, the very fact that he believes in such a god and might subsequently invoke his god is enough to prohibit a Jew from entering even a business relationship with him.

In the Middle Ages, however, we see a rather radical re-interpretation of the above norm by Rabbenu Tam, another grandson and student of Rashi and the younger brother of Rashbam. He argued that the prohibition of entering a partnership with a gentile did not apply in his own time because the Christians with whom Jews are now dealing, who although they are wont to invoke the names of their saints *(qodashim she-lahen)* in oaths, nevertheless "intend the Maker of heaven [*da'atam le'oseh shamayim*]."[42] It is clear from this comment, which had a tremendous effect on the development of Jewish-Christian relations, that Rabbenu Tam accepts the possibility of a covenantal relationship between Jews and Christians *because they both invoke the same God.* Furthermore, the God they both invoke is God as acknowledged before their respective revelations — that is, God as he is in heaven.

Of course, in Rabbenu Tam's time such a relationship was limited to the realm of commercial transactions. Jews and Christians certainly did not share any sort of political commonality. Nevertheless, the groundwork has been laid there for the constitution of a relationship, such as now exists in the United States, where Jews and gentiles (the large majority of whom are Christians) do share a political commonality as equal citizens. The religious foundation of this secular order can thus be seen as Jewishly justified. *Mutatis mutandis,* both Rabbenu Tam and Thomas Jefferson were invoking the same God — "the Maker of heaven" or "Nature's God." That is, they were both invoking the God who can be acknowledged in common albeit worshiped in very different ways because of historical revelation. There is, indeed, a "Judeo-Christian tradition," and it need not be taken as a pretext for a deistic elimination of historical religions, or a form of religious syncretism, or a Christian ruse designed to talk Jews out of their own religious singularity. What it does mean is that Jews can in good faith affirm their relationship with the American polity on covenantal grounds without having to affirm a *secularist* foundation for this secular realm. It seems to me that this justifies a Jewishly valid attachment to America, one which may be unique as regards Diaspora societies.

41. B. Sanhedrin 63b.
42. B. Sanhedrin 63b, Tos., s.v. "asur."

Postscript

Especially after the Holocaust, which began in Germany, a Diaspora country to which many Jews were very much attached, to many Jews it seems somehow inappropriate for us to be so patriotic about America. Weren't we bitterly disappointed in such love affairs before? I think of how Gershom Scholem reminded us of how one-sided the German-Jewish symbiosis really was.[43] And, especially after the establishment of the State of Israel, should we be patriots of any other nation-state except that which is now our own? These are hard questions to which I do not have sufficient answers as yet.

All I would say, in conclusion, is that the irony of the German-Jewish relationship is that it was never constituted on authentic Judaic grounds. Its justifications, even by German Jewry's greatest philosopher Hermann Cohen, were ultimately romanticizations of a society far less rooted in the Hebraic heritage than America.[44] But should America ever reject her Hebraic heritage, then we Jews could only continue living here on the basis of a secular contract, as we did and still do in so many other societies. And that would make our participation in this society much more peripheral Judaically than it need be now. And if, God forbid, America should ever deny Jews the opportunities for us to freely exercise our religious practices, let alone freely live, then the covenant between Jews and America would be broken, and faithful Jews would have no other option but to leave this society, as we have had to leave so many other societies before.

As for the State of Israel, even before there was a state in the Land of Israel, the halakhah was quite clear that dwelling in the Land of Israel *(yishuv erets yisrael)* takes precedence over dwelling anywhere else on earth.[45] Nevertheless, this does not mean that no Jewish life is possible for those who have chosen to remain in the Diaspora for the time being. Diaspora Jewish life shows no signs of simply disappearing *(shelilat ha-golah)*.[46] As long as this is the case, Jews should try to see the possible Judaic justification of all their relationships, including their relationship with this secular state. In fact, I am bold enough to think this might actually strengthen Jewish life in this country by enabling American Jews to see the light of the Torah in heretofore strange places.

43. See "Jews and Germans," *Commentary* 42 (1966): 31ff.

44. See "Deutschtum and Judentum" I and II, in *Jüdische Schriften*, vol. 2, pp. 237-301.

45. See M. Ketubot 13.11; Nahmanides, *Notes on Maimonides' Sefer Ha- Mitsvot*, pos. no. 4.

46. See David Novak, *Jewish Social Ethics* (Oxford: Oxford University Press, 1992), chap. 11.

13   The Right and the Good (2002)

The proper relation between what is right and what is good is itself a perennial ethical question addressed by philosophers and theologians in many different cultural contexts. Before addressing two different sets of text on this question, one set theological and the other set philosophical, let us tentatively define "right" as a justified claim made by one human person upon another, and "good" as that which human persons seek.[1] If so, we are inquiring into the proper relation between obligation and desire, or between justice and beatitude.

Logically, it seems that there are two cogent options available regarding this relation. Either right is greater than good; hence good must be seen as finally intending a greater right. Ultimately our desires must be directed toward our obligations. Or good is greater than right; hence right must be seen as finally intending a greater good. Ultimately our obligations must be directed toward our desires. Furthermore, both our obligations and our desires have their proper objects: we are obliged to someone; we desire someone or something. Without their proper objects, both desire and obligation sink into incoherence. Thus to separate obligation from its proper object is to desire desire; to separate obligation from its proper object is to be obliged to be obliged. In both such cases we are left with the fallacy of self-reference. The primary question involving right, then, is this: To whom am I obligated? The primary question involving good, then, is this: What do I desire? The ultimate

---

1. For right as what humans justifiably claim from one another, see Wesley N. Hohfeld, *Fundamental Legal Conceptions,* ed. W. W. Cook (Westport, Conn.: Greenwood Press, 1964), pp. 38, 60, 71. For good as that which humans ultimately seek, see Plato, *Symposium,* 206a; Aristotle, *Nicomachean Ethics,* 1094a1-5.

question of the relation of these two questions is the question of the ultimate relation of their two proper objects. And, as we shall see in due course, the greater importance of right to good or good to right does not mean that the lesser principle can be deduced from the greater one any more than the lesser object emanates from the greater one.

A third and a fourth option that are logically possible can be dismissed *ab initio,* however. As a third option, some might say that right and good are interchangeable terms having an identical referent; but that would destroy a distinction *between* right and good that has persisted in the vast majority of ethical discourses in many different cultural contexts. Such an identification would oversimplify ethical discourse and thus make it inadequate to discuss its own concerns cogently. The conceptual distinction between right and good intends a real difference between them. As a fourth option, some might say that right and good are both unnecessary terms; but that would make distinctly ethical discourse more than just simplistic; it would make it altogether impossible. Both terms are necessary for ethical discourse to be distinct from other forms of discourse such as sociology and psychology. As we shall see, ethics requires an ontological dimension for the sake of its independence, and without that distinction between right and good one cannot very well constitute that ontological dimension for ethics.

Since we are looking here at how the question of the right and the good is discussed in two different cultural contexts, which one should be considered first? The two contexts to be studied here are the history of philosophy and the rabbinic tradition. Since most readers are more familiar with philosophy — especially current Anglo-American philosophy, or at least with its cultural concerns (I am thinking of democracy as an ethical question) — than they are with the ancient rabbinic tradition, clarity might well require we begin there in our very choice of primary terms. Nevertheless, this procedural priority does not mean that the discussion of the question of the right and the good in the rabbinic tradition can be subordinated to philosophical discussion of it. The priority of Anglo-American philosophy here is hermeneutical, not ontological.[2] The treatment of these two cultural contexts and their respective texts is for the sake of analogy, not subsumption.

The most influential book in political philosophy in the last fifty years or so, certainly in the English-speaking world, has been John Rawls's *A Theory of*

---

2. As the German-Jewish philosopher Hermann Cohen put it when speaking about the literary sources of Judaism, "Those sources remain mute and blind if I do not approach them with a concept" (*Religion of Reason Out of the Sources of Judaism,* trans. S. Kaplan [New York: Frederick Ungar, 1972], p. 4). The German word Cohen uses is *Begriff,* literally "getting a grip" on the more historically remote texts.

Justice. Since justice is the most important issue of social ethics, it is important to begin with a well-known text from Rawls on our question of the right and the good: "In justice as fairness the concept of right is prior to that of the good. A just social system defines the scope within which individuals must develop their aims, and it provides a framework of rights and opportunities and the means of satisfaction within and by the use of which these ends may be equitably pursued."[3] Later, Rawls sees these "goods" as part of what he calls "a rational plan" and defines them as "those activities and ends that have the features whatever they are that suit them for an important if not central place in our life." These "rational plans must be consistent with the principles of justice." He refers to these rational plans as "the familiar values," and then supplies four key examples: "personal affection and friendship," "meaningful work and social cooperation," "the pursuit of knowledge," and "the fashioning and contemplation of beautiful objects."[4] Let us now examine what Rawls is saying with the same care with which readers of rabbinic texts have traditionally read them.

What does Rawls mean when he says that "the concept of right is prior to that of the good"? It would seem that he means logical priority. That is, since we are political beings who cannot live outside a polity of some sort or other, we have to fulfill certain necessary political obligations *before* we can be allowed by society to pursue our own desires in its space. This space is what we call "privacy," but it is framed within the more encompassing space of the polity *(res publica).* This logical priority need not be strictly chronological as well. In most cases we are already pursuing our own desires *before* we retroactively contemplate just what political conditions have made it possible for us to pursue them in society in the first place. Here is the point where it can be asserted that right *is* prior to the good.

Nevertheless, existentially, the good we desire is prior to the rights we are obligated to respect. That is because in a social contract system such as the one Rawls presents in his book, we would never agree to our political obligations if keeping them did not enable us to pursue our own desires. But our desires must be those which Rawls says "justice permits."[5] Justice, then, limits desire, since desire that does not move into action cannot be true desire. It is more likely to be a much weaker wish without true intentionality. Justice regulates an action involving more than one person, thus making it the form of every transaction.[6] Due to the need for this permission, this political dispen-

---

3. Rawls, *A Theory of Justice* (Cambridge, Mass.: Harvard University Press, 1971), p. 31.

4. Rawls, *A Theory of Justice*, p. 425.

5. Rawls, *A Theory of Justice*, p. 425.

6. See Aristotle, *Nicomachean Ethics*, 1138a4-1138b15.

sation, someone whose desires are, for example, to inflict pain on others, or to gamble with all his or her assets, or to have sexual relations with as many others as is physically possible, seems to be an unlikely candidate to freely accept Rawls's ideas of what minimal justice requires. Sadists inevitably inflict pain on unwilling victims for the sake of their own pleasure. Gamblers inevitably steal from others for the sake of their own pleasure. Sexual hedonists inevitably lie to their conquests or to their spouses; indeed, lying seems to be a part of their pleasure. Potential thugs, thieves, and liars are not the type of people who should be trusted to be parties to any contract, private or social.

That is why, according to his own assumption, it is confusing to say, as Rawls does, that "[our] rational plans must be consistent with the principles of justice." Consistency implies the good is subordinate to right. Instead, justice must be consistent with our rational plans — that is, we accept the principles of justice *in order to* be able to pursue our desires; we do not pursue our desires *in order to* be just. Justice seems to be instrumental, not an end *per se*.[7] So, perhaps it is better to explain Rawls's use of the words "consistent with" to mean that the good *qua* end must be consistent with the means to it *qua* right. That is why, it seems, Rawls equates these desires with a "rational plan." They derive their rationality from their being consistent with the principles of justice. Since justice is rational, so must be those desires that do not violate it but use it. Hence it is most unlikely that Rawls would call the pursuit of desires that will inevitably contradict the principles of justice a "rational plan," no matter how cleverly those who have such desires do indeed pursue them.

Rawls distinguishes between the right and the good by insisting that society can only prescribe right and even punish its violators. But it must not prescribe the good. Each individual should be let alone to do that for himself or herself.[8] Thus, whereas society must have a considerable amount of unanimity in the definition of right, it must be thoroughly pluralistic when it comes to definitions of the good. Accordingly, society must not interfere in the way its members pursue their own *goods*. So it clearly follows why, for Rawls, society cannot promote any particular vision of *the* good. There can be no political *summum bonum*. There is thus no real common good *(bonum commune)* — that is, society cannot make any claim upon us that is not ultimately for the sake of the individual pursuits of its members. There are only individual goods *(bonum sibi)*, although, as we have seen, the list of these goods *is* rather exclusive considering the full range of existential options readily available to-

---

7. Aristotle, *Nicomachean Ethics*, 1094a5.
8. Rawls, *A Theory of Justice*, pp. 521-22.

day. Thus Rawls says, "The common good I think of as certain general conditions that are in an appropriate sense equally to everyone's advantage."[9]

Yet the question remains whether Rawls has satisfactorily distinguished between right and good. As we have already seen, the only desires he is willing to see as being consistent with the principles of justice are those that would be taken by many to be identical with some, if not all, of the classical virtues. One could just as easily say "classical virtues" as Rawls says "the familiar values" and mean much the same thing. However, isn't justice itself one of the classical virtues?[10] If so, we must rephrase our question to Rawls as follows: Are the principles of justice affirmed only *inasmuch as* as they make room for the pursuit of our virtuous desires *(conditio sine qua non)*, or do we pursue our virtuous desires *because* they are in essence just *(conditio per quam)*? If the former, then good retains its existential priority to right, and right retains its logical priority to good. Accordingly, we have both a distinction and a difference. If the latter, however, good needs to be defined by right in the way a part needs to be defined by the larger whole *in which* it is totally subsumed. In other words, if the latter, then good itself and our desire for it need to be existentially *justified* by the political order from beginning to end. Accordingly, we no longer have a dialectical relation between right and good but the subordination of good to right alone. The only way we can maintain such a dialectical relation is when good transcends right without destroying it and, as such, neither is reducible to the other, even though one can ultimately be more important than the other.

Looking at Rawls's four examples of acceptable desires — friendship, work, knowledge, and art — we can see that none of them can really transcend the realm of justice, which is the realm of politics. In the case of friendship, it could well be argued that in the context of a liberal, secular society, who my friends are is in the greatest sense determined by our common political commitments. In the case of work, my accumulation of material property is ultimately for the sake of my political status. In the case of knowledge, my accumulation of intellectual property functions similarly. Even in the case of art, which many of us might consider the most private realm of all, works of art are commodities that are either purchased or not, tolerated or not, because of either their politically correct or their politically incorrect expressions. The fact that the state does not legally prescribe what I am to do in these four areas of human interaction does not mean that the larger society

9. Rawls, *A Theory of Justice*, p. 246. Cf. David Novak, *Covenantal Rights* (Princeton: Princeton University Press, 2000), pp. 153-58.

10. See Aristotle, *Nicomachean Ethics*, 1129b26-1130a13.

does not have ways of directing my choices therein with either approval or disapproval, incentive or disincentive. My very desire for worldly entities is determined by the social context in which I desire them.

Regarding art especially, Rawls's precise wording is important to note. It is "the fashioning and contemplation of beautiful objects." In other words, we ourselves make things for our own aesthetic enjoyment. Art is no longer a vision and imitation of something that transcends the interhuman realm of transaction.[11] In the end, here too, even what is aesthetically good — what is beautiful — must conform to what is considered right politically. This comes out quite often in public debates concerning social funding of the arts. Artists must always avoid what is taken to be obscene by their public. To be sure, criteria of obscenity vary from time to time and from place to place, yet there is no society that tolerates *every* artistic expression. (Thus, for example, many liberals who would defend Salman Rushdie's right to degrade Islam would just as vehemently object to the right of some other author to degrade, let us say, persons of a minority sexual orientation. That is because most liberals regard sexual expression to be more publicly significant than religious expression.)

What we see is that the realm of the good is confined to the realm of privacy. But the realm of privacy is not one that transcends the public realm. Quite the contrary: unless one's rights as a person come from a realm that is not politically contained, privacy is simply that area of human life that society postulates as being beneath its scrutiny. Privacy is a social entitlement, and it can be easily revoked at any time. That being the case, the private goods we desire ultimately become the political right to not only pursue them but to publicly promote them. Thus, to cite a primary example of what Rawls calls "personal affection and friendship," *my* private sexual desires ultimately become *our* political right to various forms of sexual liberation. Even though most people desire that their sexual acts themselves be hidden from public scrutiny, rarely if ever does the fact that we are engaging in them not become a matter of the knowledge of some public or other nonetheless. (Even adulterers frequently share the fact of their adultery with some others with whom they are not sexually involved themselves. Often that sharing of information is bragging. In certain social circles, adultery elicits admiration.) Privacy itself inevitably makes a public statement.

So, in the end, it seems that Rawls's statement of the priority of the good to the right is not only logical but existential as well. That is, ultimately the good is for the sake of right, and the difference between them is thus one of

11. See Plato, *Symposium*, 211cd.

degree rather than one of kind. But has this conceptual poverty missed something that could make the distinction between right and good a true difference and thus contribute to a richer vision of human existence?

Rabbinic Judaism is concerned with the relationship of humans and God and the relationship of humans between themselves and then with the interrelation of these two realms. This concern can be seen in two related rabbinic texts that very much deal with our question of the relation of right and good. The first text deals with a procedure in the Temple:

> When the priest entered to remove money donated for the sacrifices [*litrom et ha-lishkah*], he was searched both upon entering and upon exiting, and they conversed with him from the time he entered until the time he exited. This was done to confirm what Scripture stated: "You shall be innocent [*neqiyyim*] regarding the Lord and regarding Israel" (Numbers 32:22). Furthermore, it states: "You shall do the right [*ha-yashar*] and the good [*ha-tov*] in the eyes of the Lord" (Deuteronomy 6:18). "The good" means in the eyes of God; "the right" means in the eyes of man [*adam*]. This is the opinion of Rabbi Akibah. [But] Rabbi Ishmael says even "the right" is what is right in the eyes of God. And Scripture states, "and find favour and good sense [*sekhel tov*] in the eyes of God and man" (Proverbs 3:4).[12]

Here we have the interrelation of the divine-human and interhuman realms. In the divine-human realm we have the priest functioning as an official of the national sanctuary, the central religious institution. Yet there is the question of the interhuman appearance of either propriety or impropriety on his part, which reflects on his moral reputation among the people.

According to my late teacher, Professor Saul Lieberman, there is a dispute between Rabbi Akibah and Rabbi Ishmael. In his interpretation, Rabbi Akibah seems to think that the priest "is not to be degraded by such a search because this is not right [*yashar*] in the eyes of human beings." Rabbi Ishmael, conversely, seems to think "what is right in the eyes of God should also be good in the eyes of human beings." Professor Lieberman sees Rabbi Ishmael's opinion in this context as part of a general rabbinic trend that "what is right in the eyes of God will eventually [*sofo*] be good in the eyes of human beings."[13] In this interpretation, good is not the ultimate object of human desire; it is, rather, what humans most immediately experience as acceptable to them. But, for Rabbi Akibah, what is to be done as good in the eyes of God —

12. T. Sheqalim 2.2.

13. See Saul Lieberman, *Tosefta Kifshuta: Moed* (New York: Jewish Theological Seminary of America, 1962), p. 677.

that is, in the context of the divine-human relationship — must also be what is right in the context of the interhuman relationship. Human reason, then, is to be more than simply a commentary after the fact *(apologia)* of divine revelation. It has a constitutive role, not just an explanatory one; it functions *a priori*, not just *a posteriori*.[14] There is a dialectical relation between right and good for Rabbi Akibah. Each point in the relation must be satisfied, the divine and the human. But, again for Rabbi Ishmael, divine favor is sufficient, and the task of human reason is to come to accept that divine wisdom sooner or later — to catch up with it, so to speak.

This dispute is not confined to the case at hand. In what Professor Lieberman considers to be the origin of the dispute between Rabbi Akibah and Rabbi Ishmael concerning the appearance of priestly propriety, the dispute between the same two sages is about the general meaning of the terms "the good" *(ha-tov)* and "the right" *(ha-yashar)*. For Rabbi Ishmael, now placed in direct dispute with Rabbi Akibah, everything is reducible to what is right in the eyes of God.[15] That has already been clearly revealed in the Torah. As my late teacher (and Professor Lieberman's close colleague) Professor Louis Finkelstein explicated the view of Rabbi Ishmael, "he is not interested in justification [*be-hitstadqut*] before men and he is not afraid of their suspicion."[16] In our text about priestly propriety, but which pertains to their general theological dispute, it states that "the Sages concluded [*hikhri'u*] that Scriptural language is more supportive of the view of Rabbi Ishmael."[17] That is significant because later sages seemed to follow the views of Rabbi Akibah on just about everything.[18] On the more general conceptual question, though, the dispute between Rabbi Ishmael and Rabbi Akibah has resonated throughout the history of Judaism until the present day. One can only take sides, but unlike the specific case of the suspected priest, on the general question there can be no official conclusion.[19]

In the nineteenth century, when liberal Jews were proclaiming that only those aspects of the Jewish tradition that could be justified by human reason were worthy of being preserved, orthodox reaction was to reaffirm the neces-

14. See David Novak, *Jewish Social Ethics* (New York: Oxford University Press, 1992), pp. 25-29.

15. *Sifre: Devarim,* no. 79, ed. Louis Finkelstein (New York: Jewish Theological Seminary of America, 1969), p. 145.

16. *Sifre: Devarim,* no. 6.

17. T. Sheqalim 2.2.

18. See B. Eruvin 46b and parallels.

19. See my late teacher, Abraham Joshua Heschel, *Theology of Ancient Judaism,* 2 vols. (London: Soncino, 1962-65).

sity of a superrational divine revelation. Along these lines, it is illuminating to see what a major orthodox exegete of that period, Rabbi Meir Leibush Malbim, did with the ancient dispute.

> "Good" [*tov*] belongs more to the commandments that concern the relationship between humans and God [*beyn adam le-maqom*] since one does not do them because of what his mind deems right [*yosher levavo*], but only because they have been commanded by the Higher Wisdom . . . and it *is* impossible that a human being could by himself apprehend [*sheyasig*] what is good and what is evil except by means of the [Higher] Wisdom and the Torah of the Lord. . . . But, as for the commandments that concern the interhuman relationship [*beyn adam le-havero*], whose rightness [*yoshram*] is recognized by human beings, the term "right" [*yashar*] belongs. And rightness [*ha-yosher*] is a matter of [human] understanding because this [human] conduct can be apprehended by the understanding of his mind. This is the opinion of Rabbi Akibah. But Rabbi Ishmael responds that . . . even with the commandments that concern the interhuman relationship, whose rightness we can apprehend, they should not be done because of our reason [*mi-tsad sikhlenu*], but only because the Higher Wisdom commanded them.[20]

One could assume that whereas for Rabbi Akibah "the right" *(ha-yashar)* and "the good" *(ha-tov)* are two separate terms denoting two separate objects, Rabbi Ishmael regards "the right and the good" (Deut. 6:18) or "the good and the right" (Deut. 12:19) as one single phrase — namely, "right/good" or "the-good-and-the-right." This is not unique in biblical language.[21] If so, then Rabbi Akibah, who never passes by the opportunity to assign different functions to different words in Scripture, is able to assert the conceptually richer distinction between right and good about which Rabbi Ishmael is silent.[22] In fact, we can see Rabbi Ishmael having a similar conceptual problem to that of Rawls, even though, of course, his concept of right is quite different from that of Rawls: it is the right of God to command, whereas Rawls's concept of right only means human claims upon each other. Nevertheless, for both, what is right is already fully known. The good, on the other hand, with which neither

---

20. *Commentary on the Torah* (Vilna: Romm, 1922): Deut. 12:28, n. 52.

21. See Gen. 18:19 and Deut. 16:18. Cf. David Novak, *The Election of Israel* (Cambridge: Cambridge University Press, 1995), pp. 124-26.

22. Regarding Rabbi Akibah's attempts to assign different meanings to each word in Scripture, which might very well presuppose greater conceptual complexity than that of his colleagues, see, e.g., B. Baba Kama 41b re Deut. 6:13.

of them seems to be concerned in relation to the right, is what is beyond what we already know. It is what we are still seeking, getting glimpses but without any beatific vision as yet.

For Rabbi Akibah, right seems to mean a rational interhuman claim, but good seems to be what we desire that is beyond the interhuman realm, perhaps even beyond what is ascertainably religious in the interhuman realm. One could say that the theological dispute between Rabbi Ishmael and Rabbi Akibah is somewhat analogous to the philosophical dispute between Rawls (and others like him) and Plato and (others like him). Like Rabbi Akibah, Plato distinguishes between the right and the good, and like Rabbi Akibah he sees the good transcending ordinary standards of the right, thus affirming a real difference between the two. Thus he writes, "As for the objects of knowledge, not only is their being known due to the Good [*tou agathou*], but also their reality being [*tēs ousias*], though the Good is not being but superior to and beyond being in dignity and power."[23] Among the most important of these objects of knowledge are "just actions" *(dikaia)* and the other things, which "by their relation to it [the Good] . . . become useful and beneficial."[24] Transcendence is not antithesis. There is no "teleological suspension of the ethical" that we find in Kierkegaard.[25] The ethical (concerned with the right) leads into the ontological (concerned with the Good).

Although Plato sees knowledge of the Good providing the only fully sufficient foundation for human life and society, he nevertheless sees Socrates, the wisest of humans, and his interlocutors, as basically different from those for whom "there is no need to search further [*pereitero zetein*]."[26] All we have so far is "the quest for the nature of the Good itself."[27] Very much like the creative act of God for a theologian like Rabbi Akibah, whose effects we can appreciate but whose full reality itself is beyond our ken, so does Plato seem to purposefully use imprecise language to assert how the Good *is* the foundation of all being: "Say that what gives [*apodidon*] truth to the objects of knowledge, and to the knowing mind the power to know is the Form of Good [*tou agathou idean*]. As it is the cause [*aitian*] of knowledge and truth, think of it also as being the object of knowledge."[28] It would seem that we can only have a phenomenology of the search for the good and a phenomenology of the

---

23. Plato, *Republic,* 509b.
24. Plato, *Republic,* 505a.
25. See Kierkegaard, *Fear and Trembling,* trans. H. V. Hong and E. H. Hong (Princeton: Princeton University Press, 1983), pp. 54-56.
26. Plato, *Republic,* 504c.
27. Plato, *Republic,* 506e.
28. Plato, *Republic,* 508e.

traces of the good, but not a phenomenology of the good *per se* — not yet. We can only have faith in its reality.

To reduce the desire for the good to the mere establishment of human right, to confine its object to the interhuman range within which right operates, is to impoverish human existence.[29] And that ontological decision has profound ethical implications. Indeed, that bracketing of the quest of all quests might very well put even human rights themselves in jeopardy. After all, aren't human rights best secured by the most exalted vision of human nature possible for human reason to apprehend? Even though I do not think human reason can ascertain whether God is or is not, it can apprehend that human beings throughout the ages have been seekers of divine transcendence. Can any view of human nature short of that from direct divine revelation itself be more exalted? That is the case whether or not any human beings believe that any divine transcendence has shown itself to them. Because this quest is not for what is good for me, or even for us, but for what is desirable *per se,* it testifies to the truth that we are more than users of things. This preoccupation with the good *per se,* it seems to me, gives the best foundation to the most basic ethical truth: no human being can be essentially seen as an instrument of use, either by others or even by himself or herself.[30] We live in the political world, to be sure, but we desire more than what that world contains. In the words of one ancient rabbinic sage, it is "a world altogether good" *(she-kulo tov).*[31] Whether we attain that world or not, the very way we strive to attain it determines the character of our human existence more than anything else.

---

29. See Karl Jaspers, *Philosophy,* trans. E. B. Ashton (Chicago: University of Chicago Press, 1969), vol. 1, pp. 76-89.

30. See David Novak, *Natural Law in Judaism* (Cambridge: Cambridge University Press, 1998), pp. 164-73.

31. B. Hullin 142a re Deut. 5:16.

14 Is Natural Law a Border Concept between Judaism and Christianity? (2004)

Jewish Ethics and Christian Ethics

One should always be mindful of where one is speaking so as not to risk conducting a monologue. A dialogue is always preferable. To know *where* one is speaking is to know with *whom* one is speaking and *what* is worthy of our attention *when* we have some time allotted to us together.

First of all, I am speaking with fellow Jews who consider themselves "Jewish ethicists"; hence we are meeting under the auspices of what we call the "Society of Jewish Ethics." But this very meeting of the Society of Jewish Ethics is being held in conjunction with the meeting of the Society of Christian Ethics. Now there are some Jewish scholars of Jewish ethics who, I am sure, have avoided this meeting precisely because of this very conjunction. They probably remember the time in the not-so-distant past when Jewish ethics was used as a foil by many Christian ethicists — that is, when Jewish ethics was used as part of a triumphalist Christian attitude toward anything Jewish, Jewish ethics included.

At worst, Christian ethicists attempted to show how "parochial" Jewish ethics had been overcome by "universal" Christian ethics; hence the separate existence of Jewish ethics could only be seen as the obstinate refusal of a part to be subsumed (*aufgehoben*, to use the term of a Christian triumphalist like Hegel) by the larger whole.[1] At best, Jewish ethics was tolerated as a quaint expression of "proto-Christianity," which could be taken by Christians as a helpful reminder of their own historical origins — an intellectual "theme

---

1. See Emil Fackenheim, *The Religious Dimension in Hegel's Thought* (Bloomington: Indiana University Press, 1967), pp. 197-201.

park," as it were. Nevertheless, nineteenth- and early twentieth-century Jewish thinkers such as Elie Benamozegh, Moritz Lazarus, Hermann Cohen, and Leo Baeck were quick to respond to this essentially polemical stance of their contemporary Christian thinkers.[2] Not only did each of them in his own way argue against these Christian denigrations of Jewish ethics, but each of them, on the basis of universal ethical criteria, attempted to show that Jewish ethics is actually superior to Christian ethics. As such, these Jewish thinkers were not afraid to confront Kant and Hegel and their theological followers.

It is a credit to the maturity of the Society of Christian Ethics that Christian ethicists — for the most part, that is — no longer make such triumphalist claims for Christian ethics to Jewish ethicists. It is only such an attitude that makes our conjunction of meetings possible, let alone desirable. And it is a credit to the maturity of the members of the Society of Jewish Ethics that we recognize this fact and have been able to overcome what in the past was a justifiable "Christophobia." That we, both Jewish and Christian ethicists, can now discuss fundamental ethical questions in an atmosphere of mutuality rather than one of contempt, suspicion, condescension, fear, and defensiveness, that is something to celebrate — by getting down to business and discussing some real ethical issues.

Nevertheless, despite the removal of the negative impediments to true dialogue on fundamental ethical questions, have we truly opened up a new atmosphere wherein we can make progress in our understanding of these fundamental questions, let alone the more specific questions they enable us to pose? What concerns me is that perhaps we have eliminated one negativity only to replace it with another. For, at least in the old disputational atmosphere, we were doing what I think ethicists are supposed to be doing. First, we were proposing norms each of us regarded to be permanent — that is, norms thought to be true for all times. And second, we were proposing norms each of us regarded to be universal — that is, norms thought to be true for all humankind.

By proposing permanent or absolute norms, we were being faithful to what our respective traditions regarded, in the words of my rabbinic tradition, to be commandments "for all generations" (le-dorot).[3] As such, we were dealing with norms that are central to our respective traditions and not

2. See Elie Benamozegh, Morale juive et morale chrétienne, ed. Shmuel Trigano (Paris: In Press, 2000); Moritz Lazarus, The Ethics of Judaism, trans. Henrietta Szold (Philadelphia: Jewish Publication Society, 1900); Hermann Cohen, Religion of Reason Out of the Sources of Judaism, trans. S. Kaplan (New York: F. Ungar, 1972), esp. pp. 343-44; Leo Baeck, Judaism and Christianity, trans. W. Kauffmann (Philadelphia: Jewish Publication Society, 1958), esp. pp. 240-56.

3. B. Kiddushin 29a.

norms that are, again in the words of my rabbinic tradition, "only for the needs of the hour"*(sha'ah)*,[4] norms which only have a past, but no present and certainly no future. By proposing universal norms, we were being faithful to what our respective traditions regarded, once again in the words of my rabbinic tradition, to be "reasonable [*din hu*] to have written down even if they had not been written down"[5] — that is, what is reasonable to any human being who is rational. In other words, we were doing "pure practical reason" (to use Kant's term), not just engaging in historical reflection or sociological description. But by limiting either the normative duration or the normative scope of any norm, have we not thereby negated its absolute and universal prescriptiveness?

By proposing absolute and universal norms, at least in the past, we were truly speaking to a world outside the confines of our own respective traditions. In Jewish terms, we were doing more than halakhah, more than what in principle only applies to those members of our own people, and what in fact only applies to those members of our own people who accept the authority of revelation and its tradition of interpretation, application, and supplementation. To be sure, we are not engaged in a competitive struggle to convert the pagans — *the world* — to our respective theologies, as we were in the first, second, and third centuries of the Common Era. Nonetheless, in the nineteenth and part of the twentieth centuries, we were engaged in a competitive struggle to convert some newer pagans — *the secular world* — to our own respective ethics.

But, largely due to our mutual revulsion to even theoretical polemics and disputations because of their strong associations with practical violence of one form or another, instead of *confronting* one another, many of us have retreated to the safer position of engaging in what I would call "parallel discourse." That is, each of us often talks about what is ethically "interesting" in our own respective traditions, and at best we make some analogies *among* these interesting bits of closely related traditions. Thus we engage in mostly comparative work, work that is essentially descriptive. That, of course, very much befits the ethos of the academic world in which most of us earns his or her bread — and professional reputation. Many of us think, no doubt, that only such a basically relativistic attitude will enable us to continue to be tolerated by the academy. Nevertheless, the question does remain whether this academic *ethos* many of us have adopted is truly *ethical*. In other words, does this outlook suffice for the work of ethics, which, as Aristotle reminded us, is

4. B. Yoma 69b.
5. B. Yoma 67b.

not only to know the good but to do it?[6] Isn't ethics supposed to be *prescriptive?* Isn't ethics supposed to be about what *ought to be done* over and above being about what *has been done?* And isn't ethics supposed to deal with norms which cannot be relativized away so it only pertains to one time but not for all time, so it only pertains to one place but not for all places?

So, it seems to me that in order to avoid the triumphalism of the past and the relativism of the present, we Jewish and Christian ethicists should attempt to engage in *cooperative* work, which will enable us together to formulate universal norms that are not, in effect, one cultural particularity becoming universal by absorbing all others into itself, or one cultural particularity eliminating all others altogether.[7] Only in this way can we move beyond a parallelism where our respective ethical lines never intersect. Moreover, we need to do this cooperative work for the sake of an ethical intersection that is both theoretical and practical. We can only do this joint work by simultaneously resisting the *totalizing* (to use the term of the French-Jewish philosopher Emmanuel Levinas) temptation of syncretism.[8] This joint ethical work should not make us *parts of* some greater whole, which would envelop us into some new stage of historical development. Accordingly, we should always affirm the primacy of our respective traditions in a way that they will only allow us to be *participants in* a worldly arena, an arena we can and should regularly transcend rather than ever letting it subsume us, either each of us separately or even both of us together.

Moreover, this work needs to be an ethical intersection that is both theoretical and practical. In Talmudic dialectic, no two distinct theoretical views are so theoretical so as to be without any practical difference; and no two different practical views are so practical so as to be without theoretical distinction.[9] Perhaps, then, our joint enterprise should adopt the term of the German-Jewish philosopher Hermann Cohen and call itself *"die Theorie der Praxis."*[10]

---

6. Aristotle, *Nicomachean Ethics,* 1143a10, 1144b25-30.

7. See David Novak, *Natural Law in Judaism* (Cambridge: Cambridge University Press, 1998), pp. 188-91.

8. Levinas, *Totality and Infinity,* trans. A. Lingis (Pittsburgh: Duquesne University Press, 1969), pp. 35-40.

9. See B. Baba Metsia 15b-16a; B. Berakhot 22b-23a.

10. Cohen, *Jüdische Schriften,* ed. B. Strauss (Berlin: Schwetschke, 1924), vol. 3, p. 302.

The Locus of Natural Law

I think the center of our joint ethical work should be the question of natural law. But, before we can intelligently deal with this question — that is, before we can truly *intersect* in our treatment of natural law — we need to do two things. First, we need to locate the question of natural law in the sources of our respective traditions. Second, we need to see analogies to that location in the other tradition lying closest to our border. For Jews, due to reasons both theological and historical, that other tradition which lies most closely *alongside* us is Christianity. Moreover, despite my previous reservations about "parallelism," we still need to engage in that enterprise before constructing our ethical intersection. If we don't do the particular research and then the comparative work beforehand (and simultaneously as well), we risk a premature closure, which makes our present ethical reasoning and its conclusions quite inadequate to the tasks at hand. In fact, my reservations about current parallelism are over its insufficient research in the sources of one's particular tradition. As such, most parallelism is not particular enough. And, on the other hand, it is too particular in its fixation on the comparative dimension of ethics and not sufficiently cosmic in its thrust so as to be able to deal with the ontological questions our theological and philosophical forebears loved to tackle and were properly prepared to tackle. Such an ontological question is the question of human nature, the question of philosophical anthropology Kant asked: "*Was ist der Mensch?*"[11]

To let ourselves fall into such premature closure, to throw ourselves too soon into the secular world, where all the important ethical issues have to be raised today, is to leave us — Jewish and Christian ethicists — wide open to *the* secularist charge against us. That is, we leave ourselves open to the charge that all of our talk of "universal" norms is nothing but a rationalization of our very *particular* traditions and their equally particular theologies. Catholic natural-law theorists can best appreciate this point, since the term *natural law* has an immediately "Catholic" connotation for most people who have ever heard it. Thus some Catholic ethicists welcome the fairly recent interest of Protestant and Jewish thinkers in natural law.[12] If nothing else, this recent "ecumenical" interest in natural law makes the charge that natural law is really Catholic moral apologetics more difficult to make. Perhaps that is why

---

11. See Martin Buber, *Between Man and Man,* trans. R. G. Smith (Boston: Beacon Press, 1955), pp. 119-26.

12. See *A Preserving Grace: Protestants, Catholics, and Natural Law,* ed. Michael Cromartie (Grand Rapids: Wm. B. Eerdmans, 1997).

secularist opponents of any religiously inspired ethical stance on any public issue attempt to reduce natural-law arguments to projections of the "Judeo-Christian religion" — as if there were such a thing. There is a tremendous difference between a theological authorization of natural-law theory by members of a particular religious tradition and a literal derivation of natural law from the data of a particular revelation.

So, it would seem that if natural law is a border concept between Judaism and Christianity, there are three steps involved in the full formulation of that concept: one, the separate work of locating the question of natural law *within* our respective traditions; two, the comparative work of locating the question *between* our traditions; and three, the constructive work that might lead to some common theoretical agreement *together,* and even to some joint practical efforts.

As for the separate work of the location of the original question, let me now speak in the first person — first-person plural, that is — namely, as a Jewish ethicist who needs to continually do his homework before venturing out into the world where almost all significant ethical issues seem to be found today.

An affirmation of natural law can be taken as the assertion that there exists a set of norms universally binding on all humans throughout all historical time and all political space, and that these norms can be formulated through discursive human reasoning. Furthermore, a Jewish ethicist needs to take a stand on whether natural law is an *ideal* or a *presupposition.* (I would think a Christian ethicist needs to do the same, *mutatis mutandis.*) In other words, does natural law lie *on* the foreground of Judaism, or does it lie *in* the background of Judaism? Is natural law Judaism's task, or is it Judaism's legacy? Let me explain.

The fact is, no religious Jew is located normatively at the abstract level of natural law. No one could say that his or her moral life is sufficiently determined by natural-law type universality. One does not have something like natural law in hand to then go out and concretely apply it to cases waiting for its ruling at hand. Religious Jews are living according to some sort of concrete positive law already, some sort of halakhah. Moreover, this halakhah only applies to Jews. It is something formulated through a particular historical narrative. Even when we divide today's religious Jews into "traditional" or "orthodox" Jews and "liberal" Jews, particular halakhah is a reality for both groups. Indeed, even so-called secular or nonreligious Jews, when they attempt to constitute a community for themselves, have to have some kind of positive law in order to govern themselves. And if their community is to have a *Jewish* identity, then that law of theirs will have to find some sources for itself in a

Jewish historical narrative. For religious Jews, revelation is the founding and sustaining event of that historical narrative. Everything in the tradition proceeds from Exodus-Sinai toward the final redemption *(ge'ulah shlemah):* the culmination of all history, even though one cannot judge here and now how close or how far we are from that final end.[13]

As a traditional Jew who does not want to read liberal Jews — that is, Jews whose view of revelation and tradition is quite different from my own — out of "Judaism," I would say that liberal Judaism (in all its forms) needs to develop its own halakhah, which has heretofore been mostly potential rather than actual for them. Liberal Judaism needs to do that so as to have an answer to the charge of many Jewish traditionalists that it is antinomian. But I would also remind my fellow traditional Jews that our halakhah cannot claim automatic jurisdiction over the large Jewish majority who do not accept its *prima facie* authority. Indeed, according to Talmudic legend, even God himself could not impose the authority of *his* Torah on the Jewish people at Mount Sinai until they were persuaded to accept it as being in their own best interest, thus making it *their* Torah as well.[14] So, all religious Jews are living according to some halakhah, which is not only particular in relation to the larger world outside Jewry, but is even particular within Jewry itself today.

Both liberal and traditional Jews need to deal with the question of natural law from within their own particular normative domains. That is because no Jew can possibly ignore what lies beyond the border of his or her Judaism. Yet here is where there is a great divide between liberal and traditional Judaism. For liberal Jews, the universality of natural law is an ideal toward which their present, particular Judaism aspires. The best example of that is the current liberal Jewish enthusiasm for egalitarianism, especially sexual egalitarianism. Such egalitarianism is best argued for when it is based on a coherent vision of human nature in the eyes of its proponents. Traditional Jews, when they are philosophically perspicacious, clearly have a quite different view of human nature.

For traditional Jews like me, who see ourselves doing the type of rationalist theology championed by Saadiah, Maimonides, Meiri, and Albo, natural law is a general presupposition, not a universal ideal. It is something presupposed in our ethical reasoning, something we even use to propose norms in general society, but not something we look to ideally. But, how does Judaism *presuppose* natural law? In simple language, Judaism teaches that before Jews became part of the unique covenanted people by God at Mount Sinai, we

13. See B. Sanhedrin 97b.
14. B. Shabbat 88a; also see B. Kiddushin 32b.

were participants in a more general world within which there has been a consensus about certain norms always applying there and everywhere. Moreover,
not only *were* we Jews participants in that world before Sinai, we *are* still participants in that world even after Sinai.[15] "Everywhere" means that the bor-
ders of that world include as much of humankind as one can possibly encounter, however unexpectedly. Indeed, the hallmark of that normative world
is the just treatment of the stranger, the non-resident passerby, the *ger* (cf.
Lev. 24:22). Despite the fact that revelation extended our ladder all the way up
into heaven, our feet are still planted on earth, the earth "given to humankind" (*li-vnei adam;* Ps. 115:16; Gen. 28:12). Nevertheless, this normative consensus does not mean that everyone in that world has actually accepted the
authority of these basic moral norms, much less that everyone is actually living according to them. It simply means that one's society regards itself as being subject to these norms and as being judged, if only by itself, for its compliance or noncompliance with these norms.

Natural law is also a border concept between theology and philosophy.
That is evident from the fact that most natural-law theorists have regarded
natural law to be a subset of divine law. The status of natural law as divine
law, in my view, is that moral law as a divine claim comes through the phenomenon, the self-disclosure, of the "image of God" *(tselem elohim).* That is
how the general authority of God's law becomes manifest in the world. And,
to already begin our comparative work, this phenomenon was best named
by some of the Protestant reformers "general revelation."[16] Thus, for example, when Abel can be imagined as saying to Cain before being murdered by
him *"Noli me tangere!"* ("Do not harm me!")[17], one can infer from this cry
the voice of God in the background saying, "He who reviles the victim de-
spises his maker" (Prov. 17:5). God's world, specifically the world God shares
with his own human image, was "not created to be a wasteland, but constructed to be a safe dwelling" (*la-shevet;* Isa. 45:18). Moreover, contrary to
the natural-law ontology of Maimonides or Aquinas (or, perhaps, Calvin), I
do not derive natural law from any sort of cosmological argument for divine
causality of a larger nature that includes human nature. Kant has disabused
me of any such philosophical temptation. Hence what I am proposing as the
general revelation of natural law is not "natural theology" as that term has

---

15. See B. Gittin 10b; Cohen, *Religion of Reason Out of the Sources of Judaism,* pp. 115-16.

16. See Helmut Thielicke, *Theological Ethics,* trans. W. H. Lazareth (Philadelphia: Westminster Press, 1979), vol. 1, p. 165.

17. Louis Ginzberg, *Legends of the Jews,* trans. Henrietta Szold (Philadelphia: Jewish Publication Society, 1909), vol. 1, p. 109.

come to be used in Western thought, nor is it what has been more recently termed "ontotheology."

General and Special Revelation

Nevertheless, why not remain at this general ethical level? Why do Jews need the "thicker"[18] content of what some of the Protestant reformers called "special revelation"?[19] The answer here is that the general revelation of universalizable ethics is too abstract, too "thin" to be the content of a complete human life in community, either in relation to God or in relation to fellow humans.

Regarding God, at this general ethical level we are relating to God in a situation mediated by the image of God. But here is there not always the danger that God becomes for us nothing more than what Kant called a postulate of pure practical reason and, thus, less than what Anselm called "that which nothing greater can be conceived"?[20] Is there not the danger that God becomes for us something like Levinas's *l'autrui,* that "otherness" which keeps all fellow human "others" *(les autres)* out of our "totalizing" grasp?[21] Only the direct presence of God that is experienced in special revelation, and the cultic acts through which that revelation is regularly relived — only that special revelation enables us to accept God as the immediate source of our communal life, and not just a distant prop for it and, even more so, a distant prop for our ethical interaction with all humankind.

Regarding our fellow humans, in general or ethical revelation, we can only respond to their claims on our elementary justice. That elementary justice is twofold. Negatively, it means "What is hateful to you, do not do to someone else."[22] Positively, it means "His due [*gemulo*] shall be paid him."[23]

---

18. See Clifford Geertz, *The Interpretation of Cultures* (New York: Basic Books, 1973), p. 5; Michael Walzer, *Thick and Thin* (Notre Dame: University of Notre Dame Press, 1994).

19. John Calvin, *Institutes of the Christian Religion,* trans. F. L. Battles (Philadelphia: Westminster Press, 1960), 1.2.1, 1.6.4.

20. Immanuel Kant, *Critique of Practical Reason,* trans. L. W. Beck (New York: Liberal Arts, 1956), pp. 126ff.; Anselm, *Proslogion,* chaps. 2-3, in *St. Anselm: Basic Writings,* ed. S. N. Deane (LaSalle, Ill.: Open Court, 1962), pp. 53-55.

21. Levinas, *Totality and Infinity,* pp. 70-71.

22. B. Shabbat 31a.

23. See Proverbs 19:17. These two Jewish maxims, the first Talmudic and the second scriptural (from what is now called the "Wisdom Literature"), have Christian parallels (*Didache* 1.2; Matt. 7:12 and Luke 6:31). They also correspond to the introduction to Roman civil law, already found in pre-Christian sources such as Ulpan and Gaius, namely, "not to injure another [*alterm*

Nevertheless, from the general revelation of human nature we cannot respond to the claims of fellow humans on our fuller love. That is because we can only love another from out of the experience of God's covenantal love that manifests itself in special revelation. "You shall love your neighbor as you yourself [*kamokha*] have been loved; I am the Lord."[24] Here "the Lord" (named by the Tetragrammaton) is not "God" *(elohim)* the Creator of heaven and earth, but "the Lord *your* God [*elohekha*] who took *you* [Israel] out of the land of Egypt, out of the domain of slavery."[25]

The elementary justice that comes through general revelation brings with it basic norms. Pertaining to God, general revelation proscribes the worship of any creature, which is anything other than the Creator God, so that when the Lord does reveal himself, there is room in the world for that revelation to be anticipated, longed for, and accepted. Pertaining to fellow humans, that general revelation prescribes that every human person has a *prima facie* right to live in peace in the world. As for any human community that in principle advocates — perhaps even permits — the violation of these basic norms in relation to God and to fellow humans, such a community is unworthy of the moral allegiance of any human person whose very personhood is the image of God.[26] That is what any authentically *humane* community needs as its minimal precondition for both the loyalty of its members and the attention of God. That is so irrespective of how often and how many of its members in fact violate these universal norms. Minimally, such a community should be able to express its collective guilt when these norms have been violated with official sanction. For example, consider the admirable way the *Schuldfrage,* "the question of guilt," has been handled by the German people in their attempt at moral reconstitution after the defeat of the Nazi regime. This "work-

---

non laedere] and to render each his own [*suum cuique tribuere*]." See Justinian, *Institutes,* 1.3. One can also see these two maxims in Plato (*Republic,* 331e) and Cicero (*De Officiis,* 1.7; *De Finibus Bonorum et Malorum,* 5.23), which are even earlier pre-Christian sources. Jews and Christians can surely use these "pagan" formulations of the basic negative and positive moral maxims, since they in no way are derived from the polytheism of their "pagan" formulators. For justice as "just desert," which is Justinian's most general definition, and from which the negative "no harm" maxim can be inferred, see Lenn E. Goodman, *On Justice* (New Haven: Yale University Press, 1991), pp. 23-34.

24. See Lev. 19:18. See also Franz Rosenzweig, *The Star of Redemption,* trans. W. W. Hallo (Notre Dame: University of Notre Dame Press, 1970), pp. 213-14, 239; David Novak, *Covenantal Rights* (Princeton: Princeton University Press, 2000), pp. 142-47.

25. See Exod. 20:2. See Joseph Bekhor Shor on this verse for the important distinction between God as creator and God as Israel's redeemer and lawgiver: Joseph Bekhor Shor, *Commentary on the Torah,* ed. Y. Nevo (Jerusalem: Mossad ha-Rav Kook, 1994), pp. 133-34.

26. See Gen. 13:13; 18:20; 19:12-13.

ing through" (what psychoanalysts call *durcharbeiten*) of guilt pertains, of course, to what Germans did to other humans, especially but not exclusively to the Jews, but also to what they did to God by deifying Hitler in God's stead.

The reason that such elementary justice is not an ideal (as much of the Enlightenment project hoped it would be) is because even if such elementary justice were to be accepted in principle, and even if it were to be thoroughly practiced in fact, that would not bring along with it the cultural satisfaction that comes with special revelation and its tradition.[27] And it would certainly not bring with it the final cosmic satisfaction that could only come with the final redemption promised by God. As such, as a presupposition only, general revelation does not assume the Promethean type of arrogance associated with various ideologies that emerged out of the eighteenth-century Enlightenment, ideologies that set their adherents up for the great tragedy that awaits all idealists. The theologically legitimate hope for redemption is quite different from the utopian schemes that presume the world can redeem itself. But when this elementary justice functions as a presupposition rather than an ideal, it is only taken to be necessary for a communal life worthy of the image of God, not as a sufficient ground for a communal life that promises to be divine in its self-satisfaction. In other words, natural law taken as a presupposition rather than as an ideal is minimal, not maximal, in its demands and in its promises. As a presupposition only, it is certainly not salvific. It only offers *rights,* not *the good.*[28] As such, it is but a regulatory principle, preventing revealed and traditional law from falling below the bar of elementary justice, which the very presence of that law in the world requires as its precondition.

Coming to a comparison of Jewish and Christian ethics at this basic juncture, let me quote Thomas Aquinas as a Christian theologian dealing with the fundamental ethical issue of law, which is this: *Whose* voice do I obey and *how* am I to obey it? I shall then try to paraphrase what Aquinas says about Christianity in relation to Judaism on the question of natural law so that it can be understood as what a Jewish theologian might say about the relation of Christianity to Judaism on this same question.

> The Old Law showed forth [*manifestabat*] the precepts of natural law, and added certain precepts of its own. Accordingly, as to those precepts of natural law contained in the Old Law, all are bound to observe the Old Law, not because they belonged to the Old Law, but because they belonged to natu-

---

27. I use the term *cultural* as denoting a communal way of life centered in *cultus.* See Novak, *Natural Law in Judaism,* pp. 21-22.

28. Novak, *Natural Law in Judaism,* pp. 153-54.

ral law. But as to those precepts which were added to the Old Law, they are not binding [*non tenebantur*] on any except the Jewish people.

The Old Law is distinguished from natural law, not as being altogether foreign [*aliena*] to it, but as something added thereto. For just as grace presupposes [*praesupponit*] nature, so divine law [*lex divina*] should presuppose natural law.[29]

For Aquinas, "the Old Law" *(lex vetus)* is Jewish law, especially the Written Torah, the foundation of Judaism. It is what Judaism added to the pre-Judaic/extra-Judaic natural law. *Natural law, then, is that general revelation which both Judaism and Christianity have already discovered in the world rather than having brought it into the world from their own special revelations.* Thus the "grace" of which Aquinas speaks is not only what Christianity brought into the world from its own special revelation; it is just as much what Judaism brought into the world from the special revelation of the Torah. And, for Jews, that special revelation is not only the Written Torah as Scripture, but also the Oral Torah as the rabbinic tradition, the *magisterium* of the Jews, if you will. For Jews, the giving of the Torah to Israel at Mount Sinai and thereafter is taken to be the most supreme divine grace heretofore given to the world. Hence, when called to the reading of the Torah in the synagogue, Jews thank God for "having elected us from among all the peoples by giving us His divine law [*ve-natan lanu et torato*]."[30] And, after hearing the Oral Torah expounded in the House of Learning *(bet ha-midrash)*, Jews ask God for more of the "grace" *(hina)* that we have already received whenever the Oral Torah has been expounded.[31] And, for us, the final grace will be the coming of the yet-hidden Messiah and the establishment of the kingdom of God on earth as it is already in heaven.

Aquinas was a non-Jew, so the most he can say about Judaism — and to which Jews can listen in good faith — is that Judaism's "Old Law" has discovered the basic precepts of natural law in a remarkable way. To say more than that would be for a non-Jew to tell Judaism what is valid about its special revelation. That is, it would be to tell Judaism what it *ought to be*. But all that any outsider can tell the members of another tradition, and expect them to listen to, is that they ought to be upholding in principle and attempting to practice in fact what natural law requires of every human person and every human community.

29. Thomas Aquinas, *Summa Theologiae*, 2/1, 98.5 and 99.2 ad 1.
30. *The Traditional Prayer Book for Sabbath and Festivals*, ed. David de Sola Pool (New York: Behrman House, 1960), pp. 245-46.
31. *The Traditional Prayer Book for Sabbath and Festivals*, pp. 131-32.

I submit that a Jewish theologian could employ the exact same logic as that of Aquinas in looking at Christianity ethically. That is, he or she could say, along with the fourteenth-century Provençal Jewish theologian Menahem ha-Meiri, that Christianity deserves the respect of Jews because it is *lawful* (literally, "bound by divine law" — *meguderet be-darkhei ha-dattot*),[32] and that it admonishes its adherents to be *law-abiding*. But what does Meiri regard as the valid *lawfulness* (*Gesetzlichkeit* in the words of Hermann Cohen) of Christianity?[33] It would seem that he does not mean Christianity as being what Aquinas would call "the New Law" *(lex nova)*.[34] How could he? To make that type of judgment would require Meiri to judge *all* of Christian teaching to be true. But how could he do that when Christianity claims to be the "fulfillment" of Judaism? Indeed, to do that, wouldn't Meiri have to convert to Christianity in good faith, since, by such an admission, Judaism *ought to become* Christianity? That is what Meiri would have had to do if the trajectory of this type of theological judgment were to be followed to its logical conclusion. Furthermore, even if Meiri were not to become a Christian, in order to make such a judgment about *all* of Christian teaching, he would be logically required to affirm doctrines that contradict Judaism, such as the Christian doctrine that the Messiah has *already* come to the world in the person of Jesus of Nazareth, let alone that Jesus of Nazareth is divine. So the most he could do in good faith, as a Jew remaining Jewish, is to recognize that Christianity affirms a universal morality, one that is determined not by Christian revelation but only by what that revelation itself presupposes. And, in essence, that it is the same universal morality Judaism affirms and for the very same reason.

As for Christianity's assertion that its "New Law" had added to natural law not only in degree but in kind, Meiri is in no position to judge that assertion to be either true or false. But wouldn't a Christian theologian looking at Judaism on the question of universal moral law be in the exact same position? That is, how could a Christian theologian judge the special claims Judaism makes on Jews to be either true or false? Such a judgment of truth or falsity could only come from a Christian theologian who was not looking for commonality *between* Christianity and Judaism but, rather, was looking to subsume Judaism *into* Christianity. Conversely, for a Jewish theologian to judge the full claims of Christianity to be true would require him or her to become a Christian and thereby leave the normative Jewish community. And for a

---

32. Meiri, *Bet ha-Behirah: Avodah Zarah*, ed. A. Sofer (Jerusalem: Qedem, 1964), 20a, p. 46.

33. Cohen, *Religion der Vernunft aus den Quellen des Judentums* (Darmstadt: Joseph Meltzer, 1967), p. 12.

34. Aquinas, *Summa Theologiae*, 2/1, 106ff.

Jewish theologian to judge the full claims of Christianity to be false would require him or her to at least attempt to persuade any Christians he or she happens to encounter (and who will listen) to become Jews and thereby leave the normative Christian community.

In other words, in order to constitute an ethical commonality between Judaism and Christianity, any proselytizing agenda must be explicitly bracketed. For any proselytizing conducted by a member of one religion of revelation on a member of another religion of revelation would have to contrast the truth of one's own special revelation with either the falsity or the great inadequacy of the special revelation of that other religion. I might add that goes for Jews in relation to Christians too, since Jewish proselytizing of Christians is not a theological impossibility within Judaism, and it actually occurs in ways more subtle than the more obvious Christian proselytizing of Jews. Thus "bracketing" a proselytizing agenda does not mean that Christians need refuse Jewish converts to Christianity any more than Jews need refuse Christian converts to Judaism. It would seem that in order for Christians to remain Christians in good faith and not just because of ancestry, Christians need to believe that Christianity is *the* optimal relationship with God for *any* human being — Jews included. And in order for Jews to remain Jews in good faith and not just because of ancestry, Jews need to believe that Judaism is *the* optimal relationship with God for *any* human being — Christians included. In other words, this bracketing of a proselytizing agenda only means that Christians and Jews not target each other for specific conversion of the other. Concentrating on ethical commonalities, with all their limitations, can best help Christians and Jews to bracket their ultimate truth claims without having to deny them, even implicitly.[35]

Ethical Commonality

Ethical commonality between Judaism and Christianity, when located on the question of natural law, is not accidental. It is not, in the words of the late John Rawls, a mere "overlapping consensus."[36] Rather, this Jewish-Christian ethical commonality is a common vision of human nature and what the ethical implications of that vision are to be. Nevertheless, we must ask whether

35. David Novak, "What to Seek and What to Avoid in Jewish-Christian Dialogue," in *Talking with Christians: Musings of a Jewish Theologian* (Grand Rapids: Wm. B. Eerdmans, 2005), pp. 1-7.

36. John Rawls, *A Theory of Justice* (Cambridge, Mass.: Harvard University Press, 1971), pp. 387-88; Rawls, *Political Liberalism* (New York: Columbia University Press, 1993), pp. 35ff.

that essential rather than accidental consensus is limited to Jews and Christians or not.

Limiting that consensus to Jews and Christians alone would seem to recognize the fact that Judaism and Christianity share more of a common historical border than any other two traditions in the world. That common historical border begins with our sharing of the text of the Hebrew Bible verbatim. Yet that leads us into the philosophical problem of proposing a "Judeo-Christian ethic," which suggests that Judaism and Christianity constitute a joint ethical position because of the *overlapping* of their respective special revelations. But that could mean the overlapping of part of the "Old Testament" with part of the "New Testament," and then where that part of the New Testament overlaps with the Talmud. To be sure, such an ethics could be universal in scope, yet its sources could only be *inter-traditional*. As such, it could not be presented to the world as natural law, precisely because its appeal would be to the authority of two — albeit overlapping — special revelations and their respective traditions. It would not be general revelation.

The New Testament scholar and Lutheran bishop Krister Stendahl once suggested to me (significantly enough, in Jerusalem) that this "Judeo-Christian ethic" seems to be a Jewish-Christian cabal. Such a charge is of great importance today when the secular world, where all the basic ethical questions are located and where they need to be addressed if not actually resolved, is no longer "Christian" as it was never "Jewish."[37] Any ethical claims made in that world, in which we all participate, like it or not, would have to be philosophical rather than theological. But, along these lines, it should be noted that neither Thomas Aquinas nor Menahem ha-Meiri was suggesting any such theological overlapping of Judaism and Christianity. What each of them seemed to be suggesting, however, was an ethical parallel so close that it could well lead to an actual ethical intersection, one that can be *philosophically* constituted. That is, Christians and Jews can discover together some of the truth of human nature ethically and thus how that discovery leads to the formulation of certain norms given for human action in the world.

So I would suggest that the natural-law orientation of some Jewish and Christian ethicists needs to be conducted toward a universal horizon (which is, nonetheless, different than a universal ideal). That means we must locate an ethical border *around* ourselves and then *between* us and some third tradition. As such, the ethical border *between* ourselves should not preclude the constitution of another border. For the location of any such border to be co-

---

37. See David Novak, *Jewish-Christian Dialogue* (Oxford: Oxford University Press, 1989), pp. 140-42.

gent, it is important to locate just who is standing on the other side of that border most immediately. Here it would seem Jews and Christians need to engage Muslims in our common ethical enterprise: first theoretically, then practically. However, unlike what pertains between Jews and Christians, who do share the text of the Hebrew Bible as special revelation, there is no such common book upon which to historically locate any special revelation with either Jews or Christians. Unlike Jews and Christians, there is no true theological commonality if one takes "theology" to be about special revelation. That is why my notion of general revelation is not based on what is usually called "natural theology."[38] But Jews and Christians and Muslims do share the acknowledgment of God as Lawgiver. Moreover, there is in all three traditions a rationalist school of thought that recognizes a natural-law connection to the *same* divine Lawgiver. That recognition is of a universal moral law which is prior epistemologically (that is, logically but not ontologically) to the law put forth by any special revelation. That is what is meant by the *presupposition* of natural law for special revelations.

Even though the political climate today makes common practical strategies between Jews and Christians and Muslims very difficult, I think that common theoretical discussions of universal ethical concerns among Jews and Christians and Muslims are a desideratum. That is so even if the only reason for such discussions now is that they would enable Jews and Christians and Muslims to get along better among ourselves. Such discussions would also enable Jews and Christians to enlist Muslims in the ethical claims they have to make in and to the secular world. Since Jews and Christians and Muslims do not share a special revelation, such enlistment of Muslims by Jews and Christians would help rebut the secularist charge that our joint ethical claims are derived from our special revelations in conjunction, that we are in fact a Jewish-Christian political cabal with ethical rationalizations for our joint faith. In other words, conversations with Muslims on ethical issues would help Jewish and Christian ethical rhetoric to be more philosophically persuasive with the help of Muslims and the inclusion of Islam in public arguments. For arguments that can be reduced to theology cannot be made in a secular world, since acceptance of the argument would seem to entail some sort of conversion to the religion of which this special theology is an expression. Theological arguments only make sense to those who have accepted the special revelation wherefrom these arguments are derived.

---

38. Novak, "Are Philosophical Proofs of the Existence of God Theologically Meaningful?" in *God in the Teachings of Conservative Judaism*, ed. S. Siegel and E. Gertel (New York: Rabbinical Assembly, 1985), pp. 188-200.

Nevertheless, due to the present political climate in the world today, such Jewish-Christian-Muslim ethical commonality might well have to wait, even at the theoretical level (at least in public). Yet that sad fact cannot postpone the entrance of Jews and Christians and their ethical claims into the secular world. The reason the present impasse in Jewish-Christian-Muslim relations cannot postpone the entrance of Jews and Christians into secular ethical discourse — however much that entrance would be strengthened by an Islamic contingent in it — is because Jews and Christians are *already* there. The question, therefore, for Jewish and Christian ethicists is how to make our ethical claims in and to a world that is not only not prepared to acknowledge any special revelation, but is not even prepared to acknowledge any divine law at all. Can we Jewish and Christian natural-law ethicists possibly concur with Hugo Grotius (usually designated to be the founder of modern natural-law theory) that natural-law claims can still be made "even though we say there is no God" *(etiamsi daremus non esse Deum)?* Can we speak as if there is no God behind all our ethical claims?[39] That is a more complicated question, at least theoretically, than the more practical question of how Jews and Christians can talk with Muslims about ethical issues. Yet, without that universal horizon, are we not limiting our discourse to the worshipers of the God of Abraham/Ibrahim? What about those who have other gods — what about Hindus, for example? And what about those who claim to have no god — or at least no law-giving god — like so many of our Western secularists?

At this point, I think the prospects of a more universal ethical discourse are far less hopeful. The gap between secularist and theistic views of human nature is so wide that it would seem we could not arrive at any normative consensus that wasn't only an accidental overlapping consensus. It doesn't seem we could have a truly rational consensus on anything significant ethically. The gap between us is over whether or not there is a human nature whose bearers are capable of apprehending themselves as the image of God, and capable of discerning a basic divine law that rules anywhere and anytime. Could there be a common denial between secularists and theists that we are only answerable to our own desires and someone else's power to either fulfill them or inhibit them? The only possible way for us theists to bridge that gap is to show secularists that they too have some absolute norms and that their atheism offers no explanation of why they hold them. In other words, one can try to show that atheism leads to a moral nihilism that even most secularists do not really want. In this case, rational discourse is still possible, although I often think that one needs the dialogical skills of Socrates to sustain it.

39. Novak, "Law: Religious or Secular?" pp. 178-82.

It seems, then, that whereas theists — minimally, Jews, Christians, and Muslims — can engage in ethical discourse with *secularity,* we do not seem to be able to do so with *secularism* and its *secularist* proponents. Moreover, when secularists have determined that they cannot admit the political presence of religiously inspired ethicists into the world of public policy, a world they now largely control, then religious ethicists — be they Jews or Christians or Muslims — however philosophically able we may have become, need to employ more political tactics, which will better protect our respective traditions and our joint ethical stance from becoming strangers on earth. Even when we cannot convince the secularists of the truth of our common vision of human nature, even with the best philosophical arguments, we still need to make sure that those who live by this vision will not have to go into exile, either external or internal.

15   The Treatment of Islam and Muslims
in the Legal Writings of Maimonides (1986)

Introduction

When dealing with the specific questions concerning the status of Islam and Muslims for Judaism, Maimonides had behind him the development of the overall treatment of other religions in Jewish legal tradition (halakhah). It was this tradition to which he was bound as his religious heritage, and it was this tradition that he himself developed in such a way that it was never quite the same after him. Thus, in order to understand the significance of Maimonides' treatment of these specific legal questions, we must take a brief look at how that tradition developed and the options it gave a halakhist as gifted and subtle as he. Moreover, we must look at Maimonides' philosophic work to understand the full significance of the method employed in the legal decisions he made in this area especially. Elsewhere I have argued against the view that Maimonides' legal and philosophic interests were separate and distinct.[1] Certainly in legal questions such as these, where the theological issue of belief so quickly enters the picture, one can hardly ignore the fact that the same philosophic concerns which permeated his theology also permeated his treatment of this theologically charged area of law.

In biblical Judaism, religion — any religion — is seen as inextricably intertwined with national existence and culture. At this level the worship of the One God (YHWH) was seen as the unique covenant between the One God and the nation of Israel. Other nations had their own respective covenants

---

1. David Novak, *The Image of the Non-Jew in Judaism: An Historical and Constructive Study of the Noahide Laws* (New York and Toronto: Edwin Mellen Press, 1983), pp. 275ff.

with other gods.[2] Israel is monotheistic; every other nation is polytheistic.[3] For this reason, nowhere in the Hebrew Bible was any non-Israelite, any gentile, faulted for the practice of polytheism, including the cult of idolatry.[4] This being the case, Israel's relations with these other nations were not based on specifically theological criteria inasmuch as these other nations were all taken to be polytheists, but they were not all to be treated the same way by the people of Israel. As such, they were differentiated by other criteria.

Some nations were regarded as the inherent enemies of the people of Israel, in particular the seven nations of Canaan and the Amalekites.[5] They were regarded as incorrigibly antagonistic to Israel, lacking any human compassion and decency, even among themselves.[6] The fact that they were designated as "not fearing God" *(elohim)* is not so much an indictment of their polytheism as it is a moral indictment of their way of life, which seemed to place no restrictions on their cruelty and lack of trustworthiness, especially but not exclusively to Israel.[7] For this reason, primarily, they were to be destroyed by Israel.

Other nations, with whom Israel was able to conduct stable political relations, were primarily judged by the political criterion of reciprocal trustworthiness.[8] Indeed, trustworthiness *(emunah)* is the most basic criterion for the judgment of any interpersonal relationship in the Hebrew Bible, be that relationship between man and man or between God and man.[9] In the case of those nations who were subjugated by Israel, the basic criterion of judgment was their faithfulness to Israelite suzerainty and Israel's faithful guarantee of their rights as vassals.[10] The same was the case for non-Jews domiciled in Israel *(gerim)*.[11]

Only in the case of certain unusual individual gentiles was the rejection of polytheism something considered praiseworthy, but still not mandatory.[12] Nevertheless, it was realized that even such unusual gentile monotheists would have to practice public idolatry in their own societies.[13] The notion of non-Israelite monotheistic communities was not considered by the authors

2. See, e.g., Mic. 4:5.
3. See, e.g., Ps. 96:5; 1 Chron. 17:20-24.
4. See Novak, *The Image of the Non-Jew in Judaism*, pp. 108ff.
5. See, e.g., Deut. 20:16-18; 23:4-9; 25:17-19.
6. See, e.g., Gen. 13:13; 18:20ff.; Exod. 17:8-13; Lev. 18:24-25; 2 Kings 23:10.
7. See, e.g., Amos 1:3ff.; Mal. 2:10ff; 1 Kings 15:19; Hab. 2:4.
8. See Gen. 21:22ff.; 31:44ff.; 2 Kings 5:21ff.
9. See, e.g., Amos 1:3ff.; Mal. 2:10ff.; 1 Kings 15:19; Hab. 2:4.
10. See Deut. 20:10ff.; Josh. 9:15ff.; 2 Sam. 21:1ff.
11. See, e.g., Exod. 22:20; Lev. 24:22.
12. See, e.g., Josh. 2:1ff.; Job 1:1ff.
13. See 2 Kings 5:15ff.

of the Hebrew Bible. The acceptance of monotheism by any large group of gentiles was considered only in the context of their becoming part of the covenant with Israel. In post-exilic biblical texts this was envisioned as an item on the messianic agenda.[14]

In the rabbinic writings we see a rather radical development in terms of Judaism's treatment of other religions. With the emergence of the doctrine of the "seven commandments of the children of Noah" — a doctrine I have elsewhere argued emerged late in the second century of the Common Era[15] — a universal ban on polytheism and idolatry came to be accepted in Judaism. Just as Jews are prohibited to hold polytheistic beliefs or to practice idolatry, so are gentiles.[16] Although there are traces in the early rabbinic writings of the older notion that every gentile is *ipso facto* an idolator, the distinction between polytheistic gentiles and monotheistic gentiles was more and more emphasized.[17] Unlike in the biblical writings, where a gentile monotheist was regarded as an anomaly, acting above and beyond what is expected of him, in the rabbinic writings gentile monotheism was regarded as the norm, at least *de jure*, even though it was recognized that public idolatry was still common *de facto*.[18] It was recognized that polytheism was becoming less and less a matter of personal conviction for gentiles and more and more a cultural vestige. Gentiles were now judged by theological criteria. Despite this, however, the notion of a community of gentile monotheists, separate and distinct from the Jewish people, was something of which the Rabbis were unaware. Thus some obvious rabbinic polemics against the new religion of Christianity were directed against what were perceived as Christianity's compromise of Jewish monotheism, specifically through its corrupt use of the Hebrew Bible.[19]

The recognition of the fact of individual gentile monotheists is something which was already found in the Hellenistic Jewish writings. There we find the notion that these gentile monotheists are in fact potential Jews. It was recognized that the rejection of idolatry and its ideological basis in polytheism is the first step toward the eventual adoption of full Jewish identity and full Jewish responsibility for all the commandments of the Mosaic Torah.[20] In

---

14. See, e.g., Isa. 2:2-3; 19:25; 56:7; Mic. 4:5; Zeph. 3:9; Zech. 14:1ff.; Novak, *The Image of the Non-Jew in Judaism*, pp. 111ff.

15. Novak, *The Image of the Non-Jew in Judaism*, pp. 23ff.

16. T. Avodah Zarah 8:4; B. Sanhedrin 56ab.

17. See B. Gittin 45b and parallels; also, B. Yevamot 61a.

18. B. Hullin 13b.

19. See, e.g., *Ecclesiastes Rabbah* 4:13.

20. See Josephus, *Antiquities*, 14:110; Philo, *De Vita Mosis*, 2:14; cf. Juvenal, *Satires*, 14:96; Tacitus, *History*, 5:5.

the rabbinic writings we find two disparate views about whether or not gentile monotheists are potential Jews. One view holds that gentiles are obligated for seven commandments and no more.[21] The other view holds that gentiles should observe more and more of the commandments, which of course means that they are to do so and become eventually absorbed into Judaism altogether.[22]

Thus Maimonides inherited a number of options as regards Jewish treatment of a non-Jewish religion: (1) the biblical option primarily based on political and moral criteria; (2) the rabbinic option primarily based on theological criteria; (3) the one rabbinic view that gentile monotheists are potential Jews; and (4) the other rabbinic view that gentile monotheists have a sufficient religious and political life without any attachment, actual or even potential, to Judaism and the Jewish people. We shall see how Maimonides orders these options and how this ordering is philosophically determined.

Judaism and Islam

Maimonides lived his entire life under Muslim rule, and despite his eventual rise to high position under the Muslim rulers of Egypt, his view of that rule as regards Jews was often quite negative. He and his family were forced by the Almohad persecutions to leave their native Córdoba in Spain in the middle of the twelfth century (Maimonides always signed his name "Moses son of Rabbi Maimon the Spaniard") and had to roam throughout the Maghreb until eventually settling in Fustat, the old city of Cairo. In his famous *Epistle to Yemen,* written early in his career, where he attempted to comfort a Jewish community being persecuted by Muslims, he wrote,

> Remember, my co-religionists, that on account of the vast number of our sins, God has caused us to fall in the midst of this people, the Arabs [*yishma'el*], who have persecuted us severely, and passed baneful legislation against us. . . . Never did a nation molest, degrade, debase and hate us as much as they. . . . We have acquiesced, both old and young, to inure ourselves to humiliation. . . . All this notwithstanding, we do not escape this continued maltreatment which well nigh crushes us.[23]

21. B. Sanhedrin 58b-59a.

22. Y. Avodah Zarah 2:1/40c; B. Hullin 92ab.

23. Maimonides, *Epistle to Yemen,* ed. A. S. Halkin; English translation by B. Cohen (New York: American Academy for Jewish Research, 1952), p. xviii.

At the end of this epistle, Maimonides recognized that he was taking a political risk in attacking both the Muslims and the claim of Islam that it is superior to Judaism. Nevertheless, his concern for the downtrodden Yemenite Jewry took precedence over his concerns for his own safety and security.[24]

However, what is important to note, even in this highly polemical work, is the fact that Maimonides only criticized Muslim charges against the veracity of the Hebrew Bible and Jewish tradition in general. He did not criticize Islam *per se*. This should be contrasted with his treatment of Christianity. Maimonides asserted that although Jesus, unlike Muhammad, never intended to found a new religion, Christianity was still considered to be a form of idolatry.[25] No doubt he regarded its doctrine of the Trinity to be a basic compromise of the monotheism required of all persons, gentiles as well as Jews.[26]

Such is not the case with Islam. The important thing to bear in mind is that despite the political persecution of the Jews by Muslims in Maimonides' lifetime, a persecution he himself experienced and to which he himself responded more than once, Islamic monotheism was what ultimately determined his halakhic treatment of Muslims. As we have seen, the whole political criterion for determining the status of gentile emphasized in the Hebrew Bible was played down by Maimonides.[27]

This comes out in his treatment of the question of gentile wine *(stam yenam)*. According to the Talmud, Jews are not to drink wine prepared by gentiles or derive any monetary benefit from it. In the Talmud two distinct reasons are given for this prohibition: (1) It was assumed that all gentile wine has been dedicated to idolatry, even if this is not verifiable in every case.[28]; and (2) Gentile wine is not to be drunk in order to minimize social contact with gentiles, which was seen as leading to intermarriage and perhaps to idolatry as well.[29] Now it would seem that if a gentile is not an idolator, this prohibition should no longer apply according to this first Talmudic reason.[30] The ban on intermarriage, on the other hand, applies whether the gentiles were monotheists or

---

24. Maimonides, *Epistle to Yemen,* p. xx and n. 22 thereon.

25. Maimonides, *Epistle to Yemen,* p. iv; *Mishneh Torah:* Idolatry, 9:4.

26. See Maimonides, *Guide of the Perplexed,* 1.50.

27. See Maimonides, MT: Kings, 6:1ff., where the acceptance of the Noahide laws, over and above making peace with Israel, is the *sine qua non* for Jewish tolerance of any gentile nation, including Canaan and even Amalek. See the note of Rabad thereon. Maimonides' rabbinic source is Y. Shevi'it 6:1/36c; but there the acceptance of the Noahide laws is not mentioned. Cf. B. Gittin 46a, Tos., s.v. "kevan."

28. B. Avodah Zarah 29b. See Tos., s.v. "yayin."

29. B. Avodah Zarah 36b.

30. B. Avodah Zarah 57a.

polytheists.[31] In the second case the prohibition is clearly more extensive but weaker, and it was this tendency in halakhah that Maimonides followed in dealing with the wine of Muslims. Although a Jew may not drink the wine of a Muslim, he may derive monetary benefit from it. He wrote,

> A resident-alien [ger toshav], that is one who has accepted upon himself the seven commandments, as we have explained, it is prohibited to drink his wine, but it is permitted to derive monetary benefit [muttar be-haniyyah] from it. . . . And so it is with any gentile who does not practice idolatry [avodah zarah] like these Muslims [yishma'elim]: their wine is prohibited for drinking but permitted for monetary benefit. And so rule all the geonim.[32]

Furthermore, in a responsum that was probably written before the publication of his great code, the Mishneh Torah (in 1178), Maimonides stated this concerning the wine of Muslims:

> These Muslims are not far from idolatry as you mentioned. . . . Ultimately all of the geonim of the West [Spain] were lenient concerning their wine. It should be permitted to derive monetary benefit from it but no more. Permitting the drinking of it is something that has not been heard from any halakhic authority [ba'al hora' ah]. This is accepted practice [halakhah le-ma'aseh] in the presence of all the geonim of the West: when it happens that a Muslim touches our wine with a touch that could entail religious significance [nissukh], they prohibited drinking it but permitted selling it, just like Muslim wine itself.[33]

Thus, even though Maimonides regarded many of the folk practices of Muslims to be largely of pagan origin, he nevertheless held that Islam had removed the idolatrous intent which would make articles associated in any way with these practices idolatrous accessories.[34] This being the case, the only reason for the continuation of the ban is the rabbinic goal of limiting Jewish-gentile social intercourse, and that could be fulfilled by a prohibition on drinking gentile wine alone.

---

31. B. Kiddushin 68b re Deut. 7:4 and B. Avodah Zarah 36b.

32. Maimonides, MT: Forbidden Foods, 11:7. Anything associated with idolatry, even if practiced by Jews, is not to be used for any monetary benefit. See M. Avodah Zarah 5:8; B. Makkot 22a; Y. Avodah Zarah 5:12/45a re Deut. 13:18; Maimonides, MT: Idolatry, 7:2.

33. Teshuvot ha-Rambam, no. 269, ed. J. Blau (Jerusalem: Miqqitsei Nirdamim, 1960), vol. 2, pp. 515-16.

34. See Teshuvot ha-Rambam, no. 269, vol. 2, pp. 515-16, n. 28.

To appreciate the significance of Maimonides' ruling here, a ruling which was widely disputed,[35] we must examine the key terms he used in it. The resident alien *(ger toshav)* refers to a gentile who was given the right to dwell in the Land of Israel and to be protected by Jewish civil and criminal law. The Talmud indicates that the *ger toshav* ceased to be a real political status with the destruction of the Second Temple in Jerusalem in 586 B.C.E.[36] However, the Talmud did discuss anyway what was the criterion for becoming a *ger toshav*. The minimalist view was that one had to renounce idolatry; the maximalist view was that one had to adopt the whole Torah with the sole exception of the ban on eating improperly slaughtered meat *(nevelot)*. The view which Maimonides accepted, however, is that the criterion for becoming a *ger toshav* is the acceptance of the seven Noahide commandments.[37] Now the acceptance of these commandments is a universal obligation irrespective of time and place. Thus one who accepts these commandments is often referred to by Maimonides as a *ger toshav* or "like a *ger toshav*" because the obligatory character of these commandments remains even though the political privileges they entailed have been bracketed by history.[38]

How ironic that Maimonides should speak of Muslim wine inasmuch as it is well known that the Qur'an explicitly prohibits Muslims from drinking any alcohol.[39] That, however, is an internal Islamic matter, something with which Jews and Judaism need not be concerned. Clearly, many Muslims violated this Qur'anic prohibition rather openly. What is important to note is that Maimonides regarded Muslims to be monotheists who could not be judged to be those who make wine an accessory to idolatry. Furthermore, both in the responsum and in the *Mishneh Torah*, Maimonides invoked the Talmudic rule that wine not fit to be used on the Temple altar *(she-eyno ra'uy al gabbei ha-mizbeah)* — that is, wine with some admixture of honey or leaven — that this wine is exempt from the status of wine which one may not drink with a gentile.[40] Thus we can see that he even played down the whole rationale for this prohibition — namely, a bar to Jewish-gentile socializing. There seems to have been no reason to ban social contacts with Muslims.

35. See *Teshuvot ha-Rashba*, vol. 1, nos. 717, 813; vol. 4, no. 149; *Teshuvot ha-Ribash*, no. 180; *Teshuvot Tashbats*, vol. 2, no. 168; *Teshuvot ha-Radbaz*, vol. 1, no. 2.

36. B. Arakhin 29a.

37. B. Avodah Zarah 64b.

38. See Maimonides, MT: Idolatry, 10:6 (and the note of Rabad thereon); MT: Circumcision, 1:6; MT: Forbidden Relationships, 14:7; MT: Kings, 8:10-11.

39. Qur'an 5:93-94. See F. Rahman, *Islam*, 2d ed. (Chicago: University of Chicago Press, 1979), p. 51.

40. Y. Terumot 8:3/45c.

Maimonides' Response to a Muslim Convert to Judaism

We have seen that in the rabbinic writings there are two views regarding non-Jewish monotheists: (1) they are in fact potential Jews; and (2) their monotheism is a fully actual relationship with the One God and is, therefore, sufficient for them from the standpoint of Judaism. Elsewhere I have argued that the first view is the older one and the latter is later, a view largely formulated after the rise of Christianity and its separation from Judaism and the Jewish people.[41] We shall now see how Maimonides, as much as possible within the limits of halakhah as it developed up until his time, returned to the older view about gentile monotheism being in fact potential Judaism.[42] As a philosopher largely influenced by Aristotle, Maimonides used the Aristotelian ontological scheme of potency-act in his halakhic treatment of the relation between gentile and Jewish monotheism.[43]

A certain Rabbi Obadiah ('Abdullāh?), a Muslim who had converted to Judaism, wrote to Maimonides complaining that his Jewish teacher said that Muslims are idolators. The curious thing about Maimonides' response, one which a student of the the halakhah would immediately notice, is that even if the charge about Muslims were true, the teacher of Rabbi Obadiah was transgressing the rabbinic rule about taunting a convert about his pagan past.[44] However, instead of even mentioning this, Maimonides immediately made a long statement denying the charge altogether:

41. See Novak, *The Image of the Non-Jew in Judaism*, pp. 26ff.

42. Maimonides, to be sure, codified the later Talmudic bans of gentiles practicing basic Jewish rites such as Sabbath observance and Torah study (MT: Kings, 10:9 re B. Sanhedrin 58b-59a; B. Avodah Zarah 3a). He wrote, "The essence of the matter is that we do not allow him to innovate a religion [*le-haddesh dat*] and to make up commandments from his own mind. Either he should become a full convert [*ger tsedeq*] and accept all the commandments, or he should remain in his own Torah — neither adding to it nor detracting from it." Nevertheless, he also wrote this immediately afterwards (MT: Kings, 10:10): "If a Noahide wants to practice any other commandment from the commandments of the Torah in order to receive transcendent reward, we do not stop him from doing so according to its proper halakhic procedure" (see the note of Radbaz thereon). See his comment on M. Terumot 3:9 (cf. B. Baba Kama 38a). The point that emerges out of this seems to be that if the gentile observance of Jewish practices is part of an actualizing process of moving toward Judaism in stages, then it is acceptable. If, however, it is part of diluting Jewish practices for the sake of some sort of syncretism, then it is unacceptable. It all depends on the intent, and intent is clearly a teleological criterion; see Aristotle, *Nicomachean Ethics*, 1112a15.

43. Thus in the *Mishneh Torah* he refers to the Mosaic Torah (613 commandments) as "completing [*ve-nishlamah*] the seven Noahide commandments" (MT: Kings, 9:1).

44. M. Baba Metsia 4:10; B. Sanhedrin 94a.

These Muslims are not idolators [*ovdei avodah zarah*] at all. It has already been cut off from their mouth and mind. For they are totally and properly committed to the One God [*yihud ke-ra'uy*] without deceit [*dofi*]. . . . And if someone says that the house that they praise [*al-Ka'ba*] is an idolatrous shrine and an idol is hidden in it which their ancestors used to worship — what about it? Those who worship in its direction today, their thoughts are only for God [*eyn libbam ella la-shamayim*]. . . . So it is with these Muslims today, all of them, even children and women, idolatry is cut off from their mouth.[45]

Maimonides did not give unqualified acceptance to every Islamic practice. Some of them he called "their error and their foolishness" *(ve-ta'utam ve-tippeshutam)*, refusing to elaborate lest Jewish informers report him to the Muslim authorities. Nevertheless, concerning the most fundamental theological doctrine, the existence and unity of God, Maimonides argued that Islam is totally committed to it and that this commitment can be taken for granted even among the simplest Muslim believers.

If this is the case, then Islam is clearly as monotheistic as Judaism. In the case of Rabbi Obadiah, the former Muslim, his conversion to Judaism did not entail the nullification of any polytheistic belief or the abandonment of any idolatrous practice. It would seem that for Maimonides Judaism and Islam are both equally monotheistic and that monotheism is the foundation of all true religion.[46] Is Islam, then, more than potential Judaism but the equal of Judaism? If so, then what is the significance of Rabbi Obadiah's conversion altogether? What has he actually gained?[47]

---

45. *Teshuvot ha-Rambam,* no. 448 (vol. 2, p. 726). See, also his "Iggeret ha-Shemad," in *Iggrot ha-Rambam,* ed. Rabinowitz (Jerusalem: Mossad ha-Rav Kook, 1960), p. 44. No doubt something like the Muslim practice of throwing pebbles at certain shrines (see *Islam from the Prophet Muhammad to the Capture of Constantinople,* edited and translated by B. Lewis, 2 vols. [New York: Harper & Row, 1974], vol. 2, p. 29) reminded many Jews of the rabbinic description of this as a pagan practice in honor of the god Mercury (M. Sanhedrin 7:6). The Talmud rules that this practice is considered unacceptable whether done reverently or even irreverently (B. Sanhedrin 64a), and Maimonides codified this (MT: Idolatry, 3:5). However, if the act was no longer connected with pagan worship at all, then it would seem, for Maimonides, that it assumed a different character altogether (see B. Sanhedrin 64a, Tos. s.v. "af-'al-gav"). Intentionality, not historical origin, ultimately determines the character of any act. Similarly, Maimonides removed (in another responsum to R. Obadiah the Convert) any restrictions on a convert from reciting the liturgical formula "God of our fathers." *Teshuvot ha-Rambam,* no. 393 (vol. 2, pp. 548-50). See Maimonides, MT: First Fruits, 4:4 re Y. Bikkurim 1.4/64a à la Gen. 17:5. Cf. also I. Twersky, *Introduction to the Code of Maimonides (Mishneh Torah)* (New Haven: Yale University Press, 1980), pp. 485-86.

46. See Maimonides, MT: Foundations of the Torah, 1:1 and *Guide of the Perplexed,* 2.33.

47. However, conversion from Judaism to Islam — even if Islam is not polytheistic — is

The answer to these questions seems to lie in Maimonides' view of the superiority of Mosaic prophecy, whose product is the Torah. Mosaic prophecy is superior to any other prophecy, whether Jewish or non-Jewish, on two accounts.

First, Mosaic prophecy is the full expression of original monotheism. All other true prophecy, and here "true" and "monotheistic" are synonyms, is derived from it in the sense that it can only reconfirm it. Any contradiction with this original monotheism would render the subsequent prophecy false.[48] Thus Rabbi Obadiah's conversion from Islam to Judaism is a movement from derivative monotheism to the original source. Ultimately, all monotheistic persons and peoples will return to their Jewish origins. In his treatment of Jewish messianism in the *Mishneh Torah* (a part removed by the Christian censors), Maimonides wrote about both Christianity and Islam (after some rather negative comments about both Jesus and Muhammad) in the following way:

> But there is no power in man to apprehend the thoughts of the Creator of the world. . . . Thus these words of Jesus of Nazareth and this Arab who came after him were only to prepare the way for the Messiah-King and to order [*le-taqqen*] the whole world to serve the Lord altogether, as it says in scripture, "For I will unite all the peoples into pure speech, all of them to call upon the name of the Lord and to serve Him with one shoulder."[49]

In this concept of derivative monotheism, especially in the case of Islam (I shall discuss the distinction between Islam and Christianity later in this essay), Maimonides followed the lead of the earlier Spanish Jewish theologian Rabbi Judah Halevi. In his dialogue *Kuzari,* Halevi depicted a pagan king —

---

clearly prohibited in that it entails a Jew abandoning Mosaic revealed law. Such a person, for Maimonides, is an *apiqoros* — that is, one who rejects Mosaic prophecy. Also, he is a *kofer* — one who denies the full divine revelation (MT: Repentance, 3:8). Maimonides advocated rather harsh punishment for such deviants (MT: Idolatry, 10:1). Clearly he follows the rabbinic view which enabled gentile admission to Judaism (see B. Yevamot 22a), but denied Jews the right to exit from Judaism (see T. Demai 2:4; B. Yevamot 47b). When conversion was forced, however, he was rather lenient concerning the legal consquences. See "Iggeret ha-Shemad," passim; cf. also H. Soloveitchik, "Maimonides' Iggeret Ha-Shemad: Law and Rhetoric," in the *Joseph Lookstein Memorial Volume* (New York: Ktav Publishing House, 1980), pp. 281ff.

48. See Maimonides, MT: Foundations of the Torah, 8:3.

49. Maimonides, MT: Kings, 11, end, uncensored version, ed. Rabinowitz (Jerusalem: Mossad ha-Rav Kook, 1962), p. 416, citing Zeph. 3:9. Maimonides' use of Zephaniah 3:9 as his proof text is significant because this verse was also the proof text for the rabbinic view which advocated growing gentile observance of the commandments of the Torah as potential Judaism (see above, n. 22). See *Guide of the Perplexed,* 3.29.

already a philosophical monotheist — who attempts to find the true religion. He ultimately chooses Judaism over both Christianity and Islam because the latter two religions are at best derivative and, therefore, the original monotheism is no doubt the most authentic — and that is Judaism.[50] In so arguing, Halevi, and after him Maimonides, reversed the successionist claims of both Christianity and Islam. Succession is not improvement but dilution of the original revelation.

Second, the test of the most effective monotheism is not only the purity of its belief — a point where Islam is not inferior to Judaism — but also the unified political and personal order which it creates and which is singularly monotheistic in its intentionality.[51] Here Maimonides was convinced of the practical superiority of the Torah over any other form of revealed legislation. In addition, Judaism has the longest experience as a monotheistic community. Thus he continued his discussion of how Christianity and Islam prepare the way for the Jewish Messiah-King and his exalted reign, how they prepare for it but are by no means equal to it:

> How is this so? The whole world is already filled with the words of [their] messiah and the words of the Torah and the words of the commandments, and these words have spread to the farthest islands and among many obstinate [*arelei lev*] peoples, and they discuss these words and the commandments of the Torah. They say, "These commandments were true [*emet hayu*], but are already invalid [*batlu*] today, and are not to be perpetual [*nohagot le-dorot*]." . . . But when the true Messiah arises and will triumph and be uplifted and exalted, all of them will immediately return and comprehend that their ancestors inherited falsehood [*sheqer*] and their prophets and ancestors misled them.[52]

The error of the Christians and the Muslims, for Maimonides, is that they assume that the Torah is passé and that a monotheistic community can be constituted without it. Yet, despite their political power — as contrasted with the political impotence of the Jewish people — they have not been able to bring about the social and political unity and harmony which should be the

---

50. *Kuzari*, 1:4, 9-11. For Islamic charges of Jewish corruption of true revelation, see Qur'an 2:87-89, 106-8.

51. See Maimonides, *Guide of the Perplexed*, 2.40 for the integration of theoretical and practical elements *as* the evidence of divine law.

52. Maimonides, MT: Kings, ed. Rabinowitz, p. 417. See also Maimonides, *Commentary on the Mishnah*, ed. Y. Kafih (Jerusalem: Mossad ha-Rav Kook, 1965); Sanhedrin, chap. 10, prin. 9, p. 144 and n. 77 thereon.

practical outcome of monotheism. It is important to note that Maimonides regarded the Messiah-King as a political ruler who will be able, without supernatural intervention, to effect universal monotheism by putting the Torah into full practice. He seemed convinced that if the Jews had the necessary political power, monotheism would become the pervasive practical force that it is now in belief the world over.[53] The messianic failure of both Christianity and Islam is something which indicates that their monotheism (real in the case of Islam; imaginary in the case of Christianity) cannot effect a unified and harmonious world order. Hence they have not superseded Judaism, as they claim, but have rather diluted its message and missed its great monotheistic strengths. In the days of the Messiah, all the peoples — certainly all the Christian and Muslim peoples — will see Judaism as the purest and most comprehensive practical monotheism and will accept it. In the meantime, there will be certain insightful Christians and Muslims who will anticipate this messianic reality. The convert Rabbi Obadiah was one such Muslim, and Maimonides thus addressed him with the greatest personal respect as well as voicing an appreciation of how his former Islam was in effect potential Judaism, an anticipation of the true messianic realm.

Circumcision and Islam

Maimonides not only regarded Islam as an unambiguously monotheistic religion; he also saw certain Islamic practices as actually being mandated by Judaism. Concerning the practice of circumcision he wrote,

> Our sages said that the sons of Keturah, who are of the seed of Abraham, who came after Ishmael and Isaac, are obligated to be circumcised. And because today the sons of Ishmael have assimilated [ve-nit'arvu] with the sons of Keturah, all of them are obligated to be circumcised on the eighth day.[54]

To understand the significance of this ruling in Maimonides' great code of Jewish law, the *Mishneh Torah*, one must be aware of the fact that he used the term *Ishmaelite* somewhat ambiguously in his legal writings. On the one hand, *yishma'elim* or *benei yishma'el* refers to Muslims who are adherents of Islam, a universal religion, irrespective of ethnic background. On the other hand, how-

53. Maimonides, MT: Kings, 12.2ff. See David Novak, "Maimonides' Concept of the Messiah," *Journal of Religious Studies* 9:2 (Summer 1982): 42ff.

54. Maimonides, MT: Kings, 10.8.

ever, the only Muslims who are literally *yishma'elim* are the Arabs. Moreover, although Maimonides was certainly aware of the fact that there are many non-Arab Muslims, his own experience nevertheless seems to have been limited to Arabs. Therefore, in speaking about the actual doctrines of Islam, *Ishmael* refers to an abstract theology, whereas in speaking about the practices of Muslims, *Ishmael* refers to a real present cultural community. This distinction is important to bear in mind because Maimonides' high estimation of Islamic doctrine was not matched by a similarly high estimation of many of the Muslim practices he actually saw in his own time and place. In fact, as we have seen, one of his main arguments for the superiority of Judaism over Islam was that Jewish practice is more consistent with pure monotheism than Muslim practice is. An exception to this general tendency, however, is the Islamic practice of circumcision, a practice he saw among the Arabs with whom he lived and worked. Maimonides traced this practice to the literal descent of the Arabs from Ishmael who became assimilated with the Keturites. As an extant ethnic group the Keturites no longer exist. Therefore, the only non-Jewish descendants of Abraham are the Ishmaelites/Arabs. In fact, according to one rabbinic opinion, Keturah is another name for Hagar, the mother of Ishmael, whom Abraham took back and remarried after the death of Sarah, the mother of Isaac.[55] Thus, it seems, Maimonides saw the Islamic practice of circumcision, most prevalent among Muslim Arabs, as coming from Judaism and something which Judaism sees as a requirement for Arabs, and a requirement not originally Islamic. It is important to note that Muslim circumcision is not prescribed in the Qur'an, a fact undoubtedly known to Maimonides.[56]

This ruling of Maimonides caused a number of serious problems for later commentators because it seemed to contradict a number of Talmudic rulings, rulings which are supposed to be authoritative for subsequent halakhists, including Maimonides.[57]

The contradictions are as follows:

1. The Talmud explicitly states that Noahides — that is, all monotheistic, law-abiding non-Jews — are to practice seven commandments as binding according to Jewish criteria. Anything else which they practice, even if it is not in violation of these seven commandments, still does not partake of their revealed character.[58] For one group of Noahides and a large and important one

---

55. *Bereshit Rabbah* 61:4.

56. See D. S. Margaliouth, "Circumcision: Islam," in *Encyclopedia of Religion and Ethics*, 13 vols., ed. J. Hastings (New York: Charles Scribner's Sons, 1951), vol. 3, pp. 677-79.

57. See, e.g., R. Judah Rozanis, *Mishneh le-Melekh* on Maimonides, MT: Kings, 10:7; R. Aryeh Leib of Metz, *Sha'agat Aryeh*, no. 49.

58. B. Sanhedrin 58b-59a; B. Avodah Zarah 3a.

at that, Maimonides has, however, designated an eighth commandment, circumcision, an eighth commandment just as much a part of the divine law for them as the other seven.

2. The Talmud refers to the phenomenon of the "circumcised Arab" *(Aravi mahul)*.[59] There is a debate in the Talmud about symbolic circumcision *(hattafat dam berit)* of a convert to Judaism who was circumcised already prior to his conversion. (This symbolic circumcision consists of drawing a drop of blood from that place on the male organ where the foreskin had been connected to it.) Although one version of this debate reports the Hillelites — the school of rabbinic legal opinion whose view is almost always taken to be normative — as ruling that symbolic circumcision is not required, nevertheless, the other version of this debate reports unanimity of rabbinic opinion about the requirement of this symbolic circumcision.[60] Clearly the Talmud was aware of the widespread practice of circumcision among the pre-Islamic Arabs and yet did not see any Jewish religious significance in it. Circumcision was only a religious act within the context of the covenant of Israel.[61] Moreover, elsewhere in the *Mishneh Torah* Maimonides codified this view.[62] If so, then why does he in the *Mishneh Torah* passage we just examined now see a Jewish religious significance in this fact? Why should an Arab convert to Judaism, whose previous circumcision as a Muslim did have a religious significance — in a religion that Judaism (for Maimonides, anyway) regards as a perfectly valid monotheism — be required to undergo another symbolic circumcision upon converting to Judaism? Surely a Muslim convert to Judaism would not have to reaffirm his opposition to idolatry, since he had never been an idolater even in his former religion.[63]

3. The fact that the Keturites are now considered by Maimonides to have become indistinguishable from the Arab people raises another problem with Talmudic tradition. The Talmud ruled that in most cases of doubt one is to assume that what obtains for the majority obtains for the whole *(zeel batar rubbah)*.[64] Thus, for example, if a family whose members are barred from marrying with other Jews because of a strain of bastardy *(mamzerut)* became assimilated into the whole Jewish people, then the Talmud rules that their

59. B. Shabbat 135a. See M. Nedarim 3:11 and Epistle of Barnabas 9:6.

60. See T. Shabbat 15:9; B. Shabbat 135a, Tos., s.v. "lo"; *Behag,* ed. Hildesheimer (Jerusalem: Miqqitsei Nirdamim, 1971), vol. 1, pp. 205, 216; *Alfasi: Shabbat,* ed. Vilna, 53b-54a.

61. See B. Avodah Zarah 27a; B. Nedarim 31b; Y. Nedarim 3:9/38a-b; Maimonides, MT: Circumcision, 2:1 and Karo, *Kesef Mishneh* thereon.

62. Maimonides, MT: Forbidden Relations, 14:5.

63. Maimonides, MT: Idolatry, 8:9.

64. B. Hullin 11a re Exod. 23:2.

problematic background is to be forgotten.[65] Why, then, according to Maimonides, do the majority Arabs now have the obligation of circumcision of the minority Keturites? Why are the Keturites not regarded as having lost this obligation because of their assimilation with the Arabs?[66]

These are the contradictions with Talmudic tradition one can see in this ruling of Maimonides regarding Arab circumcision. However, they can all be resolved, I think, if we remember that Maimonides regarded Islam as having totally permeated the belief and most of the practice of the Arabs, who are related to the Jewish people by literal Abrahamic descent.

1. As we saw above concerning gentile observance of the commandments of Judaism, the later view is that this observance must be confined to the seven Noahide commandments only, and the earlier view (with Hellenistic Jewish precedents) is that monotheistic gentiles are in fact potential Jews and should observe as many of the commandments of the Torah as possible, as their potential Judaism. Now although the later view became the normative one, the earlier one — like so many other overruled opinions in halakhah — could not be totally and permanently suppressed.[67] Clearly Maimonides himself was partial to it and ruled that in anything short of actual religious syncretism, gentiles could practice Jewish commandments and receive transcendent rewards for such practices.[68] The fact that the Muslim Arab practice of circumcision in his day — as contrasted with the pre-Islamic, pagan Arab practice of circumcision known in Talmudic times — the fact that this practice was based on Islamic monotheism seems to have enabled Maimonides to regard it as an acceptable practical application of the Islamic monotheism he so admired in theory. The fact that he could assign an Abrahamic origin to this practice through the Keturites enabled him, it seems to me, to once again emphasize to Jews and Muslims alike the true Judaic source of all that is truly valid in Islam.

65. B. Kiddushin 71a; Maimonides, MT: Kings, 12:3; cf. also M. Yadayim 4:4; *Pirqei de Rabbi Eliezer,* chap. 44.

66. Thus Rashi (living in Christian eleventh-century France) only saw the obligation of circumcision as applying to the sons of Keturah herself (B. Sanhedrin 59b, s.v. "le-rabbot") mentioned in Gen. 25:2, not to their descendants who assimilated and lost their Keturite identity. For Rashi it is clear that the Keturites were a one-generation phenomenon as far as Judaism is concerned. See David Novak, *Law and Theology in Judaism* (New York: Ktav Publishing House, 1974-76), vol. 1, pp. 67-68, and vol. 2, pp. 221-22.

67. See, e.g., B. Berakhot 9a and parallels.

68. See *Teshuvot ha-Rambam,* no. 148 (vol. 2, pp. 282-84), and Maimonides, MT: Kings, 10:10. Maimonides permitted a Jew, no doubt for this reason, to circumcise either a Christian or a Muslim who wants this for a religious purpose, even though he was not converting to Judaism. Cf., however, T. Avodah Zarah 3:12; B. Avodah Zarah 26b.

2. There is no doubt that as a halakhist Maimonides could not always follow the practical conclusions of his philosophically conceived theology. In the
case of symbolic circumcision of all previously circumcised converts to Judaism, he had a long tradition behind him, going back to the post-Talmudic
geonim, a tradition which required this symbolic circumcision irrespective of
what the circumstances of the gentile circumcision were.[69] This is not the only
case where Maimonides as a halakhist had to place tradition before theology in
terms of practical rulings. Thus, for example, even though he codified the one
Talmudic view that gentiles who keep the seven Noahide commandments as
divine law are admitted to the world-to-come,[70] he nevertheless codified another Talmudic view — one which is undisputed — that one must tell all pro-
spective converts to Judaism that the world-to-come is for Israel alone.[71] However, the important thing to remember, in looking at Maimonides' treatment
of the question of the Muslim Arab practice of circumcision, is that despite the
fact that it should have followed from his theological premises that circumcised Muslims do not require circumcision symbolically when they convert to
Judaism, despite the fact that he had to codify the tradition which said otherwise, Maimonides still regarded Islam *per se* as being different from and superior to any other non-Jewish religion. This difference is something of which he
makes Jews, and no doubt Muslims as well, aware.

3. If one understands Maimonides' regard for Islam and its salutary influence on at least some of the practices of the Arabs who are now Muslims, perhaps an explanation of his rather strange view of the assimilation of the
Keturites and Ishmaelites can emerge. If this assimilation is simply seen in
quantitative terms, then the Keturites should be regarded as having disappeared into the Ishmaelites. However, what if the source of Arab monotheism, the overwhelming and enthusiastic Arab acceptance of Islam, is the result of the *influence* of Abraham through the Keturites? Whereas Islam traces
its roots in Abrahamic monotheism through Ishmael,[72] rabbinic tradition regarded Ishmael as an idolator.[73] It is the children of Keturah who, like the

---

69. See *Sheiltot de-Rab Ahay Gaon,* ed. Kenig (Jerusalem: n.p., 1948), 26d and 10a.

70. Maimonides, MT: Kings, 8:11.

71. Maimonides, MT: Forbidden Relations, 14:4 re B. Yevamot 47a-b. Actually the extant
text of the Babylonian Talmud does not present this problem. Maimonides' text apparently
read, "The world-to-come is only in store for the *righteous and they are Israel.*" The extant text of
the Bavli reads, "The world-to-come is only made for the righteous; *but Israel at this time* is unable to receive too much good" (emphasis mine), and see the note of R. Zvi Hirsch Chajes
thereon.

72. Qur'an 2:125-27; 19:54-55.

73. See Targum Yerushalmi on Gen. 21:9; *Bereshit Rabbah* 53:11.

children of Isaac and Jacob (the Jews), are monotheists. Therefore, it would seem that Maimonides regarded the Keturites as those who converted the Ishmaelites to the monotheism which subsequently became Islam. The Keturites may have become Ishmaelites ethnically and politically. But in spiritual terms — and for Maimonides this is far more important than ethnicity — the Ishmaelites became Keturites as evidenced by Islam and the Muslim practice of circumcision as a religious rite.[74] Unlike Isaac and his seed, the children of Keturah were the children of a concubine.[75] As such, their status is Abrahamic but clearly lower than that of Isaac and his seed. Here again, it seems to me, Maimonides took the opportunity to show his regard for Islamic monotheism and consistently monotheistic Islamic practice, while at the same time refuting any Islamic supercessionist claims of being a superior and final revelation in relation to Judaism.[76]

Islam and Christianity

In his treatment of Islam, Maimonides emphasized that it is a complete monotheism. Christianity, on the other hand, he considered to be in effect polytheistic and, therefore, a form of idolatry *(avodah zarah)*. It would thus seem that Maimonides ranked Islam higher than Christianity. Nevertheless, in one specific area at least, Maimonides expressed a preference for Christianity over Islam. When asked whether or not the Talmudic ban on teaching gentiles any more of the Torah than the seven Noahide commandments[77] still obtained with contemporary gentiles, Maimonides answered strongly in the affirmative, but then he continued,

> It is permitted to teach the commandments [*ha-mitzvot*] to Christians [*nosrim*] and to draw them to our religion, but this is not permitted with Muslims because of what is known to you about their belief that this Torah is not divine revelation [*eynah min ha-shamayim*]. When you will teach them something from Scripture, they will find that it contradicts what they have devised [*she-badu hem*] from their own minds according to the confused stories and incoherent doctrines which have come to them, and this will not be a proof to them because they possess error [*she-ta'ut be-*

74. For Maimonides' view of circumcision as a means of unifying believers, see *Guide of the Perplexed*, 3.49.

75. See Gen. 25:6.

76. See above, n. 50.

77. See above, n. 58.

yadehem]. . . but the uncircumcised ones believe that the version [*nusah*] of the Torah has not changed, only they interpret it with their faulty exegesis. . . . But when these scriptural texts will be interpreted with correct exegesis [*al ha-perush hanakhon*], it is possible that they will return to the good. . . . There is nothing that they will find in their Scriptures which differs from ours.[78]

Now it is clear from the question which prompted this response that Maimonides meant that *anything* in the Hebrew Bible may be taught to Christians. The question states: "Is every Jew obligated to refrain from teaching anything [*davar*] from the commandments [*min ha-mitzvot*] except the seven commandments or what is based on them, or not?"[79] Furthermore, "correct exegesis" seems to encompass much of postbiblical Jewish teaching as well. Muslims, as opposed to Christians, having rejected the Hebrew Bible as authentic revelation *per se,* will not be moved by scriptural proofs as would Christians. Moreover, Maimonides explicitly stated that the purpose in teaching Scripture to Christians is to attract them to Judaism — namely, that it is "likely" *(efshar)* that they will convert to Judaism if exposed to such proper teaching.

Maimonides, as we have seen, regarded both Christians and Muslims as paving the way for the coming of the Messiah, which is the full restoration of Jewish political sovereignty, the full hegemony of the Torah, and the final triumph of monotheism in human history. In the *Mishneh Torah* Maimonides spoke of the divinely mandated duty of Jews "to force" *(la-kof)* all humanity to accept the commandments given to the Noahides.[80] On the other hand, however, he emphasized there that only those "who want to convert" *(kol ha-roseh lehitgayyer)* are to be accepted as converts. Whereas the acceptance of the Noahide commandments can be seen as a political necessity which Jews should enforce when they have the power to do so, conversion to Judaism can only be a matter of inner conviction. Maimonides in this responsum also emphasized that where Jews have political power over gentiles, the gentiles' study of the Torah should be contingent upon conversion. That can be enforced, but conversion itself can only be a matter of persuasion. Now it is clear that for Maimonides the conversion of both Christians and Muslims to Judaism is a desideratum, something which Jews ought to encourage and facilitate as much as possible.[81] However, it is only with Christians that study of the He-

---

78. *Teshuvot ha-Rambam,* no. 149 (vol. 1, pp. 284-85).

79. *Teshuvot ha-Rambam,* no. 149 (vol. 1, p. 284).

80. Maimonides, MT: Kings, 8:10.

81. For Maimonides' endorsement of what seems to be proselytizing gentiles, see *Sefer ha-Mitzvot,* pos. no. 9.

brew Bible, what is their "Old Testament," could be an appropriate means to this end. With Muslims, conversely, it would do more harm than good. And the fact that these Christians are not pure monotheists as are the Muslims did not seem to detract from Maimonides' high esteem for their biblicism.

One could, of course, simply leave the matter at this point and conclude that in terms of his philosophical theology, Maimonides preferred Muslim monotheism over Christian Trinitarianism, but in terms of what we might term his historical theology, he preferred the Christian canonization of the Old Testament over the Muslim rejection of it and the total replacement of it with the Qur'an.[82] Nevertheless, I think one can infer even here a unified Maimonidean approach. This inference on my part is admittedly conjectural, but I think it is a conjecture that is not inconsistent with the overall *Tendenz* of his thought.

As far as Maimonides is concerned, the study of Scripture in and of itself is no guarantee of the philosophically demonstrable monotheism he considers the foundation of all true religion. For the nonphilosophical study of Scripture leads one to accept its anthropomorphism literally, and Maimonides thought that anthropomorphism is the ideational corollary of polytheism, a limiting of the authentic transcendence of God.[83] Now Christianity is the prime example of the error of such anthropomorphism in its original doctrine of the Incarnation and the closely related doctrine of the Trinity. As such, the study of Scripture only has immediate practical value, but on the theoretical level it requires a philosophical hermeneutic to reveal its esoteric truth *(sitrei Torah)*.

This difference between practice and theory can be applied to the difference between Christianity and Islam for Maimonides. On the theoretical level, Islamic monotheism is clearly superior to Christian Trinitarianism and, for Maimonides, although historical revelation enabled the people of Israel to emerge as the original monotheistic community, historical revelation is not the *conditio sine qua non* of monotheism. Monotheism being *ratio per se* is something which can be attained by philosophical means, although in the sense of *ratio quod nos* most people, not being philosophers, will require a historical revelation.[84] Therefore, if Muslims are pure monotheists, then it is ultimately unimportant that they derived their monotheism from historical

82. See David Novak, review of Paul van Buren's *Discerning the Way: A Theology of the Jewish-Christian Reality,* in *Judaism* 31:1 (Winter 1982): 116.

83. See, esp., Maimonides, MT: Repentance, 3:7 (cf. Rabad's note thereon); also, Maimonides, MT: Foundations of Torah, 1:7ff.; Maimonides, *Guide of the Perplexed,* 1.35.

84. See Maimonides, MT: Sabbatical Year and Jubilee, and *Qoves Teshuvot ha-Rambam ve-Iggrotav,* ed. Lichtenberg (Leipzig: n.p., 1859), vol. 2, 23b-24a; also, S. Atlas, *Netivim be-Mishpat ha-'Ivri* (New York: n.p., 1978), pp. 13-14; Novak, *The Image of the Non-Jew in Judaism,* pp. 302-4.

sources other than the Hebrew Bible. Their potential for Judaism, then, must be seen in theoretical, philosophical terms rather than in practical, scriptural ones. Christians, on the other hand, are not true monotheists, but they have accepted the practical monotheism of the Hebrew Bible. In their case proper scriptural exegesis will bring them to Judaism. Here again we see how for Maimonides Judaism is ultimately superior to both Christianity and Islam. It is superior to Islamic monotheism because it is the earliest monotheism and one which entails a far more consistent monotheistic practice than that of Islam, and certainly than the folk practices of most Muslims.[85] It is superior to Christianity and its biblicism because it has the correct, monotheistic exegesis of Scripture based on a theology which rejects philosophically untenable Incarnationism and Trinitarianism. However, since philosophy is superior to biblical literalism,[86] and since Islam does entail many acceptable practices in the light of monotheistic criteria, even this responsum, despite its preference for Christianity's biblicism, does not, it seems to me, contradict the clear conclusion emerging from looking at many of Maimonides' writings: he regarded Islam as indeed the closest religion to Judaism.

85. See Maimonides, *Guide of the Perplexed*, 2.33.
86. See Maimonides, *Guide of the Perplexed*, 2.22, 2.25.

CASE STUDIES:
JUDAISM AND SOCIAL ETHICS

16 A Jewish View of War (1974)

The Nature of War

Judaism, although possessing an intricate theoretical structure, has seen practice as the ultimate end of all theorizing. The ever-present requirements of action have demanded the enunciation of intelligible principles to determine the appropriate context and final thrust of the action at hand.[1] Since the religiously involved Jew is constantly engaged in acts, he is conditioned to ask himself two questions when he approaches any new situation: (1) What is required of me at this time and place? and (2) How is this specific requirement structured? In fact, the very constancy of this engagement in activity even made it necessary for the Talmud to establish several precise criteria for priority in the case of conflict of acts.[2]

It is to the credit of a number of contemporary American-Jewish leaders and thinkers that they view the Jew's involvement in war as a question demanding a religious stance. Such is the case, it seems to me, because the involvement of the United States in any war is not regarded as the policy of some remote entity but, rather, is seen as a situation immediately present to Jewish persons — a situation calling for a judgment of conscience — similar

---

1. Note M. Avot 1:17: "Simon ben Rabban Gamliel said . . . not learning [*hamidrash*] but doing [*hama'aseh*] is the chief thing [*iqqar*]." Even the celebrated "intellectualist" statement "Greater is the study of the Torah [than doing] for it brings one to doing" (B. Bava Kama 17a and parallels) justifies itself on practical grounds. See Maimonides, *Commentary on the Mishnah,* ed. Rabinowitz (Jerusalem: Mossad ha-Rav Kook, 1930), pp. 79, 88.

2. Such principles as "One engaged in one mitzvah is exempt from other mitsvot at the same time" (B. Sotah 44b and parallels) and "One must not do mitsvot in bundles" (B. Pesahim 102b and parallels) were necessitated by the continuous imperatives present to Jews.

to that involved in more traditional situations. This view assumes two things, one obvious and the other less so. The first assumption is that Jews are intimately and freely involved with a secular, non-Jewish regime. Not only are they the subjects of government policies, as they have been in the past, or are at present in some parts of the world, but they are now constituents in the very process of policy decision. The second, less obvious assumption is that Judaism provides Jews with theologically significant principles, which have application in situations that in the past never called for Jewish decisions at all. The first assumption is factual, but the second suggests that some sort of imperative is being sought. Therefore, the question now becomes this: Does Judaism offer any criteria to the Jew, free constituent of a secular society, who is faced with the moral dilemma of how to judge his government's involvement in an offensive war and, ultimately, what to do about it? The thesis of this essay is that Judaism does offer the morally sensitive Jew the criteria he seeks in this particular situation. I have chosen the war in Vietnam for discussion because it, more than any other war, caught many Jews in a serious moral dilemma. However, the Vietnam War is only an example of the more general problem of participation in any offensive military action.

At first thought one would suppose that the moral question of Vietnam should be analyzed by the concept of the "just war." Although this term was formulated by medieval Catholic theology, the concept itself is found much earlier in Jewish law. The Talmud classifies war into three categories: (1) *Milhemet Hovah,* a divinely ordered war, such as the war against the Canaanites in the time of Joshua, and the war against the Amalekites in the time of Saul; (2) *Hilhemet Mitzvah,* a war of necessary Jewish self-defense; and (3) *Milhemet Reshut,* a "permitted" war, where, in certain cases, Jewish national interest may be offensively pursued.[3] The deliberations necessary for the sanctioning of a "permitted" war are described in the Talmud:

> The sages of Israel approached King David and said to him, "Our royal lord, your people Israel need sustenance [*parnasah*]." He said to them, "Let them sustain one another." They said to him, "A handful of grain would not even satisfy a lion, and the wells are inadequate." He said to them, "Go and engage in plunder [*gedud*]." Immediately they consulted Ahithophel, sought the approval of the Sanhedrin [*nimlakhin*], and inquired of the Urim and Thummim oracle.[4]

3. See M. Sotah 8:7 and B. Sotah 44b. For a concise collection of many of the pertinent sources, see *Torah Studies in the Light of the Halakhah* (Heb.), ed. J. Copperman (Jerusalem: Kiryat Noar, 1962), no. 8, "Wars."

4. B. Berakhot 3b and B. Sanhedrin 16a.

One can readily see that none of the above categories applies to the question at hand. Even the most militant religious proponent of the Vietnam War would not state that it was the direct result of a command from God. On the other hand, uniquely Jewish interests were not directly involved in the Vietnam War, as they were in World War II, and especially in the Israeli War of Independence *(milhemet ha-shichrur)*. Finally, the concept of the "permitted" war, which most closely approximates this war, also does not apply, because the necessary conditions for establishing its sanction are long absent. We have neither king nor Sanhedrin. And even if they were present, they would not be applicable anyway, because the moral decision here is that of the individual Jew, not that of a Jewish state. Thus, we see that if our search is to be successful, we must be prepared to look for principles that are fundamental enough not to be solely confined within traditionally developed contexts.

We have seen that the problem in discovering the appropriate basis for moral judgment here is initially one of connection. We have not been able as yet to locate a moral connection between the individual Jew and the non-Jewish (not anti-Jewish) secular society. This context must be established before light can be shed on the specific moral judgment required. Otherwise, any sources cited might be equivocal — that is, relevant by appearance, but irrelevant as the basis for any inference of specific conclusions from general statements. If moral decisions are to be as coherent and binding for the contemporary Jew as they were for the traditional Jew of the past, we must make sure that moral reasoning does not become logically equivocal and, therefore, rooted in the subjective bias of the individual. The sources must be used as something more profound than illustrations. A good deal of the moral theorizing presented by Jewish thinkers today ignores the contextual issue and is thus of questionable application.[5] On the other hand, some Jewish thinkers seem to see no contextual change in Jewish moral decisions, and thus cannot face the real problems at hand.

Noahide Law

It is well known that Jewish tradition regarded some of the imperatives either explicitly or implicitly stated in the Torah as having an international context. While the 613 commandments are solely Jewish in context, the seven commandments of "the sons of Noah," by definition, are directed to the entire human race — to man *qua* man. Whether these laws are to be classified

---

5. See J. Neusner, "What Is Normative in Jewish Ethics?" *Judaism* 16:1 (Winter 1967): 3-20.

as "natural law" *(ius naturale)* or as "the law of nations" *(ius gentium)* or as divine law *per se (ius divinium)* is a disputed point among scholars.[6] However, the lack of certitude as to the appropriate classification of the seven commandments need not prevent our looking to them for guidance. For their givenness cannot be disputed, inasmuch as they are explicitly set forth in the Talmud.[7] There are many data to which we refer in making decisions without knowing their prime causality. I think the times require of Jewish theology that it determine whether the seven commandments are essentially grounded in man's reason, or in universal consent, or in the direct revelation of God's will. Surely such determination will shed deeper light on how Judaism views moral judgment. Nevertheless, a judgment is demanded of the morally sensitive Jew, here and now, and we must therefore look to what is already available for enlightenment.

However, we cannot simply infer a specific conclusion from the Noahide commandment of *shefikhat damim,* the prohibition of murder. First we must determine one final and crucial point of context. This will ensure that our subsequent use of texts will not be open to the charge of equivocity.

The last problem we face in this area is that the 613 commandments regulate the life of the Jewish people, and the seven commandments regulate the life of gentiles.[8] The Rabbis made it quite clear that gentiles domiciled under Jewish jurisdiction were expected to conform to their seven commandments as *enforced by the Jewish authorities.*[9] Moreover, they made it clear that certain restrictions of the seven commandments do *not* apply to Jews.[10] In other words, we seem to have clear precedents for gentiles in gentile contexts, and for gentiles in Jewish contexts. Yet we seem to be lacking precedents for Jews in gentile contexts, especially for Jews who are not only present *de facto* in a non-Jewish society, but present *de jure* as well — that is, who are free and equal constituents of that society, having full rights and responsibilities.

6. See Boaz Cohen, *Jewish and Roman Law* (New York: Jewish Theological Seminary, 1966), vol. 1, pp. 107, 271, 281, 338-39, 380, 386. For a concise background of all these terms, see A. P. d'Entrèves, *Natural Law* (New York: Harper Torchbooks, 1965). For an attempt to see the importance of this material for contemporary Judaism, see R. Gordis, *The Root and the Branch* (Chicago: University of Chicago Press, 1962), pp. 204-35.

7. T. Avodah Zarah 8.4, ed. Zuckermandl, p. 473; B. Sanhedrin 56a.

8. Cf. B. Baba Kama 38a.

9. Note B. Sanhdrin 56b: "Concerning a gentile: crimes which the Jewish courts punish by death, a gentile [*ben Noah*] is considered forewarned [*muzhar*]; matters which the Jewish court does not punish by death, a gentile is not considered forewarned."

10. See B. Sanhdrin 59a and Rashi, s.v. "mishum," and Albo, *Iqqarim,* 3.19.

However, there is a relevant passage in the Mishnah. If understood in terms of its ultimate presuppositions, it can bridge the halakhic gap of the individual Jew functioning fully in a non-Jewish society. We will then be able to apply the principle embodied in the passage, which seems to me to be a basis for inferring a judgment on our involvement in the Vietnam War. Let us examine the Mishnah text and then look at the three possible interpretations, which give successively broader groundings for the Mishnah's ruling:

> All documents deposited in the gentile courts [*arkaot she-la-goyim*], even though their sealing is witnessed by gentiles, are valid — except bills of divorce and manumission of slaves. R. Simon says even these are valid, for the ruling concerning invalidation only applies when the documents are deposited with individual gentiles.[11]

The simplest and most constricted interpretation of the text is given by the thirteenth-century *posek* (halakhic authority) R. Mordecai ben Hillel. He simply states that this is a specific rabbinic decree concerning documents. The reason he gives is that the gentiles are very careful *(makpidin)* about the signatures on documents registered in their courts.

The Gemara proper to this mishnah[12] bases the ruling on the principle of Mar Samuel, "the law of the kingdom is the law" *(dina de-malkhuta dina)*. Rashi, elsewhere, explains this principle as follows:

> All the levies and taxes and procedures regularly enacted by kings in their kingdoms are binding as law [*dina*]. For all the subjects of the kingdom freely *accept* [*mirtsonam*] the statutes of the king and his enactments.[13]

One can readily see that this principle is about certain positive laws — that is, it defines the right of the state to make specific decrees on the basis of popular consent and acceptance of authority. But it in no way presents any standard of judgment to determine whether these laws are right or wrong. As such it admits of no wide inference.[14]

Finally, commenting on a passage in the Gemara where our mishnah is cited, Rashi presents the broadest and deepest basis for the specific ruling of the Mishnah:

11. M. Gittin 1.5.

12. B. Gittin 10b.

13. B. Baba Batra 54b. See L. Landman, *Jewish Law in the Diaspora: Confrontations and Accommodation* (Philadelphia: Dropsie College, 1968).

14. See B. Baba Kama 113a.

Although sacramental matters [*kritut*] do not concern gentiles nor matters of Jewish marriage and divorce [*gittin ve-kidushin*], they are nevertheless commanded concerning the practice of justice [*dinin*].[15]

One must realize that Rashi was presenting a more fundamental grounding for the ruling of the Mishnah than the specifics of the situation actually required. This being the case, the principle he presents here has a much wider application and is not solely confined to the question of verification of documents with which this Mishnah deals. *Dinin* (the practice of justice) is a standard of judgment. In rabbinic Hebrew *dun* means to *logically infer* — that is, to perform an operation of rational judgment; it is like *krinein* in Greek, a word which has both a logical and a legal usage.[16] Rashi is presenting an extraordinary statement in depth on the role of secular order in a universe ruled by God according to his Torah.[17] His illuminating explication indicates that a non-Jewish society — in nonritual cases, of course — can be the context for Jewish action, provided that that society's legal and political order is in basic conformity with the seven Noahide commandments. This is not only a *de facto* recognition of Jews being subject to a non-Jewish regime; it is a *de jure* recognition that the state's right to rule is grounded in a law directed to the conscience of man. As such, the specific policies of that state, at all times, require a judgment of conscience by its free and responsible constituents. In the absence of the full hegemony of the Torah over the life of the Jew, the Jew is not simply abandoned to pure subjectivism, nor is he forced to search for objective standards elsewhere in the area of politics. The seven commandments indicate *that even non-Jewish law has a real religious status: complete for the non-Jew,*[18] *and partial for the Jew in exile.*[19] As such, the policies of the state can and must be judged by certain standards intrinsic to Judaism. For a Jew to look upon his involvement in the secular state with religious seriousness does not entail his prior alienation from classical Judaism. On the contrary, it presupposes a Jewish quest to do what God requires of the Jew here and now. "I am a stranger in the land; do not hide Thy commandments from me" (Ps. 119:19).

---

15. Rashi, B. Gittin 9b, s.v. "huts."

16. See H. G. Liddell and R. Scott, *Greek-English Lexicon* (Oxford: Clarendon, 1968), s.v. "krino" and "krima." For the use of *dun*, see, e.g., B. Sanhedrin 54a.

17. Cf. *Bereshit Rabbah*, beg.

18. Maimonides, *Mishneh Torah: Kings*, 8.11.

19. B. Sanhedrin 39b.

Who Is the Pursuer?

Now that we have established an authentically Jewish context for the type of moral decision required by the situation of the Vietnam War, we are finally in a position to locate some principle of halakhah that will directly apply to this case, and that will be binding on the Jewish conscience. Let us first see what alternatives of choice are present in this particular situation.

In wars there is a conflict between two distinct parties. Each side usually justifies its military activities by claiming that it is either defending itself against an offensive aggressor or is in imminent danger of attack. It is presupposed that the distinction of belligerent entities is at all times clear. The issues at stake in the war are between the two opposing parties. However, the Vietnam War was much more complicated.

Ostensibly, the conflict was a civil war between the Saigon government and the Communist-controlled National Liberation Front, the Vietcong, aided by the government of North Vietnam. The first problem we face is that the clear-cut division of entities, found in more conventional wars, was not found here. The question was whether the authentic leadership of the Vietnamese people was in Saigon or with the guerilla chiefs of the Vietcong. The policy of the United States government was an answer to this question. Our involvement in the war was justified as follows: The duly constituted and authorized government of South Vietnam is the government of Saigon. The guerilla forces of the Vietcong are, in effect, a group of illegal brigands who are attempting to overthrow this legitimate polity. Over and above our strategic interests, or whatever treaty obligations we have with the Saigon government, we are, in truth, answering the cry for help of a beleaguered nation in mortal danger. In other words, the United States policy was *ultimately* justified, not in terms of national advantage or of treaties enacted for extrinsic ends, but rather in terms of a moral principle: One is conscience-bound to act on behalf of a fellow in mortal danger. This logic can be seen in the following statement, which was issued by the State Department at the height of American involvement in Vietnam:

> Our objective in Viet Nam is a simple one — to stop North Viet Nam from attacking its neighbor. We believe that we can and will achieve victory in this sense. We seek only to assure that the South Vietnamese people have an opportunity to establish political and economic institutions of their own choosing while free from outside interference.[20]

20. *U.S. Objectives in Viet Nam,* Public Information Series (Washington, D.C.: Department of State, 1967), p. 8.

Throughout the long debate as to whether the United States should or should not have been involved in the war, even the proponents of the official policy admitted that our involvement was that of a third party subsequently entering the scene. The debate centered on the question of whether or not this third-party involvement was justified. But, it should be noted, the point of morality was introduced, not by the dissenting "doves" but by those who claimed ultimate responsibility for the military action. Therefore, no one can claim that the discussion of the moral question was irrelevant or contrived, because both sides in this debate appealed for support and sympathy in moral terms. A debate presupposes that each side recognize the rationality of the other, generally if not specifically. Thus the debate over Vietnam involved an analysis of the nature of war in general. That is why this debate is paradigmatic, even after American withdrawal from actual fighting in Vietnam.

Students of the Talmud will quickly recognize the type of reasoning outlined above as identical with the *rodef* (pursuer) principle. The following text demonstrates this:

> These are the victimizers who may even be killed if this is required to save their victims: A person pursuing [*rodef*] his fellow to kill him. . . .[21]

In our situation, the government equated the Vietcong with the "pursuer" and the Saigon government with the "pursued" *(nirdaf)*. This seems, then, to be very clear. Should the American Jew have felt that he was conscience-bound to support his government's Vietnam policy? If the line of argument we have been developing in this essay is correct, then it will seem to be at this particular juncture that the Jewish person had to exercise his faculty of moral judgment, his conscience.

However, the *rodef* principle is really rooted in another, more fundamental principle. And when we understand what this is, we will be able to see, in a truly Jewish perspective, the fallacy in the moral reasoning at the very heart of the government's justification of its war policy.

As a result, a valid inference from principle to conclusion will at last be possible. We will see that the inference is a good deal more subtle than a simple deduction from the prohibition against murder. Rather, this inference is based on a principle almost immediately present to rational man, a principle which gives, I think, the prohibition against murder its intelligibility and its rapid appeal to conscience.

---

21. M. Sanhedrin 8.9. See B. Sanhedrin 73a, which attempts to find either immediate or inferred scriptural basis for this law.

Let us look at two texts, which although dealing with the fascinating moral question of abortion, reveal a basis having much more general application.

The woman who is in extremely difficult labor: the fetus may be destroyed within her, and removed from her limb by limb, because her life has priority over its life. However, if most of the baby's body is already out of the womb, we may not harm him, because *one human life may not be sacrificed for another* [*eyn dohin nefesh mipney nafesh*].[22]

And Maimonides, in the *Mishneh Torah*, writes as follows:

. . . because the fetus is *like a pursuer* after his mother [*ke-rodef achareyha*] to kill her.[23]

Now Maimonides' comparison of the endangering fetus and the pursuer is not easy to understand. One can only become a pursuer if he is fully human and morally culpable. Why should Maimonides introduce this consideration when the particular case of abortion does not even require it? It is quite clear from several other sources that the fetus is part of its mother's body *(yerekh immo)* and can be *amputated* when necessary.[24] However, Maimonides, who chooses each word with care, states *ke-rodef,* "like a *rodef,*" and thus does not use *rodef* in the complete sense of the term. The endangering fetus is a *rodef* by analogy. Perhaps in the context of abortion Maimonides is comparing the fetus to the fully human *rodef* because the fetus, in essence, is more than a limb, but *persona in potentia.*[25]

What Maimonides may also be emphasizing, if I read him correctly, is that the principle that one life cannot be sacrificed for another is the intelligible ground for the *rodef* principle *per se.* This is most important for our problem here. There are no priorities in the value of human lives[26] unless a person (or, as in our case, a number of persons) forfeits his right to protection by denying this equality of value in his own favor. The function of society is to make this *de jure* equality *de facto* in the affairs of men. What society and any of its citizens do in the case of the pursuer is to re-establish the equality of persons whom the pursuer is upsetting. To protect or ignore the true *rodef*

22. M. Ohalot 7.6 and Sanhedrin 72b. Also see M. Niddah 5.3.

23. Maimonides, MT: Murderer and the Preservation of Life, 1.9.

24. See B. Sanhedrin 80b and Maimonides, MT: Property Damage, 11.2. Note the earlier sources — e.g., *Mekhilta,* Nezikin 8, ed. Horovitz-Rabin (Jerusalem: Bamberger & Wahrmann, 1960), pp. 275-76; B. Niddah 44b; B. Baba Kama 42b.

25. See R. Ezekiel Landau, *Noda Bi-Yehudah,* vol. 2, H. M. no. 59.

26. See B. Pesahim 25ab.

would be to deny along with him this very basis of law and right. In theological terms, the pursuer is denying his creaturely status and is usurping the authority of God. Society, in acknowledging the supreme being of God, must stop this denial. Recognition of God's existence is presupposed not only by the Noahide bans on blasphemy *(birkat hashem)* and idolatry *(avodah zarah)*, but by the general category of bloodshed *(shefikat damim)* as well.[27] Actually, in the last analysis, the fundamental principle of not sacrificing one life for another is the legal ground of the famous dictum of Hillel:

> What is hateful to you do not do to your fellow. This is the whole Torah, the rest is commentary. Go and learn.[28]

This principle, then, is basic to Judaism, and common to all reasonable people.[29] Hillel had located the ultimate ground for Judaism's encounter with the world. Maimonides, too, in another text, emphasizes the fact that our principle of the equality of human life is one of natural reasoning, something universally common:

> It is a matter of rational inclination [*davar she-ha-da'at noteh lo*] not to destroy one life for another.[30]

Now, *rational inclination* is the very same term Maimonides uses elsewhere in referring to the seven Noahide commandments, which for him are the Torah *in potentia*.[31] In other words, this principle is the intelligible ground for the prohibition against murder, and the *rodef* principle is a legitimate exception by inference:

> Concerning six areas was the first man commanded: idolatry, blasphemy, murder, adultery, robbery, and administration of justice. Even though we have them by revelation [*kabbalah*] from Moses our master, they are *a matter of rational inclination* [*ve-ha-da'at noteh lahen*].[32]

---

27. See Albo, *Iqqarim,* 3.7.

28. B. Shabbat 31a.

29. Over and above the acknowledgment of this by Christianity (Matt. 7:2; *Didache* 1.2; Gratian, *Init. D.* 1), the very same idea is found in Greek texts written long before any direct encounter between the two civilizations can be verified. See Herodotus, *Persian Wars,* 3.142, 3; Aristotle, *Nicomachean Ethics,* 1132b25.

30. Maimonides, MT: Foundations of the Torah, 5.7.

31. Maimonides, MT: Kings, 9.1.

32. Maimonides, MT: Kings, 9.1. Cf. Thomas Aquinas, *Summa Theologiae,* 2/1, q. 94, a. 2: "Omnia illa quae habet naturalem inclinationem, ratio naturaliter apprehendit ut bona. . . ." Also a. 3: "Multa enim secundum virtutem fiunt ad quae natura non primo inclinat; sed per rationis inquisitionem ea hominess adinvenerunt quasi utilia ad bene vivendum."

At this point we must realize that if the principle not to sacrifice one life for another is the basis, and the *rodef* principle is an exception by inference, the first principle is more fundamental. The benefit of a doubt *(safek)* must always be in favor of that which is more fundamental.

This is the case inasmuch as the inference is an exception — that is, a specific affirmation *(rodef)* inside a general negation (nonsacrifice of life). Therefore, logically, without the general negation the specific affirmation loses its validity, because a part is only meaningful where there is a whole. Thus, in case of doubt, negation (whole) takes precedence over affirmation (part), since a whole can exist without a part, but a part cannot exist without the whole. The principle of nonsacrifice of life stands alone; the *rodef* principle cannot. We stated above the moral claim that was made by the official spokesmen in terms of the *rodef* principle. However, we now know that this principle is logically derivative. We are in a position at last to discover whether a logical sleight of hand had not indeed been committed, whether, in fact, an inference was emphasized *at the expense* of its logical basis. In the context of the issue of abortion, where we first discovered the fundamental principle, the Rabbis were quite aware of the tragic results that can come from faulty moral reasoning. The following question arises: If a baby, most of whom is already out of the womb, is considered to now be human, and if he is threatening his mother's life *(rodef)*, why should he not be killed, if need be, on the grounds of the *rodef* principle? It is to this question that the Palestinian Talmud addresses itself:

> R. Jose ben R. Bun in the name of R. Hisda emphasized that this case is different from the case of the *rodef,* because *here we do not know who is killing whom.*[33]

In other words, where there is a doubt, the *rodef* principle is not involved. And the reason for this is most pertinent for our own situation. If, in a case of doubt, the *rodef* principle were to be applied, the intruding third party would be doing what he is accusing the "pursuer" of doing. The intruder is denying the equality of persons in his own favor. We might say, to parody a famous saying, "The arrogant rush in where the humble fear to tread."

The moral fallacy of official Vietnam policy seems to be that there was an assumption of a *rodef* situation, where in fact we did not know who was pursuing whom, as the Palestinian Talmud puts it so well. The distinction of entities, which is so important in any judgment of conflict, seems to be absent

---

33. Y. Shabbat 14, end, and Y. Avodah Zarah 2.2. See B. Shabbat 129a and parallels.

here. Both the Saigon government and the Vietcong claimed to be the authentic leaders of the people of Vietnam. We had no way of verifying who was wrong and who was right. Finally, we ourselves were in a poor position to be an objective third party, inasmuch as Saigon was and still is as much an extension of Washington as the Vietcong seems to be an extension of Hanoi or Moscow.

And this is the point which lies behind the fallacy in moral reasoning. Our involvement in Vietnam was, in fact, motivated by our own self-interest. As such the government erected a moral facade to justify an outright extension of American power. The much-used analogy to the Korean conflict was illegitimate. In Korea, it seems to me, we were acting in a genuine *rodef* situation. We were, in fact, rescuing the distinct and independent entity, South Korea *(nirdaf)*, from another distinct and independent entity, North Korea *(rodef)*. And if one looks for the factor of universal consent in moral reasoning, the United Nations sponsored the involvement in Korea. In Vietnam, on the contrary, we chose sides for motives extrinsic to the actual issue in the internal conflict there. We projected our own identity onto the Saigon regime, and then assumed that we ourselves were mortally threatened. This was not only the result of the logical fallacy of emphasizing a derivative at the expense of its basis; it was the direct moral vice of hypocrisy. In the light of the facts as we know them, and the Jewish principles we have seen in operation, the morally sensitive Jew had again the ancient option: "Avoid evil and do good" (Ps. 37:27). In this situation I could see no other alternative for the religiously committed Jew but to oppose the government's Vietnam policy, and to do everything in his power to stop that immoral war. Future wars will have to be judged on the basis of criteria similar to those outlined in this essay.

Conclusion

It may seem to the reader that I have employed a very complicated and involved method for arriving at a rather simple conclusion. Perhaps this is so. But the underlying issues have demanded such elaboration. The question of how to do God's will in a secular world is not easily answered. The simple solution would be to opt either for God's will or for the secular world. However, Judaism itself would not let us do this. The Torah is not in heaven but with us on earth; we are men and not angels.[34] And to opt for the secular world would but alienate us further from our own identity as the covenanted folk. We can-

---

34. See B. Baba Metsia 59b and B. Kiddushin 54a.

not solve our problems here and now from behind elaborate disguises. Before we attempt any solution, we must realize who we ourselves are. This chapter is an attempt to deal with this general problem in a particular case. In the analysis given above we are at the juncture of theology and halakhah. We have followed the traditional method of close analysis of texts and tight logical constructions. Each discipline intimately suggests the other; the issues of one suggest questions for the other.[35] And Jewish questions have a tendency to repeat themselves. This essay, then, like the following one on abortion, is an attempt to deal with the ancient cry: "How shall we sing the Lord's song in a strange land?" (Ps. 137:4).

35. See A. J. Heschel, *God in Search of Man* (New York: Farrar, Straus & Giroux, 1955), pp. 320-47.

17   A Jewish View of Abortion (1974)

Abortion and Bloodshed

To arrive at a Jewish view of abortion for our democratic society, we must consider two questions: (1) Is abortion permitted to Jews? and (2) Is abortion permitted to non-Jews?

Jews are bound by the commandments of the Written Torah as interpreted by the Oral Tradition, subsequently embodied in the Talmud, defined in the great medieval Codes, and continually applied to new problems by pious and learned authorities *(poskim)*. Non-Jews are bound by the seven laws of the Noahide Code.

We are concerned with the morality of abortion in our democratic society. Since the non-Jewish citizens are in the overwhelming majority, we must begin with the Noahide laws, which are a Jewish expression of *ius gentium*[1] — that is, a body of norms accepted by civilized persons and binding on humanity.

Before dealing with the specific Noahide law of abortion, we must answer four questions about Noah: (1) What is its status? (2) What is its scope? (3) How is it applied? and (4) How is it related to Jewish law for Jews — that is, to the halakhah?

Since the seven Noahide commandments are presented in the Talmud as an anonymous, publicly accepted prescription *(tanu rabbanan)*, one would assume that their source is Oral Tradition.[2]

---

1. See Boaz Cohen, *Jewish and Roman Law* (New York: Jewish Theological Seminary, 1966), vol. 1, pp. 271ff.

2. B. Sanhedrin 56a following T. Avodah Zarah, chap. 8, ed. Zuckermandl (Jerusalem: Bamberger & Wahrmann, 1937), pp. 473-74.

However, in the lengthy discussion in the Gemara, six of these seven commandments are seen as based on a single scriptural verse:

And the Lord God commanded man saying, "From every tree of the garden you may surely eat, but from the tree of the knowledge of good and evil you may not eat. . . ." (Gen. 2:16-17)[3]

Therefore, in the opinion of R. Meir Abulafia, these laws are actual scriptural prescriptions.[4]

Nevertheless, it is difficult to determine whether this inference means to actually *ground* Noahide law in Scripture *(gezerot ha-katuv)*, or only uses Scripture as a description *(asmakhta)* of a body of laws grounded elsewhere. Thus, for example, R. Saadiah Gaon refers to most of these laws as rationally prescribed, without mentioning the verse from Genesis at all.[5] Considering Saadiah's eagerness to use scriptural sources whenever possible (perhaps because of his polemics with the Karaites), one can certainly assume that he held the source of these laws to be reason.

While later medieval theologians debated the scope of reason in relation to revelation, virtually all of them agreed with Saadiah that violence *(hamas)* and bloodshed *(shefikhat damim)* are rationally discernible as prohibitions for all human beings. Even such "nonrationalists" as R. Judah Halevi and Nahmanides are included.[6] Therefore, the question before us is whether or not abortion is bloodshed. Since there is virtual unanimity that reason is the source of the prohibition of bloodshed, we can conclude that the prohibition of bloodshed for Noahides is not only *ius gentium* — that is, valid by universal consensus — but also *ius naturalis* — that is, a norm valid because it is evidently rational *(ratio per se)*. Since, as we will see below, normative Judaism considers abortion for Noahides within the context of bloodshed, abortion is a question which, Jewishly speaking, is within the proper range of human reason.

The scope of Noahide law is not limited to the seven prescriptions; rather, the seven laws were understood to be seven general categories, each one including a number of specific laws. Detailed presentations of this theory were made by R. Aaron Halevi (ca. 1290), R. Joseph Albo (d. 1444), and R. Azariah

---

3. B. Sanhedrin 56b.

4. Meir Abulafia, *Yad Ramah* (Warsaw: Shriftgisser, 1886), ad B. Sanhedrin 56b.

5. *Emunot ve-De'ot* 9.2. See *The Book of Beliefs and Opinions,* trans. Samuel Rosenblatt (New Haven: Yale University Press, 1948), pp. 327-28 and esp. n. 16.

6. Halevi, *Kuzari,* 2.48; Nahmanides' comment to Gen. 6:13.

di Fano (d. 1620), on the basis of discrepancies in rabbinic sources as to the actual number of Noahide laws.[7]

Recognizing the essentially rational nature of the prohibition of bloodshed is the moral meaning of the general truth that human life is structured toward its own self-preservation and enhancement.[8]

As such, the category of "bloodshed" covers more cases than a specific prescription against "murder":[9]

> R. Jacob bar Aha found it written in a book of the sayings [*aggadata*] of the school of Rav . . . that a Noahide is capitally guilty even in the case of feticide in the view of R. Ishmael. What are his grounds for this? It is written (Gen. 9:6), "Whosoever sheds the blood of a human *within* a human [*adam ba'adam*]." Who is "a human within a human"? This is the unborn child *within* its mother's womb.[10]

Maimonides codifies the law according to R. Ishmael's ruling, and since he does not quote the verse from Genesis, we can assume that he regarded the actual exegesis in the Talmud as merely descriptive of a truth grounded in reason.[11] The moral conclusion is primary; the actual exegesis is secondary.

Noahide Law

How is Noahide law known? How is it enforced?

The first question intrigued Moses Mendelssohn, who asked R. Jacob Emden just how the Noahides were expected to know a body of laws for which God held them responsible, if they did not have Jewish traditional teaching. But Mendelssohn already had his answer: the seven Noahide laws were rational prescriptions.[12]

If the prohibition of bloodshed is rationally evident to all *(ratio quod*

---

7. Aaron Halevi, *Sefer Ha-hinukh,* no. 416; Joseph Albo, *Iqqarim,* 3.7; Azariah di Fano, *Assarah Ma'amarim* (Frankfurt: Johannes Wust, 1698), vol. 3, p. 21. See Louis Ginzberg, *Legends of the Jews* (Philadelphia: Jewish Publication Society, 1909), vol. 5, pp. 92-93, n. 55.

8. Cf. Thomas Aquinas, *Summa Theologiae,* 2/1, q. 94, aa. 2-3.

9. Halevi, *Sefer Ha-hinukh,* no. 186.

10. B. Sanhedrin 57b; cf. *Sifra* to Lev. 12:3, ed. Weiss, p. 48a.

11. Maimonides, *Mishneh Torah:* Kings, 9.4. See Maimonides, *Sefer Ha-mitsvot,* shoresh 3.

12. Mendelssohn, *Schriften,* Jubilee ed., vol. 16, pp. 178-80, and vol. 3, pp. 43-44. Later, Hermann Cohen developed the Mendelssohnian notion of Noahide law along the lines of his neo-Kantian ethics. See *Jüdische Schriften* (Berlin: C. A. Schwetschke & Son, 1924), vol. 1, pp. 179-83, and vol. 3, pp. 345-51; and *Religion der Vernunft aus den Quellen des Judentums* (Darmstadt: Joseph Melzer Verlag, 1966), pp. 381-87.

nos), a fact emphasized as early as Saadiah and as late as Hermann Cohen, including virtually all the rationalists and nonrationalists in between, then is it possible to permit wanton bloodshed of any kind and still affirm the irreducible dignity of human life?

Man is not only a rational being but a historical being as well. Therefore, his cultural heritage informs him about his moral obligations, for law, which has been historically preserved, carries the assumption of its rationality unless proven otherwise. Our sages had great respect for those cultures which they believed were morally constituted and, conversely, great contempt for those that were not. A striking example of this is the Rabbis' admiration for the morality of Persian culture, which caused them to explain away the idolatrous Persian religion as a mere historical anachronism *(minhag avotehem),* no longer involving the true conviction of its adherents.[13]

Furthermore, the Hebrew Bible is morally authoritative for Christians, for they regard it as divinely revealed.[14] Indeed, although the Talmud prohibits non-Jews from studying Torah, it is permitted for the purpose of learning the Noahide laws.[15] Maimonides permits general scriptural study and instruction for Christians because they accept the Hebrew Bible as the word of God.[16] For him, Christians, and perhaps Muslims, could qualify for the bliss of the world-to-come by accepting the Noahide laws both as valid and as revealed.[17] In the Ashkenazic tradition, from as early as Rabbenu Tam up until R. Moses Isserles and R. Israel Lipschuetz (d. 1860), the same respect for Christianity and its moral values is found.[18]

Since orthodox Christianity (whether Eastern, Western, Anglican, or evangelical) accepts the validity of law, whether natural and revealed or only revealed, its prescriptions should be respected as moral enlightenment for Noahides — that is, non-Jews. The stand against abortion, based as it is on Scripture, reason, and history, is a consistent application of the halakhically authoritative ruling of R. Ishmael.

13. B. Hullin 13b. Concerning pro-Persian views, see B. Berakhot 8b; B. Baba Kama 117a and R. N. Rabbinovicz, *Dikdukei Soferim* (Munich: Roesl, 1867) for the textual variants; B. Baba Metsia 70b, 119a and Rashi and Tos., s.v. "Shbor Malka."

14. See Aquinas, *Summa Theologiae,* 2/1, 22, 98-100.

15. B. Sanhedrin 58b-59a.

16. Maimonides, *Responsa Pe'er Ha-dor,* ed. Amsterdam (1664), no. 50.

17. See Maimonides, MT: Kings, 8, end, and Karo, *Kessef Mishneh.* For the fullest discussion of the dispute surrounding the correct reading and meaning of this passage, see Leo Strauss, *Spinoza's Critique of Religion* (New York: Schocken Books, 1965), pp. 23-24, 273, 293.

18. For the Ashkenazic sources, see Jacob Katz, *Exclusiveness and Tolerance* (Oxford: Clarendon, 1961). Also see *Tiferet Israel* to M. Baba Kama 4.3 and M. Avot 3.14.

The enforcement of Noahide law is left to non-Jews themselves.[19] However, Jews are to encourage non-Jews to obey and enforce their own moral code. Thus, for example, Maimonides, in presenting this category of laws, justifies the action of Simeon and Levi (Gen. 34) against the Shechemites, not as revenge for Shechem's rape of their sister, Dinah, but rather as punishment of the people of Shechem, who stood by passively while their leader committed an outrage. On the basis of the first of the Noahide laws, the administration of justice *(dinim)*, the Shechemites were guilty because of their apathy.

A rabbinic legend tells of Joshua's writing the Torah upon the stones (Deut. 27; Josh. 4) in the seventy languages to remind non-Jews of their moral obligations.[20] This is my own justification for a Jewish involvement in the pro-life movement.

Unanimity about Abortion

The relationship of Noahide law to the halakhah is of especial import for abortion legislation. As Jews, do we believe in a stricter morality for non-Jews than for ourselves, or do we strive for a unified position synthesizing the principles of Jewish tradition and human reason?

The Talmud wrestled with this problem, and later the Tosafists chose the very question of abortion as an example of a unified legal position:

> R. Jose ben Hanina said that any commandments given to Noahides and repeated at Mount Sinai apply to both Noahides and Jews. If only given to Noahides but not repeated at Mount Sinai, this is for Jews but not for Noahides. It would seem that the contrary should be the case [viz., if not repeated at Mount Sinai, it is a commandment only for Noahides]. However, *there is nothing permitted to Jews which is forbidden to non-Jews.*[21]

In other words, Jewish revealed law presupposes Noahide law and then goes on to demand an even stricter morality for Jews.[22]

However, as the Noahide prohibition of abortion is unconditional, in that it does not admit the exception of the unborn child threatening its

19. B. Sanhedrin 56b; Maimonides, MT: Kings, 9, end; Nahmanides, comment to Gen. 34:13.

20. T. Sotah 8.6, ed. Zuckermandl, pp. 310-11; Y. Sotah 7.5.

21. B. Sanhedrin 59a.

22. See B. Yevamot 22a and Tos., s.v. "ervah"; B. Baba Metsia 72a; B. Kiddushin 13b and Tos., s.v. "malveh."

mother's life,[23] Noahide morality would seem to be stricter than Jewish morality. Therefore, the Tosafists proceed to use the Talmudic principle quoted above in a highly ingenious way:

> In this context one could say that abortion permitted to Jews is prohibited to non-Jews. But, some say that inasmuch as a Jewish mother can be saved from a threatening fetus, *it is possible that this is also the case with a non-Jewish mother as well.*[24]

In other words, the dispensation in the case of an unborn child threatening its mother's life *(ke-rodef achareyha)* applies to both Jewish and non-Jewish mothers, just as any other abortion is prohibited to both.[25]

Actually, two options are possible: namely, either to make Jewish abortion law as unconditional as Noahide abortion law seems to be, or to make Noahide law admit the Jewish dispensation. Tosafot clearly opts for the second alternative.

The reason for this, it seems to me, stems from the principle first enunciated in the Mishnah, "One life is not destroyed for the sake of another," a principle Maimonides explicitly declared to be rational.[26] If Jewish law refuses to declare the priority of one independent life over another, then how can it possibly rule that a dependent life (the fetus) has priority over the independent life upon which it depends (the mother)? Where a fetus threatens the mother's life, it is considered as part of her body and may be amputated as one would amputate a gangrenous limb.[27]

This does not mean, however, that the unborn child can be regarded as a "limb" of its mother in other situations as well. (Even if it were a "limb" in nonmortal situations, Judaism prohibits mutilation, self-inflicted or otherwise.[28])

To illustrate: There is the well-known Talmudic case of two travelers in the desert with one flask containing enough water for only one to survive. R. Akiba rules that the one with the water flask may save himself even if it results in the death of the other traveler. "'And your brother shall live with you [*imakh*]' (Lev. 25:36); your life takes priority [*kodmim*] over your fellow's

23. B. Sanhedrin 72b.
24. B. Sanhedrin 59a and Tos., s.v. "leyka." Cf. Y. Shabbat 14.4.
25. See B. Hullin 33a and Tos., s.v. "ehad"; Isaac Klein, "Abortion and Jewish Tradition," *Conservative Judaism* 24:3 (Spring 1970): 26-33; and G. G. Grisez, *Abortion: The Myths, the Realities, and the Arguments* (New York: World, 1970).
26. M. Ohalot 7.6; Maimonides, MT: Foundations of the Torah, 5.7.
27. B. Sanhedrin 80b and Tos., s.v. "ubar." Cf. B. Pesahim 25ab.
28. B. Baba Kama 91a; Maimonides, *Sefer Ha-mitsvot,* neg. no. 57.

life."[29] Why is this the halakhah? Because the means for saving one life are *more proximate to one person than the other*. The saving of the mother's life is more proximate than saving the life of the fetus. Once the child is born, however, both mother and child are equally proximate.

The new interpretation of the Tosafists deepens the Noahide definition of feticide put forth by the tanna R. Ishmael on the basis of the halakhah's subsequent development by the amoraim. Thus, in its relation to the developments of Jewish law, Noahide law develops a more adequate view of abortion by including the dispensation in the case of the "pursuing fetus."

Concerning the general relation of Noahide law to Jewish law, Maimonides writes, "Concerning six things the first man was commanded . . . until Moses our teacher came and the Torah was completed through him."[30] The same point has been made and developed by other traditional authorities.[31]

Thus Jewish law has illuminated Noahide law on the question of abortion. Has Noahide law returned the compliment?

I believe it has. An adulterous woman carrying another man's child petitioned R. Yair Hayyim Bacharach (b. 1639) for an abortion. Although tempted to grant her request on the grounds of certain legal technicalities, he refused such permission because "of the clear and evident consensus between us [Jews] and them [Christians] against abortion in the interest of curbing promiscuity and immorality."[32] In other words, general moral standards, universally accepted, take precedence over specific technicalities.

Indeed, R. Ezekiel Landau (b. 1713) warns against inferring any permission of abortion (where the life of the mother is not somehow at stake) from the fact that abortion is not murder in the technical sense. This is why Maimonides emphasized that the fetus is "like" a pursuer. Only in the case of mortal danger is abortion permitted; in other cases the integrity of the unborn child must be respected.[33] In the subsequent discussion, R. Landau em-

---

29. B. Baba Metsia 62a and Rashi, s.v. "imakh"; B. Avodah Zarah 6a and Tos., s.v. "vehashata."

30. Maimonides, MT: Kings, 9.1; cf. *Leviticus Rabbah* 9.3.

31. This is especially true in the Sephardic tradition. See Halevi, *Kuzari*, 2.48; Albo, *Iqqarim*, Book 1; Meiri to B. Baba Kama 38a (in *Shitah Mekubetset*) and to B. Sanhedrin 57b in *Bet Habehirah*, ed. Schreiber (Frankfurt: Hermon, 1929), pp. 226-27; Elie Benamozegh, *Israel et L'humanité* (Paris: E. Leroux, 1914), pp. 457ff.

32. *Responsa Havot Ya'ir* (Lemberg: n.p., 1896), no. 31. Cf. B. Kiddushin 12b; B. Sotah 47b; *Bereshit Rabbah* 51.1. See *Zohar*, p. 3a to Exod. 1:7. Cf., however, R. Jacob Emden, *Responsa Ya'avets* (Lemberg: n.p., 1884), vol. 1, no. 43.

33. *Noda bi-Yehudah* (Vilna: n.p., 1904), vol. 2; Hoshen Mishpat, no. 59. Cf. Heller, *Tosfot Yom Tov* to M. Niddah 5.3.

phasized that the Noahide designation of abortion as destruction of "a human within a human" applies to Jews as well.

Finally, abortion cannot be permitted on the grounds that it is not "murder" in the technical sense, for even infanticide is not murder in the sense of a humanly prosecutable crime if the infant is under thirty days old. However, no one could possibly argue that infanticide is ever permitted. Both acts are forbidden *(assur)* even if not humanly punishable *(patur), ex post facto.*[34]

A Modern Approach

This analysis is within the scope of modern halakhic thinking, which I would characterize as not only examining the various precedents within the halakhic literature, but also taking into consideration two additional factors: (1) philosophical and theological perspectives, and (2) historical background.

Many modern thinkers feel that even though authoritative conclusions cannot be inferred from aggadah, aggadic considerations can *inform* the process of halakhic decision-making. (This is one of the most important methodological points I learned from my teachers at the Jewish Theological Seminary, especially from the late Professor Abraham J. Heschel and from Professor Seymour Siegel.) Aggadic perspective is indispensable when several divergent halakhic options are possible.[35] How does one decide a Jewish position on abortion when there are both strict and lenient trends before him? This is where a philosophy and a theology of law are required by halakhah itself.

The philosophical question surrounding the halakhic precedents on abortion is this: What is the status of human life? The theological question is this: How do the covenants of God with mankind (the sons of Noah) and with the people of Israel ground the sanctity of the human person?

The irreducible status of life — namely, that life needs no justification — is a philosophical axiom which, it seems to me, underlies the opposition to the war in Vietnam, the opposition to capital punishment, and the ecology movement, which is dedicated to the integrity of all life, even nonhuman life.

An irreducible truth cannot be proven, for its truth value is not derived from a prior principle. To demonstrate an irreducible truth, one must show

34. See M. Niddah 5.3; B. Niddah 44b; Maimonides, MT: Murderer, 2.6; Maimonides, MT: Mourning, 1.7 and Karo, *Kessef Mishneh,* thereto.

35. See David Novak, "Law and Theology in Judaism," in *Law and Theology in Judaism* (New York: Ktav Publishing House, 1974-76), vol. 1, pp. 1-14. For the various halakhic opinions, both lenient and strict, see David M. Feldman, *Birth Control in Jewish Law,* 2d ed. (New York: New York University Press, 1970), pp. 284-94.

the absurdity of anything that attempts to contradict it.[36] That life is to be preserved and not destroyed is an irreducible principle. It is the foundation of all rational human action, such as the promotion of health, the establishment of society, the worship of God, and so on. The only exceptions that are rationally justifiable arise in situations where one life is in conflict with another life. To assert, however, that life's value must be justified on the basis of something else, is, philosophically speaking, to place the cart before the horse. For if life must be justified, what principle can be objectively put forward as having greater priority? This is the basis of the philosophical insight common to the Bible, Plato, the Stoics, and the Declaration of Independence — that the natural or created order takes precedence over the conventional or humanly instituted order.[37]

The fundamental question is whether the life of a fetus may be destroyed at will. If this is permitted for utilitarian reasons (overpopulation, convenience, and so on), then the right to life of the severely retarded, the hopelessly psychotic, and the senile could be questioned next. Are not the senile, the retarded, and the psychotic more "trouble" than an unwanted fetus? Reverence for life is at a low ebb, and the clamor for open abortion is just one symptom of the moral climate of our times. Jews especially, who have been the most tragic victims of the contempt for life, should be the last people in the world to support legislation that would give *carte blanche* and moral sanction to abortion. There are moral considerations that transcend even the fine points of the law and that must inform the law lest legal decisions be a respectable cover for immorality.[38]

Furthermore, the covenantal theologies of both Judaism and Christianity provide a more profound basis for the "right to life" by emphasizing not only the immanent dignity of man, but even more, the transcendent sanctity of the human person, to whom, of all his creatures, God has chosen to reveal his presence. Even the unborn can be the subjects of revelation (Jer. 1:5; Ps. 139:13-16).

A modern approach to halakhah is characterized by a concern with the historical background of the law. Jewish history is not the ground of Jewish law. That right must be reserved for revelation if halakhah is to be morally obligatory. However, Jewish history is the indispensable context of Jewish law

36. See Aristotle, *Metaphysics*, 1005b29; Thomas Aquinas, *Summa Theologiae*, 2/1, q. 94, a. 2; Ludwig Wittgenstein, *Tractatus Logico-Philosophicus*, 5.133.

37. See Shalom Spiegel, *Amos versus Amaziah* (New York: Jewish Theological Seminary, 1957).

38. Nahmanides to Lev. 19:2; also, the responsum of R. Solomon ibn Adret (Rashba), quoted by Karo, *Bet Joseph* to *Tur*, Hoshen Mishpat 2.1; cf. B. Avodah Zarah 55b.

and conditions its application. Therefore, what is the historical background of the Jewish law about abortion?

Rabbinic sources raise only the problem of therapeutic abortion. The assumption is that bearing and raising children was a great blessing in the normative Jewish communities in Israel and Babylonia, called into question only in cases of great danger to already existing life. In the one direct scriptural treatment of abortion (Exod. 21:22), the law is presented in the context of an unfortunate accident. As such, the sources seem to assume the extraordinary, unplanned nature of the circumstances involved and take a compassionate, lenient stand.

However, in the Hellenistic sources, especially the Septuagint and Philo, a harder line is taken,[39] because in the Greco-Roman world, where respect for life's sanctity could not be assumed, wholesale abortion and infanticide were being practiced. This is the historical background of R. Ishmael's ruling against abortion for Noahides. Dr. Immanuel Jacobovits, now Chief Rabbi of Great Britain, along with R. Isser Unterman, the former Ashkenazi Chief Rabbi of Israel, takes a "hard line" on the abortion question and explains R. Ishmael's ruling as follows: "Another view is that this extension of the Noahidic laws was intended, on the contrary, as a protest against the widespread Roman practice of abortion and infanticide."[40] Is our society's reverence for life on any higher level?

The tendency in Jewish law has usually been to take a strict stand when general public morality has declined.[41] The pro-abortion movement insists that abortion be permitted on demand. It is not concerned with the *occasional* dispensations allowed in Jewish law. The issue, therefore, is whether the unborn child has any rights at all.

Historical change also has an effect on two other considerations involved in abortion — namely, (1) Is the fetus a living entity *per se?* and (2) Is abortion a solution for prepartum depression accompanied by suicide threats? The assumption that the fetus is not a living entity *per se* could easily be inferred from the Mishnah in *Ohalot*, which discusses the woman in hard labor. There only the child who is born is called a person *(nefesh)* whose life cannot be violated. Furthermore, the Mishnah elsewhere notes a difference in the status of the fetus before the fortieth day of pregnancy and after. The Gemara presents various theories on the status of prenatal life based on the empirical observa-

---

39. See Feldman, *Birth Control in Jewish Law,* pp. 257-62.

40. Jacobovits, *Jewish Medical Ethics* (New York: Bloch Publishing Co., 1959), p. 181. This is based on I. M. Weiss, *Dor dor ve-dorshav* (Berlin: Platt & Minkus, 1923/24), vol. 2, p. 22.

41. See, e.g., B. Sukkah 51b-52a; B. Kiddushin 12b; and M. Berakhot, end.

tions of the ancient Rabbis.[42] However, these theories are not directly derived from scriptural decrees, which would make them irrevocable, nor are they presented as formal rabbinic decrees *(takkanot)* requiring the complicated procedure of repeal. As such, these observations are not in themselves authoritative, but rather can be modified in the light of newer scientific evidence. Thus, for example, it was an empirical assumption of the Rabbis of the Talmud that a child born in the eighth month of pregnancy could not possibly live. This affected the application of certain laws to newborn children where possible viability is a question. Nevertheless, subsequent evidence convinced R. Moses Isserles (Rema, b. 1520) that some eight-month children do live and, therefore, that there ought to be no distinction between them and any other newborn children.[43]

Again, it was an empirical assumption of the Rabbis of the Talmud that a deaf-mute *(heresh)* was essentially the same as a mentally retarded person *(shoteh)*. Nevertheless, the son of R. Moses Sofer, after a visit to an institution for the deaf in Vienna in the mid-nineteenth century, was so impressed by the responsiveness of the students that he seriously questioned whether the old empirical equation of the deaf mute with mental retardation still applied.[44]

In other words, law based on empirical evidence admits of modification when newer empirical evidence becomes available. Even though the Jewish prohibition of nonthreatening abortion is not at question in the issue of fetal life, any inferences from rabbinic sources that belittle the status of fetal life are highly suspect on the basis of the latest scientific evidence. This evidence assigns a much higher biological status to the life of the unborn child than had heretofore been known.[45] Furthermore, as we have seen, R. Ezekiel Landau believed the very designation of the threatening fetus as a "pursuer" *(rodef)* ruled out any such inferences.

The second question raised, which requires the latest scientific testimony, is whether abortion is warranted in the case of the suicide threats made by a pregnant woman suffering from what is known as prepartum depression, which many psychiatrists would consider a psychotic state. Dr. David

---

42. M. Niddah 3.7; B. Niddah 30a-31b.

43. Note to *Shulhan Arukh,* E. H. 156.4. However, some authorities tried to explain this not so much as a change in our knowledge of the evidence, but as a change in the nature of the evidence itself. See Kagan (Hafetz Hayyim), *Mishnah Berurah* to O. H. 173.2, n. 3.

44. *Shivtei Sefer* 2.21. I found this reference in Louis Jacobs, *Principles of the Jewish Faith* (New York: Basic Books, 1964), pp. 310-11. For the earlier attitude toward the deaf mute, see, e.g., M. Baba Kama 6.4, 8.4.

45. See the brief and motion filed *amicus curiae* before the Supreme Court of the United States, October term, 1971, no. 70-18.

Feldman and Dr. Isaac Klein have both argued on the basis of halakhic precedents that mental health is a valid reason for abortion.

Frankly, on this issue I am in doubt. In the first place, there are situations where the mentally ill person's demands are not to be fulfilled, especially if these demands are immoral.[46] Secondly, it is often assumed in psychiatry that what the patient *wants* is not necessarily what the patient *needs*. Dr. Carl Marlow, professor of psychiatry at the University of Miami Medical School, researched the threat of suicide as a reason for psychiatric abortion. His conclusion was that there was only a minimal risk of suicide actually taking place if the demanded abortion were not performed. Further, he states, "Most abortions performed for psychiatric reasons are at best recommended on the basis of peripheral psychoses, but are generally performed for socio-economic reasons."[47]

In summary, I believe that the matter needs much more study. *Psychosis* is a term that covers as many diverse phenomena as the term *cancer*. Hence a general ruling on the whole mental-health aspect of abortion would be imprudent. However, although not a psychiatrist myself, my three years as a chaplain at St. Elizabeth's Hospital, National Institute of Mental Health, in Washington, D.C., especially my working closely with several suicidal female patients, indicated to me that the guilt that might result from an abortion would hardly be therapeutic in the long run.[48]

Conclusion

Although my concern in this essay is with the objective moral question of abortion, it is written with deep feeling because of my own very private reasons. With one-third of our people murdered and the Jewish birthrate in both Israel and the diaspora alarmingly low, permission of abortion, for less than the most serious life-threatening reasons, is at best insensitive. And if we permit abortion for the general population — *Wie es sich christelt, so juedelt es sich!*

46. B. Sanhedrin 75a; Maimonides, MT: Foundations of the Torah, 5.9. Cf. M. Yoma 8.6 and B. Yoma 83ab.

47. Marlow, quoted in "Abortion's Psychological Price," *Christianity Today* 15:18 (4 June 1971): 41ff.

48. At present I am researching this question in the psychiatric literature. The phenomenon of suicide, which has, I think, important light to shed on the question of abortion, is the subject of my forthcoming book, *Suicide and Morality* [New York: Scholars Studies Press, 1975 — Ed.].

At a time when the hold of the Torah is so weak for so many of our people, we should by all means strengthen the only moral code many Jews still recognize — namely, the law of the secular state.

> R. Joshua ben Levi saw a contradiction between two verses in Ezekiel: "And you did *not* act according to the laws of the nations which surround you" [5:7], "You *did* act according to the laws of the nations which surround you" [11:12]. He resolved it by saying: You did *not* act according to their good laws [*metukanin*]: their bad laws [*mekulkalin*] you *did* act according to.[49]

The question of how to do God's will in a secular world is not easily answered. This is my response, on one specific issue, to the ancient cry, "How shall we sing the Lord's song in a strange land?" (Ps. 137:4).

---

49. B. Sanhedrin 39b. Cf. M. Avot 2.1 and commentators.

18 A Halakhic View of Responsibility (1982)

I categorically reject the notion expressed by some Jews, both in Israel and in the diaspora, that the whole issue of the massacre of the Palestinians and the question of Israeli involvement is a question that may be debated only by Israelis, that diaspora Jews may not have opinions, or if they may, then they must remain silent. This notion is only valid if Israel is only an *Israeli state* rather than *the Jewish state*. If that is the case, then diaspora Jews should have nothing more to do with the state of Israel.

If Israel does not bear *direct* responsibility *(zadon)* for the massacres in Sabra and Shatila, there is still the question of *indirect* responsibility *(shegagah)*.

Jewish tradition, it seems to me, indicts us on four counts.

First, the Mishnah states, "These are the persons whose lives may be saved even if another life is lost: when one pursues [*rodef*] his fellow to kill him."[1] However, the Talmud indicates that "it is different when you do not know who is killing whom."[2] To intervene in such a conflict is to choose one party in a dispute as the "pursued" *(nirdaf)* when the situation itself offers no objective evidence for so doing. Clearly, the motivation for such an act is self-interest — that is, one chooses the side he feels closer to, and then cloaks his subjective choice in objective morality.[3] I believe Israel was justified in its preemptive strike against the PLO in Lebanon. I do not believe, however, that Israel was justified in re-entering West Beirut for the express purpose of polic-

---

1. M. Sanhedrin 8.7. That this applies to non-Jews, see B. Sanhedrin 59a and Tos., s.v. "leyka."

2. Y. Shabbat 14.4/14d.

3. See David Novak, "A Jewish View of War," chap. 16 of this volume.

ing Lebanese affairs, which was obviously motivated by the desire to strengthen one Lebanese faction (the Phalange) over all the others.

Washing One's Hands of Murder

Second, the gravity of indirect responsibility is further brought out by the following. The Torah stipulates that when a murder victim is found, the elders of the nearest city conduct a rite of atonement wherein they wash their hands in a spring and declare, "Our hands did not shed this blood nor did our eyes see it" (Deut. 21:7). The Mishnah indicates that although no one would suspect the elders of the community of being murderers, they may only exonerate themselves if they can convincingly show that they did everything in *their* power to protect potential murder victims.[4] Now Israel went into West Beirut for the express purpose of preventing bloodshed. The fact is that Israeli forces, however unwittingly, made the bloodshed possible. If the elders of ancient Israel may not literally wash their hands in such circumstances, then the elders of modern Israel, especially Menachem Begin and Ariel Sharon, may not do so symbolically with their words. It is their symbolic handwashing that has so outraged many Jews both in Israel and in the diaspora. Have we so quickly forgotten others who claimed they saw and knew nothing when our people were being murdered?

Third, the Mishnah states that we may not "strengthen the hands of transgressors," and the Talmud paraphrases it by saying that it is forbidden (*asur*) to help them in any way.[5] Our tradition, furthermore, teaches that murder is universally prohibited.[6] Bearing this in mind, we should not forget just who the Phalangists are. The Phalange was founded by Pierre Gemayel (the father of Bashir Gemayel, whose murder was being avenged in Sabra and Shatila) after he visited the infamous Olympics in Berlin in 1936. Hugely impressed by Hitler and the Nazis, Gemayel founded the Phalange in their image, seeing it as the solution for the precarious position of the Christians in Lebanon. The Phalangists are Fascists with a long history of indiscriminate bloodshed. Can we claim innocence when we lighted flares for them, hoping they would only seek out "terrorists"? Considering Mr. Begin's obsession with the Nazi crimes against our people, and how often this memory saturates his rhetoric, how strange that he *is* silent about the source and in-

---

4. M. Sotah 9.6.
5. M. Gittin 5.9; B. Avodah Zarah 55b.
6. B. Sanhedrin 56ab.

spiration of his Phalangist allies! Can we be so selective in our condemnation of Nazism?

Guilt for Instigating a Crime

Fourth, the Talmud records a debate over whether one who instigates someone else to commit a crime is innocent or guilty.[7] Even though the final halakhah is that there is no formal legal guilt[8], nevertheless, there is moral guilt *(hayyav be-diney shamayim)*, and minimally *(dina zuta)*, as Rashi notes, this is the guilt of an indirect cause *(ke-gorem)*. Now I believe Ariel Sharon when he stated that the Israeli commanders explicitly told the Lebanese not to harm civilians. However, considering the mood of the Christian community immediately after the murder of so many of their own leaders, could we honestly trust them to follow such directives? Were they capable of such discretion, the type of discretion we would expect of Israeli soldiers? Indeed, as the great fifteenth-century Spanish Jewish statesman and exegete Don Isaac Abrabanel noted (no doubt based on his firsthand experience in the corridors of political and military power), when those in power set a policy, those subordinate to them are most likely to take it more seriously than ordinary suggestion.[9] Has the policy of Begin and Sharon in any way indicated to the Phalangists (or ben Haddad's militia, or whoever) that they really disapproved of the deaths of Palestinians — *any* Palestinians?

I believe that these four traditional sources indicate how un-Jewish are both the policies of Begin and Sharon before the massacre and their reactions after it.

Understanding Our Chosenness

At the heart of our Jewish moral problem here is how we understand our chosenness. The Torah states, "You are a holy people [*goy qadosh*] for the Lord your God; the Lord your God has chosen you to be his unique people [*am segulah*] apart from all the peoples. . ." (Deut. 7:6). Now our uniqueness is surely to live a life ritually distinct.[10] However, our very uniqueness has a

---

7. B. Kiddushin 43a.
8. Maimonides, *Mishneh Torah:* Murderer, 2.2.
9. Comment on 2 Sam. 12:10.
10. See *Sifra* and Rashi on Lev. 19:1.

moral significance for the nations of the world. As Isaiah prophesied, "I the Lord called you in righteousness and strengthened your hand, and I made you and designated you a covenant people, a light for the nations" (Isa. 42:6). For this reason we must take seriously the moral judgment of the nations of the world. Even though we may discard the *lies* of our enemies, we may not discard even their anger if it is based on *truth*.[11] For our chosenness requires that our morality be higher, not lower, than that of the world.[12] The world has a right to expect more of us than of any other people. Therefore, I find Jewish rationalizing about the "double standard" of the gentiles to be unconvincing.

The Talmud states, "This nation is distinguished by three traits: they are compassionate [*rahmanim*]; they have a sense of shame [*bayyshanim*]; they act kindly [*gomley hasadim*]."[13] This statement *is* made in the context of interpreting a scriptural text dealing with Jewish misconduct toward gentiles (2 Sam. 21). I find the conduct of Begin and Sharon un-Jewish on all three counts. First, they have shown little or no compassion for the genuine suffering of innocent Arabs — as well as having questionable concern for the lives of many young Israelis. Second, they have demonstrated no sense of shame over what has happened, however indirect our guilt may be. "Happy is the generation whose leader brings an offering for his indirect sin."[14] Third, they have demonstrated no plan of action to help those who have so terribly suffered in this whole episode.

On the basis of all this, I have joined along with many other American Jews, and with the Peace Now movement in Israel, in calling for the resignations of both Begin and Sharon. They have endangered the Jewish body and have tainted the Jewish soul. Their removal from public office must be part of our collective repentance.[15]

---

11. B. Baba Kama 38a.
12. See B. Yevamot 22a; B. Baba Kama 113b; B. Sanhedrin 59a; Y. Baba Metsia 2.5/8c.
13. B. Yevamot 79a.
14. B. Horayot 10b re Lev. 4:22.
15. Maimonides, MT: Repentance, 2.2.

19 Religious Communities, Secular Societies, and Sexuality: One Jewish Opinion (1998)

Religious and Social Recognition of Sexuality

Since the pioneering investigations of Freud at the beginning of this century, *most* of the old conventions concerning human sexuality have been called into question. That has required both those who advocate that these conventions be changed and those who advocate that they remain in force to devise new arguments for their respective positions. The current debate over homosexuality, especially, has called for such new arguments because the case at hand seems so radical when made by those who advocate change and so lacking in rational persuasion when made by those who advocate tradition.

Traditionally, both religious communities and secular society have discriminated against homosexual persons in three ways: (1) they have proscribed homoerotic acts; (2) they have penalized those who engage in homoerotic acts; and (3) they have denied the rights and obligations of the institution of marriage to homosexual persons who have wanted to enter it through the innovation of legally sanctioned homosexual unions. With the rise of the gay movement in the past twenty-five years or so, all three of these forms of discrimination have been publicly challenged. This challenge has been made not only by gay people but also by a number of straight people who believe that these forms of discrimination are unjust and should, therefore, be repealed on moral grounds.

Out of this challenge the following questions seem to emerge. By religious criteria, is the religious proscription of homoerotic acts just? By secular criteria, is the secular proscription of homoerotic acts just? Could there be one reason for or against this proscription that would satisfy both religious and secular criteria? Although the proscription of homoerotic acts logically entails the denial of the institution of marriage to homosexual couples, does that proscription also logically entail public penalties for these acts? In other words, could a religious community or a secular society proscribe homosexual acts, refuse homosexual unions the status of marriage, and still be consistent in not publicly penalizing those who engage in homoerotic acts?

These are all normative questions, which can be discussed only with normative coherence in the context of a community or society whose normative authority one recognizes as binding on herself or himself. Therefore, anyone discussing these questions cannot hide behind any normative anonymity. Along these lines, let me state at the outset that I am an American Jew or a Jewish American, depending on where the normative emphasis at any time is to be located. As such, I am beholden to two and only two normative orders: Judaism and the United States of America. All other normative orders to which I am beholden (for example, family, municipality, profession) are essentially subsets of one or the other of these larger normative orders. Moreover, I consider my being beholden to the normative order of Judaism, called the Torah, to be prior both chronologically and ontologically to my being beholden to the normative order of the United States. In other words, I can accept only secondary secular authority because it has been justified as being in principle (if not always in specific practice) consistent with the primary religious authority for me.[1] That is why I must first discuss the question of the religious discrimination against gay people.

The Jewish Prohibition of Homosexuality

There are few prohibitions that are more unambiguous than the traditional Jewish prohibition of male homosexual acts. Even though one could argue that the original prohibition in Leviticus 18:22 ("With a male you shall not lie as with a female") only applies to an act of anal intercourse between two males, the subsequent tradition saw the prohibition as including all sexual acts between males.[2] Hence the rabbinic term *mishkav zakhur* comes very

---

1. See David Novak, *Jewish Social Ethics* (New York: Oxford University Press, 1992), pp. 67-83. Cf. John Courtney Murray, *We Hold These Truths: Catholic Reflections on the American Proposition* (New York: Sheed & Ward, 1960), pp. ix-x.

2. For the literal definition of *mishkav zakhur* as anal intercourse between two males, see *Sifra:* Qedoshim, ed. Weiss, 92a re Lev. 18:22 and Deut. 23:18; M. Sanhedrin 7.4; B. Sanhedrin 54ab; Y. Sanhedrin 7.7/24d-25a. For a discussion of modern Bible scholarship on the subject, see S. M. Olyan, "'And with a Male You Shall Not Lie the Lying Down of a Woman': On the Meaning and Significance of Leviticus 18:22 and 20:13," *Journal of the History of Sexuality* 5 (1994): 179-206.

close to meaning what we mean today by "homosexuality."[3] And even though there is no explicit biblical prohibition of female homosexual acts, there is a rabbinic prohibition of them.[4] Thus it could well be maintained that the prohibition of homoerotic acts, be they male or female, comes under the general rubric of proscribed sexuality called by the Rabbis *giluy arayot,* literally meaning "uncovering of the genitals" — that is, for sexual acts.[5] Furthermore, however different the respective penalties might be for different homoerotic acts, the fact is that in rabbinic Judaism any prohibited act is considered deserving of divine punishment.[6]

At the level of Jewish religious observance, one could leave the matter here — that is, one could simply state that homoerotic acts are proscribed and that there is no way that this general prohibition could be repealed in a community where the halakhah has genuine governance and not just arbitrary guidance.[7] Nevertheless, the traditional sources themselves do not end their discussion of the matter here. Instead, they include two other considerations.

The first such consideration is that the general prohibition of illicit sexuality as *giluy arayot* is considered by the Rabbis to be one of the seven Noahide areas of law *(sheva mitsvot benei Noah),* which by definition are taken to be binding on all humankind collectively and on every human being individually.[8] The second such consideration is that the Rabbis also considered the general category of illicit sexuality to be a matter that "even if it had not been

---

3. For the clearest use of this more general meaning of the term, see B. Shabbat 17b, where *mishkav zakhur* includes even sex play among very young children *(tinoq),* which is most unlikely to involve penile penetration of the anus of another. For the general prohibition of any sexual contact between males, see M. Kiddushin 4.14; B. Pesahim 51a; B. Berakhot 43b; Maimonides, *Commentary on the Mishnah:* Sanhedrin 7.4, ed. Kafih, p. 122, and Maimonides, *Mishneh Torah:* Forbidden Relations, 22.2; *Sefer ha-Hinukh,* no. 209; *Tur:* Even Ha'Ezer, 24, and Karo, *Bet Yosef,* and Sirkes, *Bayit Hadash* thereon; Karo, *Shulhan Arukh:* Even Ha'Ezer, 24.1, and Phoebus, *Bet Shmu'el* thereon. Also see David Novak, *The Image of the Non-Jew in Judaism* (New York: E. Mellen, 1983), pp. 211-16, and Novak, *Jewish Social Ethics,* pp. 86-98, 109-10.

4. See B. Yevamot 76a and Tos., s.v. "mesolelot"; B. Shabbat 65a; Maimonides, MT: Forbidden Relations, 21.8 re Lev. 18:3. Cf. B. Niddah 61a, Tos., s.v. "amar R. Ami." Also cf. M. L. Satlow, "'And They Abused Him Like a Woman': Homoeroticism, Gender Blurring, and the Rabbis in Late Antiquity," *Journal of the History of Sexuality* 5 (1994): 15-17.

5. See B. Shabbat 13a and Rashi, s.v. "giluy arayot," and Tos., s.v. "u-fliga."

6. See B. Berakhot 6b; B. Eruvin 21b re Eccles. 12:12.

7. Regarding the permanent impossibility of the repeal of scriptural law that is perpetually binding *(d'oraita),* see B. Kiddushin 29a re Num. 15:23 and B. H. Epstein, *Torah Temimah* (Vilna: Romm, 1904): Num. 15:23, n. 61. Regarding the present impossibility of the direct repeal of rabbinic law *(de-rabbanan),* see M. Eduyot 1.5; B. Avodah Zarah 36a; Maimonides, MT: Rebels, 2.2-4.

8. T. Avodah Zarah 8.4; B. Sanhedrin 56ab; Maimonides, MT: Kings, 9.5.

written [in the Torah], it should have been written."[9] As Nahmanides argued about a similar area of law, even though the Torah recognizes and further specifies it, the prohibition itself is inherently rational and does not require the Torah to initially establish it.[10]

Now there is a difference between norms that are taken to be universal but *not* rational and norms that are taken to be both universal *and* rational. The former would apply only when the community that recognizes and formulates them has political power over a more general group outside itself. But in the case of norms assumed to be both universal and rational, they are taken to apply whenever rational persons understand their reasons. Persuasion is their more appropriate method of communication. They do not entail the imperialism of one community over a general group of outsiders. Instead, they apply as much to the insiders of the religious community as they do to the outsiders of the more general society.[11] Concerning such laws, the Talmudic principle is that nothing prohibited to the gentiles is permitted to the Jews.[12]

Religious and Secular Reasons

Here we can begin to see how the realms of the religious community and the secular society overlap, so that we may be able to discuss the prohibition of homoerotic acts in both localities in tandem. That overlapping, however, can be seen only when we assume that the difference between religious community and secular society is not that God is necessarily to be present in the former and just as necessarily to be absent in the latter. That is only the case when affirmation of the "secular" is taken to be essentially "secularist." Indeed, when that is the case, one cannot affirm the religious and the secular together with any coherence; one must choose between one or the other. Yet one can affirm them both together coherently when the difference between them is that in religious community one *must* affirm both the will and the wisdom of God, but in secular society one must affirm only what she or he thinks is to be socially mandated in a rational manner. One *may* only affirm

9. *Sifra*: Aharei-Mot, ed. Weiss, 86a re Lev. 18:5; B. Yoma 67b.

10. Nahmanides, *Commentary on the Torah*: Gen. 6:2, 13.

11. Throughout this essay I use the term *community* in the sense of *Gemeinschaft* and *society* in the sense of *Gesellschaft*, following the often-used distinction between the two made by Ferdinand Tönnies in his seminal work, *Community and Society*, trans. C. P. Loomis (East Lansing: Michigan State University, 1957).

12. B. Sanhedrin 59a.

what is rational as being originally the wisdom of God. For Jews, that means that among ourselves we must affirm the authority of both those commandments that do not have general reasons (like the dietary prohibitions) and those commandments that do have general reasons (like the prohibition of murder). However, in secular society we may affirm the wisdom of only those commandments (like the prohibition of murder) that apply to everyone for good reasons. All we require is that the wisdom of these commandments be capable of discussion; we do not require that the divine source of these wise commandments be affirmed by anyone else.[13] The absence of such a requirement makes the affirmation of a secular realm possible without our having to accept secularist foundations for it, however.[14]

The foundation of secular society, then, is the liberty to speak the name of one's own God in public, the liberty of anyone else to speak the name of her or his own God in public, the liberty of those who do not care to speak the name of their own God in public, and the liberty of those who have no God not to have to affirm anyone else's God. The denial of any of these liberties makes a society either anti-religious or theocratic. The difference between religious persons and nonreligious persons is that the former believe public wisdom has a divine source, whereas the latter believe it is either self-sufficient or has sources other than divine. But those who do speak the name of their God in public can do so only in connection with those commandments of their God that apply to everyone for good reasons. Anything else is questionable special pleading.[15]

In that sense, I agree with Richard Rorty when he argues that those who speak of "God's will" are "conversation stoppers" in a democratic society.[16] However, I disagree with Rorty's apparent belief that that is the only possible

13. See Maimonides, MT: Kings, 8.11, which only eliminates from the world-to-come those gentiles who do not acknowledge the divine source of universal Noahide law. Their affirmation of its rationality, nevertheless, is sufficient to ensure that they be regarded as "wise" in the sense of having practical wisdom. For the dispute regarding the correct text in Maimonides on this point, see Novak, *The Image of the Non-Jew in Judaism*, pp. 288-94.

14. See Hermann Cohen, *Religion of Reason Out of the Sources of Judaism*, trans. S. Kaplan (New York: F. Ungar, 1972), pp. 123-30.

15. This does not mean that religious persons may not request exemptions from certain civic duties — e.g., work on the Sabbath — based on their own religious laws. What they may not do is to even suggest that their own religious laws have secular authority for everyone in the society. That is why the religious opponents of elective abortion, for example, have to argue on natural-law grounds. Their adversaries, however, often attempt to expose their natural-law arguments as being in truth nothing but rationalizations for their specifically religious position. The same seems to be the case for the public argument over homosexuality, *mutatis mutandis*.

16. See his "Religion as Conversation-Stopper," *Common Knowledge* 3 (1994): 1-6.

mode of religious conversation in public. One may also speak of the wisdom of God, and that is a different mode of discourse. Furthermore, I agree with Plato that it is better to argue for a practice based on *why* it is to be done (its wisdom) than simply on *who* originally authorized it (its will).[17] However, unlike Plato, being a believer in divine *creatio ex nihilo*, I thereby believe that God is the source of both wisdom and authority, and that the relationship with this God that revelation enables is the highest good.[18] Therefore, although in secular society one need not mention the divine source of wisdom, since secular society is not itself concerned with the God-human relationship, the religious person must never forget the divine source of any wisdom.[19] For the religious person comes to secular society out of a prior community in which she or he is forever rooted and to which he or she must ever return. The essential purpose of that community is to proclaim the name of God.[20] As such, one cannot dismiss by means of Occam's razor those who see a divine source of what is rationally evident inasmuch as the affirmation of this divine source is not a superfluous premise in an otherwise self-sufficient argument. For in its original and primary context, that of the religious community, affirmation of the divine source of wisdom and authority is the most necessary premise for anything that is to be said and done. Whereas outside this community one may at best designate God as a possible cause, within the community God is the One who initiates and sustains the covenant.[21]

The Justice of the Prohibition

Let me now argue for the justice of the prohibition of homoerotic acts in terms of its wisdom, a criterion that is both religious and secular. It is secular inasmuch as one does not have to believe in a historical revelation to accept it. And it is religious inasmuch as one who believes in a historical revelation that includes it is not thereby denying the authority of that revelation by affirming the natural wisdom of this prohibition, too.

In order to understand the wisdom of this prohibition, one has to discern what the purpose of human sexuality is. At the prima facie level, there seem to

17. See Plato, *Euthyphro*, 10ae.

18. See Ps. 73:28; also, David Novak, *Jewish-Christian Dialogue: A Jewish Justification* (New York: Oxford University Press, 1989), pp. 152-54.

19. See B. Hagigah 3b re Eccles. 12:11.

20. See Isa. 43:21; M. Avot 2.12.

21. For the plausibility, but not the rational necessity, of affirming God's causality in a secular context, see Kant, *Critique of Pure Reason*, B655. Cf. Exod. 33:14-15.

be three purposes of human sexuality: (1) pleasure, (2) personal communion, (3) procreation. Thus human persons engage in sexual activities because they desire (1) the unique enjoyment of bodily union, (2) the transcendence of personal loneliness, (3) full family life. Some theorists have attempted to affirm all three purposes as three separate, albeit related, goods.[22] Others have attempted to emphasize one of them at the expense of the others.[23] However, here I would argue that all three purposes or desires are essentially one, with procreation being *primus inter pares.*

The way to see all of these purposes in unison is to assert that the purpose of sexuality is to initiate and maintain the institution of the family. It is to assert that only within the situation of family life can human persons be fulfilled, and that any situation in which family life is absent, especially when that absence is intended, takes a toll on one's humanity. In the full sense of the term, *family life* means the intended permanent union of a man and a woman, which therewith intends the conception, birth, and parenting of children.[24] As the Bible puts it, "A man shall leave his father and his mother and cleave unto his wife, and they shall become one flesh" (Gen. 2:24). In traditional Jewish exegesis, "one flesh" refers to the heterosexual couple themselves who intend to conceive a child by their union, and the child itself who results from their permanent, sustained union.[25] And from this passage, the Rabbis see all the universal (and rational) sexual prohibitions — that is, from a positive commandment they infer these prohibitions.[26]

Now the argument against this traditional definition of family life is that it is too exclusive. Specifically, it seems to exclude homosexuals, sterile persons, and celibate persons from true human fulfillment. In terms of our present topic of discussion, it can be assumed that the charge of homosexual exclusion is the most serious. (I shall return to the questions of the marriage of sterile persons and celibacy.)

The charge is most serious when made by those homosexuals who want *both* the proscription of homoerotic acts *and* the exclusion of homosexual unions from the status of marriage to be repealed. For those homosexuals, on

22. See John M. Finnis, "Law, Morality, and 'Sexual Orientation,'" *Notre Dame Journal of Law, Ethics, and Public Policy* 9 (1995): 27-39.

23. See Augustine, *De Bono Coniugali*, 9.9.

24. In the Jewish tradition that does not mean, though, that couples may not time the birth of their children and limit their number. See D. M. Feldman, *Birth Control in Jewish Law* (New York: New York University Press, 1968), pp. 46-59.

25. See B. Sanhedrin 58a, Rashi, s.v. "ve-davaq"; Rashi, *Commentary on the Torah:* Gen. 2:24; Nahmanides, *Commentary on the Torah:* Gen. 2:24; also, Y. Kiddushin 1.1/58c.

26. B. Sanhedrin 58a.

the other hand, who do not regard the permanence of marriage to be a universal desideratum, the repeal of the proscription of homoerotic acts is sufficient. However, I choose to address myself to the charges of pro-family homosexuals inasmuch as they seem to affirm the traditional proscription of sexual promiscuity that marriage entails. (Hence I assume that their appeal to be included in the social institution of marriage includes their opposition to adultery, even if both marital partners know and approve of it; "open marriage" is an oxymoron.) They request only the widening of the parameters of the traditional institution of marriage, not its elimination or marginalization. These homosexuals, then, present the most formidable challenge to both the religious and the secular institution of marriage as traditionally constituted. Indeed, they are often found in all of our religious communities, which is rarely the case with those homosexuals who see permanent sexual unions as being a heterosexual prejudice. Even in secular society, pro-family homosexuals are usually quite conservative in terms of wanting as little social change as is just. In other words, they want a place *within* religious communities and secular society, not the radical revolution of either entity. As such, they are speaking *to* us, not *against* us, who are religious and secular traditionalists. Their stated intention is to be *with* us.

Nevertheless, the reason that the definition of family cannot be stretched to include homosexual unions is that by design these unions preclude procreation. Homosexual unions do not produce children, nor do they intend to produce them. Even the insemination of lesbian women, who intend to raise their children with their lesbian partners, is not the intention of the lesbian union itself; their union does not produce the child. That is why the minimal contribution of a male, in the form of his sperm, is still needed in this situation. But I would also argue that such an abstraction of a generative substance from its source in a human person is itself an immoral use of something *personal* (unlike waste fluids) as a means to an end extrinsic to that *person* himself.[27] This is

27. See B. Hagigah 15a and Rashi, s.v. "b'ambati," where the situation of artificial insemination from a nonspouse is considered to be a grotesque accident. For the rabbinic notion that sexuality, unlike one's possessions, is personal and, therefore, may not be separated from the person as the subject of any sale or gift, see B. Kiddushin 19b and Rashi, s.v. "be-davar she-be-mammon." In the discussion following the original reading of this essay at Brown University on 7 April 1995, Professor Andrew Koppelman of Northwestern University raised the counterexample of blood donation. My answer was that the saving of human life overrides this concern for human dignity in the case of blood donation in a way that would not be the same in the case of semen donation (see B. Ketubot 19a and parallels). Furthermore, semen donation entails more of human personhood than blood donation (see B. Niddah 31a). For the issue of the extent to which one may donate a body part to save another human life, see R. David ibn Abi Zimra, *Teshuvot Radbaz,* vol. 3, no. 1052.

essentially unlike a heterosexual marital union in which two persons conceive and raise children together, and remain their parents forever, however impermanent their own relationship might actually be.

Following this point, I would add that certainly there are many differences between homosexual women and homosexual men, including their thinking on sexuality. In fact, the differences are such that homosexual women usually call themselves "lesbian" and homosexual men usually call themselves "gay." Yet one point in common that I have noted is that both groups of homosexuals seem to regard the institution of fatherhood to be at best instrumental for procreation. Artificial insemination as the preferred method of conception makes the instrumental role as impersonal as possible. Any ongoing role for fathers, working in concert with the mothers of their children, seems to suggest the *bête noire* of "patriarchy." However, if there is to be a family in the full sense of the term as it is traditionally used — that is, a miniature community including men, women, and children — then it would seem that there has to be some division of authority and responsibility between the parents. Accordingly, there should be at least proportional equality between fatherly authority (patriarchy) and motherly authority (matriarchy).[28]

If there is no intention to produce children, what interest does society have in recognizing any such union? But society does have an interest in the production and raising of children because experience has clearly taught us that society, which fulfills a natural need of human beings, intends its own transmission into the future. So it needs new citizens, and these new citizens are best produced, cared for, and raised to responsible adulthood in a home founded on a permanently intended heterosexual union. In any large-scale absence of such unions, we see major social pathology, a fact clearly evidenced by the social pathology (primarily violence in all forms) we see today in the breakup or absence of two-parent (that is, male-female) families in growing segments of our society, but especially among the poor, who are always most vulnerable to any pathology. Society's interest in traditional family life is so strong that to compromise it in any way could only seriously weaken it. That seems to me to be the best argument for the traditional prohibition of homoerotic acts and homosexual marriages.

Now this seems a better argument if we assume that homosexuality is a

28. For the notion of proportional equality, see Aristotle, *Nicomachean Ethics*, 1131a10., even though I am applying it here differently than Aristotle would — namely, assigning more authority to a wife and mother than he would. Cf. *Nicomachean Ethics*, 1138b7-10. See David Novak, *Law and Theology in Judaism* (New York: Ktav Publishing House, 1974-76), vol. 2, pp. 47-86.

matter of choice. If so, we can then argue for a familial imperative, as it were.[29] But what if we assume, as most homosexuals insist, that their homosexuality is not a matter of choice? (Of course, all sexual acts performed by nonpsychotic persons, whether homoerotic or heteroerotic, are chosen. That is what gives them moral significance, as we shall soon see.) What if by some determinism, whether natural or historical, sexuality, whether heterosexual or homosexual, is just there within one? Why should what is determined in one group of humans — that is, heterosexuals — be allowed some form of socially acceptable sexual activity (marital intercourse), but what is determined in another group of humans — homosexuals — not be allowed any form of socially acceptable sexual activity? And, following this, what if we assume that attempts to repress homosexuality or even sublimate it are contrary to the *nature* of those persons who have been *made* homosexual one way or another? The answers to these fundamental questions are largely determined by just what we mean by the term *nature*.

Contrary to Nature?

It seems to me that there are four basic meanings of the term *nature*.

First, *nature* can mean what we experience as necessity. Thus everyone would agree that the presence of sexual appetite is such a natural necessity, it is an *inclinatio naturalis*.[30] However, unlike breathing or eating, which are acts without which we could not live, sexuality is something without which we could survive. Most of us, nevertheless, would see such a life as humanly deprived. Such a choice would be seen by most of us as depriving us of a basic human need.[31]

Second, *nature* can mean realities (as opposed to fantasies) that we experience as attracting us — that is, natural ends. To use the words of Aristotle, it is not only what is necessary *(anagkaion)* but what is also advantageous *(sympheronton)*.[32] Although one could argue that the perpetuation of the species is a natural necessity in animals, most of us would regard human sexuality to be more a personal matter than a strictly genetic one. As such, for us

29. See *Sefer ha-Hinukh,* no. 15 re: Gen. 1:28; Isa. 45:18; also, Reuven Kimelman, "Homosexuality and Family-Centered Judaism," *Tikkun* 9, no. 4 (July/August 1994): 53-57.

30. For the primary *inclinatio naturalis* being the drive to live, see Aquinas, *Summa Theologiae,* 2/2, q. 64, a. 5; also, David Novak, *Suicide and Morality* (New York: Scholars Studies Press, 1975), p. 44.

31. For the notion of natural necessity *(to anagkaion),* see Aristotle, *Metaphysics,* 1015a20ff.

32. See Aristotle, *Politics,* 1254a20.

as humans, at least as an activity, it is a matter of choice, even if our inclinations are not. Our choice intends an end *(telos)* already present by nature, one which we desire to attain.[33] Our sexual acts are not just the push of a need but also the delightful pull of a desire whose good intent we happily confirm.

Based on these two meanings of *nature,* it is difficult to argue that homoerotic acts and homosexual unions are "unnatural."

As for the first meaning of *nature,* even Thomas Aquinas argued that there are cases when one's individual nature — that is, one's biological inclination — is different from that of the majority of other people. If that is the case, then such minority persons — in our case, homosexuals — are not by virtue of their inclination acting *contra naturam.*[34] Indeed, one could argue (although Aquinas himself certainly did not) that to frustrate such inclination might very well be an act (of omission, that is) that itself is *contra naturam.* And that is the argument made by what I have termed above "conservative" homosexuals. As Andrew Sullivan especially has argued based on this criterion of nature, all that such homosexuals ask for is the recognition of their rights (and for him marriage is such a right, secularly and religiously) as a definite minority.[35] The expansion of minority rights in our religious communities and in our secular society, which has become such a feature of contemporary polity, gives a renewed context to these claims inasmuch as these homosexuals are only arguing that they are *a* minority among others, not the only one.

As for the second meaning of nature — namely, what is desirable even if not necessary in the strictly biological sense — it is clear that there is a plurality of such goods of human nature. Just as biological needs have to be attended to in harmony with each other, so do human desires. Most of us would agree, I think, that a rational ordering of one's whole life requires that no single desire predominate to the extent of causing neglect of all others. As such, I think most of us would agree that, however desirable sexual acts are, they cannot be allowed to overrule our other human desires. A sexually obsessive life would be a disordered, unhappy human life. So, whether sexual desire is our most characteristic human desire, as Freud argued with his theory of libido, or not, most of us would agree that sexuality is an inherent part of human nature. It is not just instrumental.

33. See Aristotle, *Nicomachean Ethics,* 1112b12ff., and *Metaphysics,* 1072b10.

34. Aquinas, *Summa Theologiae,* 2/1, q. 46, a. 5.

35. See his "Here Comes the Groom: A (Conservative) Case for Gay Marriage," *The New Republic,* 28 August 1989, p. 22; also, see his fullest and most theological statement on the subject, "Alone Again Naturally: The Catholic Church and the Homosexual," *The New Republic,* 28 November 1994, pp. 47-55.

Now some have argued that homosexuality *per se* is obsessive and, therefore, is inherently disordered.[36] Among male homosexuals, especially, there seem to be far higher rates of promiscuous, compulsive sexual activity. However, even if this is true (although the data have been challenged on empirical grounds), it is not conclusive. For some homosexuals, especially of the conservative variety, have argued that promiscuity among homosexuals is to be taken as personally unhealthy, but that it would decrease if they were allowed to participate in the stabilizing social institution of marriage, whether secularly or religiously or secularly and religiously. (Actually there are already some religious communities that do recognize and even celebrate gay marriages.[37])

This is also important to note in terms of marriage being a form of personal communion. Not only is marriage certainly not the only form of personal communion, but most of us would agree that it is unhealthy for a person to confine all her or his personal communion to one's sexual partner, even if that partner is one's own spouse. Friends with whom one is related in nonsexual ways are for most of us an indispensable part of living well.[38] Furthermore, most of us would regard as unhealthy a spousal relationship of personal communion that was confined to sexual activity. In all of these senses of personal communion, it must be admitted that there is nothing that privileges heterosexuality.

It is only when we get to the third meaning of *nature* that we do find that heterosexuality is privileged. I take that third meaning to be the original meaning of our word *nature,* which comes from the Latin *natura,* which is itself derived from the Latin word for being born, *natus.* What is natural, then, is what is connected to birth and whose intent includes the desire to procreate in the original way — that is, by an act of heterosexual intercourse. Natality is our connection with the chain of life. Our nature is vital.

Procreation not only is the act that conceives human life, but also includes the joint rearing of children and remaining the parents of these children, minimally for as long as both parents live.[39] What is intended here is not only the present good of family life when children are physically and

---

36. See Germain Grisez, *The Way of the Lord Jesus: Living a Christian Life* (Quincy, Ill.: Franciscan Press, 1993), vol. 2, pp. 653-54.

37. For the rabbinic notion that social recognition of homosexual marriages *de jure* is worse than the presence of homoerotic activity *de facto,* see B. Hullin 92ab and Rashi, s.v. "eyn kotvin"; *Leviticus Rabbah* 23.9.

38. See Aristotle, *Nicomachean Ethics,* 1155a5. Aristotle here is speaking of *philia,* which is a nonerotic relationship.

39. Although Judaism permits divorce, it regards it as a tragedy. See B. Gittin 90b re Mal. 2:13; also, Novak, *Law and Theology in Judaism,* vol. 1, pp. 6-9.

emotionally dependent on their parents, but also the good of family life as a continuum. That continuum includes more than just the two generations most immediately present in most homes; it also includes the previous generations in the person or memory of grandparents and before, and the future generations in the person or anticipation of grandchildren and beyond.[40] Most of us want our families to remain intact, even transgenerationally. That is why the divorce of parents is so often deeply upsetting to the children, whatever their age. For the children of divorced persons often feel as though a vital connection with the living community has been broken, even when they no longer need their parents for physical support.[41]

In this view of nature, only heterosexual, marital intercourse is natural inasmuch as it intends the same relationship that minimally gave us life; maximally, it gave us our family, our first human community, in which to live; optimally, it gave us a community in which to live well. All valid intercourse, then, reconfirms the origin and value of our own lives.[42]

Finally, there is the fourth meaning of *nature*, which is nature as an inherent limit *(peras)* on activity in the world — in our case, human activity.[43] Not only is nature immanent but also specific. Each area of human activity in the world has its own inherent limits, which experience discovers and reason orders. Certainly, human sexual activity is no exception in its specifics. Here too, I think, heterosexuality and the procreative union it intends enjoy an exclusive privilege.

Procreation is necessary for the continuity of humankind. The vast majority of humans have always desired not only life but also to pass life on. Since that transmission of life is done heterosexually, one could not very well morally disapprove of heterosexual intercourse *per se*. Hence those few radical

40. See Ps. 128:6; B. Kiddushin 30a re Deut. 4:9.

41. Hence they cannot observe the commandment "Honor your father and your mother" (Exod. 20:12) with both objects in tandem. See B. Kiddushin 31a.

42. In the discussion following the original reading of this essay at Brown University on 7 April 1995, Professor Andrew Koppelman of Northwestern University questioned whether this point would be valid in the case of a child conceived through rape. In response, I pointed out that even though rape or any other illicit act of parents is to be repudiated by their children (see B. Berakhot 7a re Exod. 34:7 and Deut. 24:16), nevertheless, even a child born of an illicit union who is socially stigmatized because of that union *(mamzer)* is still required, according to Maimonides, to honor his or her parents (Maimonides, MT: Rebels, 6.11; see B. Yevamot 22a, and *Tur:* Yoreh De'ah, 240 and Karo, *Bet Yosef,* s.v. "katav ha-Rambam"). That minimally means recognition of their role in his or her coming to be. For more on the importance of parenthood as a natural institution, see Novak, *Law and Theology in Judaism,* vol. 1, pp. 72-79, and vol. 2, pp. 47-55.

43. See Aristotle, *Metaphysics,* 1022a14.

feminists who argue that all heterosexual intercourse is *ipso facto* rape cannot be taken seriously. For to follow their reasoning, the vast majority of human beings, women and men, would be required to permanently repress their sexual inclination.[44] So it would seem that even homosexuals would have to approve of heterosexuality — that is, if they value their own lives, which were conceived by the heterosexual acts of their parents. As we have seen, the best they could do is argue that because of the involuntary condition of their sexual inclination, they are exempt from any heterosexual imperative. As such, they argue that they may substitute what is sexually possible and desirable for them. Nevertheless, heterosexuals can argue against homosexuality in a way that homosexuals cannot argue against heterosexuality — that is, when they both agree that the continuity of human life is an essential end of human action. For homosexuals need heterosexuals, minimally as their parents, in a way that heterosexuals do not need homosexuals for the sake of human survival.

In order to allow that dispensation from what even homosexuals must recognize as a rational norm, homosexual theorists must argue for sexuality as an area of human activity that itself contains no limiting norms. For if sexual activity is chosen primarily on the basis of one's involuntary inclination, what possible moral limits could one inherently impose upon it? However, doesn't our moral experience begin when we learn to internalize limits on what we may do with our genitals and what we may not do with them? Isn't repression a necessary part of our introduction to social reality, only being harmful when taught in a cruel, irrational manner? Wouldn't any parent raising a child and sending a message, either explicitly or implicitly, that what the child does with her or his genitals is a matter of moral indifference be failing in his or her moral education of that child? For aren't the parents supposed to be the intermediaries between elementary narcissism and human community and society?[45] Could there be human community or society where there is unrestrained sexual activity? Isn't that why family morality begins with the prohibition of incest, from which all other sexual restrictions follow?[46]

---

44. See Andrea Dworkin, *Intercourse* (New York: Free Press, 1987), esp. pp. 126-43. For a somewhat more nuanced presentation of a similar view, see Susan Brownmiller, *Against Our Will* (New York: Simon & Schuster, 1975).

45. See Hegel, *Phenomenology of Spirit*, trans. A. V. Miller (Oxford: Clarendon Press, 1977), pars. 450, 268. Note, also, the suggestion of Martha Nussbaum in *The Fragility of Goodness: Luck and Ethics in Greek Tragedy and Philosophy* (Cambridge and New York: Cambridge University Press, 1986), pp. 370-71, that Aristotle's emphasis on the political necessity of the family (*Politics*, 1262a5ff.; contra Plato, *Republic*, 463dff.) is related to his heterosexuality.

46. See Freud, "The Most Prevalent Form of Degradation in Erotic Life" (1912), in *Collected Papers*, trans. J. Strachey (London: Hogarth Press, 1952), vol. 4, pp. 205-6.

All of these questions suggest that only heterosexuals who are committed to a permanent procreative relationship are able to argue for the inherent natural limits on sexual activity, limits that no stable community or society can afford to ignore. Even though sexual activity itself is to be done in private, its public significance is evident.

However, aren't most homosexuals like most heterosexuals in being morally opposed to rape and the seduction of children? Aren't these prohibitions limits on sexual activity?

The fact that most homosexuals are opposed to rape and the seduction of children is good, but that does not mean that homosexual theorists are thereby capable of arguing for inherent natural limits on sexual activity *per se* because of that opposition. For as we have been learning of late, often from feminist teachers, rape itself is not an act whose intentionality is erotic; rather, it is an assault on another person, using one's genitals as a weapon. Accordingly, its rational prohibition is a subset of our disapproval of violence, most of which is conducted with weapons other than the genitals. And as for the seduction of children, most of us would also regard that as either an assault on victims by those who have emotional power over them, or the robbery of their innocence and their subsequent ability to develop into adults who will have satisfying personal (including sexual) relationships.

The most that homosexual theorists can argue for, as far as I can see, is that sexual activity is an essentially private matter between consenting adults. That, however, is a necessary but not sufficient condition of human sexual acts that are morally justified.[47] It is not sufficient because, as I have argued above, it does not delve deeply enough into the public significance of sexual acts between these consenting adults.[48] For the only criterion of this minimal condition is that each party intend her or his pleasure in a way approved by the other party with whom he or she is sexually engaged at present.

However, in the Jewish tradition, pleasure itself is a desirable accompaniment to sexual activity; it is not its essential purpose. Indeed, Jewish tradition asserts that pleasure is never an end in and of itself, but its value is dependent on whether or not it accompanies acts that are either good or bad.[49] Along these lines, let it be said that all acts are transitive — that is, they intend objects outside their actors. For Judaism it can be maintained, I think, that all acts ulti-

47. For the condition of consent in mutual sexual matters, see B. Kiddushin 2b; Meiri, *Bet Ha-Behirah: Kiddushin*, ed. Sofer, 8; Maimonides, MT: Marriage, 14.8. Also, see B. Baba Batra 48b; Maimonides, MT: Character Traits, 5.4.

48. See B. Kiddushin 2b; Maimonides, MT: Marriage, 1.1, 4.

49. Cf. Plato, *Philebus*, 60dff.; Aristotle, *Nicomachean Ethics*, 1173b30ff.

mately intend personal objects.[50] Even nonpersonal objects have to be included in a valid personal relationship in order that their use be justified. The world is to be enjoyed, but that enjoyment is always for the sake of enhancing relationships that are themselves considered good.[51] Thus I am to enjoy the produce of the earth, but that enjoyment is considered to be a form of theft unless I include it in my relationship with God by using that enjoyment as an occasion to thank God.[52] So also is my sexual pleasure, which is acceptable when it contributes to my intimate relationship with my wife.[53] And that intimate relationship involves her being the mother of the children we have either already brought into the world or whom we intend to bring into the world.[54] Since pleasure can only be experienced by a self, to make pleasure an end in and of itself is to make myself the ultimate object of my acts. Hedonism, which is pleasure for its own sake, can only be narcissism. Once pleasure is shared by two persons, it is no longer just a physical sensation. It acquires interhuman meaning.[55]

So, in the end, we are left with family life, which includes (but does not subsume) personal communion and which is to be accompanied by sexual pleasure (and other pleasures as well). Homosexual unions, even if including the good of personal communion and accompanied by sexual pleasure that is not compulsive, still do not intend the core of the good of family life, which is to procreate in both the narrowest and widest senses of that term. And Judaism makes the severe demand on those who by inclination cannot and do not intend this overall good minimally to refrain from sexual activities that contradict it.[56]

Within the parameters of normative Jewish tradition, homosexuals have, it seems to me, two legitimate options. One, they may remain celibate, based on the assumption that inability to perform a positive precept (marriage) does not thereby dispense one from a negative precept (the prohibitions of homoerotic acts). Or, two, they may at least explore the possibility of therapeutic intervention in order to change their sexual orientation with those

---

50. That is why the pleasures of eating are to be included in interhuman fellowship. See M. Berakhot 7.1; B. Berakhot 45a re Ps. 34:4, and B. Berakhot 59b and Tos., s.v. "ve-rabbi yohanan"; B. Kiddushin 31ab.

51. Hence the nihilistic enjoyment of destruction *per se* is prohibited *(bal tash'hit)*. See Deut. 20:19-20; Maimonides, *Sefer ha-Mitsvot*, neg. no. 57; Novak, *Jewish Social Ethics*, pp. 118-32.

52. See B. Berakhot 35ab and Y. Berakhot 6.1/9d re Ps. 24:1.

53. See B. Nedarim 20b; Maimonides, MT: Forbidden Relations, 21.12.

54. For the notion that the character of the sexual relationship of parents influences the character of their children, see B. Nedarim 20ab.

55. Thus the initiation of marriage is an occasion of communal celebration. See B. Ketubot 7ab; Meiri, *Bet ha-Behirah*: Ketubot, ed. Sofer, 73.

56. See B. Sanhedrin 75a; Maimonides, MT: Foundations of Torah, 5.9.

psychotherapists who believe (in the face of much opposition from many, but not all, of their professional colleagues) that such change is possible and beneficial. However, I would strongly suggest that homosexual persons not enter heterosexual marriage or be encouraged to do so. Such marriages can only cause misery to both the homosexual partner (even if physically capable of heterosexual intercourse) and the heterosexual partner, who is often unaware of the true sexual orientation of her or his spouse. Because of such deceit, any such marriage is an immoral farce.[57]

Heterosexual Jews should become much more sympathetic to the plight of their homosexual brothers and sisters and not encourage them to seek deceitful and harmful "solutions" to their real predicament.

Exceptions to the Norm of Procreation

We are still left with the problem of the marriage of sterile persons and those who choose to be celibate.

As for sterile persons, there are actually restrictions in Jewish law prohibiting some individuals with certain genital deformities from marrying.[58] Nevertheless, as regards most sterile persons, they are unaware of their sterility until they have long been in a marriage. Here again, Jewish law does regard the commandment to procreate to be so important that one may obtain a divorce from a sterile spouse if he or she is determined to fulfill this commandment with a new spouse.[59] However, it seems that the tradition is so respectful of the integrity of the marital unit that where sterility is not intended, many authorities do not make such a divorce a mandate.[60] In fact, such persons are encouraged to adopt children whose parents cannot raise them or do not want to do so.[61] These children are seen as being required to practice the commandment of filial honor and respect for these adoptive parents.[62]

57. Along these lines, note how deceit can be grounds for annulment of a marriage. See M. Kiddushin 2.2; T. Kiddushin 2.4; Maimonides, MT: Marriage, 8.1.

58. See Deut. 23:2; M. Yevamot 6.5; B. Yevamot 61ab and 76ab; Y. Yevamot 6.5/7c and 8.2/9ab.

59. M. Yevamot 6.6; B. Yevamot 64a; Y. Yevamot 6.6/7c.

60. See B. Yevamot 6₄a, Tos., s.v. "yotsi"; B. Ketubot 77a, Tos., s.v. "litney"; *Hagahot Maimoniyot* on Maimonides, MT: Marriage, 15.7, n. 4; R. Isaac bar Sheshet Parfat, *Teshuvot Rivash*, no. 15; Isserles, note on *Shulhan Arukh: Even Ha'Ezer*, 1.3 and 154.10 (and Eisenstadt, *Pit'hei Teshuvah* thereon, n. 27).

61. See B. Sanhedrin 19b.

62. Usually these adoptive parents are their adopted children's teachers; hence they are to be honored as parents, since the honor due both teachers and parents is virtually identical. See R. Moses Schreiber, *Teshuvot Hatam Sofer: Orah Hayyim*, no. 164.

The hardest case is, of course, the marriage of persons who know they are sterile, usually persons who are clearly beyond the age of childbearing. But here I would say, following Wittgenstein's theory of family resemblances, that there are enough similarities to most marriages to allow such marriages.[63] Indeed, to distinguish between fertile and infertile couples *ab initio* would require a judgment to allow or not to allow marriage to be made in the case of each and every couple. However, in the Jewish legal tradition there is ample precedence for simply assuming that *most* heterosexual couples are fertile, and therefore *all* heterosexual couples are to be considered as such.[64] At the *prima facie* level, there is no generally evident difference between fertile and infertile couples. That is quite unlike the very evident difference between most heterosexual couples who are fertile and all homosexual couples who are infertile. Most men and most women are capable of conceiving a child, whereas no two men and no two women are so capable. Law is made for what is usual *(de minimis non curat lex)*.[65]

Furthermore, in a homosexual union *ipso facto* sterility is intended, which is not the case in a heterosexual union. Unlike a homosexual union, it is not meant to be a substitute for a normal heterosexual union. Indeed, most persons in this category are those who earlier in life did procreate, or they were persons who without intention could not marry any earlier in life. Indeed, in many such cases, the new spouses figuratively "adopt" the children of their new spouses. For the spouse of one's parent is functioning in many ways like one's other parent (especially the spouse of one's widowed parent).

As for celibacy, Judaism obviously recognizes that there are persons who for a variety of physical and emotional reasons are incapable of initiating or sustaining a marriage. Like any disability, this is regarded to be an unfortunate state of affairs, and persons who suffer from this disability are not to be made to feel any worse than they often already do, especially in a community where natality is so highly regarded and desired. However, voluntary celibacy of heterosexuals physically and psychologically capable of marriage is another matter. Jewish tradition does not regard this as an acceptable state of human life, and the sources are replete with statements of disapproval.[66] Nevertheless, although there are social pressures for single persons to marry,

---

63. See Wittgenstein, *Philosophical Investigations,* trans. G. E. M. Anscombe (New York: Macmillan, 1958), pars. 67, 32.

64. See M. Yevamot 4.10; B. Yevamot 42b; Maimonides, MT: Divorce, 11.20.

65. See, e.g., B. Shabbat 35b and parallels; B. Eruvin 63b and parallels; B. Hullin 11a; Maimonides, *Guide of the Perplexed,* 3.34.

66. See M. Yevamot 6.6 and *Bavli* and *Yerushalmi* thereon; also, Novak, *Jewish Social Ethics,* p. 98n. 9.

those pressures are never so severe as to exclude celibate persons from partici-pation in the religious and social life of the community. There are even un-married (and therefore presumed to be celibate) rabbis in these communi-ties.[67] My experience in traditional Jewish communities has been that most people compassionately assume that when a person is celibate, it is ultimately due to some disability rather than being the result of a real choice. The same assumption is usually made about childless couples in the community.

As for the clergy of other religions who are required to be celibate, and here one thinks of Roman Catholic clergy, a Jew need not have an opinion; indeed, she or he should not have one. Fortunately, all the Noahide laws (with the exception of the positive precept that a gentile society have a sys-tem to administer the due process of law) are negative precepts. Therefore, all violations of them are sins of commission rather than sins of omission.[68] That is why Jews are to have an opinion about homoerotic acts wherever they obtain, and, conversely, that is why non-Jewish celibacy is none of our business.

Nevertheless, I must add that the Jewish prohibition of homoerotic acts is stronger than the Christian prohibition of them precisely because Judaism does not approve of celibacy, let alone regard it as a higher form of human holiness. For if the commandment to procreate (in its full and narrow sense) is considered to be exceptionless, then any avoidance of it is considered to be wrong.[69] Avoidance by the substitution of some nonfamilial sexuality, which is a positive act, is the most severe wrong. Avoidance by, as the Rabbis put it, "sitting and doing nothing," is a lesser wrong.[70] It is also a lesser wrong be-cause inactivity is usually pursued with much less passion than activity, espe-cially activity accompanied by intense pleasure. This creates a problem for Roman Catholics (and to a slightly lesser extent for Orthodox Christians, who do require celibacy of some of their clergy), who must be prepared to ar-gue why one nonheterosexual form of life is holy and another sinful. Al-though they can do so, their argument is necessarily more theologically ar-cane than the Jewish one. And even those Protestant Christians, who do not require or even advocate clerical celibacy, are still like all other Christians who worship a God who chose to become incarnate in a male celibate body. I men-tion this because some traditional Jews have made common cause with some

67. For some restrictions on celibate rabbis, see T. Sanhedrin 7.5; B. Sanhedrin 36b and Rashi, s.v. "zaqen"; Maimonides, MT: Sanhedrin, 2.3.

68. See B. Sanhedrin 58b-59b and Tos., s.v. "ve-ha."

69. For this distinction between an avoidable norm *(mitsvah)* and an unavoidable one *(hovah)*, see Maimonides, MT: Blessings, 11.2.

70. See B. Yevamot 90ab.

traditional Christians of late over the issue of homosexuality.[71] Yet both sides should be aware that they are approaching it from different theologies at least on some points, even if their norms are practically identical.

The Penalization of Homosexual Persons

Homosexual persons have been traditionally penalized in two ways. One, their homoerotic acts have been the occasion for leveling criminal sanctions against them. And two, they have been denied the right of marrying each other.

We have already seen the reasons that the right of marriage has been denied homosexual unions. For Jews especially, the secular rationale of that refusal can be supplemented by a religious rationale. That is, the commandment to procreate, which is regarded as universal, is for Jews the commandment to reproduce new members of the covenanted people of Israel.[72] The primacy of birth is so important in Judaism that even though converts are accepted, their entry into Judaism is conceived under the legal fiction of being "born again."[73] One must also add to that the especially contemporary poignancy of the fact that even fifty years after the Nazis exterminated one-third of the Jewish people, the Jewish people, owing to assimilation, intermarriage, and a low birthrate, have not even recovered their pre-1939 population. Inasmuch as Jews have always been a small, vulnerable minority among the nations, and even more so today, it should not be surprising that many Jews believe it is detrimental to the Jewish people to recognize any kind of sexual relationship that does not minimally produce Jewish children.

For those reasons and more, there still are social (if not criminal) penalties for homoerotic acts. Thus in a traditional Jewish community, it is most unlikely that an openly practicing homosexual would be elected to a position of religious leadership. In some ways, the reaction to homosexual persons might be compared to the reaction to Jews who are married to non-Jews. While many traditional Jewish communities would include such persons in a variety of religious and social activities, they would do nothing that in any way indicated approval of the intermarriage in which such persons are living. Although there are numerous other transgressions that are being openly

71. See "The Homosexual Movement: A Response by the Ramsey Colloquium," *First Things* 41 (March 1994): 15-20.

72. See B. Yevamot 62a; Maimonides, MT: Marriage, 15.6, and R. Vidal of Tolosa, *Magid Mishneh* thereon.

73. B. Yevamot 22a and parallels.

practiced by Jews, even those who live in traditional communities, intermarriage and homosexuality have in common the fact that by design they do not produce Jewish children. That is why they are the subject of such particularly religious opprobrium.[74]

As for secular penalties against those who engage in homoerotic acts, I think there is some consensus even among those who otherwise disapprove of homosexuality that such penalties are socially counterproductive. For better or for worse, unlike religious communities which really do not have any notion of a "right to privacy" (even though privacy is protected in many situations by Jewish law[75]), our secular society has increasingly assumed that there is such a right. To effectively penalize homoerotic acts between consenting adults would entail such massive invasions of privacy that many other rights would be threatened. And these rights — which, unlike the right to engage in any sexual act with whoever agrees to do so with one — are accepted by popular opinion and tradition (for example, the right to privileged communication). Furthermore, sexual acts are the result of notions of human virtue that are better taught in subsidiary social settings than by becoming the subject of statutes of the state that are largely unenforceable. As the Talmud points out, just as there is no point in legislating to no avail, so is there no point in morally admonishing those who are clearly unprepared to listen.[76]

74. It is true that in the case of a Jewish woman married to a gentile, her children are Jews. However, the likelihood of their living a traditional Jewish life is slim. See B. Kiddushin 68b re Deut. 7:4 and Rashi, s.v. "ki yasir"; Rashi, *Commentary on the Torah:* Deut. 7:4.

75. See, e.g., M. Baba Batra 1.1, 3.7; B. Baba Batra 2ab, 60a re Num. 24:5.

76. See B. Avodah Zarah 36a and parallels; B. Yevamot 65b re Prov. 9:8; and Rashi, s.v. "lomar" re Lev. 19:17 (cf. B. Arakhin 6b).

20 Jewish Marriage and Civil Law:
A Two-Way Street? (2000)

Optimal Jurisdiction

The recognition of the institution of Jewish marriage by a secular polity, and the recognition of a secular polity by Jews committed to Judaism, is an issue of the overlapping of two distinct legal jurisdictions. The ramifications of this overlapping are long and complicated.

Judaism is basically constituted by its own law called the Torah. Judaism contains more than what is ordinarily termed "law" (halakhah); it also contains ideas (generally called aggadah, meaning "narrative"). Yet, even the exposition of ideas still requires legal justification for its valid operation in and for Judaism. Accordingly, the interpretation of ideas must be conducted within certain dogmatic limits (which are, happily, few and quite general), which are themselves legally formulated.[1] Despite the essentially legal structure of Judaism, though, the grounding of the law is not self-referential: the law does not simply present itself. The law is given by God.[2] Thus, the legal propositions of Judaism are grounded in the more elementary theological proposition that the Torah is from God *(torah min ha-shamayim)*.[3]

From God *to* whom does this law come? The law is given to a community elected by God, whose members are elected either by birth or by rebirth in conversion.[4] The founding event of this community, and the subject of its

1. See Menachem Kellner, *Dogma in Medieval Jewish Thought* (Oxford: Oxford University Press, 1987), pp. 1-10.

2. See Maimonides, *Mishneh Torah:* Repentance, 3.8.

3. See M. Sanhedrin 10.1.

4. See B. Sanhedrin 44a; B. Yevamot 47b; see also David Novak, *The Election of Israel* (Cambridge: Cambridge University Press, 1995), pp. 177-99.

tradition, is the unequivocal giving of that law by God and its unequivocal acceptance by the people.[5] That is why the law cannot be abrogated or exchanged.[6] Obedience to the law of God must always come before obedience to any human authority, Jewish or non-Jewish.[7]

The task of the Jewish community in the person of its authorized representatives, therefore, is to interpret, apply, and even augment the law of God as revealed. But the community, especially its duly empowered authorities, must never forget that the first purpose of the law is obedience to the God who gave it.[8] Only after this recognition can other purposes, even preconditions, *of* the law be proposed and effectively used by the human members of the covenant; indeed, that is their public responsibility. The discovery of the purposes and preconditions of the law must not detract from primary obedience to God's law, but they may enhance it.[9]

The law itself is God's primordial claim on the community and all its members. The law governs, both collectively and individually, the ongoing relationship between God and the community called "the covenant" *(ha-berit)*.[10] Indeed, one can see the very meaning of the word "God" as *the One who is to be obeyed above all others.* The most universal word for *God* in the Bible is the common noun *elohim.*[11] It is also used for those human powers having justified legal authority, whose essential justification is its being subordinate to the revealed law.[12] This kind of theological constitution of authority is particularly necessary in our time, when many people, both secular and religious, take religious authority to be basically "authoritarian" — that is, a projection of human power interests *onto* God. A proper theology of the law indicates how this popular impression, at least with regards to Judaism, is erroneous.

From the proper theological vantage point, it would seem to follow that Judaism's optimal polity is one where the law of God is not only supreme but has total hegemony over the life of the people.[13] The Jews ought not recognize

5. See Maimonides, MT: Foundations, 9.1.

6. Maimonides, MT: Foundations, 9.2.

7. See B. Berakhot 19b.

8. See *Bemidbar Rabbah* 19.1.

9. See David Novak, *Natural Law in Judaism* (Cambridge: Cambridge University Press, 1998), pp. 62-82.

10. See, e.g., Deut. 29:9-14.

11. See A. Marmorstein, *The Old Rabbinic Doctrine of God* (New York: Ktav Publishing House, 1968), pp. 67-69.

12. See, e.g., B. Sanhedrin 3b; B. Sanhedrin 5b; B. Sanhedrin 56b; B. Sanhedrin 66a.

13. Maimonides, MT: Kings, 11.1.

any other law than the one God has given to them. This position comes out in the following rabbinic text, which is quite fundamental:

> Rabbi Tarfon said that even where one finds that the laws of the gentile courts [*agoriyot*] are the same as the Jewish laws, one is not permitted to attach oneself to them nonetheless. That is because it is said in Scripture (Exod. 21:1), "These are the judgments [*ha-mishpatim*] which thou shalt set before them [*lifneihem*]," that is to say "before them" and not before heathens.[14]

Interpreting the same scriptural verse, it has been said, "You may judge their cases but they are not to judge your cases."[15] In other words, the Jews are to be totally governed by their own law, despite whatever commonalities their law might have with other just systems of law. Jewish law alone must rule the Jews, although some of it may rule others if they so choose.[16] Nevertheless, others may never rule the Jews, at least in principle. What is normatively sufficient for the life of the whole people could only be lessened by the addition of any other legal authority.

This is the optimal view of Jewish law and its full polity. If not utopian, however, it seems to be ideal: something that has not yet been achieved. This has never been the full convergence of both. Thus, in the days of the First Temple (from the time of Joshua to the Babylonian Exile in 586 B.C.E.), the scriptural record indicates that the nation of Israel had sovereignty — and when separated, the nations of Judah and Israel (Ephraim), respectively, were sovereign.[17] As for law at this time, though, it seems that instead of a nationally accepted written law, the people were mostly governed by ad hoc royal or prophetic decrees.[18] By the time of the return from Babylonian Captivity in the days of the Second Temple (let alone after its destruction in 70 C.E.), when the people were governed by a nationally accepted written law, their nation had already lost its political sovereignty.[19] From that point forward, Jews were governed by non-Jewish sovereign empires (Persian, Roman, etc.). As a result, the Jews have compromised the full authority of their own law due to the more politically powerful law of the governing authority.

14. B. Gittin 88b.

15. *Mekhilta de-Rabbi Ishmael*, trans. Jacob Lauterbach (Philadelphia: Jewish Publication Society, 1935), vol. 3, p. 2.

16. See B. Avodah Zarah 64b.

17. See Josh. 18:1; 1 Kings 12:20-21.

18. See U. Cassuto, *A Commentary on the Book of Exodus*, trans. Israel Abrams (Jerusalem: Magnes Press, 1967), pp. 259-64.

19. See Ezra 7:1-12; 10:5-8; see also Neh. 8:1-12.

Even now, when the Jews have regained political sovereignty in the State of Israel, that state, at least heretofore, is not governed by traditional Jewish law.[20] The State of Israel's law, like that of a Western-style democracy, is grounded in the popular sovereignty of its own people.[21] This paradigm is different, of course, from a law rooted in divine revelation and transmitted by a distinctly religious tradition (even though there might well be democratic components of this theocratic system).[22] Therefore, whatever religious law functions in the State of Israel functions as an entitlement *from* the secular state, at least as far as the secular state is concerned. Accordingly, even though the State of Israel is a Jewish state governed by a Jewish majority, Jews there who see themselves as being primarily and ultimately governed by the revealed law of Judaism still have the same problem as Jews in the diaspora: How does one live under a secular law and still maintain the supremacy of the revealed law?[23] Ironically enough, the problem is somewhat easier to deal with in the diaspora because Jewish tradition has much more experience dealing with the sovereignty of a gentile society than with the sovereignty of a Jewish society (especially a Jewish state that proclaims itself to be secular).

Current Jurisdiction

The ancient Rabbis recognized the authority of the gentile jurisdictions within which Jews had to live. Thus, the Mishnah states, "All documents which are accepted in [gentile] courts, even [when] signed [by] gentiles [witnesses], are valid [*kesherim*], except writs of divorce. . . ."[24] The later discussion of this rule in the Talmud bases it on the principle of "the law of the Government is law" *(dina de-malkhuta dina)*.[25] The medieval commentator Rashi noted that this principle not only says that gentile law has authority for gentiles, but that it has authority for Jews who either choose to, or even have to,

20. See Menachem Elon, *Jewish Law,* trans. B. Auerbach and M. J. Sykes (Philadelphia: Jewish Publication Society, 1994), vol. 4, pp. 1520-27.

21. See Z. W. Falk, *Law and Religion: The Jewish Experience* (Jerusalem: Mesharim, 1981), pp. 43-57.

22. See David Novak, *Covenantal Rights: A Study in Jewish Political Theory* (Princeton: Princeton University Press, 2000), pp. 34-35, 209-18.

23. See Izhak Englard, "The Relationship between Religion and State in Israel," in *Jewish Law in Ancient and Modern Israel,* ed. Haim H. Cohn (New York: Ktav Publishing House, 1971), pp. 168-89.

24. M. Gittin 1.5.

25. B. Gittin 10b.

partake of it.[26] Under what circumstances this involvement takes place will be examined later. Yet, this principle is not taken to be optimal but only necessary.[27] Its logic is something like that of the dictum *dura lex sed lex* — namely, a "hard" or less-than-perfect law is better than no law at all. As this principle applies to the situation of the Jews, matters of everyday justice are such that Jews cannot assume, in the absence of their own civil jurisdiction, that their real needs for civil justice can be suppressed.[28] Such an absence of Jewish civil jurisdiction could either be *de jure* or *de facto*. In a *de jure* situation, a Jewish civil court may not function in a host society because the non-Jewish state claims a monopoly on civil jurisdiction. In a *de facto* situation, on the other hand, a Jewish civil court might not function because Jews in a non-Jewish state do not trust its political effectiveness in rendering justice.[29]

The principle of "the law of the Government is the law" has a wider range than its application in the case of documents pertaining to inter-Jewish commercial relations certified in gentile courts. This principle also applies to Jews having to submit criminal matters to the jurisdiction of these courts, even matters that could entail the death penalty. Indeed, it is more likely that a non-Jewish host society would claim a monopoly on criminal jurisdiction than it would on civil jurisdiction. Many civil disputes can be settled by arbitration between the parties involved in the dispute themselves, whereas crimes against persons are usually considered to be offenses against society itself and thus the sole business of the state to adjudicate. In fact, in the not-so-distant past, Jews were frequently able to settle their own inter-Jewish civil disputes among themselves according to their own law in their own courts.

This concession to non-Jewish law is best explained by the medieval commentator Nahmanides, who wrote,

This [power to adjudicate] is based on the power of the king to make law in his kingdom. It is something by which he and all the other kings before him conducted public business. These laws are written in the royal chronicles and law books. . . . We infer this from the words *dina de-malkhuta,* namely, "the law of the kingdom," not the law of a particular king [*dina de-malka*]. This was even the case with the kings of Israel.[30]

---

26. See B. Gittin 9b.

27. See David Novak, *The Image of the Non-Jew in Judaism* (Toronto: Edwin Mellen, 1983), p. 70.

28. See Maimonides, MT: Sanhedrin, 26.7.

29. See Maimonides, MT: Acquisitions and Gifts, 1.15; see also B. M. Lewin, *Otsar Ha-Geonim* (Jerusalem: Hebrew University Press Association, 1928-1943), Gittin, pp. 208-10.

30. See Nahmanides, *Hiddushei ha-Ramban* to B. Baba Batra 54b.

In other words, a law that is simply the arbitrary whim of a sovereign does not have the moral force of law. Only a law that is part of a system of justice (what some have called a *Rechtstaat*[31]) has the moral force of law for those who live within it and under its criminal jurisdiction.[32]

The earlier medieval commentator Rashbam pointed out that royal authority (which could well be taken as the same for republican authority), whether Jewish or non-Jewish, is based on a voluntary contract between the government (whether sovereignty is individual, as in the case of a monarchy, or collective, as in the case of a republic) and the governed. Combining the views of Nahmanides and Rashbam (with whose work Nahmanides was quite familiar), one can see the most basic agreement between the government and the governed is that the governed be protected from criminal assaults against persons and their property. This agreement between the governed and government subsequently extends to the government providing the opportunity for adjudication of civil disputes that the individual parties cannot, or will not, settle between themselves. Thus, if Jews cannot always wait for their own jurisdiction to enforce their rights in civil disputes either among themselves or with others, how much more so can they never wait for their own jurisdiction to enforce their rights in criminal matters, where greater governmental power is required in order for justice to be effective.

From the primary text discussed above concerning the validity of documents, a distinction is made between non-Jewish jurisdiction for Jews in civil matters and non-Jewish jurisdiction for Jews in marital matters. The principle invoked to explain the validity of civil jurisdiction, "The law of the Government is the law," also justifies the validity of non-Jewish criminal law for Jews.[33] The whole institution of marriage is something essentially different, however, from either civil or criminal matters (even though, of course, marriage does entail civil questions pertaining to property and criminal questions pertaining to adultery). Rashi explained the difference as a result of the sacramental character of Jewish marriage *(kretut)*, something that is fundamentally different from the private contract-type character of most of civil law.[34] Another medieval commentator noted that in civil matters, the Rabbis

---

31. See Hans Kelsen, *The Pure Theory of Law,* trans. M. Knight (Berkeley and Los Angeles: University of California Press, 1967), pp. 312-13.

32. See Maimonides, MT: Robbery and Loss, 5.18.

33. See S. Shilo, *Dina De-Malkhuta Dina* (Jerusalem: Academy Press, 1974), pp. 269-74.

34. See B. Gittin 9b. Rashi also points out that because Judaism sees the establishment of a coherent system of civil and criminal justice to be a universal requirement, therefore applying to gentiles as well as to Jews, Jews can rely on any morally coherent system of justice when necessary. See B. Sanhedrin 56ab.

assumed that we can rely on ordinary, rationally evident criteria (such as the reliability of public institutions like adjudication and testimony) when these institutions are constituted within a morally respectable legal order.[35]

Jewish marriage is considered to be something much deeper and more permanent than could ever be enforced by any contract — indeed, the very agreement in which it originates is not considered to be contractual.[36] It is a covenant *(berit)*.[37] It is entered into by the parties with no *terminus ad quem* inherent in it *ab initio:* it is meant to be "until death do us part." The termination of marriage in divorce is, therefore, not something necessary within the marriage itself; instead, it is only a possibility that requires some external factor to realize it. It is the result of an unanticipated factor (such as adultery) that comes into the marriage *post factum*.[38] Jewish divorce, from the details of Jewish marriage law and derived by inference from the negative to the positive, is itself not considered to be a matter of contract, neither in origin nor in enforcement.[39] Thus, the Palestinian Talmud asserts that

> the gentiles do not have anything like Jewish marriage [*kiddushin*]. Do they have anything like Jewish divorce [*gerushin*]? Rabbi Judah ben Pazi and Rabbi Hanin [said] in the name of Rabbi Honeh, senior authority of the *Sepphoris,* that they [the gentiles] either do not have divorce at all or the parties divorce each other.[40]

This exclusive view of divorce is connected to a scriptural discussion of divorce where there is an emphasis on its direct relation to the covenant with "the Lord God of Israel."[41] Thus marriage and divorce, the mandated and desired *terminus a quo* and the possible but undesired *terminus ad quem* of a uniquely Jewish relationship, are considered to be matters too far within the interior of covenantal Jewish life to be allowed any non-Jewish jurisdiction over them whatsoever.

There are, of course, some aspects of Jewish marriage that are quite similar to aspects of non-Jewish marriages, especially as regards monetary mat-

---

35. See B. Gittin 9b.

36. See Novak, *Covenantal Rights,* pp. 133-38.

37. Novak, *Covenantal Rights,* pp. 133-38.

38. For the prohibition of initiating a marriage with the intention of subsequently terminating it, see B. Yevamot 37b; B. Gittin 90b; Maimonides, MT: Divorce, 10.21. See also David Novak, *Law and Theology in Judaism* (New York: Ktav Publishing House, 1974-76), vol. 1, pp. 1-14.

39. See B. Kiddushin 5a.

40. Y. Kiddushin 1.1/58c.

41. Mal. 2:16.

ters.[42] To assert otherwise would be fantastic. Furthermore, on the more normative level, Judaism recognizes the prohibition of adultery, the most basic violation of the marital relationship (and in some views the only justifiable ground for divorce), to be universal.[43] Adultery is a grave offense, to be punished by law, whether the adulterers are Jews or not.[44] Despite this commonality (to which I shall return at the end of this essay), Jewish marriage has such an immediately Jewish religious character that to allow any outside jurisdiction over it would be something like letting matters of Jewish worship and ritual be decided either by secular or by non-Jewish religious norms.

Although it is much easier, as noted above, to justify non-Jewish jurisdiction in civil and criminal matters, despite the hope that this not be the case optimally, one can even see the absence of non-Jewish jurisdiction in Jewish marital matters as not being absolute in the past, let alone contemporaneously.

Jewish Divorce and Non-Jewish Courts

An important exception to the general principle of excluding non-Jewish jurisdiction from Jewish marital matters is found in the following statement in the Mishnah: "A bill of divorce given under compulsion [*get me'usseh*] is valid if it is ordered by a Jewish court, but if by a gentile court it is invalid. If the gentiles beat a man and say to him, 'Do what the Jews tell you,' it is valid [*kasher*]."[45] It is important to explicate the fuller meaning of this rule in order to better appreciate how it relates non-Jewish jurisdiction to Jewish jurisdiction.

According to scriptural law, a man has the right to divorce his wife, but a wife has no right to divorce her husband.[46] The Rabbis assumed there need be some cause for a man to be able to exercise this right, but there are debates about what such a cause must be. The opinions on this subject range from presumption of adultery, to incompatibility, to the desire of the man to marry someone else in place of his present wife.[47] The tradition subsequently settled on incompatibility as sufficient cause for a man to divorce his wife if he so

---

42. See B. Yevamot 122b, and generally Louis M. Epstein, *The Jewish Marriage Contract* (New York: Jewish Theological Seminary, 1927).

43. See B. Sanhedrin 58a.

44. B. Sanhedrin 58a.

45. M. Gittin 9.8.

46. See Deut. 24:1-4.

47. See M. Gittin 9.10.

chooses.[48] Left at this level, though, it would seem that a man has almost un-limited rights in divorce, whereas a woman has no rights at all.

Even though the tradition never intended to fully equalize women and men in marriage, it did limit the rights of a man and expand the rights of a woman.[49] In a variety of ways, the Rabbis removed the right to be married from some men for several reasons. One reason would be that the marriage was improperly initiated.[50] For example, when a woman had been coerced into marriage by a man, the marriage was to be subsequently annulled by a rabbinical court.[51] Thus, the right of a woman not to be married against her will was thereby recognized. As the Talmud later pointed out, the wording of the Mishnah — "the woman is acquired [niqneyt] as a wife" rather than "the man acquires [qoneh] a wife" — is made to show that a woman is only "ac-quired" by a man if that is "not done under coercion [ba'al korhah]."[52] A co-erced marriage is institutionalized rape.[53]

Moreover, the Rabbis basically gave a woman the right to sue for di-vorce.[54] A woman had to show that her husband had not fulfilled her scrip-turally prescribed rights to food, clothing, and regular sexual intercourse.[55] If this could be shown, which would be quite easy in cases where the husband and wife no longer shared common domicile, then the rabbinical court should enforce the woman's right to either a proper marriage or a divorce.[56] If the husband refused to comply with the court order, the judges could force the husband to divorce his wife (even using physical coercion to do so).[57] Thus, marriage was, in effect, defined to give a husband more duties to his wife and a wife more rights from her husband. Subsequent authorities went so far as to include the general unhappiness of a wife with her husband dur-

---

48. See Maimonides, *Commentary on the Mishnah* ad M. Gittin 9.10; Maimonides, MT: Di-vorce, 10.21; B. Gittin 90b.

49. See Novak, *Covenantal Rights*, pp. 202-4.

50. See B. Baba Batra 48b.

51. B. Baba Batra 48b.

52. B. Kiddushin 2b.

53. Thus, the fourteenth-century commentator R. Menahem ha-Meiri noted that if there were only the biblical institution of marriage, no Jewish woman would remain a Jew. See *Bet ha-Behirah*, ed. A. Sofer (Jerusalem: n.p., 1963), Kiddushin 8.

54. Maimonides noted that the court's action in forcing a man to divorce his wife is occa-sioned by a woman's petition to the court for a divorce *(she -tav'ah ha'ishah et ha-gerushin)*. See Maimonides, *Commentary on the Mishnah*, ed. Y. Kafih (Jerusalem: Mossad ha-Rav Kook, 1963), p. 164.

55. See M. Ketubot 5.6, 6.1.

56. See B. Ketubot 61b.

57. See M. Arakhin 5.6; B. Arakhin 21a.

ing the course of their marriage (when she says *ma'is aley* — literally, "he disgusts me") to be sufficient cause for a court to order him to divorce her, although others strongly disagree with ordering a divorce for a complaint so imprecise.[58] Also, a major medieval authority required the consent of a woman to accept a divorce from her husband as a condition of its being valid. Eventually, this ruling became virtually universal in Jewry.[59] Finally, with the growing acceptance of the medieval ban on polygamy (made by the same major authority who required the woman's consent to accept a divorce), it became possible to make promiscuity on the part of the husband grounds for his wife to petition the court to order him to divorce her.

The paradox of forcing a husband to do what Scripture seems to have designated to be his free option to do is ingeniously explained by the medieval jurist and theologian Maimonides. He speculates that the coercion on the part of the court is simply a restoration of the sanity of someone who has become temporarily insane.[60] Maimonides assumes, at least at a level that might be termed the "collective unconscious," that every member of the community really wants to do what is right.[61] So, the man who refuses to comply with the order of the court is truly acting out of character. The punishing action of the court, then, is in his best interest because it restores him to consciously law-abiding action.[62] Accordingly, the husband's own best interest *(bonum sibi)* is seen in its being subordinate to the common good *(bonum commune)*. In this case, the common good of the institution of marriage itself is not well served when marriages are allowed to continue "in name only." Conversely, the common good is well served when persons are allowed to marry whomever they truly want to marry (within the range of the community, of course).[63] All of this emphasizes the communal-covenantal nature of both marriage and divorce in Judaism.

With this background in mind, one can now appreciate the force of the Mishnah's authorization of the use of gentiles to coerce a Jewish man to divorce his wife. It will be recalled that this is invalid when the gentiles do this at their own initiative.[64] Only a Jewish court can have such power over Jews in a Jewish matrimonial dispute.[65] On the other hand, what justifies a Jewish

---

58. See B. Ketubot 63b.
59. See Elon, *Jewish Law*, vol. 2, pp. 784-86.
60. See Maimonides, MT: Divorce, 2.20.
61. Maimonides, MT: Divorce, 2.20.
62. Maimonides, MT: Divorce, 2.20.
63. B. Kiddushin 41a.
64. See M. Gittin 9.8.
65. M. Gittin 9.8.

court using gentiles to enforce its own decision? The cause of such action would seem to be that the Jewish court does not have the political power to enforce its own decision. The reason for permitting this recourse is that the Jewish court can, in effect, temporarily deputize gentiles to accomplish its own ends.[66] It also seems that this is not deputizing individual gentiles but, rather, deputizing a non-Jewish court. This distinction is important because to deputize individuals to commit an act of violence (which is what coercion is by definition) would surely violate the very condition of Jews being part of a larger jurisdiction — namely, "The law of the Government is law."[67]

There are few societies that have not monopolized violence for the state in the form of police power. This police power is designed to protect private persons and their property from violence, to punish violence committed against the citizens, and to protect public officials and public property from violence. As such, the fact of gentiles being deputized by Jews is justified by the primary Jewish jurisdiction requesting an ancillary non-Jewish jurisdiction to do something the Jewish jurisdiction itself cannot do in order that justice be done. This situation is the rough equivalent of one jurisdiction asking another to return a criminal to its control because this criminal has committed an act the other jurisdiction can also recognize as unjust — even by its own criteria. Without this type of justification, though, that other jurisdiction could well regard the "criminal" whose extradition is being requested to be like a political prisoner, one whose flight from his previous jurisdiction is just, and who should be granted asylum rather than their being forced to comply with the unjust orders of his or her original society.[68]

Of course, by so doing, the Jewish court has granted jurisdiction to the non-Jewish court that, in principle, it should not have. That is why this grant of jurisdiction should be considered a sort of emergency measure, something to be very rarely invoked. Nevertheless, in countries where common law pertains, if a non-Jewish court does intervene in such a Jewish matrimonial dis-

---

66. Thus, in their respective comments on B. Gittin 88b, the medieval commentators R. Solomon ibn Adret (Hiddushei ha-Rashba) and R. Yom Tov ben Abraham Ishbili (Hiddushei ha-Ritva) noted that the gentile court is only an "instrument" in the hands of the Jewish court, rather than a full agent (shaliah), inasmuch as a gentile could not fully effect a Jewish religious act on behalf of a Jew. See M. Berakhot 5.5; B. Kiddushin 41g; B. Baba Metsia 71b. In the case of forcing a divorce, the gentile court functions like a catalyst that enables the Jewish court to complete its own enforcement of a Jewish woman's right to have her marriage terminated for just cause.

67. See B. Gittin 10b.

68. For example, Scripture rules that Jews are not to extradite gentile slaves back to their gentile masters when these slaves have sought asylum in a Jewish jurisdiction. See Deut. 23:16-17. Rashi assumes that the reason for this is because such extradition would be returning a genile slave to idolatry, something taken to be prohibited to all human beings everywhere.

pute on behalf of a Jewish court, it has created a legal precedent. So, if other cases like this come before non-Jewish courts, then by *stare decisis* what was meant to be an *ad hoc* measure becomes a factor relied upon by the legal system. The price the Jewish court pays for this help from the non-Jewish court is that, to a certain extent, Jewish marriage has become something not exclusively governed by Jewish criteria. This has profound ramifications for the contemporary institution of Jewish marriage in those societies where Jews have ready access to secular courts.

The Modern *Agunah* Problem

From medieval times up to the period just before the French Revolution, European Jewish communities had a good deal of internal autonomy, especially in handling religious matters, of which marriage is a prime factor.[69] Jews were not citizens of the states in which they lived because citizenship was confined to the Christian subjects of the Christian sovereign.[70] Jews were members of a foreign nation whose particular community had a social contract with the local sovereign.[71] These Jewish communities functioned very much as *imperium in imperio*.[72] Accordingly, it was in the best interests of both the host society and the Jewish community that the Jews keep as much of their own domestic house in order as possible.[73]

Because of this political reality in pre-modern times, it was very rare for Jewish authorities to have any need of non-Jewish authorities to intervene in Jewish matrimonial matters. Thus, the problem of the *agunah* (a wife still considered, *de jure*, to be married to a *de facto* absent husband) was almost always a problem of a husband who had disappeared (either by accident or by design), not one where a husband publicly refused to follow a court order to divorce his wife.[74] Because of the political and social power of the Jewish

---

69. See Jacob Katz, *Tradition and Crisis: Jewish Society at the End of the Middle Ages* (New York: Schocken Books, 1971), pp. 11-50.

70. Katz, *Tradition and Crisis*.

71. Katz, *Tradition and Crisis*.

72. Katz, *Tradition and Crisis*.

73. Katz, *Tradition and Crisis*; see also S. M. Nadler, *Spinoza* (Cambridge: Cambridge University Press, 1999), pp. 10-15.

74. In the Talmud and post-Talmudic legal literature, the attempts to find lenient solutions within the law for enabling the wives of absent husbands to remarry were almost always attempts to accept testimony from just about anyone about the death of the absent husband. See B. Yevamot 87b-88b.

courts at this time, such recalcitrant husbands could be subjected to very real political and social pressures to conform to the ruling of the juridical representatives of the whole community. The Jewish courts had police power over the Jews within their communal domain.[75] The Mishnah's provision for the use of a non-Jewish court in such cases of willful contempt of court was largely a legal possibility, not a political and social necessity for the most part. Membership in the Jewish community was considered by neither the Jews nor their gentile hosts to be a voluntary matter. Nationhood and one's specific status in those days were considered to be matters of birth rather than volition, matters of status rather than matters of contract.[76]

Beginning in Western Europe, all of this changed (sometimes quite abruptly) when the French Revolution and its political aftermath ended the privileges of the autonomous Jewish communities *(qehillot)*. In place of these communal privileges, Jews were now entitled to become individual citizens of the secular state.[77] As individual citizens, they now had the right to form private associations, as long as these associations were not considered to be in violation of the laws of the state.[78] Accordingly, the state cannot be called upon to enforce the basically private rules of any such association.[79] Just as citizenship in the state itself is taken to be a matter of social contract, entered into voluntarily and from which one could (at least in principle) voluntarily resign, the same is true for membership in any association entitled by the state. One can simply disobey the rules of any such association or resign from it with legal impunity. Even those who did not resign from such associations could not be subjected to any police action from within such an association itself; the most the association could do is expel such recalcitrant members from membership.[80] Indeed, were this not the case, we would have the politi-

---

75. See B. Sanhedrin 16b.

76. For this famous distinction, see Henry Maine, *Ancient Law* (Boston: Beacon Press, 1963 [1861]).

77. See Katz, *Tradition and Crisis,* pp. 11-60.

78. Katz, *Tradition and Crisis.*

79. See, e.g., *Morris v. Morris* [1973] 42 D.L.R.3d 550, 568 (Can.) (Guy, J., concurring): "We are bound to administer the law of Canada as it is written, and the power of the civil Courts of justice should not be extended to assist rabbinical courts or, indeed, any religious sects, to enforce their orders." In the same case, see 571 (Hall, J.): "In Canada all religious bodies are considered as voluntary associations. The law recognizes their existence and protects them in their enjoyment of property, but unless civil rights are in question it does not interfere with their organization or with questions of religious faith" — quoting *Ukrainian Catholic Church v. Trustees of Ukrainian Catholic Cathedral of St. Mary the Protectress* [1939] 2 D.L.R. 494, 498 (Can.) (Dennistoun, J.), citing *Dunnet v. Forneri* [1877] 25 Gr. 199, 206 (Can.).

80. In his arguments for the full political emancipation of Jews in the new secular nation-

cal anomaly of the state itself having less coercive power than a private association it has entitled.

Because Jewish associations usually have been local congregations, and considering that modern Jews have greater personal mobility than did medieval Jews, it has become quite easy for Jews in contempt of the court of one congregation to simply move, with a good deal of anonymity, to another congregation. The sad fact, too, is that many traditional Jewish congregations take no action on behalf of Jewish women who have just claims to order their husbands to give them a Jewish divorce. Adding to this communal anarchy is the possibility of a modern Jew opting for no other congregation, or moving to a congregation of those modern Jewish religious movements who do not regard traditional Jewish law to be legally binding.

The issue of Jews who refuse to grant their spouses a Jewish divorce *(get)* has become a *cause célèbre* in the contemporary Jewish community.[81] Here is where the question of the interrelation of jurisdictions comes most pointedly into focus. Although the general problem of the recalcitrant spouse is ancient, there is the specific problem of the recalcitrant spouse in modern secular society. The point of difference is that modern spouses are also participants in the specifically modern institution of civil marriage. In ancient times, when non-Jewish authorities were infrequently (if ever) deputized by a Jewish court to force a recalcitrant spouse to do what the Jewish court itself could not get him to do, the non-Jewish elements were being imported into a purely internal Jewish matter for *ad hoc* assistance, as it were. But now, in every modern democratic state in the West of which I know, all Jews are married in civil law, and most Jews *also* opt to be married by some form of Jewish religion.

This is a state of affairs that Jewish authorities accepted at the beginning of the time when Jews were first being accepted as citizens in modern, secular polities. One can pinpoint it to the year 1807, when Napoleon convened what he called, with typical grandiosity, a *Sanhedrin*.[82] This body consisted of leading rabbis in the lands under French imperial domain. Napoleon wanted assurances that the Jews, who were now losing the traditional privileges of their

---

states, the German-Jewish philosopher Moses Mendelssohn stressed the point that Jewish communities should no longer exercise formal excommunication *(herem)* of deviant members because this still smacked of the communal power Jews needed to renounce in order to win citizenship for themselves. See Moses Mendelssohn, *Jerusalem,* trans. Allan Arkush (Hanover, N.H.: University Press of New England, 1983), pp. 73-75.

81. There is now substantial literature on this subject. See, e.g., *Jewish Law Annual* 4 (1981); Shlomo Riskin, *Women and Jewish Divorce* (New York: Ktav Publishing House, 1989).

82. See S. Schwarzfuchs, *Napoleon, the Jews, and the Sanhedrin* (London: Routledge & Kegan Paul, 1979).

own communal authority, would be loyal to the new state and its overall constitution. The state had removed the monopoly of the church on the legitimization of marriage by instituting civil marriage. Thus, civil marriage was a necessity for anyone who wished to marry, whereas religious marriage was now only a purely voluntary matter once the required civil marriage had been performed. Civil marriage, therefore, became a publicly required contract in a way that religious marriage could not be. Accordingly, Napoleon wanted to know whether or not the Jews would also recognize the validity of civil marriages.[83] At the very least, this required all Jews to now become participants in civil marriage. Taken to its extreme, Napoleon's dictate seemed to require Jews to recognize civil marriages between Jews and gentiles, which is something Jewish law not only does not recognize *post factum,* but also prohibits *ab initio.*[84]

The rabbis of the 1807 *Sanhedrin* cleverly answered the most serious challenge (that of civil marriage between Jews and gentiles) by saying that they would recognize the *civil* validity of such civil marriages.[85] In other words, they did not say that they would recognize them as *Jewish* marriages (which they had no authority, of course, to do — and which I cannot imagine any one of them ever wanting to do), but that they would not interfere with the civil right of the state to recognize such marriages by its own criteria. In more traditional Jewish congregations, this hardly posed much of a problem, as most Jews civilly married to gentiles would either leave or be expelled from the congregation anyway. In more liberal Jewish congregations, though, it does pose the religious anomaly of gentiles being members of a *Jewish* congregation.

Even though the secular state has made participation in a religious marriage something *subsequent* to participation in civil marriage, traditional Jews have regarded their involvement in civil marriage as a necessity of their participation in civil society, but a necessity to which their subordination to Jewish law is *prior.* At the level of principle, this is clearly paradoxical: two separate jurisdictions, each claiming priority for itself. Nevertheless, on the practical level, there need not be troublesome confrontation because the secular state does not require one to make an ultimate commitment to its own authority. This distinguishes secular democracies from the secularism of a fascist or communist regime. All a democratic regime asks is compliance with

---

83. Schwarzfuchs, *Napoleon, the Jews, and the Sanhedrin.*

84. See B. Kiddushin 68b.

85. See C. Touati, "Le Grand Sanhedrin de 1807 et le Droit Rabbinique," in *Le Grand Sanhedrin de Napoléon,* ed. B. Blumenkranz and A. Soboul (Toulouse: E. Privat, 1979), pp. 44-45.

its civil authority.[86] This policy easily enables religious people to decide whether or not such compliance is consistent with their ultimate commitment to the authority of their God as revealed and transmitted to them by their own tradition.[87]

In the case of the recalcitrant spouse, this new state of affairs actually gives the religious community a powerful new tool in its attempts to comply with the just claims of wronged spouses. This new tool is the reality that participation in a civil marriage seems to be viewed more and more as a civil contract.[88] Because in countries like Canada and the United States clergy function as the celebrants of both religious *and* civil marriages (by officiating at wedding ceremonies that combine both aspects into one event), it could be argued that one has agreed *civilly* to initiate and terminate the marriage in compliance with both civil and religious criteria. The religious criteria are assumed to have been accepted by the tacit consent of both parties in that they voluntarily consented to be married in a religious ceremony. Lawyers in both Canadian and American courts have argued for the withholding of a civil divorce decree until "religious" impediments to the remarriage of either spouse have been removed.[89] In the case of Jewish spouses, neither party can remarry, according to Jewish law, without a properly executed divorce or annulment.[90] Along these lines, many traditional rabbis in Canada and the United States require couples before their wedding ceremony to sign a prenuptial agreement, stipulating that they will comply with the ruling of a Jewish court in the event of their filing for a civil divorce.[91]

How effective such arguments will actually be in the civil courts is still an open question. After all, it is rather tenuous to assume that Jewish marriage

---

86. Anything more than that would violate the protection of religious liberty — i.e., the right to have an ultimate allegiance beyond the authority of the State — guaranteed by the First Amendment of the United States Constitution. Thus, the Constitution recognizes religious liberty but does not create it.

87. Novak, *Natural Law in Judaism*, pp. 12-26.

88. See, e.g., *Morris v. Morris*, 42 D.L.R.3d at 553 (Freedman, C.J., dissenting), noting that "it is important to keep in mind that we are here simply concerned with a contract between two parties and the matter of its enforcement. We are not concerned with a conflict having its genesis in an order of an ecclesiastical court and thus posing the question of the proper limits of jurisdiction between a civil court and a religious court."

89. For example, in Ontario the relevant law states that one petitioning for a civil divorce must have "removed all barriers that are within his or her control and that would prevent the other spouse['s] remarriage within that spouse['s] faith. . . ." Family Law Act, S. O., ch. 4, §2 (1986) (Can.).

90. See, e.g., J. David Bleich, "Modern-Day Agunot," *Jewish Law Annual* 4 (1981): 169-87.

91. Bleich, "Modern-Day Agunot."

can be viewed as a kind of civil contract, for it seems that the legal equality of the parties essential to a civil contract is missing in a Jewish marital cove-nant.[92] The Jewish tradition seems to have no interest in equalizing the part-ners in a marriage.[93] Egalitarianism is not one of its desiderata.[94] Instead, one can see a series of normative decisions within the tradition that are designed to prevent or remedy the unjust exploitation of one party by another despite their essential differences, in this case the exploitation of a woman by a man.

In what might be seen as an eagerness to employ secular means to solve a basically religious problem, though, a number of scholars of Jewish law have uncritically compared Jewish marriage to a civil contract for this purpose. Despite undoubtedly noble intentions, their arguments are weak. Professor J. David Bleich states,

> The [get] proceedings are devoid of divine reference or other religious for-mulae. No blessings are uttered, no credos or professions of faith are pro-nounced. Execution of a get does not require that the participants sub-scribe to any particular set of beliefs. Indeed, a get may . . . be executed even if the husband has formally renounced Judaism.[95]

Despite the correct facts mentioned by Professor Bleich, his interpreta-tion of their implications for the view that Jewish marriage is, in effect, a civil contract is erroneous and misleading. First, the fact that blessings and other religious formulae invoking the name of God are not part of the writing or delivery of a get does not make it a "secular" enterprise. There are other situa-tions in Jewish law where obviously religious acts are performed and the name of God is not invoked for a variety of very specific reasons.[96] Also, not invoking the name of God does not religiously invalidate an act ex post facto, even when such invocation is required ab initio.[97] Second, although the hus-band who is giving the get need not fulfill any religious criteria, and he could even be an apostate from Judaism, that does not mean that this is a "secular" enterprise. The fact is that Judaism does not regard a nonreligious Jew, even an apostate, as being exempt from religious duties. These duties are clearly re-ligious (mitsvot), irrespective of what the subjective motives of the one per-

92. Deut. 24:1-4.

93. See Novak, Covenantal Rights, pp. 202-4.

94. See David Novak, Halakhah in a Theological Dimension (Chico, Calif.: Scholars Press, 1985), pp. 61-71.

95. Bleich, "Jewish Divorce: Judicial Misconceptions and Possible Means of Civil Enforce-ment," Connecticut Law Review 16 (1984): 257.

96. See Maimonides, MT: Blessings, 11.2.

97. See Maimonides, MT: Blessings, 1.6.

forming them happen to be. Whenever, wherever, and however some of them can be performed, they are to be performed.[98] Furthermore, even though any Jewish husband may give the *get* to his wife, the *get* itself is to be written by someone who must be certifiable as a religiously observant Jew.[99] This requirement also pertains to those persons designated to witness the writing and delivery of the *get* to the man's wife.[100]

The problem with Bleich's statement, and others like it, is that it avoids the philosophical issue at the heart of the *agunah* problem for Jews living as citizens of a democracy.[101] As distinct from ancient and medieval times, Jews are now full citizens of the regimes whose help they now seek in cases of recalcitrant spouses. Moreover, they are now participants in civil marriage, an institution in which all the citizens of the regime, Jews and gentiles alike, have equal access. As such, Jews now have more power in civil society and in civil marriage. In the short run, this seems to offer some hope of help from the state in forcing recalcitrant spouses to comply with the order of a Jewish court to either give or accept a Jewish divorce although, as we have seen, it is still too early to judge the legal effectiveness of this policy. Nevertheless, in the long run, there seem to be some important negative implications of this policy.

The Price of Secularity

On legal grounds, most Jewish authorities have stretched the meaning of the Mishnah's provision, "Do what the Jews tell you," to cover the order of a secu-

---

98. See Novak, *The Election of Israel*, pp. 189-99.

99. See Maimonides, MT: Divorce, 3.15-16; see also M. Sanhedrin 3.3; M. Niddah 6.4; B. Sanhedrin 27a concerning the religious qualifications for those designated to write, deliver, and witness the *get* and all other Jewish legal proceedings; Maimonides, MT: Sanhedrin, 10.1.

100. See texts in preceding note.

101. Distinguishing Jewish marriage law from the common law of England and its "conception of marriage as a sacrament" and a "sacred institution," Israeli Supreme Court Justice Haim Cohn wrote that "marriage in Jewish law is a contract, albeit a very solemn one. . ." (Eliot N. Dorff and Arthur Rosett, *A Living Tree* [Albany: State University of New York Press, 1987], p. 460). Unlike Bleich, whose motives are to show a particular secular aspect of Jewish religious law, Cohn, as a secularist Israeli jurist, has elsewhere stated that his intention is to show the essentially secular possibilities of Jewish law as it governs interhuman relations (see his *Human Rights in Jewish Law* [New York: Ktav Publishing House, 1984]). If Jewish marriage (and divorce), however, is "a [civil] contract," why is marriage itself deemed a religious duty (M. Yevamot 6.6), and why is divorce frequently deemed a religious duty rather than a neutral option (e.g., M. Yevamot 10.1)? To use Cohn's words against his own argument: the "solemnity" of Jewish marriage (and divorce) contradicts any attempt to see it as a "contract" at all. A contract presupposes an autonomy that is always trumped by any religious obligation.

lar court to a Jewish spouse to end a marriage according to Jewish religious law. The text literally says, however, "Do what *Israel* tells you to do." That is, it deals with a situation where the non-Jewish authorities recognize the *communal* authority of the Jewish court in the same way the court of one national jurisdiction recognizes the national jurisdiction of another court.[102] It is like a Canadian court ordering an American citizen who is a resident of Canada to obey his or her American national authorities. In principle, it is a form of extradition. Where there is, however, a constitutional separation of church and state, a secular court could not literally say "Do what Israel [the Jewish communal authorities] tells you" to any of its citizens. In the United States, as well as in Canada and other Western democracies, everyone is a citizen of the state qua *individual;* no voluntary communal association is recognized as having legal jurisdiction similar to that of the state because all Jews have been fully integrated into the secular state as citizens equal to all other citizens. That is why, as we have seen, for purposes of secular remedy to the problem of a recalcitrant spouse, marriage has to be viewed as a private contract between consenting adult individuals. A tacit part of that contract is then taken to be an agreement to fulfill certain religious requirements (both *a parte ante* and *a parte post*) when the marriage was initiated in a religious ceremony.

In terms of legal interpretation, such an elastic interpretation of a term from its original context is hardly novel in Jewish law (or in any other system of law, for that matter). This interpretation is largely the necessary function of casuistry — that is, the process whereby the law is applied to new cases, cases quite different from the situations from which the law emerged originally. When the stretching becomes quite radical, we call it a *fictio juris.*[103] Whether the new use of "Do what Israel tells you" is ordinary casuistry or whether it constitutes a more radical legal fiction is debatable. Nevertheless, it is certainly a historical departure. It represents a recognition of the new, modern secularity of marriage, something the Rabbis surely did not have in mind. The price paid for this new definition of Jewish marriage is that the secular, non-Jewish state now plays a greater role in Jewish marriage than it had previously. At a time when secular definitions of marriage seem to be veering farther and farther away from traditional Jewish definitions of marriage *per se* (Jewish or non-Jewish), this should be a cause for concern on the part of most traditional Jewish jurists. Many traditional Jewish jurists, however, seem

---

102. Accordingly, most commentators emphasize that the gentile court must recognize, either explicitly or implicitly, the authority of the Jewish jurisdiction *(dinei yisrael)* and its court *(bet din shel yisrael).* See, e.g., Maimonides, *Commentary on the Mishnah* to M. Gittin 9.8.

103. See Lon L. Fuller, *Legal Fictions* (Stanford, Calif.: Stanford University Press, 1967).

to be fascinated with the new possibilities of making Jewish law a matter of interest to secular legal systems.[104] A similar fascination transpires in the new field of bioethics, where Jewish ethicist-jurists have also taken a large interest.[105] Many jurists seem oblivious to the political implications of this new situation. At present, I see two specific areas of concern.

First, the principle of "Do what Israel tells you" should be taken to be the *ad hoc*, emergency measure it undoubtedly was and was meant to be in Talmudic times. The greater frequency of this problem today, especially because of the moral aspersions it casts on Judaism itself, requires a more general and a more radical solution than the rather artificial act of deputizing a non-Jewish court. The moral aspersions this general situation casts on Judaism are that it strongly implies that the Jewish tradition does not care about the exploitation of Jewish women by unscrupulous Jewish men (who are the vast majority of the recalcitrant spouses). Not only does it present Judaism in a negative moral light to the world; it also seriously tempts many Jewish women to opt out of the Jewish religious-legal system altogether. Why should modern Jewish women remain loyal to a system that seems so helpless to protect them from exploitation by men? Doesn't the tradition itself judge these men to be acting unjustly?[106] Such resignation from a religious community, as we have seen, can be done with ease and legal impunity in any modern democracy. Jews should be very concerned if they have to *regularly* turn to non-Jewish authorities to effect justice in an internal Jewish religious matter. The non-Jewish court was never meant to be a permanent feature of the Jewish religious scene, especially in an area of Jewish life as sacramental as marriage.[107]

Traditional Jews, who know the rabbinic sources, should be even more concerned with this non-Jewish, secular remedy to a Jewish moral problem when they (that is, in the person of their religious-juridical authorities) could largely solve the problem by the exercise of their own authority within their

104. For the pioneering work in this area, see Asher Gulak, *Yesodei Ha-Mishpat Ha'Ivri* (Jerusalem: Devir, 1922).

105. See, e.g., Immanuel Jakobovits, *Jewish Medical Ethics* (New York: Philosophical Library, 1959).

106. In this very discussion of the divorce of a Jewish woman by a husband who has been coerced to do so, the Talmud raises the question of a woman so desperate that she would even engage an individual gentile to so coerce her husband (B. Gittin 88b). Even though the Talmud concludes that there is no validity whatsoever in such a divorce, perhaps the very mention of such a possibility in this context is to emphasize the responsibility of a Jewish court to facilitate a divorce in a case where a woman's rights have been violated by her husband, so that she not be tempted to seek such a desperate solution to her just marital complaint.

107. See B. Kiddushin 2b and M. Nedarim 5.6 for the sacramental character of Jewish marriage.

community. The internal Jewish remedy, which does not require the importa-
tion of any secular authority, is the institution of marriage annulment. Annulment is the power of a Jewish court to invalidate a marriage in lieu of the
giving of a divorce by the husband to the wife.[108] This can be done when a
rabbinical court determines that there were legal irregularities in the marriage ceremony itself, irrespective of how long the couple actually lived together as husband and wife.[109] For example, the rabbinical court discovers
that the Jewish couple was not married in a Jewish religious ceremony, or that
the couple was married in a Jewish religious ceremony where the absence of
certain acts or persons means the marriage never had been valid, or there was
no public marriage ceremony at all.[110] Less easily, but still available *de jure,* is
the possibility of retroactive annulment of a marriage in which, *ab initio,*
nothing irregular happened in the Jewish ceremony.[111] Thus a court, by *fictio
juris,* can declare the object of value which the groom is required to transfer
to his bride at the outset of the marriage ceremony, to *have been* of no value
(what the Talmud calls "*hefger*").[112]

Some more conservative Jewish jurists argue that this principle of annulment is theoretical, and may only be used in the exact cases to which it was
applied in the Talmud, none of which concern a recalcitrant spouse.[113] Nevertheless, one may counter this objection with three answers. One, it is no less
radical an application of the principle "The rabbis may remove marriage
from him" (what is called "*afqa'at qiddushin*") than the use of a secular court
in a modern constitutional democracy is a radical application of the principle
"Do what Israel tells you." The logic of strict construction could equally eliminate both solutions. So, if the principle of "Do what Israel tells you" is now
acceptable in a uniquely modern class of cases, then the same more expansive
reasoning can be used to make the principle of "The rabbis may remove marriage from him" acceptable in a uniquely modern class of cases. Two, the use
of marriage annulment also returns full legal authority in Jewish marriage to
the Jews. It avoids the dangerous legal fiction — which in essence has become

108. See B. Gittin 33a; see also David Novak, "Annulment in Lieu of Divorce in Jewish Law,"
Jewish Law Annual 4 (1981): 188-206.

109. See R. Moses Feinstein, *Igrot Mosheh* (New York: M. Feinstein, 1959-), Even Ha'Ezer
nos. 74-76 for the most influential decisions made in this type *(a parte ante)* of annulment.

110. See David Novak, "The Marital Status of Jews Married Under Non-Jewish Auspices,"
Jewish Law Association Studies 1 (1985): 61-77.

111. See Novak, "Annulment in Lieu of Divorce in Jewish Law."

112. See B. Gittin 33a; B. Yevamot 89b.

113. See Aaron Rakeffet-Rothkopf, "Annulment of Marriage within the Context of Cancel-
lation of the Get," *Tradition* 15 (1975): 173-85.

a much larger political fiction — that Jewish marriage is a civil contract, something it was never ever meant to be. And three, we have an important precedent where the principle of annulment was used in a case involving a large number of people, in a way not specified in the Talmud.[114]

As for the possible objection that the adoption of this rabbinic procedure would, in effect, eliminate the use of the bill of divorce *(get)* prescribed by Scripture, there are two answers. First, it is still the fact that the vast majority of traditional Jews who terminate their marriages do so with the compliance of both spouses in the giving of a bill of divorce as prescribed by Scripture and the traditional interpretation of the specifics of scriptural law. If this ceased to be the case, there would be such a crisis in traditional Jewish marriage that the likelihood of no Jewish marriage would outweigh the likelihood of no Jewish divorce. (That is because divorce always presupposes marriage, whereas marriage only sometimes entails divorce.)[115] Second, there are ways in which the introduction of annulment would actually make Jewish divorce the more attractive course of action. For example, a Jewish court could rule that a couple must have been living apart, or already have been civilly divorced, for a period of a year or two or more before annulment proceedings can even be started.[116] Or, a Jewish court could rule that once the annulment took place, the recalcitrant spouse cannot be considered for remarriage in a Jewish religious ceremony again — a kind of permanent marital excommunication.

Of course, all of this requires a degree of unanimity in the Jewish religious community at large that is sadly absent at present. Indeed, the effectiveness of annulment depends on the acceptance of this procedure by the vast majority of rabbinical courts. It would require the type of Jewish unanimity that eventually made the medieval ban on polygamy, something permitted (although not mandated) in scriptural and rabbinic law, almost universally effective.

The growing number of cases of recalcitrant spouses in divorce proceedings might very well be a symptom of the larger theologico-political impotence of the traditional Jewish community, which cannot or will not exercise the power it possesses. This larger problem is hardly one that can be corrected by using non-Jewish institutions as a means of remedy. In the present situation, we have what the Talmud saw as an ultimate irony — namely, the sinner

114. See Moses Isserles, *Darkhei ha-Mosheh: Even Ha'Ezer* 7n.13 (Tur).

115. That might be why it is easier to initiate a Jewish marriage than to terminate it. See, e.g., B. Kiddushin 9ab.

116. Y. Yevamot 10.2/10c.

is rewarded *(hote niskar)*.[117] In the case of the modern *agunah,* the spouse who is faithful to Jewish law is prevented by a failed marriage from achieving a successful union with someone else, whereas the spouse in contempt of Jewish law effectively gets the law to assist him (or her) in what can only be seen as an act of unwarranted cruelty. The invocation of a totally internal Jewish remedy would go a long way to restoring the confidence of both Jewish women and men in the moral power of their own religious authorities.

The second area of concern raised by the secularization of Jewish marriage law involves the most pressing moral question facing marriage law today: the question of same-sex marriages. Jewish marriage has been able to relate to civil marriage because there has been enough commonality at the most basic level to make the relation plausible.[118] Heretofore, civil marriage precluded incestous and homosexual unions *ab initio,* and it has punished adultery *post factum.*[119] These factors are still a residue of the time when marriage was regarded as much more than a contract, even in an officially secular society.

With the virtual ignoring of adultery as a cause for penalty in divorce proceedings, and with the distinct possibility that Canadian and American courts will make their *de facto* recognition of same-sex unions *qua* "domestic partnerships" into literal marriage *de jure,* we may fast be reaching the point when the association of traditional Jewish marriage with civil marriage will be totally detrimental to traditional Jews.[120] The most powerful arguments for granting the right to marry to same-sex couples are made on the basis of what is taken to be the contractual nature of marriage.[121] There might come a time when Jews will be forced by the state, for all intents and purposes, not only to recognize as marriages what their tradition prohibits for Jews (like a marriage between a Jew and a gentile), but to recognize a same-sex union (in such matters as hiring practices), which Judaism teaches is prohibited to any human being.[122] Indeed, there may come a time when traditional Jews will seriously doubt whether they should be civilly married at all. After all, isn't it ironic that at the same time a small homosexual minority of the population who have heretofore been barred from marrying one another are now demanding inclusion in the institution of marriage, a much larger and growing

117. See, e.g., M. Hallah 2.7; B. Yevamot 92b.

118. See B. Hullin 92ab; cf. *Leviticus Rabbah* 23.9.

119. See, e.g., Canada Divorce Act, R.S.C., ch. D-8, § 8(1) (1970) (Can.).

120. See B. Sanhedrin 39b.

121. For a full discussion of these types of arguments, see David Orgon Coolidge, "Same-Sex Marriage? *Baehr v. Miike* and the Meaning of Marriage," *South Texas Law Review* 38 (1997): 34-38.

122. See B. Sanhedrin 58a.

number of Canadian and American heterosexual couples involved in "long-term relationships" are ignoring formal marriage, civil or religious, altogether? Clearly, both the state and religious communities have less control over spousal arrangements in our society than they had in the past.

We are also faced with the possibility that many traditional Christians and Muslims in our society will also be so opposed to sharing the institution of marriage with what they regard as a violation of natural law that they too will simply opt for religious marriage without the intrusion of what they regard as a state dedicated to undermining what they consider to be universally acceptable definitions of marriage and family. If this happens, we could be faced with a legal and political battle in our society that will make the legal and political battle over abortion, for example, look mild by comparison. In the face of all of this, traditional Jews are well advised to totally reconsider the overlapping of religious and secular jurisdictions in the institution of Jewish marriage. Its liability might now have far outweighed its benefits. To employ the metaphor used in the title of this essay: What is now a two-way street might have to become a one-way street again in order for the Jewish traffic to move toward its true destination.

21 Can Capital Punishment Ever Be Justified in the Jewish Tradition? (2004)

The Death Penalty and Moral Responsibility

Debate over the death penalty is of such practical import in our society that it would be irresponsible for me to simply report opinions regarding it in my own tradition. The import of this question requires responsible citizens in our by now heterogeneous society, coming from their respective traditions, be they religious or secular, to at least suggest a judgment *on* the death penalty emerging from their tradition. A question of such immediate moral concern makes a greater and more specific claim on our judgment than any question only motivated by general curiosity. Indeed, merely reporting what one's tradition has said *about* a current moral controversy, like the one concerning the death penalty, usually shows that same moral controversy can be found within his or her own tradition. As such, leaving the discussion at the merely descriptive level allows the reporter to evade responsibility for what the answer *of* his or her tradition ought to be *for* the question at hand here and now. At the descriptive level alone, one can get away with concluding that "some Jewish thinkers are in favor of the death penalty and others are opposed to it."[1] But that is hardly enough. In other words, the political implications of any public discussion of the death penalty are too significant for any such discussion to be left in such an irrelevant academic corner.

Moreover, even though the Jewish tradition I discuss here is only morally authoritative for us Jews, its wisdom can nonetheless provide guidance, even if only by suggestion, for those of other traditions. This is especially so when

---

1. For a discussion of these views, see David Novak, *Jewish Social Ethics* (New York: Oxford University Press, 1992), pp. 174-80.

they discover analogous patterns of moral reasoning during a process of authentic multicultural dialogue. Out of this process of multilateral guidance could emerge a unilateral conclusion having real governance — that is, a theoretical conclusion leading to real political and even real legal results. Furthermore, in the process of becoming more normatively focused, such specific judgments, only tentative and suggestive at present, should still have some direct relevance to a particular situation or case of deep moral concern. It takes no stretch of the imagination at all to see the death penalty as a matter of such particular concern for us all due to the terrible events of September 11, 2001. Of course, even had these events not occurred, we would have other events on which to focus our particular concern. Nevertheless, the events of September 11 have very much eclipsed them.

How could anyone here or elsewhere, when the death penalty is so much as mentioned, not think of the victims and the victimizers who came together on that by now infamous date of September 11 in a global *danse macabre?* A death penalty was decreed and enacted, even entailing the suicide of the immediate perpetrators. Yet, some of the victims and some of the less immediate victimizers survived the killing. What are we to do with them? In the case of the victims who survived, our immediate response must be to offer them financial aid and emotional comfort. But do we not also owe them — both the living and the dead — justice? In relation to the victimizers, who are still living and at large, are we not required, in the oft-stated words of President Bush, "to bring them to justice"? The question is, of course, just what sort of justice we are to bring them to. And, to cite the most important case that could possibly face us, what could we justifiably do if we were to capture Osama bin Laden or one of his close associates in the leadership of al-Qaeda? Could we try him or them in a court of law? Who could sit in such legal judgment of him or them? What could be the maximum punishment meted out to him or them if and when found guilty? In terms of this last question, the question immediately following is this: Could we justify executing him or them on moral and legal grounds? What does Judaism say — or better, what *could* Judaism say — about this? Surely, Jewish pride in having a true teaching *(torat emet)* requires that Jewish thinkers not remain mute or non-committal, especially when asked for their opinion by others.[2]

Of course, we are assuming that Osama bin Laden and the leadership of al-Qaeda are being charged as war criminals. And, of course, there are the precedents of the 1947 Nuremberg trials of the Nazi leaders, and the 1962 trial of Adolf Eichmann in Jerusalem. In both of these cases, the accused were

2. Novak, *Jewish Social Ethics,* pp. 225-39.

tried in a court of law as opposed to simply being killed upon capture. Thus it was assumed that the accused had violated a law for which they were responsible before the time of their crime *(nulla poena sine lege)* and were thereby responsible for its legal consequences after their crime. And that means that the victors in a war had the right to try those of the vanquished whom they could indict for instigating the crime of killing whole populations. Dealing with this crime is different in kind from the way the victors have often dealt with those who simply killed enemy combatants in what could be seen as a program of conquest. The "crime" of failed conquest, if that is even the right word for it, has more often been "punished" by political and economic sanctions against the offending nation than by legal sanctions, like the death penalty, against its leaders. In both the Nuremberg and the Eichmann trials, it was assumed even before it was formally concluded that we may punish such wholesale acts of murder with the death penalty.

The reason for the death penalty in such cases was best expressed, I think, by the late political philosopher Hannah Arendt. Despite her rather ambivalent relationship with her own Jewish heritage, she nevertheless expressed views, as we shall soon see, which have strong foundation in the Jewish tradition, whether she knew it or not. In the epilogue to her still controversial book of 1963, *Eichmann in Jerusalem,* she formulated what she thought should have been the justification for the death sentence against Adolf Eichmann for the crime of genocide. Dramatically speaking in the second person, as if she herself were the presiding judge pronouncing the death sentence against Eichmann, she wrote, "And just as you supported and carried out a policy of not wanting to share the earth with the Jewish people and the people of a number of other nations — as though you and your superiors had any right to determine who should and who should not inhabit the world — we find that no one, that is, no member of the human race, can be expected to share the earth with you. This is the reason, and the only reason, you must hang."[3]

The Death Penalty for Ordinary Murder

I would like to place Hannah Arendt's great insight about the death penalty for the crime of genocide in the context of the exceptionally rich tradition of moral experience and reflection of the Jewish people, something she herself did not do. And how she responded to the program of terror implemented by Adolf Eichmann and those with him is, to a large extent, the way we can re-

---

3. Arendt, *Eichmann in Jerusalem,* rev. ed. (New York: Penguin Books, 1965), p. 279.

spond to the program of terror initiated by Osama bin Laden and those with him. By so doing, we can develop her insight with greater precision, and we can better connect it to the moral distinction that needs to be made between the murder of individual human persons for reasons extraneous to their essential humanity (homicide), and the murder of persons for the sole reason of removing them, and everyone like them, from humankind itself altogether (genocide). Making this great moral distinction should lead to even greater legal differences between homicide and genocide.

Although all Jewish norms can be derived from either specific biblical commandments or the general biblical mandates warranting legislation by Jewish authorities, Jewish reflection on the meaning and purpose of these norms takes place in the Talmud and its related literature. Surely such is the case with Jewish reflection on the death penalty. All of it comes from the Talmud. And, quite significantly, this reflection takes place during a time when, according to the Talmud itself (and some other cognate sources), the Jewish people did not have enough political sovereignty to enforce the death penalty on anyone.[4] This means that Talmudic reflections on the death penalty were either reflections on what had transpired in previous Jewish history, or what the Rabbis hoped would transpire in future Jewish history with the restoration of Jewish political sovereignty, or what the Rabbis either approved of or disapproved of in the surrounding gentile societies, especially those gentile societies under whose rule Jews were living at the time. In the case of these gentile societies, the Rabbis were in effect telling them rabbinic views of their judicial practices, even though it is quite unlikely these societies were interested in what the Rabbis thought of them and their laws, and were even less interested in listening to the practical guidance their thoughts about them implied. As we shall see, though, things today in this area of political consultation might very well be different.

It is important to note that the legal situation of the Jews today, especially when it comes to our relation to what the tradition mandates concerning the death penalty, has not changed essentially. That is, even though Jewish political sovereignty has been regained in the State of Israel, the State of Israel is not governed by traditional Jewish law, certainly not by traditional Jewish criminal law, by which the death penalty is prescribed. Such is not the case in the Jewish state, and even less so in the worldwide Jewish diaspora. On the one and only occasion that the State of Israel ever judicially executed anybody

---

4. See Y. Sanhedrin 1.1/18a and 7.2/24b; B. Sanhedrin 41a and Shabbat 15a; also, John 18:31; H. H. Cohn, *The Trial and Death of Jesus* (New York: Ktav Publishing House, 1977), pp. 31-32, 346-50.

— and that "anybody" was Adolf Eichmann — it was *not* done according to the governance of Jewish law (halakhah). Nevertheless, even though we Jews have no jurisdiction for the specific application of the Jewish law of capital punishment, we are able to look to the Talmud more selectively for guidance in how the death penalty should or should not be applied where there is such jurisdiction. That guidance should function in the form of rational persuasion. Moreover, unlike the Jews of the Talmudic period, we Jews who live in secular democracies like the United States and Canada are not just offering guidance from our tradition to societies in which we are essentially outsiders. Instead, because of our full citizenship and cultural presence as well, we are in a position to offer some guidance to our own societies in areas of law where we are both subjects and objects of the overall political process of which law is the most authoritative part.

Before we come to the rabbinic speculation on the death penalty that can be most directly applied to the events of September 11, we must see how the Rabbis looked at the death penalty in what might be seen as more ordinary circumstances, which are when one private citizen murders another private citizen. Only after looking at what is ordinary can we better appreciate rabbinic speculation on what is clearly much more extraordinary. We must understand the legal reaction to homicide before we can understand the legal reaction to genocide. In some ways they are similar; in others, different. By his declaration of a war of extermination on Jews *qua* Jews, Americans *qua* Americans, and Christians *qua* Christians, Osama bin Laden and his close associates have taken responsibility for what is in our eyes — but not in his — the crime of genocide.

In the context of dealing with ordinary homicide, no traditional Jewish thinker could be opposed to capital punishment in principle, since it is clearly mandated by Scripture. To all humankind Scripture mandates, "Whosoever sheds human blood, by humans shall his blood be shed" (Gen. 9:6). To Israel (that is, what came to be solely identified as the Jewish people) Scripture mandates, "Whosoever strikes a man dead, he shall be put to death" (Exod. 21:12), and "Whosoever kills another human being, he shall be put to death. There shall be one penalty for the alien and the native. . ." (Lev. 24:21-22). Nevertheless, there is debate in the rabbinic tradition as to how widely applicable these laws are, especially the laws applying to Jewish murderers in a Jewish polity.

Despite the scriptural mandate for capital punishment, certainly for premeditated murder, there is a great debate regarding the extent to which this mandate could be put into actual practice. Thus two of the most influential sages of the second century of the first millennium, Rabbi Tarfon and Rabbi Akivah, stated that had they been in the Sanhedrin — the Jewish supreme court — when Jews did have the political power to administer capital punish-ment in their own community, no one would have ever been executed.[5] They would not have been executed because almost none of them *could* be exe-cuted according to the law. Clearly, for theological reasons, these rabbis could not justify this opinion by declaring their opposition to the scriptural man-dates of capital punishment. Scriptural mandates may never be repealed be-cause the law of God cannot be corrected by humans; it can only correct them.[6] Instead, later sages explained their opinion by arguing that they would have interpreted the laws of evidence so strictly that, in fact, if not in princi-ple, it would never be possible to officially sentence anyone to death.[7] In other words, being stricter as regards the laws of evidence *de jure* enables one to be more lenient regarding the death penalty *de facto*. In effect, then, they would make the mandate for capital punishment a null class, which is a legal fiction. And, if anyone asked why Scripture would mandate what is in effect a null class, they could answer that the purpose of the law is moral instruction about the gravity of the crime of homicide. As was said about another such law, one involving the death penalty for a juvenile delinquent, where some rabbis also argued for a null class, stating "it never was applied and never will be," the purpose of the law is theoretical — namely, that those who study it are to "be rewarded for ethical reflection about it" *(darosh ve-qabbel sekhar)*.[8]

It is important to connect the legal views of Rabbi Akivah especially — who was the most prominent of the early rabbis — with his theology. One of the cardinal points of his theology is that the essence of humanness is that humans are created in the "image of God" *(tselem elohim)*, which seems to mean that there is a sacred dimension to human life itself: human beings are the objects of particular divine concern or providence.[9] So, even though the victim of homicide is designated by Scripture to be made "in the image of God" (Gen. 9:6), and that is the reason his murderer is to be executed, the murderer too is no less made in the image of God. As such, even the execution of the murderer, to use the words of Rabbi Akivah in another vital context, is "as if one diminished [*k'ilu me'et*] the divine likeness."[10]

Moreover, if Kant's second formulation of the categorical imperative —

5. M. Makkor 1.10.

6. See, e.g., B. Kiddushin 29a re Num. 15:23.

7. B. Makkot 7a.

8. B. Sanhedrin 71a.

9. M. Avot 3.14.

10. *Bereshit Rabbah* 34.14, ed. Theodor-Albeck (Jerusalem: Wahrmann, 1965), p. 326. See B. Yevamot 63b. Another version of this idea says that "one indeed destroys [*hareh hu mevatel*] the divine image" (T. Yevamot 8.7). Cf. T. Sanhedrin 9.7 re Deut. 21:23.

namely, that a person always be treated as an end-in-himself-or-herself
(*Zweck an sich selbst*) — is taken as a secular version of the doctrine of the image of God *(imago Dei)*, then we would certainly have to dispense with the
most frequently cited reason for the death penalty.[11] That reason is that by executing one murderer now, we deter many would-be murderers from mur-
dering in the near future. Following the theology of Rabbi Akivah and the
philosophy of Kant, we could not execute anyone for this reason, inasmuch as
it would be taking one human life for the sake of saving other human lives.
But that is unacceptable because it means the life of the murderer is being
turned into a means for the end of another life. Similar logic is at stake in the
rabbinic principle that one is "not to set aside one human life for another"
(ein dohin nefesh mipnei nafesh), unless that one life is directly threatening the
life of another.[12] And, as another rabbinic text famously put it, "Whoever destroys even one other human life [*nefesh ahat*], Scripture ascribes guilt to him
as if [*k'ilu*] he destroyed an entire world [*olam mal'e*]."[13]

The opposing view, enunciated by Rabban Simeon ben Gamliel, argues
that if this legal fiction, which makes capital punishment for homicide a null
class, were actually in force, the effect would be to "increase murderers in Israel."[14] The usual interpretation of this more stringent view is that it assumes
that capital punishment as a real social institution is required for the deter-
rence of homicide. Thus, in what seems to be a view consistent with that of
Rabban Simeon ben Gamliel, another sage, Rabbi Hanina the vice-High
Priest, argued that Jews need to pray for the success of the Roman government. But isn't this the same Roman government that destroyed the Temple,
the religious center of the Jewish people, and the same Roman government
that squashed Jewish sovereignty by its defeat of the army of Bar Kokhba? His
reason, nonetheless, is that without such governmental authority and power,
"a person would swallow his fellow person alive."[15] Surely he had the widespread Roman use of the death penalty in mind. And, as is best known from
the execution of Jesus of Nazareth, the Roman government often used capital
punishment as a way of maintaining political order because of what they believed to be its deterring effects as well as the effect of eliminating those likely
to again cause trouble for the Roman authorities.

Conversely, those sages who would have probably been closer to the more

11. See Kant, *Groundwork of the Metaphysics of Morals*, trans. H. J. Paton (New York: Harper
& Row, 1964), pp. 95-99.

12. M. Ohalot 7.6. Cf. M. Sanhedrin 8.5; Novak, *Jewish Social Ethics*, pp. 168-69.

13. M. Sanhedrin 4.5. See Maimonides, *Mishneh Torah: Sanhedrin*, 12.3.

14. M. Makkot 1.10.

15. M. Avot 3.2.

lenient views of Rabbi Tarfon and Rabbi Akivah at times expressed their disapproval of how easily, carelessly, and guiltlessly the Romans used the power of capital punishment.[16] Indeed, one could see Jewish revulsion at the prevalence of capital punishment in their society, which they did not control politically. This revulsion was a major factor in their decision to rule quite differently what they hoped would be the future society they would control politically and legally according to more accurate criteria of justice.

For this same reason, the Romans removed the power of capital punishment from their Jewish captives, since, presumably, this power over life and death was inappropriate for a captive people to administer for themselves or for anyone else. All killing was to be done by the Roman rulers alone and for their purposes alone. In fact, when Jews did regain the power of capital punishment for a while from their Christian host society in fourteenth-century northern Spain, they seem to have adopted the view of the political necessity of capital punishment, even dispensing with some of the stricter standards of evidence of the earlier rabbinic tradition.[17] This dispensation was justified on the grounds that the needs of political order required it. One could no longer assume, as much of Jewish tradition did assume, that homicide was extremely rare among the Jewish people. As the Rabbis had to admit in another dispensation from a traditional Jewish law pertaining to homicide, "the murderers had increased."[18] Nevertheless, it could also very well be argued that this departure from the tradition of greater caution in capital cases was required by the Christian host society — namely, that Jewish legal practice be consistent with Christian legal practice. If that is the case, then this Jewish departure from the tradition of caution should not be taken as a precedent for what Jews should do when they do not have to conform to the standards of others — that is, when Jews either have a state of their own or are full citizens in a state that is neither Jewish nor Christian but fully secular.

The main aspect of the Jewish law of homicide that makes capital punishment very rare — something, by the way, never disputed in principle even by seemingly pro-death-penalty jurists of the view of Rabban Simeon ben Gamliel — is the practice of *hatra'ah,* or "forewarning." This practice assumes that the only way one can assume malice aforethought in the crime of homicide, thus differentiating it from what today we would mostly consider to be manslaughter, is if the criminal had been explicitly forewarned by the same

16. See, e.g., B. Gittin 28b.

17. See Y. Baer, *A History of the Jews in Christian Spain,* trans. L. Schoffman (Philadelphia: Jewish Publication Society, 1978), vol. 1, pp. 232-33.

18. M. Sotah 9.9.

witnesses who witnessed the crime itself.[19] In other words, we need explicit evidence that the fully conscious intention of the criminal had been to violate a law of whose content and consequences he or she was fully aware. This fore-warning consists of the witnesses explicitly informing the criminal just about to commit the crime of three things: (1) the fact that the act he or she is about to commit is proscribed by the Torah; (2) the exact punishment for which he or she will be liable if he performs the proscribed act; and (3) the exact status of the would-be victim in a case of a crime of aggression. The explicit evidence also includes verbal indication by the would-be criminal back to the same would-be witnesses just before committing the crime that he or she intends to commit the crime anyway. Accordingly, the burden of proof is on the accuser, on the prosecutor, to show that the person charged with homicide explicitly demonstrated that he or she was *compos mentis* in the most complete sense possible. Yet it is extraordinarily difficult for this to happen. Even when crimes are actually witnessed by others, the presence of these others is rarely known in advance. In fact, foreknowledge of the presence of witnesses by a would-be criminal would probably deter all but the most foolhardy from actually carrying out criminal intentions.

Whether what might be termed this legal "ritual" was ever actually practiced by the Jews is difficult to say. Nevertheless, its actual practice would be extremely rare for another reason, which is the biblical commandment "You shall not stand idly by the blood of your neighbor" (Lev. 19:16), which the Rabbis interpreted to mean a positive obligation to rescue someone from imminent mortal danger.[20] That being so, wouldn't two witnesses who could get close enough to warn a would-be assailant just about to attack his or her would-be victim be in a position to save the would-be victim from homicide — even if that meant killing the would-be assailant rather than wasting precious time warning him or her against committing the crime? As such, could one not assume that the practice of *hatra'ah* might have been invented by those who agreed with Rabbi Tarfon and Rabbi Akivah that the law of the death penalty be, in effect, a null class? Also, since the practice of *hatra'ah* is not disputed in general — there only being dispute about some of its more specific aspects — it seems that the only difference between those rabbis who seemed to be anti-death-penalty and those who seemed to be pro-death-penalty is that the pro-death-penalty rabbis would interpret the laws of evidence somewhat more leniently than the anti-death-penalty rabbis, epitomized by the view of Rabbi Tarfon and Rabbi Akivah as interpreted by later scholars.

19. B. Sanhedrin 40b-41a.
20. B. Sanhedrin 73a.

Comparing the traditional Jewish law of the penalty for homicide with current American legal practice in this same area, or at least current American legal practice in most states and in federal jurisdictions, indicates that we execute criminals far more easily. Such practices as self-incrimination and the use of circumstantial evidence (that is, the absence of eyewitnesses) to cause a conviction for homicide, which we find in our own society's legal practices, are proscribed by traditional Jewish law.[21] Moreover, this greater stringency of the Jewish law pertaining to the death penalty is even the case with what the Rabbis envisioned to be the standards Jews could accept and respect when practiced by gentile societies. Here the Rabbis assumed that one could be convicted for homicide on the testimony of one witness rather than two, and without the forewarning of *hatra'ah*.[22] Nevertheless, even here, there would be far less capital punishment than in our society today because the chance for error in judgment would be far less.

Of course, here again, because of the primacy of Scripture (which influenced common law cases until the twentieth century) no one could advocate on traditional Jewish grounds that the death penalty, especially for the crime of homicide, be abolished. But on these same traditional Jewish grounds, one could argue that the law of capital punishment is more symbolic than real. This is especially convincing when one questions whether the death penalty really is a deterrent and that without its active practice, chances increase of a greater number of homicides. Here again, Jews might question the depth of the commitment of our society to the sanctity of human life. This is also at the heart of the rabbinic principle that "when there is any doubt regarding human life [*safeq nefashot*], the benefit of the doubt should be in favor of the human life" — even when that human life is very likely the life of a murderer.[23] That does not mean, though, that we might not devise other ways to protect society from those whose guilt and presumed danger to society are less than perfectly ascertained. That is, this concern for human life does not rule out the institution of imprisonment, even for a life term.

Public Crimes

The Rabbis were also aware of some basic differences between what might be termed "public crime" as distinct from what we have seen as "private crime."

21. See A. Kirschenbaum, *Self-Incrimination in Jewish Law* (New York: Burning Bush Press, 1970).

22. See *Bereshit Rabbah* 34.14.

23. B. Shabbat 129a and parallels. See also B. Sanhedrin 78a and Tos., s.v. "be-goses."

By public crime I mean a crime ordered by the leaders of a society — even if that society be a band of pirates, whom one can judge al-Qaeda to be, even when governments who support their operations deny they do so. Indeed, a pirate used to be placed in the category of "enemy of the human race" (*hostis humani generis*).[24] The crime is even more public if it is ordered after a public declaration of intent by the leaders of a society, and it is most public when it is directed toward the extermination of all the members of another society — that is, *genocide.*

Concerning the ordering of a crime, note the following rabbinic dispute:

> One who says to another, "Go and kill another person [*ha-nafesh*]," the one who killed is liable [*hayyav*], but the one who sent him is exempt [*patur*]. Shammai the Elder in the name of Haggai the prophet says "The one who sent him is also liable." This is based on Scripture, "You killed him with the sword of the Ammonites" (2 Samuel 12:9).[25]

The killer here is King David, who, it will be recalled, ordered his general, Joab, to place his soldier Uriah the Hittite, the husband of the king's paramour Bathsheba, in a battle situation where Uriah was certain to be killed.[26] The king's orders, though, were followed unquestioningly by Joab, who again and again proved that his loyalty to his king took precedence over everything else, even over the divine law of justice.

Subsequent discussion in the Talmud, however, qualifies this dispute by assuming that the first (anonymous) sage is not saying that the one who instigates a murder is totally innocent.[27] Rather, the dispute is over the extent of guilt. Haggai the prophet (as reported by Shammai the Elder) is assumed to assign direct guilt (*dina rabba*) to the instigator of the homicide, whereas the first sage is assumed to assign indirect guilt (*dina zuta*) to him. Furthermore, there is an attempt to argue that the citation of the charge against King David made by the prophet Nathan is no source of law for other cases because it involved a special case of divine revelation for David alone.[28] Clearly, the editors of the Talmud accepted the principle "There is no agency for sin" (*ein shaliah le-dvar aveirah*), whose purpose seems to place direct responsibility on the actual perpetrators of a crime, and not allow them to divert responsibility onto those who had been "bad influences" on

24. See Arendt, *Eichmann in Jerusalem*, p. 261.
25. B. Kiddushin 43a.
26. 2 Sam. 12:1-24.
27. B. Kiddushin 43a.
28. B. Kiddushin 43a.

them.[29] As for these bad influences, the most that they could be guilty of in a human court is the violation of the scriptural norm "You shall not place a stumbling block before the blind" (Lev. 19:14), which the Rabbis interpreted to mean leading the morally obtuse astray, but by no means relieving them of their moral responsibility thereby.[30] Here leading someone astray is much less of a crime than the act of the one who chose to be so led astray — that is, one who should have known better. The question is whether or not a king is an ordinary instigator of a crime committed by someone following his orders and over whom the king, as commander-in-chief, has the power of life and death.

The fifteenth-century Jewish statesman and theologian Don Isaac Abravanel, contrary to the drift of the Talmudic discussion, considers the prophetically condemned act of King David to be paradigmatic. In fact, he sees another example of such officially ordered — but not directly implemented — murder in the case of the priests of Nob, who were murdered according to the order of King David's predecessor, King Saul.[31] Thus he writes, "The reason for this is because he was a king, and no one violates his command. Therefore, it is as if [*k'ilu*] he himself killed him."[32] Kings have the power of life and death over their subjects, and even though later rabbis ruled that one should die rather than kill someone else due to an unjust decree, the fact is that very few people would risk their lives by defying someone as powerful as a king.[33] And it helps our appreciation of this insight to know that Abravanel was a man who held high state posts in Spain, Portugal, and Venice, and who thus had intimate knowledge of how political power operates in the world. Political power, when unencumbered by moral and legal restraint, frequently operates as terror. Abravanel more than the other Jewish thinkers on these questions certainly knew that from his own experiences of state.

What we learn from this is that the essential difference between private and public murder is that in private murder we are to punish the direct perpetrator of the crime far more severely than the instigator of the crime; whereas in public murder, which is the murder ordered by political leaders (however informally the political state or organization might be structured), we are to punish those who ordered the crime at least as severely, and often more severely, than we are to punish the actual perpetrators of the crime. The

29. B. Kiddushin 42b.
30. B. Pesahim 22b.
31. 1 Sam. 22:9-19.
32. *Commentary on the Earlier Prophets:* 2 Sam. 12. See Maimonides, MT: Laws of Murder, 4.9.
33. See B. Pesahim 25b; B. Sanhedrin 74a.

actual practice of the Nuremberg court, which followed this kind of logic, concretized Abravanel's biblical speculation so as to make it a real precedent in law.

Abravanel is silent on the question of whether the errant kings of Israel, Saul and David, could be tried before a human court, or whether their judgment is to be left to God alone. Since in the biblical account, David was indicted by the prophet Nathan but not by human judges, it would seem that his judgment and those of other kings would have to be left to God's own ways of rendering justice, ways only known and only made knowable by a prophet. Nevertheless, rabbinic opinion is divided on this question. One view is that only God is above the king, so only God can judge him.[34] But another view is that the king is both to "judge and be judged" *(danin oto)*, or, as a later sage put it, "If he is not to be judged by others, how can he judge them?!"[35] This latter opinion seems to have been preferred by later theologians.[36]

If we accept the validity of human judgment of a king (or any political potentate), who is justly authorized to judge him? If humans are to judge him, then those humans who can judge him now are to be preferred to those humans who might be able to judge him better but later. Justice delayed is often justice denied. The most effective justice is the justice that can be done at present. Following this logic, it would seem that the optimal judge of such a public criminal would be a court authorized by his own people. In fact, wouldn't their judgment of their own leader restore their national honor, which the terrorist — even genocidal — acts of their leader had so tainted? Thus, if rabbinic tradition permits a king to be judged by his own people when judgment is called for, then isn't this permission in effect a mandate to the people to judge their king? Along these lines, the great medieval Jewish jurist and theologian Maimonides argues that the people of the biblical city of Shechem were guilty for not having judged their crown prince when he openly abducted and raped Dinah, the daughter of the patriarch Jacob (Gen. 34:1).[37] Because of this dereliction of public duty by the Shechemites, the brothers of the victim were entitled to effect justice themselves. The implication of this interpretation is that if the people of Shechem had done their public duty, the brothers of Dinah would not have been entitled to avenge the crime committed against their sister, which they recognized to be something "not to be done" (Gen. 34:7) — that is, not to be done anywhere and to be

34. Y. Sanhedrin 2.3/20a re Ps. 17:2.
35. B. Sanhedrin 19a re Zeph. 2:1.
36. See Maimonides, MT: Sanhedrin, 2.5.
37. Maimonides, MT: Kings, 9.14.

punished by anyone when the local authorities are either incapable or unwilling to take appropriate judicial action.[38]

Wouldn't a trial of Eichmann — or, optimally, of Hitler — by the German people have provided the world with the most satisfying form of justice? And wouldn't a trial of Osama bin Laden by an Islamic court, whose law he claims to be following, be the optimal venue for his trial? Wouldn't that be an act of supreme theological and political responsibility? Yet in order for this trial to take place, the criminal would first have to be apprehended by his own people. If they could not or would not apprehend him, then they are in no position politically, and probably legally as well, to try him. The will to justice that the execution of justice requires was not there and is not here. The sad fact is that the Germans did not apprehend Adolf Eichmann in 1961, although that capture would have been easy; and bin Laden has operated with and was protected by the militantly Islamic regime of the Taliban in Afghanistan. Furthermore, no other Islamic regime seems willing to or even interested in apprehending bin Laden and his associates.

That leaves the apprehension of a genocidal war criminal either to an international court or to a court of the people targeted for genocide who have, nonetheless, survived and, in some cases, like that of the Jews, have even become more politically powerful after their survival. The fact that there is no international court (and that includes, it seems to me, the newly constituted International Court of Justice) capable of meting out what most would consider full and swift justice rules out any real hope that such a court could be trusted with a criminal as dangerous as Osama bin Laden. Accordingly, we are only left with a court of the survivors, who seem to be the second-best alternative in principle, but the only real alternative in practice.

A good biblical precedent for this judicial alternative is the execution of the Amalekite king Agag by the prophet Samuel. The Amalekites were a people who engaged in what we would today call terrorism. They indiscriminately attacked the "faint and the weary" (Deut. 25:18) — that is, they killed noncombatants for no military reason. In fact, later biblical tradition saw the plan of the Persian prime minister Haman to "utterly destroy" *(l'abbdam)* the Jews (Esther 3:9) to be the result of his being a literal and spiritual descendant of Agag. He was "Haman the Agagite, persecutor of the Jews" (Esther 3:10). Now it seems that optimal justice would have been fulfilled if the Amalekites themselves had executed their terrorist king. In fact, Maimonides, who is the only medieval theologian to fully codify the rabbinic laws pertaining to the conduct of the state, rules that even the Amalekites would be spared mass de-

---

38. See Maimonides, MT: Sanhedrin, 26.7.

struction by the people of Israel if they would repudiate their terrorist tradition and adhere to universally applicable laws.[39] Two of these laws are the rule that every society judge and convict its own criminals *(dinim)*, and the rule that every society prohibit murder *(shefikhut dammim)*.[40] Thus, in order for the nation of Amalek to redeem itself, it would have to execute justice against itself in the person of its leader. The fact that they did not do this, and the fact that Saul the king of Israel wanted to compromise with a fellow king, required that the prophet Samuel, who was the judicial leader of the people, try and convict Agag himself, even though this unusual case called for unusual methods of execution. He justified his act by stating to Agag at the time of his execution, "Just as your sword made women childless, so may your mother be made childless" (1 Sam. 15:33). Samuel did to Agag what the Israelis later did to Adolf Eichmann and what the Americans should do to Osama bin Laden — if they ever have the opportunity to do so.

Public Forewarning

The second difference between private and public murder centers on the question of forewarning *(hatra'ah)*. It will be recalled that if a murderer is tried according to traditional Jewish law, then he or she must have been forewarned by the witnesses to the crime, and that he or she must have verbally indicated full awareness of the contents of the forewarning. However, certain rabbinic sources may enable us to see things differently in cases of public murder, especially genocide, and especially when the leaders under consideration have announced their program in public.

The first relevant opinion in the Talmud, albeit an opinion subsequently judged to be a minority opinion, is that a rabbinical scholar, then called a "fellow" *(haver)*, does not require forewarning in order to be convicted of a crime for which premeditation is an essential factor.[41] Premeditation *(mezeed)* can only be assumed when the person about to commit the crime is fully aware of the prohibition of the act about to be committed, fully aware of the legal consequences if the act is committed, and fully aware that the object of the act — the would-be victim — is the true object of the prohibition (that is, in the case of murder, the witness must inform the would-be assailant who the would-be victim is). In addition, the would-be assailant must indicate that he

---

39. Maimonides, MT: Kings, 6.4. See Novak, *Jewish Social Ethics,* pp. 187-201.

40. B. Sanhedrin 56b.

41. B. Sanhedrin 8b.

or she knows that the would-be victim is the true object of the prohibition.[42] Anything less than this full awareness makes the crime subject to the penalties for inadvertence *(shogeg)*, very much akin to what we now call manslaughter, which are always something less than the death penalty. Therefore, in the case of someone who knows the law and is also considered to be quite perceptive, we may assume that such a person has already been forewarned for any prohibited act he or she may be tempted to perform. Surely, the ruler of a society, a maker of public policy, or a political leader falls into this already-forewarned category.

Despite the fact that the view that learned persons do not require forewarning is a minority view in cases of private murder, in cases of crimes of negligence not involving murder, there is a majority opinion that public officials are already forewarned by virtue of their public office *(ke-mutrin v'omdin)*.[43] Perhaps one could conclude that the above opinion (that of Rabbi Yose, son of Rabbi Judah) was only rejected in the case of a private murder committed by a public official, but that it might apply to a case of a public murder being ordered by a public official. Such a process of contextualization, what some have called casuistry, is very common in the ongoing process of rabbinic jurisprudence.

An even better source, though, is the rabbinic opinion that states that before one can be convicted to be punished by the death penalty, one has to have "permitted himself for death" *(hiteer atsmo le-meetah)*.[44] What does this rather opaque phrase mean? There are three interpretations. One: It means that by accepting the forewarning, yet violating its proscription anyway, the would-be criminal has sentenced himself or herself to death.[45] Two: It means that the forewarning could even be uttered by the would-be victim to the would-be assailant just before the crime is committed.[46] (This is what some rabbis imagine Abel did just before being murdered by his brother Cain.)[47] Three: It means that the murderer forewarns himself or herself *(hayah matreh b'atsmo)*.[48] In other words, the would-be murderer defies the law he or she knows, violates the victim whose protected status he or she knows, and takes

42. Maimonides, MT: Sanhedrin, 12.1-2.

43. B. Baba Metsia 109ab. See Maimonides, MT: Employment, 10.7 and *Magid Mishneh* thereon.

44. B. Sanhedrin 40b.

45. B. Sanhedrin 40b, Rashi, s.v. "hitir" thereon. See T. Sanhedrin 11.4.

46. B. Makkot 6b, Rashi, "mi-pi atsmo" thereon.

47. See Louis Ginzberg, *Legends of the Jews,* trans. H. Szold (Philadelphia: Jewish Publication Society, 1909), vol. 1, p. 109.

48. Maimonides, MT: Sanhedrin, 12.2, *Kesef Mishneh* thereon.

responsibility for his or her act in advance. Clearly such an act of self-recognition places the would-be murderer in the class of a "defiant rebel" *(mumar le-hakh'is)*, which designates someone who violates the law out of conviction and not just out of appetite or even mindless passion *(mumar lete'avon)*.[49]

Would not a public murderer who, like Hitler or bin Laden (or, to a lesser but still culpable extent, Eichmann), orders public murders out of conviction, and who does so because of a publicly declared ideology — wouldn't such a leader qualify as one who is already forewarned? Don't their very public speeches and publications (Hitler's *Mein Kampf* immediately comes to mind) make any argument about their lack of full awareness ridiculous? Hence, I think a good case can be made for answering yes to this question. In fact, unlike the public murder of a private citizen conducted by King David, in which the king issued his death sentence for Uriah in a secret memorandum, and which was certainly not genocidal, the publicly justified acts of Hitler and bin Laden — with their frightening appeals to a law above what most persons would consider the natural law of God — seem to fit the joint category of publicly initiated murder *and* publicly declared and justified (that is, by the political leader) genocide. In such cases involving enemies of the human race, one could make the strongest possible argument for the death penalty that could come out of the whole Jewish tradition of moral and legal reflection for the sake of immediate justice in the world.

Nevertheless, I cannot in good faith conclude without recalling that one of the greatest sages quoted in the Talmud, Rabbi Meir, taught that God suffers even when the blood of the guilty *(damam shel resha'im)* has to be shed.[50] Perhaps in order to enable human judges to imitate the divine Judge, Rabbi Meir's teacher, Rabbi Akivah, ruled that human judges have to fast on the day the convicted criminal is being executed.[51] This is, no doubt, meant to be an act of atonement *(kapparah)*, like fasting on the Day of Atonement *(yom hakippurim)*. It is an act of atonement for what is necessary to do for justice, but which is tragic nonetheless.

---

49. B. Sanhedrin 27a.
50. M. Sanhedrin 6.5.
51. B. Sanhedrin 63a re Lev. 19:26.

22 A Jewish Argument for
Socialized Medicine (2003)

My concern with the question of socialized medicine and a Jewish approach to it has been greatly heightened by my experience in Canada during the last six and one-half years. I now hold citizenship in this country along with the American citizenship conferred upon me by my birth in the United States. I proudly retain my American citizenship because of what this country has done for me and my family going back a number of generations. I have not ceased to be an American, but as a Canadian I have a new basis for comparison of morally significant phenomena in my two countries.

As is well known, Canada provides health care for all of its citizens and residents. The United States, as is equally well known, does not provide universal health care. We all know that there are approximately 40 million Americans without any regular health care who have to depend on the arbitrary charity of public and private institutions. That sad fact came home to me almost twenty years ago when I had to take my wife to a hospital emergency room in New York City. There I saw the large number of poor people who had to use that emergency room as their primary health-care facility — that is, after the staff there could take time away from the paying patients. In our case, many of their more serious health problems had to wait for treatment until my wife's less serious problem was treated. Why? Because she had health insurance and they did not. They either never had any health insurance at all, or they had had it and lost it because it came with the jobs they had lost. So, despite all the problems faced by Canadian health-care services — such as the elective surgery for which I have been waiting now for almost a year — I firmly believe that health-care delivery in Canada is fundamentally just and health-care delivery in the United States is fundamentally unjust. As an American and a Canadian, the question I need to address is why this belief of mine is rationally justified. But, more importantly, as a Jew, I need to base this belief of mine on the authoritative sources of the living Jewish tradition.

Problems with Medicine

I shall begin with a rather shocking rabbinic text, one that has embarrassed many Jews, especially because of the long Jewish involvement in medicine. The Mishnah states that Rabbi Judah said in the name of Abba Gurya, a man of Sidon, "The best of the physicians belongs in hell [*tov she-ba-rof'im le-gehinnom*]!"[1] In his Talmud commentary, Rashi, the great eleventh-century French commentator, gives four reasons for this seemingly harsh judgment.[2] First, physicians are not apprehensive about disease and let sick people eat food that is only fit for healthy people. Two, physicians do not pray — literally, "break their hearts" — to God. Three, there are times when physicians actually kill humans. And four, physicians have the power to heal the poor, and they do not heal them. Each of these reasons for a harsh indictment of ancient medicine could be applied to modern medicine as well.

Preventive Medicine

The first reason addresses what might be considered preventive medicine. In ancient times, this was a much greater factor in medicine than it has been in modern times. Even though Rashi was a medieval thinker, he was still much closer to the ancient world than to the modern world, so he could identify more easily than we can with the situation of medicine in the ancient world assumed by the Mishnah.[3] Back then, physicians probably engaged as much — and maybe even more — in prescribing healthy living to their patients as they did in treating the bad effects of their patients' often unhealthy lives.[4] Today, except for the annual physical examination that most of us older than

---

1. M. Kiddushin 4.14.

2. B. Kiddushin 82a, Rashi, s.v. "tov she ba-rof'im."

3. See Rashi, *Commentary on the Torah*, ed. C. Chavel (Jerusalem: Mossad ha-Rav Kook, 1982), Exod. 15:26.

4. In Aristotelian terms, the first type of medical practice is a form of distributive justice — that is, who deserves/needs what. The second type of medical treatment is a form of corrective justice — that is, restoring what originally belonged to someone and has been taken away (see *Nicomachean Ethics*, 1130b-1132a19). This concept is important to invoke here so as to prepare the reader for the analogies between the practice of medicine and the practice of justice discussed later in this essay.

fifty get from our private physicians, or that insurance companies occasionally require us to undergo, the majority of people deal with physicians on a crisis basis. Rashi reminds us that physicians ought to be our teachers even before they are our rescuers. If preventive medicine was wanting in his day, how much more so is it in our day, when physicians are required by HMOs to see more and more patients in less and less time.

Religious Medicine

The second reason for Rashi's condemnation of physicians brings up a delicate problem, especially in a multicultural, secular society like ours. Can we expect our physicians to pray? Of course, if one regards the practice of medicine to be something totally mundane, something that is no different in essence from having one's car repaired, then the relationship of the physician to God is unimportant. But the fact is that few of us regard our bodies, which physicians treat, to be a commodity like our cars. We *are* our bodies, which we cannot treat like a thing. To say I own my body is to say that I created or acquired my body, which is untrue. My body is not *mine;* it is *me.* It is personal. Moreover, I cannot destroy my body without destroying myself. I am not related to my body as something detachable from myself, like anything I have made or acquired. Therefore, either my body/myself has been purposely made by someone greater than myself and all those like me, or my body/myself is only an accident. But, if I regard my being made as an accident for which no one is responsible, how can I act purposefully and responsibly myself? Certainly my own projects, my own self-created purposes are not powerful enough to overcome the basic absurdity of the universe of which I am but a tiny part. Therefore, how the physician looks upon his or her own body/self is of great importance in determining how he or she looks at my body/self. Our bodies and the bodies of all others have enough sanctity to dispel the notion that we are but things, but not enough self-sufficiency to embrace the notion that we are gods. Since we did not make or acquire our bodies, they are not things. Since we did not make or acquire ourselves, we are not gods.

Since few of us regard our bodies to be a mere commodity, few of us would regard a physician, to whom we allow the most intimate access to our bodies next to that of our mates, to be a mere mechanic. A physician comes closest to God in our experience of bodily dependence in the world. That, of course, opens the physician up to the temptation of thinking he or she really is God. In fact, a large part of the current appeal of the field of "biomedical ethics" stems from our fear that physicians, due to their vast power derived from the vast expansion of medical technology, have been "playing God" in an unlimited way that is unbecoming any mortal creature. We want physicians to be answerable to standards not of their own making — that is, not made by them for their own self-interest. The great power of physicians also helps to explain the staggering cost of medical malpractice suits in the United States. It seems to many that litigation is the only real check that ordinary citizens have on what would otherwise be medical omnipotence. Perhaps the Jewish tradition had the "God complex" temptation of physicians in mind when it occasionally made some negative remarks about medical practice.[5]

The irony is that the vast expansion of medical technology has made physicians much less likely to think of themselves as mechanics. In our so-called secular age, we use the term *miracle* more often than did our supposedly more religious ancestors. How many times have we heard the term *medical miracle* used in ordinary discourse and in the media? Needless to say, quite often. Given this, the question really is not "secular" versus "religious" medicine. When medical treatment is a serious matter of life and death, the question is better asked: Whose God? Whose God is the physician's? Whose God is the patient's?

Many years ago, as a young rabbi here in Washington, I visited a woman in the hospital on the day that she was to have a very serious, life-threatening operation. I asked her how she felt, and she told me, "I have absolute faith in my doctor!" Since she also asked me if what she said was right, I told her, "Save your absolute faith for God, and hope that your doctor is doing God's work." Being a religious person, she did not argue with me on that point. Not ever having met her physician, though, I cannot say whether I could have said the same thing to him — namely, "Have faith in God and hope you are doing God's work."

It would seem, nevertheless, that most of us would not want to be treated by a physician who thought he or she was God. Why not? Because it is clearly not true, and any physician who thinks he or she is God is not likely to have the patient as the object of his or her prime concern. Those who lie to themselves are in a bad position to be truthful with others and likely will fail to recognize these others for what they truly are. Instead, such physicians will be much more concerned with their "God-like" reputation.[6] It would seem that the best physician, for us patients, is one whose concern *for* us is greater than his or her power *over* us. It is best for both patients and their physicians to regard themselves as participants in a process that no human creature either

5. See, e.g., 2 Chron. 16:12; M. Pesahim 4.9. Cf. Sir. 38:1-14.

6. For a modern critique of this whole mind-set, see Robert Mendelsohn, *Confessions of a Medical Heretic* (Chicago: Contemporary Books, 1979), pp. 123-40.

has been able to initiate or will be able to conclude. No human creature has the creator's unique power either to create life or to create life beyond death. This perspective best prepares patients to expect only partial care and, even more, only partial cure from their physicians, and physicians to expect only partial success for their patients. After all, life itself can be seen as a terminal disease. Even if a miracle does occur, which means something beyond our normal expectations, the physician is its conduit, not its creator. Minimally, that means patients would want physicians who do not think they are God, and who therefore do not expect worship from us. In other words, medicine should avoid idolatry, which for Judaism is the sin of all sins.[7] Both the patient and the physician are part of the same process, and the pre-eminence of the physician over the patient is only a difference of degree, not a difference in kind. They are both members of the same species, not only biologically but morally and spiritually as well.[8]

Maximally, from a Jewish perspective, the converse of medical idolatry is that both the physician and the patient have a positive relationship with God, what Judaism would call a *covenant*. But in a secular or even a multicultural society, a positive relationship with God is neither something that patients can require of their physicians nor that physicians can require of their patients. Conversely, the rejection of idolatry is indeed something that any human can ask of any other human. It is rationally demonstrable. In other words, one can say, "From the very meaning of the name 'God' — even if you are not sure there really is a God — it is obvious you are not God." However, a positive relationship with God can come only from the acceptance of God's revelation to a particular community in history. One cannot argue someone else into faith the way one can — at least theoretically — argue someone else out of idolatry. Only God can inspire faith. Even the coercion of a good argument will not work here. So, even in a secular context, where one cannot assume one's physician will be of the same faith or any faith, one still can be wary of physicians whose faith is in themselves and who expect similar devotion from their patients.

Careless Medicine

Rashi's third reason for condemning physicians is that they can and do kill. Of course, Rashi could well be referring to medical carelessness, the type of malpractice we all dread, when the physician has not taken the proper pre-

---

7. See B. Kiddushin 40a re Jer. 6:19; also, Mendelsohn, *Confessions of a Medical Heretic.*
8. See Benjamin Freedman, *Duty and Healing* (New York: Routledge, 1999), pp. 152-86.

cautions in treating the perilous situation in which patients often find themselves.[9] Here is the stuff of malpractice suits, which now so often elide the difference between human fallibility and human culpability. Nevertheless, taking Rashi's comment as not only insightful but prescient, we are reminded of the situation today in which some physicians insist that it is now their duty to enable patients to end their lives in voluntary death just as much as it always has been their duty to enable patients to continue their lives voluntarily. This transformation of physicians from angels of life into angels of death, which means turning them into executioners as well as practitioners, goes against all traditions about medicine.

For most of us, medicine always should be about, maximally, the saving of human life; minimally, the comforting of human life — but never about the deliberate termination of human life.[10] (Physicians who perform non-lifesaving abortions are in this category too.[11] And I would even put in this category physicians who administer lethal injections for the state in cases of capital punishment.) This new situation, though, is a corollary of the divinity that some have invested in modern, technologically advanced physicians. Like all false gods, the creator is actually the creature. As such, the real creator here, which is human projection, can demand of its divinized creature, which is modern medicine, that it deliver what its creator wants, even if it is a request for self-immolation. Idolatry is involved here too, since one only would turn one's body over to the life-and-death power of a person one considered a god. The other alternative, the physician as mechanic, does not explain the fascination of a Dr. Kevorkian.

Commercial Medicine

Rashi's fourth reason for the condemnation of physicians — that they fail to heal the poor — brings us directly to my main topic: how societies should authorize and fund medical treatment for their citizens and residents. I have analyzed Rashi's other three reasons first, since I believe all four reasons hang together in a logical sequence. That is, ignoring preventive medicine can lead to the notion of medicine as, in essence, a miraculous intervention in a crisis, and this can lead to regarding one's death-bringing powers to be on a par

9. For notions of medical malpractice in rabbinic sources, see T. Gittin 3.8; T. Baba Kama 9.11.

10. See B. Shabbat 151b; David Novak, *Law and Theology in Judaism* (New York: Ktav Publishing House, 1974-76), vol. 2, pp. 98-106.

11. See B. Sanhedrin 57b re Gen. 9:6; B. Sanhedrin 59a and Tos., s.v. "leeka"; Novak, *Law and Theology in Judaism*, vol. 1, pp. 114-24.

with one's life-bringing powers — that is, one may exercise medical power in the most powerful way, be it for life or for death. And, finally, this in turn can lead to regarding the practice of medicine as a type of entrepreneurship practiced by pagan gods, who solicit increasingly opulent offerings from their worshipers in return for favors granted.[12] (In contrast, the ordinary mechanic, by only promising ordinary services, usually gets more ordinary reimbursement from his or her customers.)

Medicine as a Sanctified Profession

Rashi's condemnation of medicine as commerce seems to presuppose a prohibition of physicians' selling their services, and thus that they have no right to withhold their services from individuals who cannot pay. But where is this prohibition actually stated? It is a principle of Jewish law that one is not condemned for committing a sin unless that sin already has been prohibited.[13] Furthermore, if there is such a prohibition, is there also an imperative for one to become a physician who then may not sell his or her services on a *quid pro quo* basis?

There is a specific biblical prescription to save a human life, even if that requires intervention on the part of the rescuer. "You shall not stand idly by your neighbor's blood" (Lev. 19:16), which means you shall intervene by all means possible to save someone whose life is in danger.[14] This is considered a positive commandment of the Torah. Like all commandments of the Torah pertaining to interhuman relations, there is both a right and a correlative duty, or a claim to which there is a required response.[15] The right or claim is that of the person in mortal danger. This right is that person's claim on whomever has the power and the opportunity to rescue him or her from mortal danger to do so unconditionally. The duty or response is that of the person who has the power and opportunity to rescue the other person who is mortally threatened. The Torah, as the law, recognizes the right *(zekhut)* to be rescued from harm and thus commands rescue as a duty *(hovah)* to be performed by whomever is capable of doing so. The question now is this: May one claim reimbursement for his or her performance of the duty of rescue?

12. See Plato, *Euthyphro*, 14d-15a.

13. B. Sanhedrin 54ab.

14. Lev. 19:16. See B. Sanhedrin 73a; Maimonides, *Mishneh Torah:* Laws Regarding Murder, 1.5 re M. Sanhedrin 4.5.

15. See Novak, *Covenantal Rights* (Princeton: Princeton University Press, 2000), pp. 3-12.

There is a principle in the Talmud that answers this question: "The commandments [*mitsvot*] are not given for monetary benefit."[16] In other words, no one is to be paid for the performance of his or her duty, be that duty to God or to another human being. That being the case, if the practice of medicine is the performance of the duty of rescue, then it would seem that physicians — and, in fact, all those we today call "health-care professionals" — may not receive compensation for their services. But if this is indeed the case, then one might ask, Is a person expected to lose money in the performance of his or her divinely mandated duty? Wouldn't physicians be losing money by performing their duty for free? Wouldn't the performance of this duty for free take one away from the process of otherwise earning a living? It is true that some rabbis teach that one's reward for performing a commandment is to be found in the world-to-come, but not in this world.[17] However, should someone else benefit from my *regularly* performing a commandment on their behalf in this world while I am penalized for it by being prevented from making a living because of it? In the case of acts not specifically mandated by the Torah, I can accept payment for services rendered without any such theological impediment.

At the most extreme level, no human being has the right to ask another human being to die for him or her.[18] The most that can be said is that one human being has the right to die for another human being if he or she so chooses.[19] To make such a choice is commendable, but not to do so carries no penalty. Accordingly, no human being has the right to be rescued at the expense of the life of his or her rescuer. Nevertheless, no human being has the right to deprive another human being of the property — or means — necessary to rescue himself or herself from death. So, for example, if saving my life requires destroying some of your property, I have the right to destroy your property. You certainly do not have the right to withhold your property from me if it is needed to save my life.[20] However, you also have the right to compensation from me for your monetary loss.[21] Another example is pertinent as well: Even though there is a duty to give charity to the poor, the Rabbis decreed that this should not exceed twenty percent of one's annual income, the

---

16. B. Rosh Hashanah 28a.

17. B. Kiddushin 39b re Deut. 5:16 and 22:7. Cf. Tos., s.v. "matnitin" thereon.

18. B. Baba Metsia 62a re Lev. 25:36, the view of Rabbi Akiva, which is to be followed in any dispute he had with a colleague (see B. Eruvin 46b and parallels).

19. See Y. Terumot 8.4/46b; David Novak, *Jewish Social Ethics* (Oxford: Oxford University Press, 1992), pp. 111-14.

20. B. Sanhedrin 73a.

21. B. Sanhedrin 74a; M. Baba Kama 10.4. Cf. Maimonides, MT: Torts, 8.14.

reason being that one's generosity should not impoverish oneself or one's family.[22]

So, if this is the case, why can the physician not say to the patient, "As I am benefiting you with my services, you should benefit me by contributing to my support through paying a fee"? How is this any different from the grocer who rescues me from starvation by supplying me with food, for which nobody suggests I should not pay him or her — at least if I have the money to do so? Nevertheless, Jewish law follows the opinion of the great thirteenth-century Spanish-Jewish theologian-jurist Nahmanides (himself, like many of the medieval rabbis, a physician), who stated,

> As for the matter of payment for medical services [*sekhar refu'ah*], my opinion is that it is permitted to accept payment for the time and effort expended [*sekhar betalah ve-tirha*], but not payment for the actual medical prescription [*sekhar ha-limud*] since that involves the possible loss of life, and the Torah says "You shall return it to him [what he has lost]" — Deuteronomy 22:2. As for the performance of any commandment [*mitzvah*], it is to be for free [*be-hinam*].[23]

Yet how can one distinguish between the effort expended in the practice of medicine and the actual practice itself, which is prescription of one kind or another? Furthermore, the notion of payment for one's time expended is my loose translation of the Hebrew *sekhar betalah,* which literally means "payment for doing nothing." In other words, we are supposed to be paying the physician for not doing something other than conducting his or her medical practice — that is, for not doing whatever he or she would be doing if he or she were not a physician. This assumes, however, that we know what else a physician would be doing and what he or she would be willing to accept for not doing it.[24] Considering the amount of time and effort it takes to become a physician, the actual calculation of what this *other* profession might pay him or her, let alone what he or she would accept for not engaging in it, seems to be highly imaginative precisely because these alternatives do not exist. So, in order to make the *professional* distinction between a grocer and a physician a

22. B. Ketubot 50a; also T. Arakhin, 4.24-26. Even when performing commandments that are duties owed to God, where one is required to spend his or her money for the objects involved in these acts, one is not required to impoverish oneself because of them (see M. Negaim 12.5; M. Keritot 1.7; T. Niddah 9.17; also, B. Shabbat 118a; Maimonides, MT: Sabbath, 30.7).

23. Nahmanides, *Torat ha'Adam:* Inyan ha-Sakkanah, in *Kitvei Ramban,* ed. C. Chavel (Jerusalem: Mossad ha-Rav Kook, 1963), vol. 2, p. 44. The Talmudic source for the analogy of returning lost property and restoring life is on B. Sanhedrin 73a.

24. M. Baba Metsia 2.9.

real difference, one must view the practice of medicine as something very different from an ordinary job, even an ordinary job that benefits other people.

In the carefully worded text quoted above, Nahmanides states that he is expressing his own opinion. In rabbinic parlance this means that he has no explicit source for what he believes the law to be. Nonetheless, he cannot simply create a law *de novo*. As a rabbi he has no charismatic authority.[25] Therefore, his opinion in fact must be an inference he has made from an authoritative source in either the Bible or the Talmud (of which the Mishnah forms the basic text). His source is a statement in the Mishnah about judges who take money from the litigants who stand before them seeking justice.[26] The Mishnah rules that their judgments are null and void because, as one of the major commentators points out, this is considered to be akin to the violation of the biblical commandment "You shall not take a bribe."[27] In the ensuing discussion in the Talmud, the reason for this ruling is traced back to a statement of Moses: "See, I have taught you [statutes and ordinances] which the Lord my God commanded me."[28] From this the Talmud infers "Just as I taught you for free, so you should teach for free."[29] But, of course, Moses' authoritative teaching is what Jews call *hora'ah* — and what Catholics call *magisterium*.[30] As the verse itself states, it is authoritative because it comes from God. Moses is able to teach for free because of what God gave him for free, not as a reward for his righteousness, but as a message for the people to whom he is privileged to be God's messenger. In the Jewish tradition, Moses is the arch-rabbi, always being called *Mosheh Rabbenu,* "Moses our Teacher," whose rabbinical authority is primarily juridical. (In traditional Jewish communities, the primary — indeed, the essential — function of the rabbi is still that of judge, even though rabbis always have performed other "clerical" tasks as well.)

Medicine as a Calling

What do rabbis and physicians have in common to the exclusion of other socially useful professions? Their commonality is that each profession is meant to be a "calling" *(vocatio)* — that is, they are not mandated by ordinary commandments. Thus, in the case of saving human lives, the commandment

25. See B. Menahot 29b.
26. M. Bekhorot 4.6.
27. Deut. 16:19; B. Bekhorot 29a and Tos., s.v. "mah" re B. Ketubot 105a.
28. Deut. 4:5.
29. B. Bekhorot 29a.
30. See Y. Berakhot 4.5/8c re 2 Chron. 3:1.

"You shall not stand idly by the blood of your neighbor"[31] applies to anyone who happens to be in a situation where he or she can save somebody else's life. But where is one commanded to prepare for and devote himself or herself to the *profession* of saving lives, a profession that will clearly take all of one's time and energy? Based on his definition of the practice of medicine as a uniquely commanded activity, Nahmanides writes, "Any physician who knows this science and art [of medicine] is obligated [*hayyav hu*] to heal, and if he prevents himself from doing so, he has shed human blood."[32]

It would seem that even though everyone is commanded to save a human life whenever and wherever possible, to dedicate oneself to this as one's profession, one should regard himself or herself to have been *individually* called by God. Why? Because the profession of healing, the ongoing activity of *being* a physician, is an individual case of imitation of God *(imitatio Dei)*.[33] In the Torah, God says about himself, "I am the Lord your physician."[34] That is why, it seems, the Talmud refers to the individual practice of medicine as being a "dispensation [*reshut*] that is granted [*nitnah*] to the physician to heal."[35] Who gives this dispensation? God, the author of the law of the Torah, who is also the arch-physician. It is a dispensation because without it one might well think that the human practice of medicine is usurping a uniquely divine role in the world.[36]

This also might be why the practice of medicine is not called a "commandment" *(mitsvah)*. It only applies to someone who believes himself or herself to be *individually* called by this imperative. Hence we apply to it the word *reshut,* which very often means an option one can choose or not choose with legal impunity.[37] Unlike ordinary commandments, there is no way anyone else can tell whether somebody has been so commanded, so called. Whether one feels called to be a professional participant in the divine process of healing is too intimate a matter to be the subject of a general commandment.

Here the comparison of a physician to a judge can be developed further.

31. Lev. 19:16.

32. Nahmanides, *Torat ha'Adam,* p. 42.

33. Even the attendance to the need of the sick *(biqqur holim)* that is required of ordinary nonprofessionals is considered to be *imitatio Dei.* (See B. Sotah 14a re Gen. 18:1. Cf. Maimonides, MT: Mourning, 14.1 re Lev. 19:18.) Nevertheless, this *imitatio Dei* is not an individual option.

34. Exod. 15:26.

35. B. Baba Kama 85a re Exod. 21:19.

36. Nahmanides, *Commentary on the Torah:* Lev. 26:11; also, David Novak, *The Theology of Nahmanides Systematically Presented* (Atlanta: Scholars Press, 1992), pp. 83-87.

37. See, e.g., M. Whevuot 3.6.

There is a general commandment to practice justice — "Justice, justice you shall pursue" — which the Talmud interprets to mean seeking out the best possible judges.[38] Nevertheless, there is no general commandment for one to be a judge. That decision too is an individual case of the imitation of God, for in the Torah God also is designated as "the judge [ha-shofet] of all the earth."[39] In other words, just as a judge must feel individually called to heal the body politic in order to be adequate to the sanctity of the human community, so a physician must feel individually called to heal the human body in order to be adequate to its sanctity. Moreover, without the notion that the judge in the act of true judgment becomes, in the words of the Talmud, "a partner [shutaf] in the work of cosmic creation,"[40] the execution of justice becomes more and more mundane, more and more a matter of mere social utility.

The comparison of a physician to a judge is helpful in justifying universal health care, which means, among other things, that physicians do not work for fees directly paid to them by their patients, or even by private insurers of their patients. If judges were to be paid by those appearing before them for justice, then the judges would be in violation of the prohibition of taking bribes. Therefore, the Talmud answers that the judges in Jerusalem, who dealt with civil disputes involving Temple property, were paid out of Temple funds.[41] Later jurists argued that this payment of judges by the community, which made them civil servants, was the fact in the vast majority of Jewish communities everywhere. As the great twelfth-century French theologian-jurist Rabbenu Jacob Tam pointed out, the judges are not being paid by the litigants, and therefore the community is obligated to pay them, since they have no other source of income.[42] An approximate contemporary of Rabbenu Tam, Rabbi Judah the Barcelonian, mentions a special fund designated by the community for that purpose.[43]

Interestingly enough, on the very page of the Talmud where the distinction between private and public payment of judges is being worked out, there is a reference to the fact that physicians do take fees from their patients, and the text associates this with the sin of taking bribes.[44] This probably means that the community had much more control over the allocation of justice than it did over the allocation of medical services. Jewish physicians probably

38. Deut. 16:18; B. Sanhedrin 32b.
39. Gen. 18:25.
40. B. Sanhedrin 5b.
41. B. Ketubot 105a; see M. Sheqalim 4.1.
42. B. Ketubot 105a, Tos., s.v. "gozrei gezerot"; also, B. Bekhorot 29a, Tos., s.v. "mah."
43. Tur: Hoshen Mishpat, 9.
44. B. Ketubot 105a re Deut. 16:19.

were competing with non-Jewish physicians in a larger social context where there was no such thing as physicians being communal employees. Nonetheless, following the comparison of medical practice with judicial practice, it would seem that if the community did have the power to institute universal health care, which means making it a public service rather than a private option, then it would behoove the community to do so.

Like judges, physicians are supposed to be licensed by the community.[45] Licensing or communal authorization is another, legal meaning of the Hebrew word *reshut*, which, when used for theological purposes, as indicated above, refers to the divine *dispensation* for physicians to participate in what is taken to be the superhuman process of healing. So, if the community believes it has the right to license those who administer either justice or healing, does it also have the right to refrain from so doing? I think not. Therefore, it seems that communal authorization of those who are doing God's work *(imitatio Dei)* is a social duty. Could one not infer that this social duty also should include paying the salaries of health-care professionals as a regular retainer? In our day, we might ask this question: Since society funds all kinds of medical research, because doing so eventually will benefit all its citizens, does not society have a prior duty to fund medical treatment for all its citizens, since doing so will benefit them much more immediately? Only a society that had no money for medical research, no National Institutes of Health, could say in good faith that it had no such duty, or that it could not fulfill such a duty.

Following the comparison with the administration of justice, could we not say this: Just as the administration of justice — the protection of citizens from possible harm by other persons and the rectification of real harm caused by other persons — is society's unique duty, so shouldn't the delivery of health care, which protects citizens from possible harm and rectifies real harm, also be society's unique duty? In injustice, citizens are harmed by criminals; in the lack of universal health care, citizens are harmed by disease. If this analogy seems far-fetched, it is interesting to note that the greatest medieval theologian-jurist-physician, the eleventh-century Spanish rabbi Maimonides, compared a fetus threatening the life of its mother *in utero* to a criminal threatening the life of his or her victim.[46] Putting aside the question of whether the fetus in Jewish law is what we would call a "person," certainly, *in utero*, the fetus is functioning impersonally.[47] Unlike the literal "pursuer" *(rodef)*, the "pursuing" fetus has neither intelligence nor will. But we still can compare the personal and the imper-

45. T. Baba Kama 9.11.
46. Maimonides, MT: Laws Regarding Murder, 1.9 re B. Sanhedrin 72b.
47. M. Ohalot 7.6. Cf. M. Niddah 5.3.

sonal, the protection from injustice and the protection from disease. (In other words, the life-threatening fetus is like a diseased organ of the mother's body that, if need be, must be amputated to save her life.)

Nonsectarian Medicine

The last question to address is this: What does all of this fascinating information and reflection from the Jewish tradition have to do with the health-care situation in the United States today? Why should multicultural American society be bound by anything the Jewish tradition says? The answer requires making two essential distinctions: one, the distinction between commandments that could be addressed only to Jews and commandments that could be addressed to any human being; and two, the distinction between governance by one's own law and guidance from someone else's.

The Jewish philosophic tradition makes a distinction between what are called "rational commandments" *(mitsvot sikhliyot)* and "revealed commandments."[48] Some theologians have noted that virtually all the commandments that pertain to interhuman relations are in the category of rational commandments — that is, commandments that are readily acceptable to ordinary human reasoning and that do not require that one affirm any singular revelation in history by becoming part of the community that has accepted that historical revelation.[49] Thus, for example, Maimonides rules that the benediction *(berakhah)* recited before most commandments stating that God is the One "who has sanctified us by his commandments by commanding us to do such and such" is not said before the performance of any commandment done for the direct sake of another human being.[50] It is not that Maimonides thought these commandments have a human source in place of the divine source. Rather, it seems Maimonides thought that the more direct source of these commandments is what human reason can directly discover about the legitimate claims of one human being upon another, even though God is, of course, the ultimate source of these commandments.[51] So, perhaps some of what the Jewish ethical tradition puts forth indeed can make a moral claim upon non-Jews, simply by virtue of their being rational persons created in the image of God.

---

48. See Saadiah Gaon, *Book of Beliefs and Opinions,* trans. Samuel Rosenblatt (New Haven: Yale University Press, 1948), 3.3.

49. See M. Baba Batra 10.8; Israel Lifschuetz, *Tiferet Yisrael* thereon, n. 84.

50. Maimonides, MT: Benedictions, 11.2; Joseph Karo, *Kesef Mishneh* thereon.

51. See B. Yoma 67b re Lev. 18:4; David Novak, *Natural Law in Judaism* (Cambridge: Cambridge University Press, 1998), pp. 89-91.

But, even if one does not see the Jewish ethical tradition making any moral claims upon non-Jews, it still might inform one's moral decision-making, even if only by analogy. In other words, the Jewish ethical tradition may offer some moral guidance, even in instances where it cannot claim moral governance in the form of literal moral/legal obligation. An ancient Jewish legend indicates that the reason that the Torah was given in the Wilderness, in a place that belonged to no one *(hefqer)*, is because God wanted the nations of the world to be able to partake of the Torah.[52] But the Torah was given twice: once at Mount Sinai shortly after the Israelites left Egypt, and then again on the Plains of Moab just before the Israelites were to enter the Promised Land. At the second giving of the Torah, the people were commanded to write it on stones for all to see.[53] In this version of the legend of the Torah being given to all nations, it is stated that the nations of the world sent notaries to copy the Torah for themselves.[54] But how much of the Torah was written for them to copy? One rabbi said all of it. Another rabbi said, "They only wrote what the nations would want."[55] The example that is given by this rabbi is how to conduct oneself in war to avoid bloodshed if at all possible. According to the first rabbi, by copying all of the Torah, the nations were now to be judged by it for their noncompliance with its governance. But if the Torah written for them was only the Torah that would appeal to their moral reason, then the Torah was only a source of guidance for them. As such, they were in the words of the Talmud "those who did even when not actually commanded to do so."[56] Thus even in terms of guidance only, I think the Jewish ethical tradition has much to offer those who want health care to be based on something more morally elevated than the practice of individual autonomy or the heteronomy of collective ownership of human persons.

Judaism offers neither the capitalist notion of medicine nor the socialist one. Neither of these alternatives is sufficient to ground the respect for the sanctity of the human person as a being created in the image of God that is so rationally appealing. That is why the Jewish ethical tradition, which is based on this respect for the sanctity of human personhood, both individual and collective, is so attractive — if only for its insights, rather than its authority; its guidance, *rather than* its governance.

---

52. *Mekhilta:* Yitro re Exod. 19:1, ed. Horovitz-Rabin (Jerusalem: Bamberger & Wahrman, 1960), p. 205.

53. Deut. 27:8.

54. T. Sotah 8.6.

55. Quoted from a text by my late revered teacher, Saul Lieberman: *Tosefta Kifshuta* (New York: Jewish Theological Seminary, 1973), p. 700.

56. B. Kiddushin 31a and parallels.

Index of Subjects and Names

Index of Scripture and Other Ancient References